STEVEN J. ROSEN

BLACK LOTUS

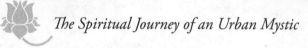

The Spiritual Journey of an Urban Mystic

HARI NAMA PRESS

First printing 2007
Cover and interior design by Barbara Berasi

Main photograph on cover
and small photograph lower left on cover:
© 2006 Lawson Knight/Lakshmivan das ACBSP
www.photoswami.com

Printed in the United States of America
ISBN softbound: 1-885414-23-4

Library of Congress Control Number: 2006935480

Persons interested in the subject matter of this book
are invited to correspond with the publisher:

Hari-Nama Press
PO Box 76451,
Capitol Hill, Washington, DC 20013
www.ifast.net/hnp

To
Mother Pearline
and Uncle Nanda
(Norman Anderson),
for setting him on the path.

And to His Divine Grace
A. C. Bhaktivedanta Swami Prabhupada,
for taking him along that path
with a loving hand.

CONTENTS

ACKNOWLEDGMENTS

I N THE WRITING OF ANY BOOK, there are usually a number of people who must be given due credit, and this book is no exception. Though it is not possible to mention everyone who contributed to this process, I would like to direct the readers' attention to a few. First of all, Bhakti Tirtha Swami himself must be thanked. Had he not lived such an exemplary life, I might not have been inspired to write this book. In addition, I felt his guidance every step of the way. Nagaraja, senior editor of *Back to Godhead*, the magazine of the Hare Krishna Movement, should be recognized, too, for in allowing me to write a feature article on Bhakti Tirtha Swami (November/ December 2005), he helped me to crystallize my thoughts about the Swami's life and work.

Others gave me content and encouragement: Most significant were Bhakti Tirtha Swami's close family and friends, including Frances Myers, Julia Henderson, Margarite Brooks, Bernadette Satterfield, Paul Favors, and especially his niece, Renita Allen, who worked closely with me on early drafts of the manuscript. Ronnie Cooper and Lester Sandifer (his childhood friends), Ron Bey, Bill Miner (his roommate at Princeton), Melvin McCray (a colleague from the same school), Lila-smaranam, Sri Ishopanishad (Isis), and Jagannath Pandit, were also quite helpful. Interviews with his mentors and teachers, including Vivian DuBose Jordan, E. Randel T. Osburn, Jan Carew, and William Hall were an invaluable asset.

Let us not forget Radhanath Swami, Bhakti-charu Swami, Giriraja Swami, Danavir Maharaja, Mahabuddhi, Kalakantha, Krishna-kshetra, Hridayananda Maharaja, Satsvarupa Maharaja, Sesha, Riddha, Rasikananda, Bhakti-jana, Bhumi-pati, Rupa-vilasa, Amogha-lila, Vakreshvara Pandit, among others. Their love and appreciation of the Swami, captured in personal interviews, make their appearance in this book.

Finally, the work could not have been completed without Vraja-lila Ma, Ekavira, Ekendra, Kamagiri Ma, Nanda Sunu, Jambavati, Parvati, Jason Pearson, Lakshmi-nrisimha, Hladini Shakti, Sahadeva, Kaishori, Neil Chakrabarti, Lawson Knight, Shrivas Pandit, Prabhupada Lila, Vasudeva, Brahma-muhurta, Kalpa-vriksha, Purusha-sukta, Ananda Vrindavan, Krishnanandini, Anubhava, Indrani Ma, Chintamani, Madhava, Lila-katha, Jo Lynn Wells (Bhadra), Ishvara, Sikhi Mahiti, Varaha, Yashoda, Dhira Nitai, Kripa, Aja, Murari, Raga, Madhvacharya (and Kunti), Raghunath (John Giuffre), Anna Sapritsky, Mirabai Sapritsky Giuffre, Subal, Grahila (for the index), Madhurya-Kadambini and her Russian biographical materials in translation, and others too numerous to mention.

Let it be said at the outset that the beauty and devotion found in the following pages belong to our great Vaishnava forebears, behind whose giant footprints I attempt to walk. Luminaries, such as Bhakti Tirtha Swami, who was undoubtedly advanced on the path, should not be held accountable for those who lag behind—people like me. And yet, I write this book. As a consequence, the reader may find imperfection, lack of clarity, or imperceptiveness in the following pages. If so, the fault lies with me alone, and it should not detract from the remarkable journey that will now unfold before you, nor should it diminish your estimation of this extraordinary individual known variously as John Favors, Ghanashyam, Bhakti Tirtha Swami, Gurudeva, and so on. Rather, his giant shoes may have been several sizes too big for my tiny feet, even if I labor diligently to follow in his footsteps.

Special note to his disciples: I recognize that I do not speak for Bhakti Tirtha Swami's many disciples and that my view is simply that of a loving Godbrother. For this reason, the mood and general tenor of the book might seem unfamiliar or even strange to the average disciple. On this score, I apologize and ask you to please bear with me: the perspectives and insights of a well-meaning Godbrother have value, and may reveal a side of Bhakti Tirtha Swami that is edifying in numerous ways.

That being said, the disciples have their own special relationships with him, and, no doubt, many of them will eventually release books to share their memories and realizations. Bhakti Tirtha Swami himself remained focused on his service of producing literature, even up to the time of his departure. He left Hari-Nama Press with volumes of additional material and a directive to continue their publishing work as he continues to guide and inspire them from within their hearts. Hari-Nama Press will thus publish additional material in the future that focuses on Bhakti Tirtha Swami's work and mission—but more, much of this material will be expressed from a disciple's point of view, with all the love and emotion characteristic of such relationships.

FOREWORD

HIS HOLINESS BHAKTI TIRTHA SWAMI
(written one month before he departed this world)

IN MY HUMBLE OPINION, Steven J. Rosen (Satyaraja Dasa) is, in many ways, one of today's leading Vaishnava scholars in the Western world. His forté, as I see it, is in utilizing the rich Vaishnava culture of ancient India to address contemporary issues and modern-day concerns. By masterfully drawing on Vaishnava predecessors and their philosophical conclusions, he is able to access truths and perspectives that bring contemporary scholars and practitioners together—to analytically examine and appreciate the tradition for the benefit of all.

In his own personal life, he shows this harmony between scholarship and practice by himself being a most humble practitioner since 1973 and by writing thorough, well-researched texts. He was initiated into the Gaudiya Vaishnava tradition by His Divine Grace A. C. Bhaktivedanta Swami Prabhupada, the founder and spiritual master of the International Society for Krishna Consciousness (ISKCON), in 1975. Since then, Satyaraja has written over twenty books; served as the founder and senior editor of the *Journal of Vaishnava Studies*, an academic quarterly esteemed by scholars around the world; he is an associate editor for *Back to Godhead*, the magazine of the Hare Krishna Movement; and he was recently asked to write a textbook on Hinduism as part of the Introduction to the World's Major Religions series (Greenwood Press), which will be in universities and research libraries throughout the United States and much of Europe.

As if all of this publishing isn't enough, he still finds time to mentor fledgling (and senior) devotees and to advise academics on courses at major universities, where his books are often used as required reading. Still, with all this, I see Satyaraja as "a work in progress"—not only in the sense that he is always fine-tuning and honing his talents, which is evident with each of his newly published books and magazine articles, but especially in that much of the world is as yet unaware of his great contributions, nor do they understand the depth of what he has offered to the global community already.

So when we initially discussed writing my biography, not only was I extremely humbled and honored, but I could not imagine a more qualified person in ISKCON to render the task. This is especially true because my life has been somewhat mysterious and complex, taking part in both the rich Vaishnava tradition and in a desire to communicate that tradition in a contemporary setting. I know that Satyaraja understands this and will express it in a clear and accessible way.

As I write this foreword—which is most probably only a few days before I leave this body—I think of two specific goals that I want this work to accomplish. First of all, Satyaraja's writing of my life story should draw greater attention to the works of my spiritual mentor, Srila Prabhupada, who is also Satyaraja's spiritual mentor. And, secondly, I pray that it will draw attention to the many contributions that Satyaraja has made through his own writings.

Some may question the very idea of a spiritual biography. Traditionally, every religious tradition wants to explain its existence through the lives of those who have benefited through its practice. Usually, religious biographies are written about saints and others who deeply embody the tradition. Sometimes, however, biographical works are written about humble practitioners, people who, through their own struggles, show how anyone can traverse the path of the sages.

For my disciples, this book may serve the former purpose. For friends, well-wishers and Godbrothers, it may assist in the latter. In either case, I am hoping that it in some way aids the readers' understanding of Krishna Consciousness, the profound Vaishnava tradition that is at the heart of the spiritual pursuit. Vaishnavism is not about "my religion versus your religion"—it is about the science of the soul. This is what should come through in these pages.

By writing this book, Satyaraja will help me to live on and on for many generations as a servant of humanity. I want nothing more than this opportunity.

I am so honored to have had Satyaraja as a close friend. He has repeatedly touched me in a very deep way. This has gone on for years —he has offered much to me personally as well as to the international community through assisting me in my work. He has even taken time out of his extremely busy schedule to write the foreword to one of my earlier books, and he has assisted my editors in numerous ways. I am eternally indebted to him, especially now, since he is helping me to die on the battlefield, wherein I am able to continue to serve my spiritual master not only up until my last breath, but even after that.

I love you Satyaraja, and your wonderful wife and child who support you so nicely in your life and work. I look forward to meeting up with you in the spiritual world to continue the beautiful relationship that we have nurtured in this one.

INTRODUCTION

*"Through Bhakti Tirtha Swami's great efforts, his spiritual
legacy will live on and endure throughout posterity."*

—ALICE COLTRANE

BHAKTI TIRTHA SWAMI (1950–2005), the "urban mystic" at the center of this book, was a person of singular determination, a courageous and bold teacher of spiritual science. His work took him around the world, particularly to Eastern Europe, behind the Iron Curtain, where he surpassed all others in sharing divine wisdom, often risking his own life, and to Africa, where kings and queens acknowledged him as a high chief and recognized him as a spiritual leader. He was esteemed in the International Society for Krishna Consciousness (ISKCON) as well. Here he was a respected *sannyasi*, a monk in the renounced order of life, and a guru, with disciples of his own. He was the world's first African-American Vaishnava spiritual master, and he published many books, too, explaining how to apply the eternal principles of God consciousness in the modern world. His books use the language of conflict resolution and depth psychology, as well as that of the New Age. They foster spiritual advancement through principle-centered leadership techniques and inner realizations. In addition, he had a tremendous ability to touch people on a deep level, to change lives, as thousands of friends and disciples can attest to.

I

Setting the Scene: How Did He Get Here?

Back in his youth, when he was known as John Favors, or simply as "Johnny Boy," he had always dreamed of going to Africa. He had roots there. But he could only trace his ancestry back a generation or two, when the family had already arrived in the United States, specifically in Alabama. Years later, as a student at Princeton in 1968, he had adopted the name Toshombe Abdul, identifying even more with his African heritage. By the time he graduated in 1972, his professors had arranged an expense-paid trip for him to Africa, along with a teaching position at an important institution of learning. But it was not to be. He didn't go where they wanted him to go. Instead, he joined the Hare Krishna Movement.

Shoot forward to the end of 1979: He had recently become a monk in the renounced order of life (*sannyasa*) and started to think deeply about how to best use his African-American identity to convey the truths of the spirit. That is to say, as a spiritually gifted black man he perceived the importance of communicating with others of his race, and to thereby share with them the treasure he had received from the Hare Krishna Movement. Thinking along these lines, he finally went to Africa.

As the hot sun greeted him at Murtala Mohammed International Airport, Nigeria, there was a sense of coming home, even though he had never been here before—at least not in this life. Nonetheless, this was a triumphant return, of sorts, for impressions deeply embedded in his psyche, as well as ancestors whose genes permeated his body, whispered of his connection with a land long forgotten. And though several generations of separation had dimmed the memory, he was now returning with a gift, something the people of Africa would embrace with full enthusiasm. He was bringing them Krishna Consciousness.

But for the moment, as he stepped off the plane, he was overcome with a barrage of emotions, seeing Africa's sea of faces, set alight by her sweltering heat. As a black man from Ohio and a child of the

'60s, he knew well about Pan Africanism, which claims that diasporan black people throughout the world are forever linked with Africans through a common experience of oppression and slavery. But he was even more convinced of his real identity as a spirit-soul; he knew that ultimate truth transcends bodily identification.

Yet here he was, in Africa, exposed to its people, its beauty, its exotica. How did he get here? He finds himself remembering childhood folktales about the Congo and also colorful stories of Madagascar; he sees truth in a village in Nairobi and the heavens on a mountaintop palace of Kabare. Gradually, he will experience the problems and the miracles of life in Africa. After some time, spiritual and political leaders in Warri, Nigeria will make him a high chief, a rare privilege for a Westerner reaching maturity in the ghettoes of Cleveland. Again, how did he get here?

This book seeks to answer that question, but not before acquainting the reader with the "Krishna Consciousness" that the Swami was bringing to Africa. This was no sectarian religion—it was not the "Hinduism" that had long existed among the African people, having arrived there in the nineteenth century along with hopeful immigrants. Rather, this was the ancient tradition known as Sanatana Dharma, or "the eternal function of the soul," also called Vaishnavism—the worship of God in His most confidential feature, as Vishnu, or Krishna. As far as Bhakti Tirtha Swami was concerned, he was bringing to the people of Africa the subtle thread that ties together all religious truth.

He was not interested in one religion as opposed to another, the sectarian battle that foists one aspect of spirituality to the forefront while belittling or even demonizing all others. He was interested in the science of God consciousness, the underlying reality at the core of all genuine religious revelations and the process by which one can awaken one's love of God. Spiritual adherents of all religious traditions can apply the principles taught by this pristine Indic system with equal benefit.

The Hare Krishna Movement

The movement that brings us this precious fruit of India's ancient spiritual heritage was incorporated in New York City in 1966, though it sprouted from the seeds of a religious and cultural system that is thousands of years old. These seeds were brought West by His Divine Grace A. C. Bhaktivedanta Swami Prabhupada (1896–1977), Bhakti Tirtha Swami's spiritual master. Prabhupada founded a movement called the International Society for Krishna Consciousness, which has theological roots that can be understood in terms of two historical paradigms, one modern and the other ancient.

The modern form of the movement reaches back into sixteenth-century Bengal, when Chaitanya Mahaprabhu (1486–1533)—the revered religious ecstatic who fully embodied the movement's teachings, practices, and goals—vibrated a song of universal love. This song's main chorus centered on the chanting of the holy names of God, especially the Maha-mantra, or "the Great Chant for Deliverance": Hare Krishna, Hare Krishna, Krishna Krishna, Hare Hare/ Hare Rama, Hare Rama, Rama Rama, Hare Hare.

What does the mantra mean? Again, the implications of this uniquely transcendent prayer are not sectarian but universal. The word "Hare" is the vocative form of "Mother Hara," another name for Radha, Krishna's eternal consort and the very embodiment of devotional service (*bhakti*). Essentially, this refers to God and the potency by which one can serve Him—regardless of one's chosen religious tradition. Rama is another name for Krishna, meaning "He who gives His devotees the highest pleasure." Thus, in brief translation, the chant may be rendered as follows: "O Lord! O energy of the Lord (Radha)! Please engage me in Your divine service!" While Chaitanya favored this most selfless prayer, he taught that the recitation of any of God's names would have similar effect.

The thing that Bhakti Tirtha Swami liked most about chanting is that it puts one in direct touch with the Supreme. It pierces through all physical, mental, and intellectual layers of existence, situating one on the spiritual platform. This is because God's name is absolute—it is one with His essence—a fact that is realized when one's chanting is perfected.

This ultimate oneness between God and His name, of course, is distinctly spiritual, and it also reveals a fundamental difference between matter and spirit: Material substances are relative, i.e., in the material world a thing and its name are *not* one and the same. They are two individual items. On the other hand, in the spiritual world, which is the exact opposite of the material world, the reverse must be true—an essential oneness engulfs all. This is not to say that there is no hierarchy in the spiritual world, with various gradations perceivable by spiritual adepts, but rather that a sense of oneness and difference exist simultaneously. Through chanting, an accomplished practitioner develops an awareness of God's absolute and spiritual nature, i.e., that there is no difference between the *nami* ("the named one") and the *nama* ("the name").

Absorption in the otherworldly nature of Krishna and His name is the heart of Vaishnava mysticism, leading to love of God. But it is not a random or haphazard exercise. Rather, it is a detailed science, with many rules, regulations, and ancillary practices that serve to facilitate perfect chanting. By absorbing oneself in the holy name, one becomes *spiritualized*, totally engulfed in God's energy. Because chanting the name of God is so much emphasized in Vaishnava texts, practitioners focus on chanting as a central devotional method. Thus, deep meditation and great emotion accompany (1) Japa (soft chanting on beads, similar to the Christian rosary), (2) Kirtan (loud chanting or singing), and (3) Sankirtan (congregational chanting or distribution of the holy name). As we will see, Bhakti Tirtha Swami excelled in all three forms of this practice at various points in his devotional life.

This practice of reciting mantras is rooted in earlier Vedic texts—the

Vedic literature constitutes the scriptural legacy of ancient India, detailing the science of love of God—where glorification of God's names is recommended as the most effective form of self-realization for the modern age. In fact, it was seen by spiritual adepts as the open secret of the Vedic tradition, the hidden jewel of the Indian scriptures.

In the late fifteenth century, European kings sent their heroic explorers in search of new routes to treasure-filled India. Many returned home on ships laden with silks, spices, artwork, and magnificent jewels. But they bypassed India's real treasure, which was just then being widely distributed by Lord Chaitanya. Prior to Chaitanya's time, a reawakening of Krishna-*bhakti*, or devotion to Krishna, had swept the subcontinent, drawing on centuries-old Sanskrit texts and vernacular poetry composed by Chaitanya's immediate predecessors. Now Chaitanya and his followers were filling in the missing pieces by showing how to put this deep theology into practice and by emphasizing the power of the holy name. In this way, Chaitanya pioneered a great social and spiritual movement that continues to spread its profound influence worldwide.

At the very least, Chaitanya transformed India in four respects: philosophically, by establishing the logic of a personal Absolute named Krishna and the need for rendering loving service to Him; socially, by opposing the blindly rigid caste system and setting in place a universal doctrine that is open to all; politically, by organizing India's first civil disobedience movement—predating both Gandhi and Martin Luther King by centuries—against a repressive government; and, most important, spiritually, by teaching and demonstrating that love for Krishna is the secret meaning behind all Vedic texts, the cooling balm to heal all the world's woes, and the ultimate nonsectarian truth for which everyone is searching. Bhakti Tirtha Swami took hold of this truth and stretched it to its limits, particularly in relation to social reform and personal application.

Chaitanya Mahaprabhu's nondenominational movement came to

be called Gaudiya (Bengali) or Chaitanyaite Vaishnavism, but, as stated, it was deeply rooted in the much older tradition of Krishna-*bhakti*. To this end, it makes use of standard classical texts, like the Upanishads, *Bhagavad-gita*, and the *Srimad-Bhagavatam*. And, in this sense, it is quite orthodox. It claims affiliation with the prestigious Brahma-Madhva-Sampradaya (lineage), and can trace its teaching to Brahma, the father of the created universe. This is the second historical paradigm by which ISKCON can be understood. In this context, it is called Sanatana Dharma, or "the eternal function of the soul," as mentioned above. To briefly clarify: Chaitanya Mahaprabhu did not begin his mission to teach something new. Rather, his purpose was to reveal deeper, esoteric truths found at the core of the ancient Vedic tradition—a tradition that transcends sectarian concerns. Again, his teaching embodies the original spiritual truth found in all religion. Thus, it is not merely Hindu dogma, but, rather, a transcendental science that benefits everyone, regardless of one's religious or sectarian affiliation.

Even the chanting, as mentioned above, is not peculiar to Vaishnavism—it can be found as a general principle in all religions. This was something that Bhakti Tirtha Swami emphasized in his teaching: Mohammed counseled, "Glorify the name of your Lord, the most high." (Koran 87.2) Saint Paul said, "Everyone who calls upon the name of the Lord will be saved." (*Romans* 10.13) Buddha declared, "All who sincerely call upon my name will come to me after death, and I will take them to paradise." (*Vows of Amida Buddha* 18) King David preached, "From the rising of the sun to its setting, the name of the Lord is to be praised." (*Psalms* 113.3) And the Vaishnava scriptures repeatedly assert: "Chant the holy name, chant the holy name, chant the holy name of the Lord. In this Age of Quarrel there is no other way, no other way, no other way to attain spiritual enlightenment." (*Brihan-naradiya Purana* 3.8.126)

Prabhupada brought these teachings to the West, claiming that his only credit was that he did not change anything, but delivered what he had received "as it is." God's revealed word, Prabhupada told his followers, is the Absolute Truth—"For our part," he said, "we can only follow this Truth and convey it to others, without interpolation or change." Moreover, unlike other gurus and God-men from India, Prabhupada was adamant that a human being should not be identified with God—he claimed that he was merely God's humble servant, and that he was ready, willing, and able to teach others how to serve in this same capacity. Bhakti Tirtha Swami inherited this mission from Srila Prabhupada, as did others, and he brought it to various parts of the world, particularly to Africa.

Of course, the Hare Krishna Movement had already appeared in that continent by 1969. This was due to the diligent efforts of Shakti Mati Devi Dasi and, later, in 1971, Brahmananda Swami, before Bhakti Tirtha Swami had arrived there. The work was carried on by Pushta Krishna Swami and others, all disciples of His Divine Grace A. C. Bhaktivedanta Swami Prabhupada. Indeed, Prabhupada himself had been to Nairobi several times, and had journeyed to South Africa in 1975. But all of these endeavors had been confined to South and East Africa—West Africa had to patiently wait for Bhakti Tirtha Swami's arrival in late 1979. Once there, he was able to spread his master's mission in an unprecedented way, both because of the color of his skin and because of his unique characteristics, from personal charisma to purity of purpose.

A Black Lotus Emerges

The book's title deserves brief explanation. A lotus is a specific kind of lily; but it is also an ancient and universal symbol of spirituality and can be found in the writings of the Aryan Hindus, the Buddhists, and the Egyptians as well. It was adopted as a Christian emblem by Greek and Latin Churches, who eventually replaced it with the water lily. In India, where it is perhaps most well-known as a sacred symbol, it is viewed in a philosophical way that is particularly pertinent in our present context and thus worthy of scrutiny.

The roots of a lotus, say ancient Indic texts, are found in mud, while its stem grows up through surrounding water and its beautifully scented flower lies above its liquid source, basking in bright sunlight. In a similar way, a true spiritual practitioner, while taking birth in the mud-like quicksand of the material world, rises up above its dirty waters, untouched by its considerable contaminants. This lotus-like phenomenon is poignantly demonstrated in the life of Bhakti Tirtha Swami, who, though born in the ghettos of Cleveland, rose to prominence as a true spiritual leader, as we shall soon see.

Though there are other water plants that bloom above the water, it is only the lotus that, because of the strength of its stem, commonly rises eight to twelve inches above the surface. Similarly, though others have risen to great heights on the spiritual path, Bhakti Tirtha Swami's contribution was truly unique, given his strength of character and the kind of person he was. Thus, while there are white, red, blue, pink, and even golden lotuses, there is only one black lotus, and that's what this book attempts to bring to light.

Bhakti Tirtha Swami's urban roots made him especially sensitive to the needs of the downtrodden, and so he championed not only the cause of equal rights for blacks but also for disenfranchised women, homosexuals, children—and for all marginalized factions of society. This he particularly fought for in the Hare Krishna Movement, but he did so in general as well. His compassion and far-reaching spiritual vision has left a significant mark on the movement of which he was a part and on the outside world too. Exactly how this is so will be revealed in the following pages.

It is interesting that the names by which he was known in the Hare Krishna Movement tell us much about who he actually was: For example, Srila Prabhupada gave him the name "Ghanashyam Dasa," which means "servant of the blackish cloud." The name Ghanashyam refers to Krishna, God, who, in His original form, is as beautiful as a dark rain cloud, with a complexion to match. Prabhupada had thus acknowledged his disciple's beauty as a charismatic black man, an African American with marked exquisiteness both materially and spiritually. But more, in giving him this name, he predicted that his then fledgling disciple would eventually take Shyam (another name for Krishna), to Ghana, or that part of Africa, among others, where Bhakti Tirtha Swami did indeed ultimately spread Krishna Consciousness.

Also, "Bhakti Tirtha," the name he was given at his *sannyasa* ceremony, when he became a life-long monk, was highly appropriate as well. This is so because he was like a true *tirtha,* or "holy place," in that such places are like bridges to the spiritual world. The word *tirtha* is conceptually linked to the Sanskrit, *tirthankara,* or "bridge-builder," the idea being that a spiritual teacher, too, is like a bridge to the spiritual realm, for they give people facility to get there. He, especially, was like a bridge, using *bhakti,* or devotion, to bring people to Krishna. Hence, "*Bhakti Tirtha.*"

Along related lines, his style of conveying Krishna Consciousness emphasized the importance of "bridge-building," so that outsiders would have easy access to the philosophy. Accordingly, he drew on varied sources and revolutionary methods to express traditional truths. These were his "bridges" to get people to the other side. His intense desire to do this was a product of his compassion, which inspired in him ever-fresh methods of bringing sincere souls to the lotus feet of Krishna.

For a brief period in ISKCON's history, in fact, he was known as Srila Krishnapada, which, again, indicates his favored position at Lord Krishna's lotus feet and his ever-broadening capacity to give shelter to others. Of course, he was also a "swami," which indicates one who is able to control his senses. As we shall see, his life as a devotee reveals these qualities in abundance.

But there is more. "Krishnapada" was a recurring theme in Bhakti

Tirtha Swami's life. Sometimes he knew it, and sometimes he did not. Let me explain. We have already indicated the more common usage of the term Krishnapada, wherein it is viewed as one who has taken shelter at Lord Krishna's lotus feet. However, the word has another meaning, as we discover later in this book. *Krishnapada* can also mean "black foot." And in this sense, yet again, the word is graphically linked to Bhakti Tirtha Swami: He was born with a black birthmark on his left foot, a distinguishing bodily characteristic remembered by close family members and friends. More, it would be a tumor under this very birthmark that would eventually take his life. So Krishnapada has been with Krishnapada throughout.

Bhakti Tirtha Swami's story, of course, goes far beyond thought-provoking coincidences, or even divine truths, regarding his name or title. It is a story of victory over obstacles, of a pious childhood that was punctuated by poverty and racial discrimination. It is the story of a true spiritual seeker who achieved an extraordinary level of accomplishment and then enthusiastically shared his gain with all who would have it. This same treasure will also be shared with anyone who enters into the mood and message of this book.

One last point: Some readers might question the propriety, or even the need, of telling Bhakti Tirtha Swami's life story, and they may wonder why he would encourage such an enterprise, as he does in the Foreword. After all, a Vaishnava is characterized by his humility, and a humble person would naturally be disinclined to have others focus on the details of his or her life. And this is certainly true. Indeed, there is a saying that, "for the Vaishnava, self-praise is as good as death." Still, there is a caveat, an exception, when the writing of one's own biography—or the willingness to allow another to do so—would not only be approved but enthusiastically endorsed. This exception manifests when the story has a purpose larger than itself, when one's life might convey the truths of Krishna Consciousness.

The medieval Vaishnava text *Brihat Bhagavatamrita* (2.1.107-109), written by the sage Sanatana Goswami, makes this clear when it describes the value of autobiographical narrative, saying that, at times, there is no literary device as effective in explaining spiritual reality. This was also seen in the final pastimes of Srila Prabhupada, Bhakti Tirtha Swami's own spiritual master. When, in 1977, Srila Prabhupada was preparing to leave his mortal frame, his then secretary, Tamal Krishna Goswami, expressed his belief that the world could be further enlightened by Prabhupada's life story. His divine master agreed, explicitly stating who his biographer should be (Satsvarupa Dasa Goswami) and enumerating various childhood stories that might be included in the text. So Prabhupada's own example shows that a Vaishnava could endorse his own biography, at least if the story might serve the greater good of humankind.

Bhakti Tirtha Swami, similarly, saw his life in terms of what it could do for his fellow human beings, how it could be used to enlighten and instruct. In this spirit, he came to the conclusion that his story should be told, and that I should be the one who tells it.

Black Lotus thus attempts to convey a taste, a drop, of the Swami's journey and accomplishments, just to whet readers' appetites. To do more would be impossible. The full story, due to its enormity, variety, and spiritual intensity, resists comprehensive treatment, and omission has been necessary for a number of reasons. This being the case, be prepared for mere glimpses of the Swami's life, although my historical lens and attention to detail might make it seem more complete. In other words, the Swami's tale unfolds with necessary gaps, perceived between the light and shadow of the material world, with implications that will be understood only according to the realizations of individual readers. Additionally, this is not a book for scholars or historians. Rather, it better serves as a template for those on a spiritual quest—it is not for those merely seeking knowledge, but for those who are also seeking love. Without any further adieu, then, let us pay close attention to the black lotus now blossoming on these pages.

CHAPTER ONE

THE FORGOTTEN TRIANGLE

"God prepares great men for great tasks by great trials."

—JOHN BAPTISTE GRESSETT

I T WAS THE LATE-1950S and a cold winter day in Cleveland, Ohio. Even so, one particular neighborhood, known as the Forgotten Triangle—East 82nd Street and Kinsman Road, to be exact—managed to find some warmth. Although the area had gone through hard times and was populated by impoverished but hard-working people, mainly African American, there was a group of families attending a birthday party for nine-year-old John Favors, and that helped them break through the cold. The warmth generated by this energetic young boy's bright smile gave everyone hope, even if their day-to-day life was commonly interrupted by racial discrimination, difficult conditions, crime, and indigence. This smile would grow as the boy aged in years. And everyone who saw it would know the same warmth, the same energy, gracing that small ghetto on the eastside of Cleveland where he spent his early years.

Lotus Roots

John's African roots impacted on his life in numerous ways, not only in those early days in Cleveland but even during his soul-searching spiritual journey in the Hare Krishna Movement and while a high chief in Nigeria as well. Understanding the history of blacks in America, therefore, is integral to understanding who he was and what motivated him on various levels.

Though there are multiple versions of the story, it is perhaps best to begin by mentioning the recent work of scholars such as Ivan Van Sertima and Barry Fell, who demonstrate through archeological, linguistic and other means that there was a significant African presence in the Americas prior to Columbus. According to this understanding, early African Americans were skilled navigators, explorers, statesmen, and educators, whose expedition to the Americas was distinguished by the desire to share knowledge with the locals, never exploiting or foisting imperial designs upon them. These Africans did not come as slaves.

The more common version of postcolonial history, however, runs something like this: In the early seventeenth century, some 15 to 20 million Africans were brought to America and traded for crops. Initially, they were used as workers and, worse, they were seen as commodities—they had no legal rights and were treated like thoughtless livestock, animals with no feelings, no voice, and useful only while they served the purposes of their "masters." This went on for over 200 years.

The American Civil War (1861–1865) engaged north against south, with Americans killing each other for various reasons, not least for the abolition of slavery. Early black activists, such as David Walker (c. 1785–1830), Frederick Douglass (c. 1817–1895), and Harriet Tubman (c. 1819–1913), some of whom rose from slavery, were prime movers in the advancement of human rights issues. Eventually, with the victory of the north in 1865, the 13th amendment of the Constitution abolished the use of humans as slaves. Nonetheless, the oppression of African Americans continued, if not as slaves then as second-class citizens, or as an inferior race. Forced to live in the compromised setting of ghettos, they generally had little food, poor sanitation, and were deprived of education and other opportunities. Though the northern states would become known for more subtle manifestations of such racial prejudice, it reached exaggerated proportions in the South, with blacks not being allowed to use the same restrooms, buses and schools as whites. Inferior education kept them in the lower echelons of society, and if they endeavored to better themselves they were often beaten, tortured, or killed. Consequently, they usually settled for less, and, when finding work, had the most difficult of jobs—usually involving hard labor; and because morale was down, there was little hope for social or economic progress.

Just after the Second World War, African Americans worked harder than ever in their struggle for dignity and equality. Animated by a handful of agreeable Supreme Court decisions on education and segregation, blacks, in general, were now more confident about the future, and they more forcefully demanded their civil and human rights. Leaders like Paul Robeson (1898–1976), Ralphe Bunche (1900–1974), and Martin Luther King, Jr., (1929–1968) helped the Civil Rights Movement realize its goals.

When John Favors was five years old, Martin Luther King, Jr. received his Ph.D. in Systematic Theology from Boston University, setting King on his way to becoming a widely accepted voice for blacks worldwide. Later that same year, on December 1, 1955, Rosa Parks, who had been active in Civil Rights for quite some time, refused to give up her seat to a white passenger on a segregated bus in Montgomery, Alabama. Although she was temporarily arrested for her act of defiance, she set a precedent that resounded throughout the world. She stood up for dignity and equal rights, even as she sat firmly in her seat. These were the beginnings of significant breakthroughs.

By the end of the 1960s, even though progress was clearly being made, many African Americans became impatient, rioting in black ghettoes across the country. Inner-city districts like Harlem or the south side of Chicago provided the setting for heart-rending and violent rebellions. Among the most lethal were those in Los Angeles (1965), Detroit (1967), and even in Newark (1967), the year before John started school at nearby Princeton. After the death of Martin Luther King in April, 1968, the explosive expressions of rage became even more chaotic, as opposed to the carefully orchestrated, nonviolent demonstrations of the early Civil Rights Movement. Many blacks were taking their cue from Malcolm X (1925–1965), whose militant message of black consciousness often conflicted with the more peaceful teachings of Dr. King. This dichotomy between "action by any means necessary" and the more long-term and nonviolent approach to life marked the African-American legacy inherited by John Favors.

He watched closely as Dr. King, among others, pioneered a major social revolution for African Americans, as already mentioned. And he took part in it, as much as he could, for in King's time, young Johnny was just coming of age. Significantly, King's main influence, after Christ, was Mahatma Gandhi, the Hindu saint who based his teachings on the principle of *ahimsa*, nonviolence, which is central to Vaishnava thought. The connection between King and Gandhi will have meaning in the spiritual journey of John Favors, who in fact met Dr. King on several occasions, a series of fortuitous events that will be explored in Chapter Two.

Dr. King taught that prejudice and social inequality could not be overcome by hatred or force. Apropos of this, he practiced and preached Gandhian techniques of nonviolence as a way of dealing with aggressors. In the end, of course, King himself was murdered, but the Civil Rights Movement had tremendous impact in the Western world, and the rioting eventually subsided. Because of his initial work, and that carried on by others, conditions over the last forty years have improved for most African Americans, though some, indeed, would argue otherwise.

Urban Origins

John's story begins in Cleveland, a city whose origins go back to 1786. One of the first black settlers in the area was George Peake, who arrived in 1809. African Americans would slowly trickle into the area and, by 1860, at least 800 lived in a Cleveland community of over 43,000.

It was in the 1930s that Pearline Hill relocated to the area. She had lived in Alabama as a little girl, with family in both Leighton and Sheffield. Her mother's name was Julia Whiteside, and her father's was Eddie Earl Hill. She loved her life in the south, even if it was, at times, difficult. But she wanted to experience other parts of the world as well. For her that meant traveling up north, where she would at first live with her uncle and then raise a family of her own. She watched the political and economic structure of Cleveland change after World War II. Its black population had expanded to 250,000 by 1950, which was the year that John was born.

The Congress of Industrial Organizations, which helped African Americans get jobs, minimized various aspects of discrimination, particularly in hospitals and hotels. By 1967, the large African-American population and voter increase ushered in Carl Stokes, the first black mayor of a major city. Meanwhile, many whites left Cleveland, destroying the economic base before new African-American jobs could accommodate the fall. But we get ahead of ourselves.

One of the more downtrodden neighborhoods in the area was known as the Forgotten Triangle, though some writers refer to it as a quiet, urban, working class community on the eastside of Cleveland. This is where Pearline was able to find a home. The half-shuttered housing estates there have upbeat names like "Renaissance Village," but like many depressed urban areas in the States, they are now a mere shadow of what they once were. Many of the homes, including the one in which John Favors was raised, are no longer there. The area has been left behind by the shallow and largely jobless economic recovery of recent history.

The Forgotten Triangle is very inner-city. At the time—the 30s, 40s, and 50s, when Pearline was raising her family there—it was a fairly dense neighborhood with many homes. The area was like a suburb, with nicely kept front lawns, though the houses were somewhat ramshackle by higher-class standards. Still, the families were basically happy, enjoying simple and close-knit lives. There were a good number of businesses up and down the Kinsman area (beauty shops, cleaners, ice cream and beer parlors), bordering the Triangle, and most people commuted by using local buses. It was the type of 1950s atmosphere where, after dinner, a family or a group of friends could take walks around the neighborhood and were friendly, saying hello or nodding as they passed each other by. Though outsiders would think twice before passing through the district, those who lived there found it safe and homey, even pleasant.

John Favors reminisces about his childhood home and about his mother as well:

> I remember how we grew up never locking our doors, even though we lived in the ghetto, in an area that could be considered dangerous. It was my mother's policy to never lock her doors. It was somewhat similar to her heart; her heart was always open to everyone.

Nearly a century ago, the Forgotten Triangle was a lively industrial center where neighborhood residents walked to their jobs at plants and factories. In fact, one of John D. Rockefeller's first oil refineries was located there in the 1880s, making it an important area for local commerce. In addition, the neighborhood was home to one of the busiest railway lines in Northeast Ohio, the Pennsylvania Railroad, which instigated new development throughout the years. But with the decline of production and the closing of the railroad, the Forgotten Triangle was more or less forgotten.

The Favors Household

Pearline married Paul Favors, and their family came of age on 79th Street and Holton Avenue, in the heart of the Forgotten Triangle. But Paul passed away prematurely, from tuberculosis, with Pearline lovingly caring for him until the day he died. Unfortunately, the couple never did have children. Nonetheless, years later, she eventually had a subsequent relationship that gave her John Favors. There were five siblings as well: Frances, John's eldest sister, was born in 1936; Julia a year later; Margarite in 1941. Bernadette took birth in 1945, with Paul Jr. making his appearance just two years later. Finally, John greeted the Favors household on February 25, 1950.

Mother Pearline was clearly the matriarch of the family, caring for all six children with the kind of love found only in mothers. John's father lived separately and was rarely in attendance, though he would sometimes arrive on weekends or for special family trips. He had a son from an earlier marriage, Isaac, whom Pearline's family really didn't know. John did, however, meet his elder half-brother later in life and also resolved issues with his father.

The family sometimes got together for day-long outings to Mentor Headlands Beach in Mentor, Ohio. They would bring picnic baskets, delight in the adjoining state park, relax on the beach and go swimming. Although John himself didn't swim, he thoroughly enjoyed these family jaunts—it seemed the people closest to him were all getting together for some spirited, good-hearted fun, and he liked that. His sister Margarite and her now ex-husband Carl Evans—who was something of a father figure to John—along with their daughter Floretta, would often come along. On other occasions, his eldest sister Frances, with husband, son, and daughter, would all get together with his immediate family for a Mentor adventure.

Mentor Headlands is a mile-long, natural sand beach and a popular summer spot for people looking to get away from their day-to-day grind. It is the largest natural sand beach in all of Ohio, part of the Cleveland Lakefront State Park that spans the entire Northeast Ohio Lake Erie coastline. All members of the family have fond memories of these trips.

But the glue that held it all together was Mother Pearline. Her love superceded all difficulties and her positive attitude overshadowed family problems. Most significantly, her religious—specifically Christian—enthusiasm, along with her caring and nurturing way, informed all of her activities, and this left an impression on the children, giving them a keen sense of right and wrong. Her warm and affectionate temperament served to build character and conscience in her offspring, who became strong, principled people as a result of her solid but tender upbringing.

John has fond memories of his mother:

> She had so many wonderful characteristics. For example, she was famous for giving speeches at church as well as for making announcements. Many of my earlier speeches were actually written by her. When I ran for student council or gave other speeches, she would not only help me as a speech writer, but she would have me go over the speech right in front of her and would give me ideas of how to present the subject matter. Her education was minimal, but she made up for it in spirit and enthusiasm. And love.
>
> My mother was known for her extreme kindness. And when any of our friends came to our home who didn't have proper shirts, pants, or shoes, she would simply go into her room, take her own clothes, or mine, or Paul's, or our sisters', and give it to them. Even though we were as poor or poorer than many others in the neighborhood, she always had an air of abundance. I was almost a teenager before I realized that we were actually poor.

She was a very good cook, too, especially at making pastries. Often she would prepare delicious baked foods, like her cakes and donuts, making them available to everyone in the neighborhood who would stop by. She would do housework and everything herself, even after going out and working other full-time jobs. She would come home and do all the cleaning and the cooking, with an amazing amount of energy. Mother was a very fabulous dresser as well. She was particularly known for her hats, shoes, and pocketbook. Even though she was living a humble life of relative impoverishment, one would never know it by her demeanor and her lifestyle. She loved concert music and, from time to time, she liked to go to operas. And she had a very regal walk, very queenly. She would walk with a strut, with a slight hip movement, while holding her head cocked up high in the air. If you saw her, you would have definitely thought she was an aristocratic person.

She also had this power that everyone who met her always stayed in touch. Even when our own girlfriends or boyfriends broke up with us, or even when some of the marriages went bad, the partner would still see themselves very much connected with my mother and would still regularly visit her, call her, etc. Once my mother met them, she would consider them eternally part of her family. And she evoked that kind of love and affection in them, too. In her later years, she loved to travel, and was always very active. I remember her organizing clubs and being the kind of person who, when young boys or girls fought, would find a way to break it up and get the adversaries to come together in order to form some kind of healthy club or reconciliation. She was always concerned about others in that way, making their problems her own. Her famous mantra, often used on the phone when she greeted people or in person as well, was "peace and love." We always had this mantra ringing in our ears, and my mother was well-known as a person who was a carrier of love and peace.

She was extremely selfless. And in many ways I think this spoiled us. For instance, even all the way up until the time she became ill with cancer, or whenever I would visit her and most of the children, she would stop things to cook for us. Not only would she cook but even after cooking, she would herself wash the dishes and plates. (When I think about it now, I realize how much we overtaxed my mother.) Here I was a grown man and when visiting with her, she would immediately want to feed everyone. She was completely selfless, and she taught that to her children, not only by words but by example.

While on 79th Street Pearline regularly brought her troupe to Second New Hope Baptist Church (which in the 1980s was changed to the New Community Apostolic Faith Church). It was right up the block, so they would often walk down a short alley to attend Church and Bible classes there. When the children were quite young, however, the family moved to 82nd Street, which is where John was born. The Favors continued to attend the same church, though, for Reverend J. W. Allen, the family's pastor, was an inspiration and encouraged their religious household.

To understand John's childhood experience, it would be useful to visualize the surrounding area and neighborhood in which he spent his formative years. His sister Margarite remembers their pleasant childhood dwelling:

We lived on 82nd street in an unusual looking house. It was actually idyllic in many ways. It had a white picket fence and, as I recall, everything was whitewashed—my mom really believed in whitewashing things. There was a tree in front of our house, which was also whitewashed about halfway from the bottom.

Along the fence that separated our house from the house directly next to us, there were morning glories. Our mom loved flowers and would often talk to us about those things, about flowers and God's many gifts of nature—how they opened up in the morning, showering the Lord's blessings on us. The morning glories would wind around the fence—close to the front of the house. Closer to the back were sunflowers. Just outside of the back door, there were some hedges and a rose bush. To this day, I have never seen rose bushes that big.

My mom worked pretty much exclusively for an important Anglo or Caucasian family. I think their name was Mr. and Mrs. Dix. I remember she used to have to take the rapid transit to get there. She would walk up to 79th street and take the rapid transit out to Shaker Square. While there, she cleaned for them. That was her job, and she worked hard at it. What is really strange is that we now have family that lives in the area where my mother cleaned. At that time, Shaker Heights was a place where only the wealthy Caucasians lived.

Kinsman, the general area in which John lived, was also the name of a main street, which ran from east to west. At the time, one could catch Cleveland Transit System (CTS) buses to travel downtown or up to 55th street to East Technical High School, where John, for a time, was a student. Walking south on E. 82nd Street toward Kinsman, one would find Ronnie Cooper's house—he was one of John's best friends for much of his youth. If one walked east on Kinsman from E. 82nd Street, one would come upon an old bridge leading to Woodhill Park. Interviewees describe the scary experience of walking over that bridge—in general, it wasn't a safe area. There were tales of bodies that were found under the bridge, and so John and his many friends tended to avoid it altogether.

The park had an outdoor skating rink, swimming pool, and snack bar. Many of the neighborhood children participated in sports, spending much of their time in the playground. John occasioned the place as well, but he preferred his own neighborhood environment.

His niece, Renita Allen, remembers:

Most of the neighborhood children were good skaters and would dance on skates. But my uncle didn't play in the park that much. He played in the area in front of the house, and he liked to read, especially as he got older.

The houses had large porches where the children and families would gather. The street was lined with trees and Uncle lived in a single-family white house trimmed in green. The porch led to the living room and off from the living room was grandmother's [Pearline's] room.

There was a wood burning stove in the dining room, which heated the house and at times served as a second cooking place for large family gatherings, of which there were many. It was also where grandmother would sit in her rocking chair. I remember moments of oiling and brushing grandmother's scalp and hair while she would rock and sing deeply moving spirituals. Off of the dining room was another bedroom and off of the kitchen was still another bedroom that was used by Uncle Paul [John's older brother] to cut hair for friends and family—he did this more as a hobby than as anything else.

The kitchen was always filled with the aroma of food cooking or baking. Whenever one entered the house, one was always offered something good to eat. Many days you would find the kitchen filled with neighborhood children who were waiting for the homemade donuts to come out of the oven, or the cinnamon rolls, yeast rolls or cookies that were about to be served. When one walked out the backdoor, there was another door on the left, which opened up to a steep staircase. This led to the area that use to be an attic but which had been remodeled as living quarters—another bedroom. This area was rented out to other families when the children were younger. This is the area where Uncles John and Paul would reside as they grew older.

In the backyard, there were cherry and apple trees, which all the children climbed on, or they would alternately swing on a tire, *hung from a rope tied to the tree. At times Uncle would push us in the tire. There was a doghouse that was used by Leo, a hound dog, and later "Whitey," named for his long white hair, who would walk uncle, Paul, and Bernie [their youngest sister] to school. He was also the dog that Uncle would carry in and out of the house when the poor pooch became too ill to walk. This was a labor of love because Uncle's allergies would act up whenever he carried the dog. There was also a garden full with greens, onions, cabbage, tomatoes and other vegetables. We would pick fresh vegetables and eat them raw. The yard was fenced in, but the doors to the house were left unlocked most of the time. Cousin Frankie lived next door; Uncle John's good friend Lester Sandifer lived immediately across the street.*

West of E. 82nd, Kinsman would take you past the area butcher shop, and to several smaller stores and churches, and on the corner of 79th and Kinsman was Kinsman Elementary School, where John attended in his earliest days. It was located across the street from a brick fire station. The school site later became a field that would house a local carnival in the spring and fall. In the 1960s, the first public housing development "Garden Valley" was built in the neighborhood on E. 79th.

Travelling north on 82nd Street, you would come to the corner of Ottawa. Here you would pass Mother Jefferson's house on the way to the store. Two doors down was the home of the Allens, who later became relatives when John's eldest sister Frances married Horace Allen, Renita's father.

Says Renita:

When you reached 79th Street, you would cross the street and proceed north to Second New Hope Baptist, which was on the other side of the rapid transit stop. One could see Rawlings Junior High School from there, also located on 79th & Rawlings, where John had *the pleasure of meeting Martin Luther King Jr. Often, John would walk north on 79ᵗʰ and cross Woodland, proceeding on to Quincy to attend choir rehearsal or Bible studies with Ms. DuBose.*

"Ms. DuBose" refers to John's first mentor. She was a pivotal person in his spiritual journey, and much of the next chapter will be devoted to his experiences under her guardianship and care. But first, let it be underlined that Mother Pearline's "Forgotten Triangle" was highlighted by remembrance of God. One might think that in the midst of racial discrimination and poverty, God would seem a million miles away, or at least easy to forget. Indeed, in the face of hardship many tend to focus only on day-to-day needs—to the exclusion of spiritual needs—but this was not the case for Pearline and her immediate family and friends. For these residents of the Forgotten Triangle, God was remembered all the more.

A famous dictum tells us that "If God likes you, He gives you everything, but if He loves you, He takes everything away." This means that His special mercy often comes in the form of "tough love." The methodology of such love involves allowing its recipient to suffer in an attempt to strengthen his character and resolve, and to bring him to a better place. It is a deeper kind of love, for it views the larger picture; it doesn't seek to soften or divert the natural hardships of life, which is what we instinctively try to do for our loved ones. Rather, tough love looks to the ultimate betterment of its recipient, whatever pain it might take to get them there. In the case of God and His children, He sometimes puts them in difficult situations so that they might rise to the challenge, so that they can accomplish things they might have otherwise deemed impossible.

How does this relate to those in the Forgotten Triangle? Due to providence or other circumstances, some people find themselves ensconced in difficult situations, with little facility and fewer assets. Nonetheless, such people—sometimes *because* of their difficult situation rather than in spite of it—have a unique opportunity to become ever more conscious of their dependence on God, and, consequently, to do amazing things. As John F. Kennedy reminds us, "When written in Chinese, the word 'crisis' is composed of two characters—one represents danger, and the other represents opportunity."

Mother Pearline took full advantage of this opportunity. She may have lived in the Forgotten Triangle, but she had a "triangle" of her own, consisting of the Father, the Son, and the Holy Spirit—and it was this triangle that enriched her life; it was this that she bequeathed to her children.

CHAPTER TWO

LIFE-ALTERING EXPERIENCES

"Miracles are not contrary to nature, but only contrary to what we know about nature."

—SAINT AUGUSTINE

MOTHER PEARLINE had difficulty giving birth to John. For a not-so-brief moment, it seemed he didn't want to come out into the material world. But that was the last problem he ever gave her. From then on, he was almost too good to be true. As a child, he rarely cried, and as he got older he was soft-spoken and gentle, extremely well-behaved. He never caused trouble, and he was always ready to assist family members and friends. His sister Bernadette, who was a bit of a good-hearted mischief-maker and somewhat confounded by her brother's relentless piety, would periodically try to test his character. To give but one example: For most of John's youth, he had an aversion to insects. Knowing this, Bernadette took hold of a few ants, and, when he wasn't looking, tossed them down his back. He shook them off, ran a short distance, and then mildly turned to her, saying, "I'll pray for you."

29

Prayer was common in the Favors household. It was Pearline's modus operandi, and the children inherited it as one might a family heirloom. Along with prayer, of course, comes preaching, the desire to share one's inner wealth. Naturally, then, basic but heartfelt spiritual philosophy, as heard in church services, permeated the Favors household. Even the young children did their best to convey the gospel. Interestingly, young Johnny Boy was marked by a speech impediment—though it would almost entirely subside when he spoke on religious subjects. By using stuttering as a device, it seems, the Universe was saying, "Let me direct your attention to what comes out of this young boy's mouth—you're going to want to hear this!"

His sister Margarite remembers his speech impediment along with his general goodness.

> John stuttered so badly. He would start to talk and, as he would try to get a word out, he would stomp his little foot like he was trying to make it come out by force. He would get so upset that we would want to finish the words for him because he was our little brother. But in the midst of all of this there was just a sort of peacefulness about him. We were talking recently, his other siblings and I, and none of us could remember him getting a spanking. It was not that he did things and got away with them; he didn't do anything that warranted a spanking. He was an extremely good-hearted kid, and that stayed with him his entire life.

John's elder brother Paul once explained in writing how John's birth was actually an answer to his prayers. In this brief note, he mentioned the stuttering, too:

> I am told that as a child I would play games with an imaginary little brother. I would pull him in my wagon, talk to him, and save him candy and cookies, even before his birth, only to have them pilfered by someone, probably by one of my sisters.

When asked what became of these goodies, I was told that Johnny Boy ate them. Young but not dumb, I knew better; but, oh, what a surprise (and an answer to my prayers) when the next child born to my mother was a boy! Naturally, he had to be named John Edward Favors, better known as Johnny Boy. These were to be the beginning of happy and sad days for me.

It brought joy to my heart to see my brother play, make friends and grow up, but he had an impediment. It caused him to stutter and blink at times while stamping his foot. This bothered me because he was made fun of, sometimes. I told him to take his time, collect his thoughts, and then speak. I love him with the impediment, maybe even more because of it.

John himself often spoke about his stuttering:

I was born with a speech defect, and sometimes I could not even speak at all—my stuttering was actually that bad. For most of the younger part of my life, I was commonly embarrassed to speak out or raise my hand in class because, when I did, students would almost inevitably laugh at me. They would tease me because it would sometimes take me minutes—literally minutes—just to get one word out. But the most astounding thing was that, even as early as eight or nine years old, when I would start speaking about God—I was a child evangelist at this time—I would not stutter. But almost immediately after I stepped off the stage, the lectern or the pulpit, I would have difficulty with speaking.

Even today, although I have given thousands of lectures, I still feel nervous when I speak, even though the stuttering is almost completely gone. Sometimes it's not there at all. The amazing thing is that once I start speaking and gaze out into the crowd, I seem to almost immediately relax and go outside of myself. In other words, when I am in front of a crowd, I am in my element. The larger the crowd, the more important the audience, the more I find myself energized and able to deliver something that will affect most people who are in attendance. Perhaps it is similar to being a musician; the bigger the crowd, the more receptive and responsive the crowd, the more the musician can give and share something with everyone. He empowers and enthuses the crowd and it is as if the crowd somehow empowers him.

This has helped me to appreciate how my speech defect is one of the great boons and blessings given to me in this lifetime; it helps to remind me that I am not the controller. It also helps to remind me how delicate each moment is—we're not in control, and the Supreme Lord, who is in fact controlling us all, can change things instantaneously, at His will. When a person has a chronic stuttering problem, he never knows when he may find himself unable to speak or at least unable to get a word or sentence out smoothly.

During this time, in my youthful years, most of my lectures would be on topics of faith, tolerance, and love. Sometimes I would give campaign speeches, since I ran for elections in my various schools and in many different organizations. In most cases I would win the election, and I often won based on the presentation—a stutterer versus calm, trained speakers. Just imagine that! My confidence was definitely enhanced by Ms. Vivian DuBose Jordan, one of my first mentors. She knew just what to say—her wisdom and faith could move mountains.

When John was ten years old, his music teacher, Vivian DuBose Jordan, an elderly woman who was, even at that time, well-established in Cleveland public schools, inspired him to become a child evangelist, often appearing on local radio and TV stations. John, for his part, was a well-groomed, determined little lad. Perfect attendance and exceptional marks characterized his days at school, eventually leading to a full scholarship to Princeton, and Vivian marked him: "Here's an intelligent and stable child, just suitable for doing the Lord's work."

His First Mentor

A stammering young boy, John was naturally reserved about speaking in public. But Vivian would have none of that. She was relentless, giving him unending encouragement and a sense of urgency about the importance of sharing spiritual knowledge. "You know, John," she told him, "my own father, who has been a minister for over forty years, has a speech defect himself. He stutters, yes, but this did not stop him from his ministry." She also told him about Moses: "John, one of the greatest personalities in Christian history was Moses, who served God in unimaginably important ways. But you should remember that Moses himself felt that he was totally unqualified to do this. He had a very unusual speech defect—he was such a stutterer—and yet he is remembered as the perfect instrument of God. He was used to perform many miracles. His whole existence is a confirmation that if one simply makes himself available to the Lord's service, then one can be used to do things far beyond their normal capacity."

John remembers Mrs. Vivian DuBose with great affection:

She didn't have any children of her own, and her father was a minister. They lived in a rather middle-class, or upper-middle-class neighborhood. However, she was teaching underprivileged students— myself and the other students—in a ghetto area. She obviously had tremendous compassion to reach out and to be so concerned with all of us. Perhaps because she didn't have any children of her own—that might have helped her to take us on as if we were her own children. But it went beyond that, certainly. She just radiated love and a sense of doing the Lord's work.

There we were, a group of children from a ghetto area, who had been detected, highly appreciated, and deeply helped by this wonderful, creative, spiritual lady.

She took special interest in me, it seemed. She groomed me for

*preaching, just like my mother did. The main places I would speak
were at mental institutions, prisons, reformatories, on radio shows,
as well as in Bible classes and at churches. At the prisons I would
often explain how the prisoners, in one sense, were more fortunate
because they were confined and were aware that they were confined.
Most people, I told them, are not aware that they are prisoners of
the body and mind, and prisoners of the material world. Since they
are thinking that they are free men and women, their confinement
is even worse, because they are captured by the illusions of freedom
while they are in fact highly controlled and deeply incarcerated, if
in a more subtle way.*

*Also, I would often discuss the material body as being in a dis-
eased state. In a sense, just having a material body is a sign that one
is sick. Unless and until one realizes one's spiritual dimension—realizes the soul within the body—one is anything but in a healthy
state of existence. So when I would visit mental institutions or hospitals, as a little preacher, I would try to remind the people there
that we are all diseased in some way or another. I would tell them
that we have to get to the root of the ultimate disease—we have to
free ourselves from birth, old age and death, from the misconception that we are these material bodies.*

*Also, when I would give class at the Bible study group, we used flip
charts and various pinups made with flannel that helped convey basic
teachings. This was Vivian DuBose's genius. She created certain paraphernalia to help discuss various concepts and ideas. It gave us some
visual aids to help us in preparing our presentations and it helped
others to understand and to appreciate what we were offering.*

One of John's best friends at the time, Lester Sandifer, also reflects
on the impact their early mentor had on them:

*Growing up we had some very good direction from a spiritual
mentor, Vivian DuBose, or Vivian DuBose Jordan. She guided and*

directed us in a religious sense. We had our own personal little ministry at the time. We would go to different churches and speak for five or six minutes as part of the service. Seeing these little kids speak with knowledge and passion impressed people. Not knowing what format to go by, she would tell us to just let God speak through us. So we did. That was something that John and I did together. We shared that.

Going around to nursing homes and penal institutions was also part of that same ministry as a youth choir member. He and I sang under the direction of Vivian DuBose. Again, we were part of a youth choir. This choir went around and sang, sometimes preached. We sang down at the public square. It is a bit different in Cleveland now, but we were under the direction of Vivian DuBose Jordan and we sang as a youth choir. Later, after we parted ways with the junior high choir, we were involved in what was then called a young men's youth choir. It was still a Christian choir and we still made several contributions throughout the neighborhood by going to different institutions and just sharing. That was very, very touching—to see how someone would take their precious time to share spirituality with others, when some people thought there was no hope for them.

Mrs. DuBose had a morning Christian program where she invited John on a couple of occasions. I distinctly remember that. I cannot recall how many. The topics I don't remember, either, but it always centered around some religious teaching. But even at that time it seems he was destined to be a leader. It is easy to look back and see how that was formed. His radio personality developed at that time—he was an impassioned speaker and deeply sincere. Vivian DuBose, especially, brought that out in us.

Vivian DuBose was a short woman, with a little extra weight and a beautiful smile. She was kind but firm, a bit like Pearline. The difference was her air of authority—she was a teacher and a recognized preacher, with her own radio talk show, whereas Pearline was mom, and that's what defined her. The children recognized that Mrs. DuBose ran a tight ship, and they didn't joke in her presence. She normally wore long skirts and dressed plainly; she was strongly conservative, determined, and ready to convert the world to Christianity.

As John says, "She was eager to share her message and her realizations, and wanted others to be good Christians, like she was. She didn't just believe in prayer, she believed that prayer necessarily produces results. A lot of her ministry, in fact, was centered on prayer, asking God for various things, to work His various miracles."

Vivian talks about the early days and her exceptional student:

I was on the television and the radio in those days. This is because, when I came to the Cleveland schools, they were noted for their boys' choir, and, being a music major, I got to be in charge of the choir. We did all kinds of performances and even went to Washington D.C., at the request of political leaders. John was in that choir. Every year, the city of Cleveland asked us to come and sing downtown in the square. We would sing Christmas carols. The television spot that I had for my choir was how I initially got on television, but then I got my own local show, for preaching the message. This was when I was with Kinsman Elementary School, where John attended. I started teaching in 1943 and taught until 1987. When I started teaching, our average class size was 50-55 students. The desks were bolted to the floor. Sometimes the children had to sit two to a seat. These were the days of ink bottles and ink pens. We had to maintain discipline with the "board of discipline" for those who interrupted class.

Boys usually flock to boys, but John was always a loner to some degree, very quiet and unassuming. After school, I had a Bible class. It was on 71st Street and we met on Monday, Wednesday and Friday, right after school. I would drive over and pile all the children into the car. John was always in that Bible class. One day, I wasn't able to get to that class, and I knew that it meant so much to the children.

So I asked my father, who was also a minister, if he would get there early and make sure the door was open. Well, to shorten the story, my father did not get there in time. However, he told me later that when he did get there, the door was open and that the children were singing and praying. John had taken charge of the session. After it was all over, I asked them how they got in, and John said that when they arrived, the doors were closed and we had children arriving from different neighborhood schools, including older kids from the junior high school. John said that he climbed on top of their shoulders and jimmied that top window open. "I jumped in," he said, "and I unlocked the front door and all the children came in."

When asked if John's determination and leadership qualities came from his mother, Pearline, Vivian expressed a different idea:

I think it was a gift from God, and that's that. God earmarked that little fellow for what he's been doing. He's a servant of God, and the thing about it was that some members of the family would tease him and do different things to break his faith and get a reaction, but he would never budge. They knew he was an unusual boy. John was born for that job—I'm convinced he was always a true servant of God, and has been so since I first met him, way back when he was just a boy. I knew him from the time he was ten until the day he died. He would send me all his books, and though I didn't have time to read them all, I felt that God was telling me to do so, that His being was in these books. John was a chosen vessel of God, to spread the good news to the world. He did this until death. Even when he was dying, he was still teaching. People were still coming to visit him and he was still making time to preach.

Vivian herself was brought to God through the experience of miracles, both in her own life and in the lives of others. She says:

What brought me to God was a nerve condition that caused me to have severe pains in my right temple. Nothing the doctors were doing helped, not even a little. I was healed at a church service in 1951. That was what led me to believe in God. From then on I felt a calling to the ministry. My ministry was basically helping children and teaching Bible classes to children a few days a week after school.

Seeing is Believing

Vivian DuBose Jordan's teaching and example augmented something John had already received from his mother: faith in prayer. She was coming from a Baptist if also decidedly Charismatic tradition. The word "charismatic," in this context, is an umbrella term for Christians who believe that God offers certain supernatural gifts to sincere practitioners, such as healing miracles and glossolalia, or "speaking in tongues." They believe that just as early Christians had had access to these otherworldly phenomena, so too should contemporary Christians, though it can only be accessed, they say, through intense prayer and austerity. Their belief is based on numerous decrees by early Church fathers, such as Irenaeus (ca. 130–202), who wrote, "When God saw it necessary, and the church prayed and fasted much, they did miraculous things, such as bringing back the spirit of a dead man." Similar statements are attributed to Origen (ca.182–251), Eusebius (ca.275–339), and Chrysostom (ca.347–407), among others. These were Church luminaries with whom John Favors would eventually become familiar as he studied Christian mysticism.

For now, he merely inherited the essence of their wisdom in terms of Christian revivalist religion, especially popular among American blacks at that time. Here we find prayerful if also ecstatic revelries in which people are healed of some serious illness or otherwise reap the benefits of intense prayer sessions. As a result, those involved come to depend on miracles as evidence of God's work in the material world. For John and many of his local contemporaries, the poverty that was part of their daily experience was counterbalanced by a spiritual tradition rich in wonder and spectral occurrences.

This tradition came to life in the presence of Vivian DuBose Jordan, whose deeply religious personality and vibrant, energetic approach to spirituality enthralled her young students. With Vivian, religion was not a part-time enterprise—she was totally immersed in her daily devotions and in praying with great concentration. This made the prayer meetings, which John attended regularly, take on greater importance, imbuing them with ever-broadening mystical dimensions. Through Vivian's determined example, he began to view prayer differently, convinced that it could change the external world, that spirit could somehow envelop and manipulate matter. In his own words:

> When I was a boy, praying with Mrs. DuBose, I came to see the power of prayer, and this changed me for life. Now, there were about fifteen children in the prayer group on the average. Sometimes there would be a few less; sometimes there would be two or three times that amount. But normally there was a core group of about fifteen children. We were all either in junior high school or approaching that age, so we were around the ages of ten years old or a little older—young teenagers. Some adults would also come to some of the sessions, but in most cases it was a very small number. It was mainly children, almost always. One of the prominent kids in our group was my very best friend, Lester Sandifer, who lived across the street from me on 82nd off Kensington Street.
>
> Lester was very talented. He was a fair-skinned chap; rather attractive. He was a clever person who later became quite an orator. He was something of a flashy dresser, a talented singer, and also seemed to have a good support system from his immediate family. Another person who was a part of the prayer circle was a girl named Eleanor. She had a very powerful, professional voice, even though she was such a young kid. She had a voice like a professional opera

singer. Others in the group I can barely remember because it was so long ago. But these two I particularly remember because they were among the most prominent in the group.

The nature of the group's interaction was like a powerful underground cell, in as much as we all had our own lives as students in school, as children playing in the neighborhood, as young folks connecting with our various families. But it was more like our real identity was with each other, coming together in this house that had been converted into a Bible study center. Even when we were at school or at home, we all had this inner awareness that we were on a mission, that we were constantly involved in trying to grow spiritually and in trying to connect in a deeper way with God.

One of the miracles we witnessed involved a boy who had a withered arm; he wasn't really a part of our group. As a matter of fact, most of us never saw him until the day he came to the Bible center. He lived in the neighborhood, nearby the center. Now, Mrs. Vivian DuBose constantly wanted to test the power of prayer, or, I should say, she wanted to show others how powerful praying could be. Much of her ministry on her radio shows were testimonies of how people had prayed and how they had gotten all kinds of extraordinary results.

In the case of the boy with the withered arm, I became a believer. We were all extremely affected by this experience. We were surprised, but at the same time we weren't surprised. You see, in our Bible study group almost every week we discussed the power of prayer—and we all believed in it.

Still, even though there was a constant sharing of miracles, this one was exceptional—I mean, it would have made a believer out of anybody, bar none. The way I was personally affected was that there were several times in early periods in my life when I was really trying to give up the idea that there was a God. Whenever I questioned the spiritual path, or tried to find ways to avoid my spiritual calling,

I would often reflect back, especially to these two experiences—the withered arm and the blind lady, which I'll soon mention. This would once again revitalize my faith and increase my commitment to maintain my steadiness on the spiritual journey.

Anyway, the short version is that we gathered in prayer, and then we all saw it happen. Clearly, this wasn't a collective illusion. A room full of young kids saw it right before their eyes. This boy regained the normal size of his hand—I remember as we watched the hand grow out, we were all astounded, with tears of joy. The atmosphere in the room was so intense, and the young boy was just crying with happiness and disbelief. Then, after the session was over, he immediately ran home to inform his parents and to show them what had happened. I never saw this boy again. Up to this day I never found out exactly how this impacted on him after that. Nor do I know how this impacted on others, his family, or people around him. But at least my close friend Lester, who was also there, reminisces with me about this. Many years later, Lester and I would meet from time to time. I know that this experience, as well as the other miracles we encountered together—all in our association with Mrs. Vivian DuBose Jordan—had a permanent affect on our consciousness. It has kept us both very God conscious personalities, extremely open to otherworldly possibilities in the universe.

The setting of the Bible study group was in a lower income area, a two-story building with an upstairs that had a series of small apartments. Downstairs, on the ground floor, was one large room, like a loft space, and this is where the classes were held. There were no furnishings to speak of, except chairs, and the walls were bare. The room could hold perhaps 65-70 people, but it was rarely filled to capacity. John reflects on this simple setting where his early realizations took place:

Even though this Bible study group was such a simple place, it was

*something very special for all of us because it provided a place where
we could meet and really reveal our hearts. It was like a big secret
that we had, even though it wasn't a secret. But it was a chance for
us to literally tune in to a whole other dimension of reality and a
chance for us to feel very safe and secure as we prayed together and
as we moved about as special ambassadors who were on a spiritual
mission. Even though we were so young, we felt that we had great
responsibilities in the world and that we were specially blessed to be
able to have this opportunity to be workers of higher consciousness.*

This large room had become a venue for miracles, and faith in
God flourished for the young boys and girls who attended. John was
particularly moved by the healing of one particular blind woman,
mentioned earlier, whose eyesight, it is said, returned as a result of
this small prayer group. Because of this and his experience of the boy
with the withered arm, which happened only a few months earlier,
he developed a deep faith in the supernatural. He says:

*Most of us didn't know the blind woman, though we had seen her
around the neighborhood. She was "the blind lady." Mrs. Jordan,
I think, was the only one who actually knew her. The lady was one
of Mrs. Jordan's fans, someone who frequently listened to her radio
programs. That day, we were all seated together in the Bible class.
There were a larger number of us than usual, about 35 people or so.
However, only about three or four of us had this vision of the lady
being healed. You see, it was a little different than the "withered
arm" incident. That fellow was right in the room with us, but this
woman stayed in her own home. This is a phenomenon known as
"distant prayer."*

*Mrs. Jordan informed us in a dialogue that went something like
this, "We know that Jesus has no favorites. We know that he has
come into this world as the son of God and that he has said that
those who believe in him can do as he has done and even greater.*

He has also said that whoever calls on him and whatever one asks in his name—this shall be given. So, today we are gathered here to call upon the Lord to show His mercy and give His blessings to this lady who is blind. Out of selflessness and compassion, I want you all to pray with great intensity."

Mrs. Jordan continued, "I have asked this lady in her own home to pray with us from 4 PM to 6 PM. She is going to be praying in her home and we are going to be praying here." After about 45 minutes of intense praying, Lester Sandifer, me, and one or two other people, who I do not recall, began to have visions of this lady. Oh, they were real—we corroborated each other's stories down to the clothes she was wearing. First Lester spoke, "I see her going to her closet. She puts her hand on the door and opens it up; she goes and sits in a chair in the closet. Her hands are over her eyes and she is praying." After that, my own dialogue went something like, "Now I see her shouting and crying. She has taken her hands off her face and she is in total ecstasy because now she can see everything around her. She is thanking God like anything for being so kind to restore her sight. She is humbled; she is grateful; she is amazed and also somewhat frightened to see so many unfamiliar images all around her. She doesn't know whether she is dreaming or whether this is a real experience. But as the experience persists and she is able to see, she realizes that it is not a dream, but that prayer has facilitated her in such a powerful way." Remember, we were innocent, sincere boys, intensely religious. We were highly impressionable. But this was definitely something more than we bargained for.

After that, we had a dialogue where another child in the audience stepped forward and said she could see the woman on the telephone calling her close friends and relatives. The lady was crying and explaining to them that God has been so kind. He has given her back her sight.

When Mrs. Jordan heard us explain what we were seeing, she was excited and very happy. At the same time, she later mentioned how she was somewhat skeptical, thinking that these young kids have such faith in God—what if this lady has not regained her sight? What if these kids were just making up what they felt they saw? Or what if their desire to see this lady healed was so strong that it caused them to hallucinate?

Thinking in this way, she decided to call the lady, only to hear her screaming and crying on the phone and thanking her so much for invoking the power of God in her life. Of course, the next day Mrs. Jordan informed us about how she had had some doubts and fears, and that she had called the lady so she could know for sure. As soon as she got the lady on the phone, she told us, she knew the Lord had definitely answered the prayers of her Bible prayer group. That next week, the lady spoke on Mrs. Jordan's radio show giving her testimony of how she was healed through the power of prayer. She mentioned specifics that we saw in our visions. How could she know what we were seeing?

These two mystical events—the boy with the withered arm and the healing of the blind lady, which were not so far apart from each other in terms of time—played a major role in increasing the faith of all of those who were a part of the Bible study. These are the experiences that have lived on with me year after year. It is not something you forget. I'm sure that anyone who has experienced something similar would say the same.

Mystical Background

The reader may legitimately wonder if these otherworldly and miraculous claims hold any validity. There is certainly reason to have doubt. But if we think about it, we will admit that there is more to what we see around us than meets the eye, and that the great mystery we call "life" is bound to have certain metaphysical dimensions. Therefore, the above stories (and others like them) might just as easily be true, and the people involved given the benefit of the doubt. In addition, the reader might suspend disbelief in order to understand or empathize with the people under discussion, with their faithful disposition and their spiritual belief system. In this way, one might begin to appreciate what they were feeling or experiencing as the events took place. Whether or not the stories are everything those present believed them to be, they were clearly life altering.

The greatest miracle workers, such as Jesus and the biblical prophets, or, in the Vaishnava tradition to which John would later become privy, Chaitanya Mahaprabhu and the distinguished spiritual masters in his line, have always had deep philosophy and long-established traditions as a backdrop to their actions. Their miraculous feats are grounded in supernatural truths that are based on profound scriptural treatises and elaborated upon by brilliant philosopher-saints. Vivian DuBose Jordan and John Favors take part in such a well-established tradition. Baptist faith healers and miracle workers have a long and respect-worthy spiritual history. But there is quite a bit of fraud in that tradition as well, and John gradually became aware of this.

That being said, there is ample proof that prayer works, and that there is a definite connection between prayer and healing. Many scientific studies have pointed in this direction. In his 1994 book, *Healing Words*, for example, Larry Dossey, M.D., co-chair of the Panel on Mind-Body Interventions of the Office of Alternative Medicine at the National Institutes of Health in Washington, D.C., explores the effects of prayer and meditation on physical illness. Much of his evidence showed conclusively that prayer can have an effect on everything from sleeping patterns to wound healing.

Results occurred not only when people prayed for explicit outcomes, but also when they prayed more generally, when they simply desired good for someone. An innocent attitude of prayerfulness, a sincere attempt at holiness, and a feeling of empathy, caring, and compassion for the person in need—this is what formed the necessary background to accomplish acts of religious healing.

There are those who will want to know if Dossey's work is really provable by scientific methods. He assures us that it is, but with caution. For most people, he claims, prayer should be used to augment traditional or even allopathic healing methods, which also have their place in God's world. Still, given all that we now know about the traditional prayer techniques of established religious traditions and the contemporary work undertaken by Dossey and others, there's little question—prayer can be extremely effective, far beyond the levels once thought possible.

According to Dossey, experiments with prayer and healing already offer credible evidence that there is a link between the two. These experiments tend to "level the praying field," says Dossey. "They show that prayer is a universal phenomenon belonging to every race and creed, and these studies, therefore, affirm tolerance." In other words, anyone can pray, in whatever way they are comfortable, whenever they want to connect to the Absolute—and this is likely to help heal and even cure those for whom one prays. Vivian and John, indeed, would be pleased with Dossey's findings.

Alien Encounters

There was one other formative experience in the early life of John Favors, one that involved alien possession. Though for outsiders this experience might be more questionable than the results of the healing prayer sessions conducted under the direction of Mrs. Vivian DuBose Jordan, it was indisputable to his family and friends, who witnessed it for themselves. For John, the alien encounter further confirmed that there are unseen forces in the universe, subtle energies of which most people are unaware. If the combined incidents of the boy with the withered arm and the blind lady showed him that prayer is powerful and that there is a divine being who hears prayers, the "possession" of his cousin Edward Pruitt helped him to realize that, even in the material world, there are hidden dimensions of reality. Here he tells the story:

My cousin's name was Eddie. He was a very friendly and jovial kind of person. We all played together as kids—Eddie and his brother David, Greg Green, my brother Paul. Eddie's father, my uncle, was an elder in the church, and his mother, my closest aunt, was an extremely caring and loving person—both were deeply spiritual people. Now, at that time I was probably only about nine or ten years old. I knew next to nothing about extraterrestrial existence, except from a few TV shows or hearing some conversations and such. So this was my first encounter with any type of extraterrestrial entity.

I look back now and I can see how this was just an experience in a continuum of paranormal experiences that would be a major aspect of my life, opening me up to other possibilities. It was interesting, but the alien who possessed Eddie's body could read minds. Now I understand that it was actually a walk-in. My cousin lost waking consciousness for almost two weeks. Also, the being that occupied his body was disturbed by light. So, in other words, my cousin laid in his bed for two weeks time; he didn't eat or drink anything—though his parents tried to feed him—and had very little movement. His body was being occupied by this other presence. His voice was somewhat different, too, and the intellect was totally different. Now, my cousin was somewhat of a jokester, and so, at first, when the possession came upon him, we all thought he was playing with us. But, of course, after we all saw that he didn't get out of the bed and didn't eat and was talking in a very unusual way, it was clear that something strange was going on.

Being relatively simple people, we at first thought that he had some type of mental breakdown, but it was far from that. It was more of a mental break "up," because his level of perception and intelligence became far beyond that which he normally possessed. Some of the qualities that manifested in this trance state, which we would now call a walk-in state, were that he was clairvoyant, clairaudient, and telepathic. Again we were young; my other cousin was about eight or nine years old. So we found it quite entertaining that he could read our minds, or that he would inform us of things in advance—maybe ten or fifteen minutes before they would happen. He would tell us about people who were going to come into the room, things that were going on in other geographical areas.

His mission, he said, was to play his role in bringing about peace. He spoke about being in connection with other beings who were visiting the planet at that time, but he gave us some indication that he was somewhat of a renegade. He had broken off from them for some time, he said. It was as if he was on his own type of exploration that had brought him into the particular environment and into the body that he was now occupying.

Eddie was only twelve years old at the time. But while seeming to be quite young and youthful, because of his body, there was an unusual maturity—this was not the Eddie we had come to know. He just laid there, eyes closed, day and night, babbling, at times, but at other times answering questions and displaying knowledge far beyond what we deemed possible.

After he was in this trance for maybe four or five days, several people in the neighborhood and other relatives became aware of this and would come to visit. Most came to visit just based on curiosity, but also disbelief. His parents just wanted him to return to his normal state. It was confusing for them to see their son in what seemed to be an almost comatose state, not eating, not moving, confined to a bed, and speaking in an unusual way that had little meaning to them. Doctors were brought in, but no one knew what to make of it.

I remember quite clearly that one of my cousins was afraid to come into the room. You see, my sister, her friends, and some of my cousins used to tell lots of lies; it was a kid thing, you know. And several times during that two-week period, they would come into

Eddie's room and, surprisingly, he would expose something devious that they had said or done. So one of my younger cousins was somewhat afraid to come into the room because she was concerned about what might be revealed; she was terrified of his knowledge.

At some point my auntie and uncle became very disturbed, thinking that their son would never come back. The being inhabiting Eddie expressed great sympathy and sadness for their feelings, since he occupied their son's body. He seemed to be in a somewhat ambivalent state, wanting to continue what he had come to the planet for, wanting to use the body for what it was supposed to be used for, but at the same time feeling definite compassion for the plight of the parents.

At one point this tension became quite intense. The being in Eddie's body informed us that he was going to have to leave and go back to his particular dimension or planet. He apologized to us for any difficulties or problems that he had brought to the family and for any things he had exposed that disturbed us. He also seemed to feel that he had made a mistake by leaving the particular group that he was supposed to be with and felt that now he could understand better why he was not to go on his own in this particular way.

About five minutes or so after expressing his sadness for any confusion that he had caused, he wished us goodbye and then left. After he left the body, in less than forty seconds my cousin's subtle body entered back into the physical body. He had no recollection of what had happened for the prior two weeks. He was quite amazed that we were all standing around the bed looking bewildered and concerned. At that time we were crying both because the being was leaving and because we saw Eddie come back to us—tears of confusion, sadness and happiness. We were young kids and could feel the alien's sadness. Almost out of control, we found ourselves crying as he was leaving the body and returning back to his own home.

The other unusual thing was that when he did get out of the bed after only two weeks time, in which he hadn't eaten or gone to the bathroom, his feet seemed to have grown. Everything else was the same in terms of his physiognomy, but his shoes were too small. He just remembered having a terrible headache and lying down in bed. That was all he could recall.

John's friend Greg Green was in Eddie's room at the time, too, and he corroborates the above story:

It was the early '60s, but I remember the incident very clearly. It was a Tuesday. I was coming home from school, and I saw that Eddie's family had just returned from the hospital, I believe. They were leading him up the stairs along the side of the house, to his room. So I went along. I got in trouble that day, I remember, because I got home at 5:30. In those days, you were supposed to be home at 3:30, right after school. But this was so intriguing, so strange, that I just got carried away.

It came out on this day that Eddie was possessed by a being from another universe. At one point, Johnny Favors and I were sitting on the edge of the boy's bed. I remember it was completely dark in the room. Eddie demanded it—he told his parents, in this strange, otherworldly voice, that he couldn't take the light, even though his eyes were closed. Now, at one point, while lying there, Eddie made a sudden move, and I got scared. So I jumped off the bed, knocking over an ashtray. At that point, Eddie spoke, saying, "Why are you earthlings trying to hinder me?" Apparently, loud sounds and bright lights upset the alien; he couldn't tolerate it while in Eddie's body.

He knew we were there. He would call us by our names "Johnny Boy, Gregory Green Boy." Eddie's brother David was present and a few others, Ernest, Tracy, were there too—he called us all by name. And yet it wasn't his voice. Also, he knew things he couldn't possibly know. He described the clothes I was wearing, the color of my shirt, the trousers. Now, mind you, it was pitch black on this particular *day. Well, it was night when we entered the room; maybe it was the second day when I again came over to see how he was doing. I couldn't see him, but he proceeded to describe what I was wearing. And he would sometimes announce people before they came in. He would know who was in the house, who was coming over, and, like clockwork, they would enter the room, just when he said they would. He would also talk about his home in a distant galaxy, and how he betrayed the others to search out things on his own. But he was here on a peace mission. That's what he told us.*

Now, I've had many years to think about this, and, believe me, there were times when I tried to block it out. But it was real, and there are a number of us who were there to confirm it. So I'm quite sure about this, at least at this point in my life. Here's the thing, though. A young kid like that—he could pretend for an hour, maybe two. But this went on for over a week. No kid plays with his parents, relatives, and friends for that long, pretending to be from outer space, without eating or going to the bathroom … and predicting things. No. I'm sorry. Kids snap out of it pretty fast when they're hungry. No, this was the real deal.

Here's another thing: Eddie had huge hands before the incident. And he had just purchased a pair of comforters—a shoe that was in style at the time. After this happened, his hands were noticeably smaller, and his feet had grown. He couldn't wear the shoes anymore although he had just bought them two or three weeks before, and they had fit just fine. I remember him bragging about his great new shoes. And then this happened. So that was really strange. His body changed. Still, when he snapped out of it, he remembered nothing of the week or two that he was possessed. I'll tell you how it ended. Eddie was a muscular kid, and he had too much body mass. This is what the creature inside him said. Struggling with that, and not wanting to disrupt Eddie's life and family any more, he left.

Suffice it to say, the entire Kinsman community was startled and confounded by the boy they previously knew as Eddie—he exhibited strange symptoms and seemed to have the power of prophesy. They lined up outside the house, anxious to get in, so that Eddie might give them some insight into the ups and downs of their lives and into their future in general. Naturally, since most neighborhood folk were Christian, they interpreted the incident a little differently. To them, it was the Holy Spirit that inhabited the young boy they knew so well. God, they said, had taken over his body to show His power and glory. Frances, John's eldest sister, for example, was certain that this must be the case. But others were equally sure that it was alien possession.

Back to Earth

The mysterious episodes described above should not give the impression that Johnny Boy was anything other than a normal youth— exceptional, yes, but normal all the same. That is to say, he playfully interacted with his neighborhood friends, bicycled in the area, pulled harmless pranks on local people. He had an active imagination, enjoyed comic books, music and the usual recreational activities for boys his age. He drew quite well, and, at times, engaged in competitive sports. His mother and Vivian DuBose Jordan sparked in him a profound religious interest, it is true, and his thirsty mind was ever interested in learning the details of new subjects, in experiencing all that life has to offer. But, by and large, he was much like the other kids—if also a notch above them.

His family and friends have fond memories of his playful early days. Lester Sandifer, one of his closest friends from Kinsman Elementary School and on into his teenage years, had this to say:

We made our own go-carts and scooters. I don't know if you recall the skates that you had to hook on to your feet and have the key to turn it to tighten them up. We took those and got some two-by-fours and old milk crates—at that time they were wooden—and we made scooters and go-carts. So we had our own innovative ways of enjoy-

ing ourselves as far as fun is concerned. We all read comic books, too. Sometimes we traded off comic books with each other, and then, based on what was going on in the neighborhood, we played marbles or something like that. I know John did have a collection of marbles. We went to the movies, but not that often. The movies were somewhat of a treat in those days. I do remember a show that was part of our local neighborhood—it was called the King Theater.

Ronnie Cooper, another of John's best friends, remembers the fun they had as they came of age:

We used to go to a place called Halnorth. It was a movie theater. The rodents there were so bad we used to joke about them. We used to say we were going to get two bags of popcorn—one for us and one for the rodents. As far as music, we were into the Motown sound, especially as we got a little older, like when we were teenagers. We would have talent shows at East Tech. Some of the older guys from the neighborhood would usually win because they were real talented, you know, like Paul's friends, who were two or three years older than Johnny and I. The music at the time was Motown. Johnny Boy and I loved the Temptations, Four Tops, Smokey Robinson and the Miracles. There was a restaurant where we used to dance called Jets Restaurant. It was on 79th and Holton, with a jukebox, you know? We would bring our girls there and dance. Just kids having fun. My mom had a variety store just across the street.

Carmen Sledge, an early girlfriend who was also star cheerleader for a well-known local basketball team called the Scarabs, saw another side of his musical taste:

We liked quite a bit of classical. Sometimes we would go to Severance Hall, across from Case Western Reserve University. There were a lot of classical performances there. John loved anything with strings. He loved culture, the arts. He was so sensitive to what was going on.

John and his friends were into clothes, too. As kids they would love to dress as grown-ups, and as they matured they liked to stand out, both as an act of artistic expression and, of course, to attract the ladies. John, in fact, is remembered as quite a flashy dresser. Says Ronnie Cooper:

And he always had a high sense of fashion. Johnny, Lester, and myself, as pre-teens and teens, would wear white pants and a black bell-out shirt. That was Johnny Boy's idea. One Easter we dressed up in red blazers, black trousers, white shirts and black ties just to stand out, just to be unique or fashionable. You see, in our neighborhood, there were rummage sales. And we would go to thrift stores. We would get things like used sweaters or beaver hats, really "in" at the time.

Now, being cool guys, we couldn't be seen going into these kinds of places, you know what I mean, or we would get the reputation of not being so cool anymore. So, on our way in, we would look down one side of the street and make sure nobody was there, and look down the other side and make sure nobody saw. Then we would dash into the rummage sale and get what we had to get. Then on the way out, we would pry the door a little way open, put our heads out there to make sure nobody saw us coming out, and then dash out. This way, the younger kids would still be impressed with us, as would the neighborhood girls.

John remembers his flair for fancy attire as well:

In high school, I would often get the award for best dresser, or sometimes for the person, you know, most likely to succeed. But what was really amazing was that, although I would wear very attractive and unusual clothes, I would get them from a second-hand shop. We were so poor, but that didn't matter—I was dressing elaborately and getting all the things I needed. My mom just taught us how to make due, and also how to work around not having a lot of money. This is how I would get the best dresser award: by going to Goodwill, rummage sales, or Salvation Army, I would get old clothes that I would put together in creative ways.

But his greatest assets were his intellect and his heart. Despite childhood playfulness and a penchant for fancy dress, he took life seriously and was determined to excel at whatever he put his mind to. From his earliest days in school until his final days on earth, his personal example was one of enthusiasm, determination, hard work, and loving care.

For example, his perfect attendance, class participation, and general friendliness toward the other kids made him especially liked at Kinsman Elementary School. This set the tone for his tenure at Rawlings Junior High, too, where he eventually became the primary officer of the student council and received numerous citations and awards in academics, social studies, art, and Junior Olympics. He seemed unstoppable—if he tried for it, he succeeded. Reflecting on those early school years, he says:

My elementary school and junior high school—and my high school, too, come to think of it—were all in ghetto areas. The facilities were lacking. Most of the students were quite poor and generally came from broken homes. Unfortunately, many of them, especially in the middle school and in high school, took drugs, and they tended more toward partying than learning. They were more into being cool and having fun than into being serious students. I liked to play, but I took school seriously.

I always held positions on the student council, and I ran for various offices—I was quite active all the way through my early school days, from kindergarten and on to Princeton. I was popular and at the same time my speeches were usually pretty good. I don't recall the people that I ran against. But usually they were rather

popular, too. Still, somehow or other, every election that I partici-
pated in I won. A lot of it had to do, of course, with the wonderful
speeches prepared by my mother, Pearline.

She was really articulate, spunky and creative. Not only would
she write most of the speeches for me, she would also have me prac-
tice in front of her and then she would give me critiques. Well,
it worked. The students—and teachers too—were often quite im-
pressed by the speeches. Overall, though, when I reflect, I really
didn't do much when I was in office. Most of the activities were
controlled by an overseer. Even though I was student council presi-
dent, there was usually an adult who would be the student council
advisor. That person would be very active in helping to organize
and oversee things. But it seems like I was a good politician, want-
ing to get into office—I knew I could do a good job. And I wanted
to help people, and I knew that to help people you had to have some
power, some facility. This idea about the importance of political
status might have originated in my work with Leodis Harris.

Social and Political Activism

Leodis Harris, now an attorney but during John's early years a
judge in the juvenile court of Cleveland, specifically in Cuyahoga
County, was an important early influence. Harris served as a judge
there for eighteen years, and was a highly respected individual. He
first met John Favors, he says, in church. They were members of the
Second New Hope Baptist Church, and Judge Harris was particularly impressed by John's mother. He remembers her as an outspoken
preacher and as an eloquent poet—she would often recite her well
thought-out verses in the context of prayer, something all the local
church-goers looked forward to. John was just a young kid at the
time, but Harris found both the boy and his mother to be outstanding individuals. The good judge reminisces about those days, which
took place more than forty years ago:

Well, back then I was running for the office of City Council in Ward 16 and the church was located in that area. That's how I met John, along with his family and friends. This was a deeply religious family—his mother especially. At the time, Jackie Russell, who had been in office for a number of years, seemed unbeatable. Now, his administration pretty much ignored the children. Part of my campaign was to ask for improved recreation facilities in that neighborhood, especially for the children. Because of this, I attracted a lot of kids—they just came in, or their parents sent them in, which helped me.

Now, Johnny Boy was always a moralist—even as a child—which set him apart from the other kids. Some kids were kids, you know—running, playing, doing whatever kids do. He wasn't about that. Oh, he did all of that, too, but there was something more serious about him. He was always the moralist, trying to set things right, trying to keep things under control. He had a dignity about what we were doing. It didn't matter that he was just a kid. That was him. He had natural integrity.

John's good friend Lester Sandifer remembers Harris too, and the impact he had had on both him and John:

Going back to our junior high school days, John and I were involved in a campaign for a respected young lawyer who was running for councilman. His name is Leodis Harris; he eventually became a judge. I can recall John and I as being part of the campaign to elect Leodis as councilman of Ward 16. We had a flatbed and we were running around with it, doing our thing for the cause. We had no idea what the campaign really was—we were kids. We just knew that here is an African-American lawyer, and we wanted to see him get into office. We could relate because of the skin color—it was kind of like we were getting into office.

I remember the times we were passing out leaflets, John and I, and also riding around on that flatbed. From a large speaker on the truck we had music playing; it was Ray Charles' song, "Hit the Road, Jack." You see, at that time the incumbent was Jack P. Russell, councilman of Ward 16. He was a long-term councilman for that ward—a white guy. At that time, Ward 16 was a mixed neighborhood, though it was heavily ethnic. It was pretty hard to unseat Jack Russell. And, actually, at that time, it didn't happen, but we did campaign hard and strong.

With political interest often comes social awareness. For John, such awareness began to blossom at Rawlings Junior High, when he met Martin Luther King for the first time. Of course, he merely shook the legend's hand, as did so many other young African Americans in the area. King's visits to Cleveland were few, and so, when he initially came there in the mid-1960s, large crowds ushered in to greet him. John may have been one of many, but for him this experience sparked deeply rooted feelings of racial distinction. He felt pride in his people, and resolved to learn more about their history and plight.

At this point he became particularly serious about schoolwork, wanting to distinguish himself as an outstanding young black man. His close friend Ronnie Cooper remembers this period in his life:

John began with Upward Bound around the time he met Dr. King. This was a program for gifted kids, to enable them to move ahead, to prepare them for higher education. I would go over and visit him at Case Western Reserve. This was a college that John attended in the summertime. He was still at Rawlings Junior High, but they had these programs that were called College Bound programs. He was interested in really make something of himself, for his family, for his people. So he was a part of that program while still in junior high. He had the intellect, enthusiasm, and determination to do it. He was really exceptional.

William Huffman, the director of junior and senior high schools for most of Ohio, also noted John's exceptional nature. He predicted that in a few years the young Favors dynamo would hold the office of Cleveland's mayor. His prediction was broadcast in local newspapers, much to the pleasure of Pearline and her kin. Such accolades were not uncommon, nor was it unexpected when John was accepted for the Upward Bound program.

Established in 1966, which is when John took part in it, Upward Bound was designed to prepare low-income and potential first-generation college students for successful school years and future work opportunities. All students, grades nine through twelve, who were attending Cleveland and East Cleveland public schools, were eligible for participation in the program. This was a year-round undertaking, including a summer residential component lasting six weeks, at which time a simulated college environment was constructed where students often lived in university residence halls, received intensive academic instruction in mathematics, natural sciences with laboratory, reading, study skills, and foreign language. They also participated in the Health Careers Internship Project or the Community Service Project, which basically meant summer jobs at local health facilities. John took full advantage of these opportunities.

He began to associate with people working for Civil Rights, progressive thinkers who were as aware of black history as they were of spiritual truth—both subjects that attracted his attention. One such person was the Reverend E. Randel T. Osburn, touted as the first cousin of Martin Luther King. Actually, Osburn was the cousin of Coretta Scott King, who, of course, is King's widow, and he was quite accomplished in his own right. The founder of the Martin Luther King Youth Foundation, which developed and sponsored programs that eventually generated considerable funds for employment training and youth development, Osburn's major claim to fame was his work with the Southern Christian Leadership Conference (SCLC), and John was excited to meet him. Here he talks about his then newly found mentor in glowing terms:

> *I was awestruck at times when I heard Reverend Osburn give impassioned and eloquent speeches. It was also amazing to see him negotiate with major corporations, trying to get them to humanize their policies. He assisted in many boycotts and marches, and was quite fearless. He was a born leader, cool, determined, and dedicated to the mission and direction of Martin Luther King, particularly in his work with the SCLC.*

The SCLC's main objective was to coordinate nonviolent protests throughout the South. It was established in 1957 by Martin Luther King, Ralph Abernathy, Fred Shuttlesworth, Bayard Rustin, and others. These are the men who gathered for the Southern Negro Leaders Conference on Transportation and Nonviolent Integration (soon to be renamed the SCLC) and released a manifesto. In it, they outlined a series of proclamations to federal officials, calling upon white southerners to "realize that the treatment of Negroes is a basic spiritual problem. . . . Far too many have silently stood by." They beseeched black Americans to "seek justice and reject all injustice," and to "dedicate themselves to the principle of nonviolence no matter how great the provocation. . . . Not one hair of one head of one white person shall be harmed."

Back when John was seven, he had heard about the founding of the organization and that Dr. Martin Luther King, Jr. was its initial president. But it wasn't until John's years in junior high that he had the pleasure of meeting Reverend Osburn in person, for at that time Osburn taught at Case Western University, where John attended the Upward Bound program. The Reverend took close note of young John Favors. In fact, as time went on, he introduced the boy to Dr. King. Reverend Osburn tells the story:

John eventually became the leader of the Youth Division of the SCLC. We handled the entire Midwest region. He had a lot of progressive ideas, things that were alien to young black people of the time. He was a visionary, even then. For instance, he felt that black people should be engaged more in the right to vote. This was unheard of at the time. So he was at least ten years ahead of his time. Dr. King told me that personally. I'll tell you the story.

One night Dr. King and I were talking at Howard Johnson's at 107ᵗʰ and Euclid in Cleveland. It must have been 1967. That's where we stayed when we were in town. Anyway, we had invited some people to come in to meet Dr. King. Everyone wanted to meet him. Most would just shake his hand and walk away, grateful to have met such a celebrity. Not John. When John walked up to shake his hand, he paused for a minute and said, "Dr. King, why don't you use the word 'black' instead of 'negro?' And why do you wear Western dress rather than a dashiki?" So whereas most people were happy just to meet Dr. King, John actually challenged him.

At that point, Dr. King looked up at him with a bit of surprise: "Who are you, young man? What have you done for your people lately?" Though King was somewhat taken aback by John's bold questioning, there was a bit of admiration there as well. You see, John was on this kick of liberation and standing up for his people. So King pointed out to him, "Who have you liberated lately?" But he liked the boy's gumption. Feeling a bit embarrassed, I guess, John just left the room with the others who came in to shake Dr. King's hand. I'm sure he hoped he hadn't offended Dr. King.

After John left, King and I were talking about the conversation, and he said to me, "You know, that young man is really headed somewhere. He's at least ten years ahead of his time." I could under-stand that he was actually impressed with John. King also noticed his stuttering. He said, "Did you notice how he stuttered all the way up to the time that he was ready to really take me on? But once he started to take me on philosophically, he came into his own. He spoke like a true leader." We laughed about that for quite a while.

East Tech and Beyond

John often spoke about his time in East Technical High School, though he didn't stay there very long. He was there for less than a year when his excellent grades, perfect attendance, and the important people who were watching him made sure that he received special opportunity by going to Hawken prep school. His brief stay at East Tech, however, almost changed him for the worse. In his own words:

East Technical High School led to a big shift in my mentality, my life, but in many ways it wasn't a very good shift. I was getting involved with girls at that time. You know, a young guy with an eye on the ladies. It was a period in my life when I developed a taste for hanging out with social deviants, too, you might say. Basically, I wanted to fit in, and I became something of a rebellious teenager. So I started to hang with other rebellious teenagers, but, at the same time, we were all very popular—the guys you wanted to be with.

It was in high school that I really started trying to run away from God because I wanted to try to be like a normal person who just engaged in basic sense gratification. I wanted to be like everyone else. But somehow or other, it was difficult—like I was destined to engage in a spiritual path. I tried, but I just couldn't fight it.

East Technical High school was just that, a high school focused on technical things. It was much more than academics. Although it definitely had some good teachers and good students, the school was in the heart of the ghetto and, therefore, was really substandard.

East Technical High School was the first public trade school in the Greater Cleveland area. It was one of only five technical high schools in the country when it opened in 1908. The idea behind the school was to combine a general education with technical training in specialized fields. It eventually became one of the city's most important secondary schools for children from the ghetto, specializing in inter-scholastic athletics and winning city championships in football, basketball, and track, particularly during the days when future Olympic stars Jesse Owens, Dave Albritton, and Harrison Dillard attended.

Originally, the school was co-educational. It became all-male, however, in 1929, when its female pupils were transferred to John Hay High School. Nonetheless, it went co-ed again in 1952 when Central High School and East Tech were merged. The old building was made of brick with a Gothic facade, and it was located on East 55th Street. Eventually a new establishment was built across the street in the fall of 1972, but John attended while it was in the original location.

A predominantly black school, his opportunities would have been limited, to say the least, and by his own admission, as cited above, had he stayed there he might not have gravitated to the best kind of association. As fate would have it, however, he would quickly be transferred to Hawken, where his life would change in innumerable ways, not least in the realm of opportunity and multicultural experience. Reverend Osburn elaborates:

> I just know that there are whites who still, to this day, believe that, without our involvement in the Southern Christian Leadership Conference, and Dr. King's involvement as President of the organization, he would have never gotten into Hawken. But I hasten to add that it couldn't have happened without the distinct qualities he brought to the table—that's what prepared him and that's what really mattered. You talk about miracles: For John Favors, given his background and the neighborhood he came from, with its various disadvantages, getting into Hawken—now that's a miracle.

CHAPTER THREE

THE PRINCE OF PRINCETON

"A mind is a fire to be kindled, not a vessel to be filled."

—PLUTARCH

BEFORE ARRIVING AT PRINCETON, John was "prepared" by going to Hawken School in Gates Mills, Ohio. Founded in 1915, Hawken is a high-class preparatory establishment with an exceptional reputation, and John felt lucky to be there.

Five days each week he would take the same path to the rapid transit, emerging at the end of the line, which was Green Road. There he would pick up the bus to go to Hawken. It was a lengthy trip compared to the comparatively short walk to East Tech. But it was lengthy in yet another way—it was a journey through various worlds, from the downtrodden of the Forgotten Triangle to the posh, upper crust of white aristocracy.

At that time—1967 to 1968—Hawken was an all-male school, with a well-established academic and athletic record. Few there would have suspected John's impoverished background—his second-hand clothes, judiciously purchased at Cleveland's best thrift stores, allowed him to fit in. His very presence at Hawken, in fact, signaled his distinction among his peers, setting him apart from other blacks, and also indicating an academic ability that surpassed many whites.

He ran track and wrestled, and participated in class debates. In one such contest he assumed the role of Carl B. Stokes, who was running to become the first black mayor in the United States. Given John's background as a child evangelist and as a seasoned lecturer—compliments of Mother Pearline and Vivian DuBose Jordan—there was really no competition to speak of. John won hands down. Later that same year, Carl Stokes indeed became America's first black mayor.

One of John's classmates at Hawken, Birkett Gibson, tells us about the school and his time there with John in the late 1960s:

> It was the class of 1968 at Hawken. Nowadays, I'm director of alumni relations there. It's a second career for me after over thirty years in the automobile business. I love it—it's great fun. A little background: The school became co-ed after the mid '70s, but John and I were already gone by that time. In those days, we wore coats and ties to school every day. We had chapel morning and evening. It was rigorous academically. One hundred percent of the class matriculated to college.
>
> John came as a post-grad senior student in the fall of 1967 to Hawken School. He was transferred from East Technical High School in Cleveland, from a program called Upward Bound that worked with minority students to provide scholarships for them. Hawken was the first independent school in Cleveland to have enrolled an African-American student—but that goes back to 1962, amid some raised eyebrows, I might add. In my class, the class of 1968, we had two African-American students: John Favors, as he was known at

the time, and an exchange student from Liberia, who was one hell of a soccer player. We had a smattering of Jews and Catholics, but overall the culture was white Anglo-Saxon Protestant.

Now, mind you, John grew up in a neighborhood in Cleveland called the Forgotten Triangle. It's on the East Side of Cleveland, which was, in its day, a very industrial neighborhood. But as the factories aged and became obsolete, they weren't replaced or refurbished. It was a run down kind of place. Poor, poor, poor. It was from this background that John came to Hawken.

I would guess it took at least forty-five minutes for him to get there every day. In the class of '67 we had another East Tech student, Greg Watson, who came for a post-grad year; he did very well and played football with them. Maybe John had heard about Greg Watson. Greg lived in the same neighborhood that John did, but I don't know if they knew each other. So John, being one of a handful of African-American students at Hawken, had to make huge cultural adjustments, but, in fact, he seemed to do it with ease and grace. He wasn't intimidated.

He was well-rounded—a serious student and yet also on the wrestling team with me. He was into it. He was coordinated and physically quite strong, but he wanted to learn the skills of wrestling as well. He realized that there was a science to everything, a way that things are supposed to be done. He always worked very hard and was a great member of the team. He was always friendly, too. We kidded about his wardrobe a little bit. He tended to be, well, I don't want to say "flashy," but he wasn't a herringbone, tweed, or button-down kind of guy, if you know what I mean.

The amazing thing is that it was a school of mainly WASPs and that he was a black guy from the ghetto—it must have been culture shock for him. But he was smart and affable. People liked him and he knew it.

John's professors were fond of him. Peter Relic, in particular, saw

tremendous virtue in the Hawken newcomer. Relic was Head of the
Upper School as well as chief advisor to the students. He was also
involved in school athletic teams, so he knew John in several capacities. Their most significant interaction, however, came through
Relic's "Political Philosophy" course. Relic says:

*John is unforgettable. Although we're talking about thirty-five years
ago, I remember him vividly—he was intelligent, gentle, friendly,
probing with his curiosity. He was never rude or impatient, never
put anybody down. He was truly exemplary, as a student and as a
person. A wonderful human being.*

*If I could apply two words to him, even when he was a kid, it
would be justice and compassion. These are the words most obvious from his participation in my political philosophy course, too,
which John absolutely loved. The course dealt with a whole range
of Western philosophers. And what we did was relate the philosophers to each other, and then to political action, and then to ourselves, in contemporary philosophy and society. For example, we
would study Montesquieu, and then we would try to understand
how his theory of separation of powers in government related to
Madison, and how that related to the formulation of the American
republic. This would lead us into exploring ourselves in the current
day, with what was going on with the Vietnam War, and so on.*

*John was unreal in that class—he was so attentive and respectful.
His contributions were phenomenal. I taught the students to listen
to each other, which also meant to listen to yourself, to listen to
your heart. And John got it. He really understood, and he led the
others in this. They understood through him. He thrived in that
environment, and he always came back to justice and compassion—these were his topics.*

*These recurring themes stayed with him throughout. When, years
later, he came to visit us in East Hartford with two friends, he sat
with my wife and I over dinner. He was already a Hare Krishna*

leader, and he had two friends with him, two assistants. Over dinner, I discovered that the two men were previously inmates in prison. He hired them to give them an opportunity, to help them get on their feet. So even years later I saw his sense of justice and compassion, giving these two ex-cons a chance. He mentored them, helped them. He was a role model for them. This was the kind of person he was.

Howard P. Baker, known to Hawken students as "Dean Baker," took a liking to John, too. A prominent figure in the school, Baker taught at Hawken from 1964 to 1969, before he moved on to a higher position in another institution of learning. His field was American history but he was the "college counselor" as well, helping graduates place themselves in schools of their own choosing. In January 1968, he wrote a telling letter to Princeton's administrative offices, which clearly worked in John's favor.

His letter outlined the student's underprivileged background, emphasizing that despite all disadvantages, "he excelled in schoolwork, had perfect attendance, and was liked by both professors and other kids." He writes that John "arrived at Hawken in the summer of 1967 for a special course on Geology." This was "part of a program that enabled specially qualified inner city students to participate with suburban students in a meaningful course of enrichment." He notes that it was the Cleveland Board of Education that selected John for this opportunity, which was quite an honor. He remembers that, during this time, "John was part of a ten-day field trip to Colorado, which was the young man's first opportunity to see some part of the country other than the Cleveland-Hough area."

Because of John's successful performance in this summer school experience, Baker muses, "a Hawken parent volunteered to pay all of his expenses if he were enrolled here." His letter recollects how John, as a young boy, would sing Christian songs with his Bible study group at the Warrensville Workhouse, a correctional facility in Cleveland. He relates how John spent his time off and every holiday recreating his experience at the Workhouse, sharing Christian values with inmates in neighboring prisons. Naturally, states Baker, John "came to Hawken to help himself, but his goal is also to help his entire race. And he isn't waiting for the distant future to do this, for he has become a fine tutor in the Hawken inner city tutoring program in the Hough-Glenville area."

He ends his letter by saying, "John is a thoughtful, determined, mature young man who is going places, and he has the emotional stability and motivation to succeed among the most aggressive and competitive. Any college would indeed be fortunate to have him as a member of their class of 1972!"

John's impact at Hawken is felt to this day. James S. Berkman, Chief Head of Hawken School, had this to say:

> *He could be found studying in the library during his free time, as Hawken does not have formal study halls. He managed his time well, and found time to participate extensively in athletics and extracurricular activities at school. Being admitted to Princeton University upon graduation in June of 1968 rewarded his hard work. He fully embraced Hawken's central belief of "Fair Play" and definitely lived the Hawken Mission in his daily life serving others: "That the better self shall prevail, and each generation introduce its successor to a higher plane of life."*

John talks about the importance of his time at Hawken:

> *The change to Hawken was much more abrupt than when I finally went to Princeton. Whereas East Tech was a school of all blacks, Hawken was a school of all whites. Only three or four people of color in the entire school. The students in general were wealthy white kids; they were getting new cars every year. Many of them were from Shaker Heights and Lyndhurst, wealthy suburbs where homes had like 20-30 rooms. What was surprising to me when I*

visited their homes was seeing their maids. My own background
was more similar to that of the maids than to the students I was
visiting. Actually, my own mother was a maid and she used to work
in wealthy people's homes.

It was a huge cultural shock to now be in this environment with
the rich and even the super rich. But I was quite shocked to find out
that people are people, no matter how you cut it. They were having
tremendous relationship problems, just like the rest of us. They were
often bored, depressed, and involved in heavy competition with
each other. It taught me that human nature is the same wherever
you go. People have needs, desires, confusion, bad times, good times.
With that as a basis, I started looking more deeply into the essential
nature of things. If people are basically the same, at least on the face
of it, if we have similar likes, dislikes, attitudes, wants, needs—
regardless of our racial and cultural backgrounds—then who are
we really, underneath it all? This directed me more toward psychol-
ogy and philosophy, subjects that I would explore even more when
I arrived at Princeton.

New Kid on the Block

John entered Hawken late, having been transferred there from
East Tech in the midst of his high school years. Consequently, most
of the students there saw him as "the new kid on the block." They
had, for the most part, risen together through grade school and knew
each other quite well. But John, in addition to being black, knew
few people at the school and ended up spending quite a bit of time
by himself.

His initial stay at Princeton was similar. Upon arriving, he didn't
know anyone on campus, and there were few minority students to
lighten that deficit. Still, he did receive some solace. For example,
Carl A. Fields, the first African-American dean at Princeton, and in
the Ivy League, had been at the school since 1964 as Assistant Director

of Student Aid. He made history in 1968 when he became Assistant Dean of the College. In addition to his other duties, he served as a counselor to Princeton's first major wave of African-American students, which included John.

This eased John's transition to campus life. He was also encouraged to learn that a black man had actually received a Princeton degree as early as 1947. His name was John Howard, and he went on to higher studies at Columbia University. Moreover, the rebellious attitude of the 1960s sounded a clarion call for black men and, eventually, for black women, too. It ushered in thunderous social reforms and the attendant opportunities that went along with them. The reverberations were felt throughout America, and no less at Princeton. Always attentive to the sounds of the times, John saw an opening, and knew he could use this to eke out a place for himself.

He talks about how he ended up at Princeton:

As I was preparing to leave Hawken, the principal said I could go to any university I wanted, mainly because I fit in the minority category—they needed to accept a certain number of minorities at these Ivy League schools. At the same time, he felt I wouldn't be a risk. He said that any admissions office would realize that what I did at Hawken—academically and in terms of exceptional attendance, in my earlier school years—shows that I had what it takes to excel. I did extremely well in subjects that were new to me, courses like physics and math, for which I should have had a foundation but didn't—so they were naturally harder for me. Remember, I came from the ghetto schools, and so I really had no background in these subjects. But somehow I still passed.

It was interesting. My hard work paid off, but, on another level, it almost seemed irrelevant. We just waited until the admissions office sent out my acceptance. That was the situation: you don't have to work too hard at the end; you give all your records and then people come to recruit you.

Anyway, I chose Princeton. Although I was interested in those higher-level schools—Harvard, Yale, Brown, Oxford—Princeton offered me a full academic scholarship as well as money so I could go back and forth—I could go home for the holidays. They really wanted me, and they gave me a package deal I just couldn't refuse.

They were concerned because they had so few minorities, Indians, Africans, Latinos, etc., at that time. They were trying to be magnanimous, but they were also very clear, "Look, nobody fails in this school. We don't need a bad record. We may accommodate minorities, but you guys have got to pass." They told us that directly. They would give us whatever we needed, but we had to do well, to be serious.

And my case was very unusual because I had gone to these ghetto schools. I didn't really have any English or grammar courses, until Hawken, and I was one of that school's first black graduates. So they were sort of taking a gamble with me. It was different for the other students. In many cases, their uncles or fathers were presidents or deans of universities, or they were just plain wealthy, so they knew they were going to get in and they knew they were going to have a good job because, after school, they were going to join their father's company. Obviously, that wasn't going to be the case for me.

Princeton: Pertinent Pre-History

Located in Princeton, New Jersey, Princeton is the fourth-oldest institution of higher education in the United States. It is considered one of the nation's foremost universities, with a significant undergraduate college and graduate school, important departments of architecture, engineering, and public and international affairs. John would major in psychology, but also show interest in courses focusing on the international community, race relations, politics, and law.

The campus, located on beautifully landscaped grounds, boasts a large number of antique, English-style buildings, some dating back to the late 19th and early 20th centuries. The visual impact is tremendous, particularly for someone coming from an inner-city environment, like John. One can only imagine his first impressions when he arrived and saw the idyllic, country setting, with strong, well-taken care of trees, lush flowers and blossoming vines. His hopes and aspirations must have run wild as he contemplated the cultured, blue-blooded ambience of Princeton, with clerisy and wealth merging in a fantasy-like smorgasbord of possibility. He talks about the campus:

The Princeton campus is beautiful. I was taken aback by its storybook-like setting. Princeton, New Jersey, is a wealthy area in general. It has beautiful homes and people with a lot of influence and power. The campus is gorgeous but rather small when you contrast it to campuses like Harvard, Cornell, and others. The architecture is extremely elegant and artistic, though. The grounds were always kept up extremely nicely—meticulously. Living accommodations varied. Some of the buildings were new or renovated, but most were older and well maintained. Some had fireplaces and created an atmosphere. Overall, I'd say it smacked of a rather elitist architectural tradition, for which Princeton is well known.

The presence of African Americans in the Princeton area dates back to the eighteenth century, when blacks worked as slaves on large farms and in homes as agricultural and domestic servants. Even the free blacks in the community were said to be descendants of these slaves. Though the college actually had a regulation that forbade the students to bring personal servants with them, they tended to hire local black residents as personal "employees." After slavery was abolished, many blacks stayed on in Princeton, though they weren't allowed to go to school there. These were the people who would soon form an active African-American community, maintaining a pivotal role in the area's growth and development.

During the 19th and early 20th century, Princeton University was known for its emphasis on southern white leadership. Throughout

much of its history, the area, and the university in particular, had
been described as a northern town that has its spiritual heart in the
south. In other words, the social attitudes associated with the south
were given free reign and support at the university and in the town
that surrounded it. As John observed:

> *Probably some of my greatest fears at that time revolved around the
> fact that Princeton was a southern Ivy League school, very conser-
> vative, and I wasn't sure how I would fit in socially. But there were
> some minority students, though few and far between, and on week-
> ends, especially, we bonded and had exciting parties. So I would
> very much look forward to these weekend respites.*
>
> *Most of the earlier students were from very wealthy families
> from the South. My own roommate was a gentleman from one of
> the wealthiest families in South Carolina. That was my first year
> there. On his application he wrote that he wanted to live with a
> minority student. So he had me as a roommate. The first dormitory
> in which I lived had a suite and next to the suite was one small
> room. This small room was originally the slave quarters. What
> would happen is that the wealthy boys would come for their stud-
> ies at Princeton and would bring their slaves along with them to
> wash their clothes and to take care of other things. It was quite an
> environment. There were constantly confederate flags hanging from
> the windows of the rooms as a reminder of the South wanting its
> independence. The place was not receptive toward northern values,
> especially toward minorities.*
>
> *Of course, one of my fears also was that I would become a
> bureaucrat or some snobbish Ivy Leaguer and forget about some
> of my basic roots. But that never happened, especially since I was
> very active in the Third World Coalition with other minority
> students. I was one of the co-founders of the Third World Cul-
> tural Center, which was the center of people of the Third World
> at Princeton.*

Black is Beautiful

John's second year at Princeton saw him focus more on psychology and parapsychology, subjects that would have great meaning to him as the months turned into years. He started to make close friends, too. He met Philip Hollman, John Semida, Eric Vinson, and Bill Miner in their freshman year, and the five young students decided to room together as sophomores, a living situation that lasted until their final year at school.

Semida remembers that John Favors always dressed in a suit and tie during that first year—he was clean-cut and serious about his schoolwork. That was his focus. But his second year at Princeton saw a pronounced involvement in black nationalism, says Semida. This is not to say that he didn't still excel as a student, but rather that his worldview was changing. It was at this time, too, that he began to shed his more conservative dress in favor of Afro-centric clothes, also at times donning the rebellious attire of a student of the '60s. Bill Miner says, "We were all black, urban newcomers to campus. And it was the late '60s—Dr. King had been killed that spring. This was something fresh in our minds. In fact, there was a very, very active black student union, and I remember John being a big part of it, as was John Semida, and, maybe to a lesser extent, myself."

Melvin R. McCray, one of his colleagues at Princeton, eventually became a well-known producer on WABC television as well as an award-winning editor for World News Tonight, working with Peter Jennings for many years. McCray wrote in the *Princeton Alumni Weekly* (1981):

I saw John Favors for the first time at the introductory meeting of the Association of Black Collegians (ABC) in the fall of 1970. As ABC's president, he delivered an impassioned speech on the role of blacks at Princeton. Though only 5' 9", he was an imposing figure in his leopard-print dashiki and matching fez-like hat, with walk-

ing stick, pipe, bushy afro, and full beard. At that time he called himself Toshombe Abdul, and he spoke with the force and dynamism of Malcolm X.

Adopting the extremely temporary name Toshombe Abdul—he used it for almost two years—was John's way of acknowledging the importance of his black roots. At the time, many young African Americans were taking on such names for similar reasons. Toshombe, originally "Tshombe," is the name of a famous family in the politics of the Congo (ex-Zaire). It is from the Lunda or Ruund language, a Bantu language spoken mainly in that area, but also in Angola and Zambia.

John would have seen the picture of Moise Tshombe on the cover of *Time Magazine* in the winter of 1961 and felt a sense of pride. The article said that "the Christian, anticommunist, pro-Western Tshombe was elected president of Katanga in August of 1960," and that he declared to his people: "We are seceding from chaos." The *Time* article goes on to report, however, that Tshombe was accused of treason. The world would later find out, in 1967, that he was sentenced to death in absentia. On June 30th of that same year, his plane was hijacked to Algeria, where he was jailed and eventually died from heart failure in 1969. Still, his face on the cover of *Time* indicated a changing world for black people—for the better. As for John's second name, the word *abdul* means "slave" or, more accurately, "servant of"—it is the Arabic equivalent of *dasa*, the Sanskrit affix with which John would later become so familiar.

McCray tells the story of how John came to be the president of the Association of Black Collegians, leading to the spirited speech mentioned above:

It went like this: After the assassination of Martin Luther King, black students wanted to suspend classes, to take a day and reflect on the importance of what just went on. They wanted to have a "teach-in." In other words, they wanted to hold seminars, lectures, classes about the life of Martin Luther King, what he meant to the country, and so on.

The faculty objected, "We don't ever suspend classes; we just don't do that." But the black students were adamant. "No, no. We're not asking—we're telling you. We're not going to go on with business as usual. Forget it." And so there was a real showdown.

As a matter of fact, the students went right to Bob Goheen, the then president of Princeton. They went to his house, being led by Favors. One night, they assembled and confronted him, and I guess it was somewhat frightening because there were some in that group who really wanted to do damage. These were passionate students with a cause. They were just extremely upset that the administration was stonewalling them, in a sense, saying, "Absolutely not, and under no circumstances will we suspend classes." And, so, the black students felt they were being disrespected.

This was really the first major showdown between the black students and the administration. Well, Goheen didn't make a decision right then and there, but he listened to them, talked with them, and tried to understand what exactly was moving them. Anyway, it was during that confrontation that the then president of the Association of Black Collegians wilted. I think it was as a result of him not stepping up to the plate. He backed down, which is understandable. He didn't know how this would impact on his stay at Princeton.

But Favors took over. He seemed fearless. When I met him, he had just taken over, and he gave this impassioned speech. . . . Favors stepped in and filled a void and became the president of the ABC on campus. Eventually, Goheen heard them out and reversed his earlier decision, and classes were suspended in favor of the teach-in. This wasn't all due to the ABC students, though. What happened was that a black dean who was on campus, Carl Fields, made a call to Goheen and asked him to reconsider, which he did. Fields

*explained that these youngsters were not just trying to get out of
class, to skip out on school. This "teach-in" really meant something
to them. And so Goheen understood. Whatever the case, this positioned John Favors as an important person on campus.*

It was during John's second year at Princeton, too, that he became
friendly with certain leaders in the Black Panther Party, formed in
1966 by Huey P. Newton and Bobby Seale. He was interested in how
they interpreted the ideals of the Civil Rights Movement, how they
transformed it into the Black Power Movement. The Panthers set up
clinics and free breakfast programs in the ghetto, and this appealed
to John. He sometimes helped out in between classes and on weekends. But their aggressive rhetoric and militaristic methods exposed
them as extremist, thus alienating segments of both white and black
society, including John, who was looking for a more balanced approach to global concerns.

While the Panthers proved too radical for his tastes, black nationalism was more to the point. Here was a political and social movement
with which he could align himself, remaining true to his own conscience as a thinking, even-minded and compassionate individual. The
movement can be traced back to Marcus Garvey's Universal Negro
Improvement Association (UNIA) in the 1920s, which sought to
give economic stability to blacks, and to infuse in them a sense of
community and camaraderie. As opposed to being assimilated by the
American nation, black nationalists preferred to promote a separate
identity for people of black ancestry.

John found this a sensible approach to his black background, and
to this end, as 1969 turned into 1970, he joined the Student Nonvi-
olent Coordinating Committee and other activist groups on campus.
He was elected student body president in 1971 and chairman of the
Third World Coalition in 1972, a group that he had co-founded.
Semida remembers:

The Third World Center. Blacks, Hispanics, Asians, Indians—we formed a coalition, a social, cultural center that staged dramatic performances, enjoyed communal activities, performed functions, and provided association for students of the Third World. John was one of its founders. I believe it was his brainchild. And the center goes on to this day; it's a self-sustaining entity. He set it up. He wanted people to know that they could depend on each other—that we were there for each other. That's the kind of visionary he was."

And yet he longed for a conception that would transcend bodily identification altogether. Although he didn't know it then, this transcendent worldview would have to wait for the blossoming of his interest in yoga and Eastern philosophy, which was just beginning to emerge in his early college years. Soon, these interests would coalesce with his Christian background and his passionate search for the truth, ultimately manifesting in his life as a devotee of Krishna.

Bring in the Girls

If John's eyes were focused on schoolwork and on civil rights for students—if his vision centered on doing well and on the pros and cons of the black experience—they were also on girls. Both John Semida and Bill Miner describe him as something of a lady's man in his early days at Princeton. But then something happened. He went through a metamorphosis, of sorts. Says Semida, "He might have been a lady's man in the first two years, but he then became less interested in that stuff. He started to move in a more spiritual direction." Bill Miner muses on the exploits of five young men at school:

It all starts at these dining halls, where students get to know each other. This was Woodrow Wilson College, part of Princeton, and so we all went in and got this fantastic four-room suite. That's where Favors, Semida, Vinson, Hollman, and I stayed for two years. Wonderful, wonderful place. It was kind of a new living system at

Princeton, having some of the newer buildings—the newest build-
ings on campus. These were new one-, two-, three- and four-bed-
room suites. We had the largest of the bunch.

What you have to envision is four small bedrooms, one bath-
room, and then a pretty good-sized communal living room—all
modern, all classy. It was like a large suite in a fancy hotel. And
like I said, it was fairly new, but it was kind of bare-boned. So we
decorated it with what we had at the time. It was pretty tacky stuff
by today's standards; we had psychedelic lights, beaded curtains,
and tie-dyed things. So we were extremely normal for the time. The
thing was to attract ladies, which it did. Now, John was into girls,
too, but he was more serious all around. He was a kind person; he
wasn't into using people. In other words, he wasn't into just being a
Casanova, or exploiting women; he was into real relationships.

Still, we entertained a lot in this suite. Princeton is a lovely
campus, but it's also pretty remote, and if you're from Cleveland
and Washington, D.C., which is where we were from, it gets boring
after awhile. So we used our suite as a party room, and other groups
did, too. We let people use it. But I think we got a pretty good
reputation for having a well-decorated, extremely accommodating
place; we had a good sound system and we were very hospitable,
with parties almost every weekend.

In the beginning, there were no minority women on campus.
There were no women—period—for quite a while; Princeton was
just starting to accept women students. There were quite a few,
though, in the small town of Princeton. We also had girlfriends
brought into campus on weekends from Rider College in one direc-
tion, and then we had Rutgers in another direction; those were the
closest schools. Rutgers was co-ed, and it was a big school. So we
were pleased with that.

Vicki Harrington was one of John's girlfriends while he attended
Princeton. But this was not an on-campus romance. The couple

met while she worked for the Black Economic Union, which was a summer job in Cleveland. The Union was founded to provide jobs for college students, especially minorities. John and Vicki, then, mainly saw each other during summer vacations, when John returned to Cleveland and she was working there. The couple had much in common, particularly a concern for the future of blacks in America and an interest in African roots: Oladeji Aquah, as she was known by her African-American comrades, was, in many ways, a suitable partner for Toshombe Abdul.

Vicki became part of the family, an abiding relationship that outlived the romance. To this day, she is the best of friends with John's sister, Bernadette. Says Vicki:

We were Africans in America and I was attracted to people who had the same causes and goals as I did. We were both somewhat militant, reading the same kinds of books, into the same worldview. He was a very important person in that area. There was something that set him apart; something different about him. I think, basically, he was more nonviolent. That was one thing. He generated a kind of love and understanding. He was like Dr. King in that respect.

And he had this whole spiritual thing happening. Now me, I was more into revolutionary activity, spiritual or not. My main thing was changing the world. He wanted to get the job done, too, making a change and striving for peace, and he was determined. But overall he was more peaceful, or, let's say, he wanted to accomplish his goals by peaceful methods. My passion took shape in other ways. Now, on another but still related issue, even though we were really close, he gradually lost interest in sex. It was strange, and kind of embarrassing, too, but his spiritual dimension was really taking over. He was sweet, intelligent, good-looking—all good qualities. But he became more interested in God than in women. That was difficult for me.

Another of John's girlfriends while at Princeton was Juanita

Ray-Crame, who was a student on campus. Her memories of John—particularly his fascination with black culture but also his overriding passion for things of the spirit—corroborate Vicki's. She thinks back almost thirty-five years:

I met him one day walking on campus in October, 1969. I was lost and he offered to help me find my way to class. You could imagine the scene—we were on the beautiful Princeton campus. There were few women there; I think my year was the first to have girl students. He saw I was lost and didn't know where to go. So he gallantly approached, with his big, bright smile, and offered his help. A prince to the rescue. And so we chatted—it went on and on. We just hit it off.

It was kind of a unique situation, because, as I said, Princeton had just gone co-ed. And if there were few women, there were very, very few African-American women. In fact, as I remember, there were only twelve of us. So it was really easy to spot us on campus.

Anyway, we stood there for some time and talked up a storm— he was very pleasant. He literally was the first person I ever saw wearing rose-tinted glasses. They were in the shape of diamonds— wire-framed glasses, with a deep, rose-colored lens. I remember him as a very peaceful person, too, even then, at that first meeting. His energy was very calming and he wasn't frenetic like a lot of people I had recently come across. And he was really easy to talk to . . . with a good sense of humor. But he wasn't sarcastic or cynical. And that was one of the things I really liked about him, because there was so much cynicism in the air at the time, with the racial tension, Vietnam, and what have you.

And he was well versed in many areas. You could talk to him about things that were happening politically, things that were happening socially, spiritual subjects, psychology. He was a deep thinker. I remember eventually going to his room, because we became friends. It was a good-sized suite, and I remember that, the other guys, his roommates, would all be into watching the football game on the television and all of that, but he preferred to read, or to have good conversation. He was unique in that way. He socialized, and did things with the guys, but you got the feeling that this stuff didn't mean as much to him. Mundane activity was all the other guys had, but he was into so much more. He wanted to make a difference. He didn't want to waste time.

So our relationship developed from that—it was a deep friendship. We went out a couple of times, for a few months. I wouldn't say we were actually girlfriend and boyfriend, but we enjoyed each other's company. We went out mostly to dinner, to maybe have a nice meal . . . because we both liked to talk. We had conversations about spiritual things, God and metaphysics. This was one of the things that we clicked on. We discussed books constantly, like The Prophet, *by Kahlil Gibran. We talked about Edgar Cayce and reincarnation, the law of action and reaction, vegetarianism, yoga, meditation. Stuff like that.*

John also remembers his days at Princeton, with particular attention to girls on campus:

When I first came to the campus in 1968 it was all male, and during my second year the school became co-ed. In the early days we used to bring in busloads of women from places like Vassar, Radcliffe, and some of the other established girl schools. It would be a bit of a frenzy because during the week it was only men on campus and then, come the weekends, there was an influx of women.

The setting was in the dormitory, the suite where I had four other roommates. We had a very nice living room with a bar. The whole suite had been fixed up in such a way as to create a sensuous atmosphere. It was a den where we would attract women. That was our plan. So imagine the scene: I was with a small group of friends and we were listening to jazz music with the lights down in a very relaxed atmosphere. We were taking some mild intoxica-

tion, mainly alcohol, and some were also smoking marijuana. We weren't really into drugs. Now, there was this very beautiful girl sitting next to me on the couch, and I was telling her how beautiful she was . . . but then something strange happened. I found myself telling her that physical bodies are only temporary and that the soul inside the body is an eternal part of God. Love is not merely two people coming together to enjoy each other or to see what they can get from each other. Real love is only possible when God is in the center. I told her that spiritual love is what life is really all about, and until we learn how to love God, our love for each other could only be shallow, or a shadow of real love. Without God, love becomes lust and it brings negative reactions.

My friends, who were sitting nearby, were holding their ears, covering their mouths, and trying hard not to laugh. They knew where I was coming from, but they also knew that I was definitely going to blow it with this girl.

Professors, Psychology, and the Paranormal

John's early days as a child evangelist began to merge with his sense of global politics—his intense desire to change the world—which was augmented by a newfound interest in psychology and yoga. Yoga, in fact, was all about controlling the mind—so the two subjects melded well for him. He decided to focus on psychology as his major, realizing that, for him, the mind seemed to hold the secrets of desire and aspiration, conditioning and inspiration. He believed that his early experience of religious miracles, alien possession, and even racial prejudice could be understood in terms of subtle forces that center about the mind.

This is not to say that his prior mystical experiences and the way people treated him because of his color were not tangible realities in the external world, but only that they could be better understood by exploring their psychological dimensions. He began to think in

terms of *why* people do the things they do, why they believe in some
things and reject others. He wanted to know what motivated people,
leading them in particular directions—he wanted to know the limits
of human potential as well as the mind's impact on that potential.
Psychology and parapsychology seemed to hold certain answers.

Psychology is a science dealing with mental processes and behavior. Howard C. Warren, in his informative *Dictionary of Psychology*
(1934), gave four definitions of the word, ranging from "a branch of
science that investigates mental phenomena or mental operations" to
"the science concerned with the mutual interrelations of organism
and environment through transmission of energy." He also defined it
as "the science of the self." This last definition spoke to John's growing interest in psychology as a central human concern, as an underlying spiritual principle.

Ultimately, psychology is the science of the soul, and, in its earliest
manifestation this, indeed, is what it focused on. John was aware of
this, and it naturally enhanced his interest in psychological sciences.
True, the word "soul" was ill defined in the early days of psychology,
and in many quarters it is still a vague concept. The words "mind,"
"intellect," and "inner living being" were often used interchangeably
by early psychologists, who were, after all, not theologians but rather
doctors who specialized in human behavior. Because of this vague-
ness in terminology—and because of the limitations of psychology
in general—John was not content with his chosen field. Rather, he
preferred to journey into the more experimental realms of parapsychology, which is the scientific and scholarly study of unusual events
associated with human experience.

He explored the subject with considerable gusto, hungering for
the association of anyone who could enlighten him on this or related
topics. Friends would see him securing books on parapsychology like
a man kept away from his favorite foods. Soon it became obvious
to him that scholars from various fields and disciplines were finding

interest in the subject as well. He noted that physicists were interested in parapsychology because it implies that man has a fundamental misunderstanding about space and time and about the transmission of energy and information. Psychologists see in it unexplored methods of perception and memory. Philosophers view it as addressing age-old intellectual problems, such as the role of the mind in the physical world and the nature of subjective reality in an objective world.

A long-held, philosophical assumption, John noted, is that subjective and objective worlds are completely distinct, with no overlap. Subjective reality, or so the theory goes, is merely an individual's perspective; it is something that doesn't necessarily exist outside of one's own perceptions. Objective reality, on the other hand, is in the outer world for all to see. It is something that is usually viewed as being true in all circumstances.

The premise of parapsychology is that the hard and fast line between subjective and objective reality may not be as hard and fast as once thought. The dichotomy between the two might instead be part of a spectrum, with aspects that sometimes read as subjective and, alternately, as objective. Specialists tend to call such phenomena "anomalous" because they are difficult to explain in terms of current scientific models.

These anomalies fall into three general categories: (1) Extra-sensory perception, which refers to the ability to gather information that is beyond the normal reach of the senses, is the first and perhaps most popular form of parapsychology. ESP, as it is also called, is a concept that includes telepathy, clairvoyance, and precognition. (2) Psychokinesis, also referred to as PK, is the second category often associated with parapsychology. This is when an individual is able to directly interact with physical objects through mental powers, whether by moving such objects with one's mind or otherwise engaging them in subtle ways. Finally, there is (3) the study of the self as surviving bodily death, including near-death experiences, apparitions, and reincarnation. It quickly becomes clear why these subjects held such fascination for John.

His courses at Princeton reflected this new passion. While he took certain electives, like a drawing class, which was instigated by his friend Bill Miner, an architect, his main concern was philosophy and psychology, metaphysics and spirituality. All of this, of course, was always tempered by his interest in race relations, international affairs, and politics, which filled out his course schedule. He also took "Elementary Swahili" at Livingston College, part of Rutgers University. This was a special course taught by Al-Amin Mazrui, an expert on African culture, Islamic studies and numerous dialects, and so John managed the inconvenient commute, mainly because Princeton agreed to pay the weekly travel expenses. John was thorough and persistent—he wanted to know the language in case he pursued race relations and politics in Africa, which he had been considering for quite some time.

But the classes that meant the most to him were clearly the psychology classes, from which he tried to understand the more subtle aspects mentioned above. In these classes, he pursued his professors and their knowledge without distraction.

John often came to know his professors personally. He was never satisfied with the usual exchanges of formal classroom settings. Rather, he wanted to converse in private, to augment whatever he learned in class with something extra. It was as if he wanted to get an inner understanding, to extract from his professors deeper truths that they didn't cover in class. Richard Falk, Professor of International Law and Practice at Princeton's Woodrow Wilson School, who is now professor emeritus of international law at Princeton, was among his favorite teachers. From 1967 to 1975 Falk was Chairman of the Consultative Council for the Lawyers' Committee on American Policy Toward Vietnam and since 1981 has been a member of the Consultative Council for the Lawyers' Committee on Nuclear Policy.

Another cherished professor was Henry Reed, whose pioneering work on dreams, intuition, and super consciousness captured John's attention. When Reed began his career as an Assistant Professor of Psychology at Princeton University, he quickly developed a name for himself because of his work on memory and dreams. While at the C. G. Jung Institute he was inspired to revive in contemporary form the indigenous ritual of dream incubation, asserting, in scientific language, that divinities can speak to us in dreams. He is now Senior Fellow at the Edgar Cayce Institute of Intuitive Studies, where he regularly provides training, consultation and research. These were the caliber of men with whom John wanted to associate, and his later life as a spiritual leader was marked by what he learned from them.

In addition to the above, mention must be made of William S. Hall, John's psychology professor at Princeton prior to his thesis work. Hall received his Ph.D. from the University of Chicago in 1968, so he was a young man when he served as John's professor. Perhaps because of this nearness in age, he befriended his young student, whom he remembers even to this day. Professor Hall's research focused on the use of animal models of communication to understand the neural basis of human language learning. His current work is on the emergence of functional auditory-vocal pathways. Hall talks about his course at Princeton:

Usually we covered such theorists as Piget, Jean Piget, or Piaget, for cognitive development, and Freud, for psychoanalytic concerns —we also covered such topics as the place of intelligence, and for that we would look at the work of Alfred Binet and others.

John was an incredible student, attentive, bright, alert, a pleasure to have in class. His work was always exceptional.

Bill Miner remembers a project that he and John had worked on together. This took place while John was in Professor Hall's class:

I vividly remember him doing a lot of research in hypnosis and in psychology, and we would discuss it. Now, I'm an architect and I was an architecture major. We spent a lot of time talking about various environments and the psychological impact of the world you live in, the town you live in, the neighborhood you live in, and the dwelling that you live in—how it impacts on you as a person.

And I would talk to him from the architectural side and he would talk to me from the psychological side, and I do remember us doing one experiment together. This was in our junior year, and I had to take a very significant final exam—in architecture it's all projects. In psychology you can learn from experiments. So we wanted to do a project together. We decided to build an environment for mice, laboratory mice, and to establish very different tactile fields within this, somewhat like a maze. One environment would be very hard, cold, and dark. Another portion of it would be softer, lighter colored, and a little more spacious. We wanted to see the animals' preferences, how much time they spend in these various locations. We wanted to see if there was a tendency to be in one environment in the day, in another environment in the night, in another one to sleep in, and another one to eat in. These were all mice, and we used different mice. We just sort of verified the responses . . .

We were aware that not only will different beings, whether mice or humans or what have you, react differently in different circumstances, but even the same person or entity will act differently at different times. It's a hard thing to ascertain. So I can't say that we made any major breakthroughs. But I do remember us having some very in depth discussions about the impact of one's environment on one's psyche—the ability to know satisfaction, the ability to function. John found this especially interesting.

One other very interesting thing—and a little bit humorous—is that John became a very accomplished hypnotist while at Princeton. I saw this on several occasions: John would take a willing subject and put them in a hypnotic state. He would make very

*deliberate suggestions, such as, "When we are done eating tomor-
row night . . . when somebody says a specific word, you're going
to do the following, like go get some milk or something like that."
Nothing, you know, harmful. I remember on many occasions, we
would be sitting in the dining room, and everybody at the table
knew what he had done the night before—except the subject. And
I swear to God the people he put under hypnosis would do exactly
as he had suggested the night before. They had no idea what was
going on, and, you know, it was a gas. We really marveled at his
ability to do that . . . and some people even feared him because of
it. But it was always in good sport.*

Eric Vinson, one of John's other roommates, corroborates his fascination, and even expertise, with hypnosis:

*Yes, he used to use hypnosis techniques to help students with their
work. He would assist them in coming up with thesis topics or
have them focus on an assignment where they would get their work
done—all with hypnosis. Also, some of Princeton's psychology professors approached him to study his hypnotic abilities, which also
at times included mental telepathy. John would get a piece of paper
and write a color on it. Then, he would have someone on the opposite side of room write down a color, too, and, behold, it was
the exact same color! I saw him do this too many times for it to be
coincidental.*

John's interest in hypnosis could be traced to a link between psychology and the yogic truths he would soon explore with full enthusiasm. He often spoke about the connection:

*My senior thesis involved psychology and yoga—it attempted to
show the more subtle manifestations of psychological science, and
how it was more developed in the East. I did the research while
hypnotizing people—this was an important part of the study. I*

would take them, in different levels of consciousness, to different places, different avenues of reality. Sometimes, I would take them back to different times in their life, so they could experience it more fully. This is not uncommon. Sometimes psychologists or psychotherapists use hypnotherapy to help people with certain blocks, and they take them back to previous experiences, so they can work them out. This is so the patient might become free from some anxiety, some issue, or some sense of stagnation.

I would take people back to earlier times and I became quite good at it. And then I took people back to previous lifetimes, and we would record some information. It seemed indisputable. So this developed in me a real interest in reincarnation. I would read so many books about life after death, like the work of Ian Stevenson and others, because I could see that there was some evidence that it actually existed. They take people back and there's no other way to explain it. The subjects under hypnosis speak languages they don't know in this life; they speak of places, countries, people they don't know. How would they be able to speak those things? Sometimes the experiments are done on children, and they are brought back in time, under hypnosis, and they start speaking other languages. Reincarnation is really the only explanation. This is parapsychology and this is what I was into—I made it the focus of my senior thesis.

So I was changing. By this time I was a leader of the student council and people saw me as a revolutionary, involved in revolutionary politics and concerned about civil, national and international issues. And I was into these things, but something else was emerging during this period. I was meditating and praying, and the real me was beginning to come out again.

The Long Awaited Dissertation

John's senior thesis, completed in April, 1972, was entitled, "Yoga and Western Psychology, Or, Does Mankind Have a Future?" It was

263 pages, divided into nine chapters, of everything he had learned up to that point, taking the best of East and West. But more, the work represented a major turning point in his life and thought. He was moving away from the outer world of race relations, politics, and social concerns. He was, as he would often say, going back to his spiritual roots. Reverence for an all-knowing God was rising up again in his soul, and prayer became a mainstay of his daily activities. But while in his youth his spiritual moorings were somewhat haphazard, he now approached it in a more structured, scientific way.

He started to experiment with yoga, the Indic tradition of "linking with God," which is the literal meaning of the word. Unlike many of his contemporaries, he was not interested in the practice as mere bodily exercise, which was quite popular then, as it is now. He was reaching for *samadhi*, or complete absorption in the Supreme. And meditation, too, was not a passing fancy, something he would do for a few minutes when he had extra time. Rather, he tried to incorporate deeply contemplative techniques throughout his day. He used his knowledge of the mind, too, gleaned from reading numerous books on psychology, to augment his meditations, as he took the long journey to the center of the heart.

The thesis reflected this merging of spiritual interests. A brief breakdown of its contents runs as follows:

Chapter One, entitled "Does Mankind Have a Future?," explores six factors that endanger life on our planet: The possibility of nuclear war, overpopulation, pollution, depletion of resources, poverty, and oppression due to alleged inequalities. He briefly shows the interrelation of all six, bringing to bear his interests in global politics, the environment, race relations, and social welfare. Establishing a basis for the chapters that follow, this section asserts that men and women in the modern world must rethink their approach to life. Otherwise, the future will be dismal for all.

The next chapter, "Essentials of Indian Philosophy," is an attempt to acquaint the reader with India's historical and philosophical background, thus setting the stage for an understanding of yogic spirituality. The basic principles of yoga will be offered as an alternative to the modern epistemology and cosmology so detrimental to our postmodern world, a destiny clearly chalked out in the first chapter. Interestingly, John's findings here reveal that India's philosophical and religious heritage are among the world's oldest and most profound, and that her initial language, Sanskrit, is the earliest of the world's dialects. This is high praise from someone who was immersed in Afrocentricity, Pan-Africanism, and the Moorish sciences, to be explained in the next chapter. John was clearly developing new allegiances.

Chapter Three, "The Yogi's Solution for Incoherence and Transformation," picks up where the previous chapter leaves off. Having explained the roots of yogic tradition, John now elucidates the specifics of yoga itself, showing how its practice and function could avert international and intra-national conflicts on numerous levels, from war in the outer world to the wars that people fight within their own minds and hearts.

Chapters Four, Five, and Six treat "Hatha Yoga," "Raja Yoga," and "Jnana Yoga," respectively. The first of these three describes specific bodily exercises to help gain mastery over body and mind—but with the clear goal of becoming a servant of God. To have a finely tuned instrument, i.e., a fit body, can be dangerous, especially if one then uses that body for sense gratification—this could distract one from the goal of attaining the Supreme. But if that same finely tuned body and mind are harnessed for God's service, that would be considered the perfection of yoga. "Raja Yoga," for its part, extends the discussion of yoga to meditation techniques, also bringing to light Freudian and Jungian ideas about consciousness and how yoga might impact on these ideas. The "Jnana Yoga" section explains the place of the mind in yoga and meditation, and also explores parapsychology in relation to these subjects, specifically bringing in reincarnation and other Eastern concepts.

Interestingly, Bhakti Yoga, or the "Yoga of Devotion"—the path that John would later take up as his life and soul—is conspicuous by its absence. On pages two and three of his thesis, he introduces his readers to Bhakti, explaining it as the highest yogic process. But he does not elaborate. As of the writing of this thesis, he had already met the devotees of Krishna, and he was regularly attending temple functions. Thus, he would have understood the importance of Bhakti, so fundamental to Krishna devotion. But it was as if it was his own special prize, a secret gem that he was not ready to share with the world. "The most evolved soul," he writes in his thesis, "is attracted to the path of Bhakti Yoga." And then he falls silent. He gives full chapters to the other yoga systems, and only a brief mention to this greatest of all yogic paths.

Chapter Seven more fully explains the interrelationship of yoga and parapsychology. In this section, John looks at psychic phenomena first by categorizing its various components and then by exploring various prevailing theories or explanations of them. After this, he critiques the above theories in terms of yogic philosophy, with particular attention to the astral plane, the astral body, and astral senses, showing how ancient India had long understood the nature of subtle existence.

Chapters Eight and Nine, "Dreams" and "Life After Death," focus on Freudian and Jungian research into dreams and the unconscious mind, comparing it to the findings of yogis from ancient India. These chapters also elaborate on how one's inner self, the soul, survives death and travels on to other existences after the demise of the body. This final section goes into great detail on how this is so. Briefly, John explains the law of action and reaction, known in the East as *karma*. He tells us that every soul must enjoy or suffer the results of his or her actions. And that this is carried out by the Law of Conservation of Energy, which states that energy can neither be created nor destroyed. That is to say, the soul, the energy in the body, lives on after death, reaping the rewards or punishments of its current acts in a future birth.

Post-Graduate Studies

Among all of John's professors, his favorite, perhaps, was Jan Carew. Born in 1920 in Guyana, South America, and educated at Howard and Western Reserve Universities in the United States, Charles University in Prague and the Sorbonne in Paris, Carew is renowned as one of the founders of Pan-African Studies as a field of learning. He is Emeritus Professor of African American and Third World Studies at Northwestern University, and has taught courses on literature, history, agricultural technologies, and the origins of racism in the Americas at Princeton, Rutgers, Northwestern, George Mason, Illinois Wesleyan, Lincoln, and the University of Louisville. He is the author of numerous novels, essay collections, histories and memoirs, along with a number of stage, radio and television plays, children's books and novellas for young people. And John thrived in his association. Carew has tender and affectionate deliberations about their exchange:

I believe I first met John Favors in 1968 or '69 when he was in my summer preparatory class. I structured this class specifically for incoming minority students. That year I had a group of about forty kids. It was a new thing at Princeton, so he attended that summer to prepare for entering Princeton.

This was not a class to prepare them academically, mind you, but rather to equip them for dealing with some of the daunting challenges they would have to face. Emotional and psychological challenges, racial challenges, as well as new subjects, at least to them, like mathematics and literature.

Now, I must say that I liked John immediately. You see, for the black students, members of the black faculty, such as myself, were not only professors, but we were like father figures for them.

John, like the others, shared personal problems with me; he talked about adjusting to a primarily white school. And sometimes I would get these students to go abroad. It gave them perspective. So what I did with John, I worked out a special program for him to go to Jamaica for a semester. He stayed with my sister there. Her husband, Warren Thorpe, was the headmaster of a very elitist grammar school called Meadow Brook High school, and John stayed in the headmaster's house. You see, by doing that he was able to discover that the problems of the poor in Jamaica were more daunting than his own. This was so good for him. Perspective. It had a very good psychological affect on him.

Also, spending time in a society where the majority of people were black, you know, in Kingston, Jamaica, well, it was a different experience for him. It wasn't just black people who couldn't make it, like in Cleveland. It involved the whole culture, overwhelmingly black. It was like opening his eyes, showing him that people have hard times wherever you go. And that he had black brothers and sisters who were suffering for other reasons, not just because they were held down by whites.

So that was an important trip for him, which lasted for half a year. He stayed there for six months. Then, after that, he finished and graduated from Princeton, at which time, a friend and colleague of mine, Ulrich Cross, founded a law school at the University of Dar 'Es Salaam. The Prime Minister of Tanzania had invited him to establish a law school at the University of Dar 'Es Salaam. This is in East Africa.

Now, I suggested that John go there. I wanted to set him up and Ulrich was eager to have him come. He could have studied law, eventually getting a teaching position. He could have been a huge educator, or a politician. At that time John was thinking about specializing in international law, especially as it related to the newly independent African countries. And he had tremendous potential.

But he didn't go; I didn't hear from him again until he came to my house as a Hare Krishna high priest. Not that this was surprising. He always had an extremely dominant spiritual dimension, and it was just a matter of seeing where it would take him.

Years later, John himself would often reminisce about the opportunities afforded him by Jan Carew and the Princeton faculty:

Interestingly, Reverend Osburn, one of my early mentors, was training me in nonviolence and social reform. But, some few years later, when I was at Princeton, I was mentored by a famous international writer, revolutionist, and political and educational consultant, Professor Jan Carew, who introduced me to revolutionary politics, guerilla warfare, and he began to connect me with such thinkers around the world. It was a clear choice, but both options were material.

This was a major turning point in my life—I had to decide whether I was going to get involved in creating a better world through politics, international law, and revolution, or whether I was going to move away from physical revolution altogether. This is the point at which I decided to get involved in a revolution for higher consciousness. It was during that last year at Princeton, actually the last few months at Princeton. This is when I made the decision to walk away from my material career, where I was studying psychotherapy, international relations and, on the side, revolutionary politics. Instead, I was drawn to the spiritual journey. I saw clearly that real change had to begin at home. It had to first be inside, and, in the most profound way, it had to be spiritual.

I saw that even the people I respected, people who were acknowledged experts in psychology, for instance, or people who were dedicated to the goals of civil rights, politics, or what have you, all allowed themselves to become distracted. They all seemed to miss the point, as great as they may have been in certain ways. Their material attachments made them fall short. So I knew I had to pursue change in a different way, in a spiritual way.

This professor, Jan Carew, had personally arranged for me to go to Tanzania to work with the chief justice of the country. Then I was to go to China to study in well-known revolutionary circles, and then to interact with the United Nations. The president of Princeton, Robert Goheen, personally secured the money for my future studies from special alumni, even though I was going to be leaving the States. This was unheard of. Money had to be kept in America, for internal programs. But, they made an exception for me—they were that confident in my success.

But, as I said, I was at a turning point, and I knew, even if it was going to let them down, I had to get into a more spiritual lifestyle. So I not only left Princeton and put my material pursuits on hold, but I also did not accept the money, which shocked them. The money and the planning were considerable.

It was at that point that I worked for one year with the office of the Public Defender in New Jersey, helping to oversee penal reform programs. I lived almost one full year simply going to work and coming back home and just reading and chanting. At some point, I gave all my possessions, suits, collectibles and things of this nature away, gave the house back to the owner, shaved my head, and went to join the Hare Krishna Movement.

Just prior to his joining the movement, his chosen fields of endeavor, particularly in relation to employment, revealed him to be an extremely conscientious individual, truly concerned with humankind, if not in an ultimate spiritual sense then at least in terms of altruism and offering general help. For some time, he was the director of seven drug rehabilitation centers under former Mayor Carl Stokes of Cleveland. He was also special assistant to Stanley Van Ness, Public Defender for the State of New Jersey.

John was aware that the position of Public Defender in New Jersey had been held by some of the most respected names in the state's

legal community. The first Public Defender was a man named Peter
Murray, whose untimely death in 1969 led to the appointment of
Stanley C. Van Ness. Here was a man who had been the governor's
counsel and was active in national efforts to reform court procedures.
He also became the state's first Public Advocate when that agency was
created in 1974. John worked under him and watched him closely. He
was looking for integrity and for people who mean what they say.

The Epitome of Absurdity

John reflects on the first time he saw devotees of Krishna:

*It was in Boston at Harvard Square. It was extremely cold, almost
ten below zero, and these Hare Krishnas were bundled up on the
street corner chanting. There were seven or eight of them, including Satsvarupa Maharaja and some older devotees from the Boston
temple, though I didn't know it then. I thought it was just a bunch of
rich white kids out for some fun—strange fun, but fun all the same.*

*At this time, in 1970 or 1971, I had been attending Princeton
and was on my way to a game at Harvard. After returning several
hours later, after the game, I noticed the devotees still chanting on
the same street corner and thought that these people were either
extremely crazy or had something incredibly deep. Their determination was impressive. I remember my exact thought: "This is
the epitome of absurdity." And yet I sensed that it was more than
absurd. It was complete dedication.*

*I could barely tolerate the outside temperature for five or ten
minutes before running into a building or car for some heat. Despite the cold, they just kept chanting, dancing and even jumping.
Just from their appearance, I could observe something very unusual
and special. After briefly giving it some thought, I let it drop.*

But not for long. His burgeoning interest in yoga and Eastern
mysticism found him pursuing teachers of various traditions. He

temporarily settled on Sri Chinmoy, a spiritual master from Bengal who had attained some fame as the guru of numerous celebrities and as interfaith chaplain for the United Nations. Having found his "eternal master," John quickly returned to Cleveland, to an unnamed mentor—later revealed to be Norman Anderson, a spiritual adept described in the next chapter—telling him that he had finally found his teacher. John relates the story as follows:

> *I had been visiting different yogis and spiritualists, taking initiation from this guru and that guru. Anytime I heard of some guru or spiritualist, I would go to learn from them. One teacher who instructed me for four or five years in the late 60s taught me a variety of disciplines such as Raja Yoga, Hatha Yoga, Ashtanga Yoga and other mystical practices. Nevertheless, he always told me that he was not my actual teacher or guru.*
>
> *I next met another teacher, Sri Chinmoy, joined his group, and took initiation in New York. After returning to my previous teacher in Cleveland, I told him, "Now I have met my guru and I've taken initiation." I thought he might be proud of me. He simply laughed, saying, "This teacher only has a little impersonal realization at best, and it is not what you think." I replied, "But he is advertised as the jagat-guru, the spiritual master of the universe." He laughed again, saying, "The position of this particular personality is not something very serious."*
>
> *When I initially met Sri Chinmoy, I was excited at the prospect of having found my guru. But now I was disappointed to hear that he was not the real article. You see, I deeply respected my previous mentor from Cleveland, and so I took it quite seriously when he denounced my new teacher.*
>
> *One day, that same mentor from Cleveland asked me, "Do you really want to know who the jagat-guru is?" and I replied, "Yes, yes, yes, I really want to know." Then he repeated more emphatically, almost teasing me, "Do you really want to know?" Again I*

answered, "Yes." Actually, he was cautioning me, realizing that
my life would have to change after hearing this truth. He asked
one last time, "Do you really want to know?" With all sincerity, I
said, "yes." He finally answered, "The spiritual master of the Hare
Krishna Movement, Srila Prabhupada—he's the real jagat-guru."

"WHAT?" I asked, incredulously. "You're referring to those
people who wear bed sheets and jump up and down in the streets
with strange-looking paint on their faces?" I immediately remembered the first time I saw them chanting in Boston, in the cold. I
questioned him, "You mean that they have deep philosophy and a
special spiritual mentor?" He answered in the affirmative. He explained Srila Prabhupada's position as the spiritual master of spiritual masters. He then further explained, "When Prabhupada came
to the West, the many other spiritual leaders who knew something
of his level of excellence and position should have assisted him in
his mission. I have always told you that I am not your guru because
I am not. You're supposed to be involved in Bhakti, devotion to
Krishna, as taught by Prabhupada. Still, everything I've shown you
will help in the future with the work you'll have to do."

This completely astounded me because I had always looked for
ultimate truth and now this particular spiritual authority informed me of a higher truth available in the Krishna Consciousness Movement. This new dilemma required deep reflection. From
my observation of the Hare Krishna devotees, I could understand
that their practice was not some extracurricular, yogic experience.
It demanded a commitment beyond weekly meetings and a few
asanas. This I knew. Following these Hare Krishnas would mean
a total shift in my lifestyle and mindset. I searched for ways to
avoid dealing with the situation, unable to believe that such high
knowledge could be found among these strange people in the streets.
After attending Princeton and preparing for a career in the United
Nations, I could hardly accept that higher knowledge meant wear-

ing a bed sheet, painting your face, and jumping in the streets for the rest of your life.

John attended a few "Sunday Love Feasts" at the Brooklyn Hare Krishna temple. Here he had his first taste of *prasadam* (vegetarian food offered to the Lord in sacrifice and then distributed as sacred edibles), along with his first sampling of introductory Krishna Conscious philosophy classes and spiritual chanting sessions—these were also part of the Love Feasts. It's something that he really enjoyed, and so he casually invited the devotees to visit him at Princeton.

Within weeks, they arrived: A troupe of four enthusiastic chanters led by Sudhanu Prabhu unexpectedly knocked on his dorm door. They had been regularly attending peace rallies and college campuses to distribute their brand of Vaishnava spirituality to the masses, and they just showed up one day at Princeton unannounced. But when John opened the door and saw them in full regalia, he greeted them with his signature smile.

Ushering them in, he started to phone up his friends and invited some neighboring schoolmates. The devotees, now making themselves at home, did their thing. They proceeded to engage in demonstrative Kirtan, congregational chanting of Krishna's names. Soon they were cooking a *prasadam* feast and explaining the eternal truths of Krishna Consciousness. They also spent the night. By the time they left, John was all the more convinced of the age-old philosophy of the Vaishnava sages.

He invited the devotees back several times, and he now regularly attended their temple, not only on Sundays but during the week as well. At Henry Street, where the Brooklyn temple was located, he had had engaging interactions with others who had been practicing for several years. One was Mahamuni Dasa, who helped him to see the virtue of personalistic Vaishnava philosophy. John was coming from the Sri Chinmoy outlook, which was heavily influenced by vague notions of an amorphous divinity and a goal of becoming one

with God. Mahamuni helped bridge the gap, explaining that imper-
sonalism is but a preliminary step on the path of God realization,
and that merging with the Supreme is a stepping-stone to a mood of
divine service. "Vaishnavas don't want to *be* sugar," said Mahamuni,
"they want to *taste* sugar." John listened and understood.

CHAPTER FOUR

ENTER THE DARK LORD

"In reading the lives of great men,
I found that the first victory they won was over themselves . . .
self-discipline with all of them came first."

—HARRY S. TRUMAN

JOHN'S INVOLVEMENT WITH KRISHNA was part of a personal continuum. He did not view his newfound faith as antithetical to Christianity, nor did it in any way contradict the truths he had learned from the Bible. Rather, his lifelong commitment to God and the spiritual pursuit was augmented, or enhanced, by his discovery of Vaishnavism, which he also saw as the perfection of yoga. In other words, Krishna Consciousness was an extension of his earlier spiritual path.

He was convinced that he had now found the science of the soul, a methodical approach to the nurturing of his inner life. All sectarian religion, of course, is a step in this direction, and Christianity is no exception. But he had now come to the source, the nonsectarian origin that was carefully handed down from master to disciple in an unbroken chain of highly qualified teachers. It is this original spiritual science that gradually manifested as the many religions of the world, usually in some abbreviated form.

Krishna Consciousness, as John saw it, was like a fossil, perfectly preserved from a purer time, when humankind was focused on God. The great Krishna Conscious teachers of the past had devised spiritual technologies by which one could reach perfection. They encoded these truths in carefully worded scriptures and in time-tested techniques that gradually unlock the secrets of the spiritual world. These were the precious gems that John now cherished.

This was the postgraduate study of religion. John liked Prabhupada's analogy: If the Bible could be seen as a pocket dictionary, then the Vedic literature was the unabridged version. For example, throughout his life, John had wondered about "the Father," that enigmatic entity to whom, in the Christian Bible, Jesus prays. John believed in this elusive "God," but he wanted to know more about Him. God's kingdom was also mentioned in the Bible—this was a higher realm that John had heard about for his entire youth and for much of his early adulthood. But what did he really know about it? The paucity of information supplied by biblical literature was troubling to him.

He was extremely pleased, therefore, to learn that the Vedic literature reveals considerable details about Jesus' Father and about the spiritual kingdom from which He comes. Only in this ancient, esoteric tradition do practitioners find minutiae of God's self-existent nature and His multitude of forms. The Lord's kingdom, too, is not described merely as "great," as it is in the Bible, but specifics about this greatness are fully delineated—higher and lower planetary systems in the transcendental kingdom are graphically described.

Naturally, then, John was grateful to the individuals who introduced him to this tradition. There are two people, in particular, who influenced his initial allegiance to the Krishna Consciousness Movement: Norman Anderson, briefly mentioned in the previous chapter, and Eva Coleman, John's fiancée. Their guidance, compassion, natural wisdom and inherent spirituality led him to join a movement in which he would soon become a global leader. Before elaborating on

his specific evolution as a devotee, therefore, let us first briefly explore
these two consequential personalities and their impact on his life.

"God is a Blue Dude"

Norman Anderson was born November 2, 1922 in Paduka, Kentucky to John Isom Anderson and Willie Billingsley, African Americans
of southern extraction. As a child, Norman was introduced to Vedic
teachings by his grandmother, who was from India. He thus imbibed,
early on, the culture of black America along with that of East-Indian
exotica. Because of this, he says, he was a vegetarian for most of his life,
which is why, in his own words, he "smelled like roses."

After the family relocated to Cleveland, he attended and graduated from Central High School and then joined the US Navy, which
afforded him some modicum of travel and worldly experience. Afterwards, he married Bernice Bowers. They had three children—Norman
Jr., Arturo, and Marita—and one stepchild (Elizabeth Bowers).

Throughout his life he maintained an interest in history and philosophy, but always as it related to the spiritual quest. As far as his personal journey, he was inclined to Islam, eventually moving on to the
intricacies of Moorish Science, explained below. Moreover, he maintained that he was introduced to Krishna Consciousness in 1954, in
a psychic exchange with Srila Prabhupada, the movement's founder,
before Prabhupada ever came West. Whatever one makes of this, his
devotion to Prabhupada's mission lasted until his dying day.

When Norman was in his 40s, he saw Prabhupada in New York's
Bowery, soon after the spiritual master had indeed arrived there in
the 1960s, and it frightened him. He saw "Prabhupada's power," as
he put it, and was taken aback. The subtle energy was too intense,
and he fled. When Prabhupada came to New Vrindavan in 1974,
however, Norman drew the courage to come and see him, and, after
that, he resolved to spread the teachings of this *jagat-guru*, or "universal world teacher," for the rest of his life. Norman passed away at

Meridia South Pointe Hospital in Cleveland as a resident of Willow Park Nursing Home on April 11, 2000.

John's relationship with Norman goes back to the late '60s, though he only began to accept him as a mentor while at Princeton, on summer breaks when he returned to his hometown. Many of the local teenagers were enthralled by Norman, who was quite a bit older. To the inquisitive youth of Cleveland he seemed like a wizened mystic, a man of the world who knew secrets of God and the universe.

He had a certain mystique that made him a pied piper for young black soul searchers, in particular. Though Norman's education was minimal, he made the most of available literature and was basically self-taught. He was someone who could convey spiritual science in a nonsectarian way, which made his approach appealing to the seekers of the '60s, who regularly came to hear from him. John was one of these seekers, and, as already mentioned, Norman directed him to the Hare Krishna Movement.

Although Norman's background in theology remains obscure, he had a profound knowledge of the Moorish sciences, which he used as a basis to explain universal spiritual truths. The Moors were the medieval Muslim inhabitants of al-Andalus, which refers to the area in and around the Iberian Peninsula, including present-day Spain, Portugal and the Maghreb, whose indigenous culture is often called "Moorish."

In its most contemporary form, the teachings can be traced to Timothy Drew, a native of Newark, New Jersey, who, in 1913, claimed that all blacks were of Moorish, i.e., Muslim, descent. He thus advocated a "return" to Islam as the only way blacks could attain true spiritual redemption. The actual creeds of Moorish Science, however, draw as much from Buddhism, Christianity, and Freemasonry as they do from Islam, and practitioners who study the science deeply are well-versed in all of these.

The origins of Freemasonry are shrouded in myth, legend and obscurity, but its connection to Moorish Science is indisputable. Freemasonic lore and symbols have been traced to ancient Egypt and Phoenicia, and even to the Templar Knights. But its most significant debt is to Islamic mysticism, that is to say, Sufism, whose esoteric tradition connects the Masons with the Moors of North Africa.

Norman Anderson brought all of this to bear in his explanation of ultimate reality. His command of Moorish history, along with its related Freemasonry and Sufi leanings, was profound. But he added something extra—he introduced yoga and Eastern thought to practitioners of Moorish Science. And John liked it.

Ron Phillips Bey, a close friend of John's, remembers Norman's impact on their close circle of friends:

> We all converged around Norman, somewhere around 1971. He was into Moorish Science, which is the science of mystical Islam, basically. It involves a lot of esoteric readings of scripture, internal truths, high spiritual sensibilities. But Norman brought other ideas to the table too.
>
> This is what happened. I saw Johnny Boy downtown one day in Cleveland. They used to have street festivals when Carl Stokes was in office and they would block off all of Euclid Avenue. This is '71—I was just getting out of the service, so it was probably in June. Now, Johnny Boy and I went to East Tech together. We had known each other for quite a while. Anyway, on this festival day, I saw him walking down the middle of Euclid Avenue. He was on summer break from Princeton. I think he had one or two more years after that.
>
> At this time we were both studying the spiritual sciences—we had been looking into this stuff since our days at East Tech. We were reading as much as we could. The Prophet, Hiram E. Butler's Solar Biology, which is about parents' consciousness when a child is being conceived and how it affects the child. Self-mastery and the Cycles of Life was another title. The Teachings of Don Juan, Science of the Breath, The Kybalion, Hermetic Philosophy.
>
> That was our background, and we were eager to catch up, to see

what new stuff to get into. I had just come back from the Marine Corps, and I asked John what he was studying. He told me he was studying parapsychology at Princeton and that he was going to be an attorney, in a field involving international law. The parapsychology part I understood. It had meaning to me. So I said, "Wow, we do some of that too at the Moorish Science Institute."

We were in the midst of this noisy street festival, but we understood that this was of central importance, that we were discussing matters of the spirit in the midst of all this. People would be selling stuff on the street. There was music and dance. That's when Cleveland had a very vibrant downtown. Some of the retailers would have their wares out on the street. All the stores were doing brisk business, and the streets were super-crowded.

It was in this context that I invited him to come up to some meetings at the Moorish Science Institute. They were on 89th and Cedar, or maybe 83rd. He started to come up there religiously. He would hook up with Isis, Eugene Barker Bey and myself. At the time, I was engaged to Isis and we married shortly after. We would go up to the Moorish Science Institute, which later changed to the American Moorish Institute, on Sundays from two to four in the afternoon. They would talk about the science of the mind and metaphysics. After that we would go to another church, I think it was the Science of the Mind people.

To make a long story a bit shorter, this is where Norman comes in. I had actually been seeing him all my life because he was related to the ladies who owned the building. Small world. So, gradually, we started going to Norman's house instead of always going to the Moorish Institute, mainly because the guys at the Institute were speaking highly of Norman. He blew people away with the knowledge he had. So we started going to meetings at Norman's house on Friday nights, also. It was the summer of 1971, and John was really into it.

Now, Norman introduced yoga into Moorish Science. And

Radha and Krishna—he had their pictures on the wall.

And he had a little chair with mirrors in it. I remember that. Besides this one distinct chair, he didn't have any furniture, only pillows on the floor. He didn't have anything. He didn't care about anything—except Truth. We would study with him and he would talk about . . . the yoga of the mind, instead of the yoga of complete surrender to the Godhead. But Norman would tell us that the highest yoga was Bhakti-yoga, the yoga of Krishna Consciousness.

He tried to take us there gradually, though, explaining all kinds of preliminary yoga systems and only hinting about Krishna—God is a beautiful blue boy, he would say, and then go on to relate it to the Moorish science, Sufism, mysticism, and what have you. On top of all this, he had us studying practical water cure and the Yogananda series of books. He was quite eclectic.

Eugene Barker-Bey, another close friend from John's inner circle in those days, remembers that summer, too:

John was doing something to help people when he came home during the summer. He was working in a program mentoring kids on 105th and Sinclair. He had a grant, I believe, where he assisted children or kids in an outreach-type program, mainly African-American children.

It was during this period—I would say it was the summer of 1971—that we started going to classes together at the Moorish Science Institute. Through that, we came in contact with Norman Anderson. Now, when Norman came in, there was an upheaval. He brought in some foreign elements, like yoga. There were people who were upset by this, but Ron, John, Isis and me—we ate it up.

His apartment, at that time, was on 101st. Now, I grew up on 102nd and Sinclair. Ron grew up on 101st and Sinclair. And Patricia, or Isis, stayed on 102nd and Sinclair on the other end. So we were all quite close. Anyway, John came in that summer and was mentored by Norman like the rest of us, maybe even more so.

Larry Holt, also known as Lila-smaranam Dasa, knew Norman well, having been one of his son's closest friends:

What can I say about Norman Anderson? He took care of himself—he was in shape—even though he was an older gentleman at that time. He commanded respect when he walked down the street. He had an aura of aristocracy. When I first met him, I went to his place to study. I remember when his apartment was at 91st and St. Clair, on the Northeast side of Cleveland. It was a middle class neighborhood.

I was just astounded by the pictures he had on his walls. He had pictures of Radha and Krishna, the female and male aspects of divinity, from the Krishna tradition. He had a picture of Lord Brahma, the first created being, and he had various transcendental art decorating his apartment, which was sparsely furnished. I thought such humble dwellings seemed like a contradiction for a person who was so stately. Really, he was living in poverty—he didn't have a couch or a stereo or a TV. I mean, these are things most people have, even if they're poor. He didn't care, though. He was about spiritual things instead.

Even though he mainly explored mysticism and Moorish Science, and that's what he talked about, he also talked about Krishna. He said, "Krishna is God. He is a little blue dude."

"Huh?" I would think, "What's he talking about? God is a little blue dude?" And yet something rang true. I mean, why not? God could be whatever He wants to be. Why not a beautiful boy of darkish hue? The thing Norman did was this: he gave God a personality, a face. And that was important to us; we responded to that. We had been taught in the Christian Church that God was spirit—so you naturally assume that He must be formless or some such. The opposite of material form is no form. But Norman taught us that the

opposite of material form is spiritual form. Interesting, huh?

He would show us pictures from Prabhupada's books, from the scriptures, like Srimad-Bhagavatam, *or the* Krsna *book—he would point to the pictures and say, "Here is a picture of God, right here."*

He would talk about things from different traditions, but he was really trying to steer you to Krishna Consciousness, at least if he felt you had the intellectual capacity to understand it. You see, he didn't talk about Krishna to some people. He would talk to them about Islam and that's that. He saved the esoteric Vaishnava tradition, Krishna Consciousness, for his prize students. He saw that as the highest of teachings.

Norman's greatest service, perhaps, was when he conveyed Srila Prabhupada's true status to John, as explained in the previous chapter. Many years after this incident, John repaid the favor by initiating Norman into the eternal tradition of Vaishnavism, giving him the name "Nanda Maharaja," which is the name of Krishna's father in the spiritual world. Once initiated, John always referred to him as "Uncle Nanda," showing him the respect due an elder and the love appropriate for a mentor.

The End of Romance

Eva Coleman was John's fiancée, having met him during his latter days at Princeton. A yoga instructor who was almost ten years his senior, she was largely responsible for his internal journey to the land of the Ganges. In fact, the emphasis on yoga in his Princeton thesis was inspired by her studies with Sri Chinmoy and Swami Satcidananda, two popular Eastern gurus of the period. Together, John and Eva would listen to John Coltrane's "A Love Supreme" and Alice Coltrane's recorded mantras; relish the moods and tones of Ravi Shankar and Ali Akbar Khan; meditate according to various traditions and discuss the ancient sages of Vedic India. Eva's association ignited John's Eastern passions, even as the two young seekers lit the exotic Indian incense that changed the fragrance of their destiny. Says John:

My fiancée was Eva Coleman. She was a powerful yoga teacher who lived in New York. When I initially joined the Hare Krishna Movement, we were coming to the temple together. That was my last year in Princeton, 1972. She was a disciple of Sri Chinmoy, had studied with Swami Satcidananda, and was in contact with Sai Baba. The more I got involved in Krishna Consciousness, the more I realized that it wasn't going to work between us.

She was quite psychic and, one day on our way to the temple, she had a clear vision that we were going to separate in the near future—that I would renounce the world, including her, in favor of the spirit. She was also clearly aware of the connection we had had in a previous life. A short time later, her vision of my leaving to become a monk surely came true.

The first day that I chanted sixteen rounds of Japa—Hare Krishna, Hare Krishna, Krishna Krishna, Hare Hare/ Hare Rama, Hare Rama, Rama Rama, Hare Hare—on beads, Vaishnava rosary, I was in her house. This Maha-mantra, chanting Hare Krishna, was a new kind of prayer for me. "O Lord! O Energy of the Lord! Please engage me in Your service!"

In my youth, I was involved in serious praying, no doubt, but usually for something material. It was not selfless chanting for service to God. At best, it was to heal someone or for some other altruistic goal. Here, the mantra is completely selfless; it asks for nothing in return—only to be engaged in God's service. This appealed to me. I could see that all praying should eventually graduate to this level, that the Maha-mantra was the culmination of the prayerful mood.

Anyway, at Eva's place, I sort of locked myself in a room so I wouldn't be bothered. After I finished the rounds, I came out and I knew what I had to do. It was clear to me that as much as she and I were attracted to each other, my spiritual calling was such that I wouldn't be married in this life. We had some short discussions after this and we both agreed that I had to do what was necessary.

So I left her house and never talked to her or heard from her again—we were both clear that this would be best for each of us. She exhibited extreme selflessness by not trying to stop me or not trying to draw me back in. She felt that this was a sacrifice we both had to make for attaining God Consciousness.

There is another story involving Eva Coleman in which she was the immediate catalyst for John's entry into Krishna Consciousness. If Norman Anderson gave him verbal disapproval of Sri Chinmoy and pointed him in the direction of Prabhupada and Krishna, Eva gave him something tangible that would change his life forever.

It came in the form of vinyl—it was a record album called "Happening," in which Prabhupada chants the Maha-mantra and explains its meaning for the benefit of his listeners. Eva had purchased the album during one of their jaunts to the Henry Street temple, and she thought her mate might get more out of it than she did. John listened to the recording carefully. As he heard Prabhupada's voice, it stirred something deep inside. It was strangely familiar, as if he had known it for many lifetimes. He felt a connection to Prabhupada that was inexplicable, and he started to weep. He and Eva looked at each other one last time, and went their separate ways.

Brooklyn, 1972

Bhakti-jana Dasa was a Caucasian disciple of Srila Prabhupada who had been deputed by his guru to open a temple in Harlem, New York. He was chosen because he had been raised in a predominantly black neighborhood, and there were few African-American devotees in the New York area, none of whom wanted to take on the project. And so the loving chore devolved upon Bhakti-jana. Even still, there was rumbling in the ranks. Bhakti-jana was, after all, white. Would he be able to convey Krishna Consciousness to black people in Harlem?

Consequently, he arranged a meeting with Prabhupada himself and a group of mainly black devotees. The idea was to have Prabhupada affirm his mission in Harlem, to state that he wanted Bhakti-jana to perform the task, and to discuss racial discrimination, a phenomenon that had unfortunately cropped up in the Brooklyn temple. This concerned many devotees, particularly those of color, since the basic philosophy of Krishna Consciousness centers on the distinction between body and self, asserting that living beings are absolutely *not* their bodies. This being the case, devotees tend to de-emphasize bodily distinctions, except for in practical matters of service, and view it as hypocritical when adherents do otherwise. But the latter is exactly what was going on, at least in certain quarters.

John, although a newcomer to Krishna Consciousness, was interested in exactly where the meeting with Prabhupada would go, and he managed to slip into the room at the last minute. Once there, Rasikananda Prabhu, an articulate African-American devotee, began to express grievances to Prabhupada, but then cut himself short. Says Rasikananda:

> *There was a group of dissidents, the black devotees on one side, and Prabhupada and his early white followers on the other, like armies arrayed for battle. In the room were Markendra Rishi, Shyamaka, Lokamangala, Abhinanda, Balaka, and so on—really dedicated black devotees. And they were anxious to bring up the problem of racial hypocrisy to Srila Prabhupada.*
>
> *But when everyone was in the room, the black devotees felt that their concerns were somewhat trivial, and they melted away. They had come to talk to Prabhupada about racial prejudice in the temple, about Bhakti-jana's involvement in the Harlem project, about living separately, outside, maintaining a job, or continuing with music careers. But facing Prabhupada, all of this seemed to lose meaning. Not that it wasn't important—it was! It's just that when one is in the presence of a pure devotee like Prabhupada, one*

can only think about serving Krishna purely. All problems become
totally insignificant, and that's what happened.

Rasikananda managed to insert one question about married couples living outside the temple, perhaps in a separate building. Up
until that point, most devotees felt it mandatory to live together in
the *ashram*, or at least in a community setting. Prabhupada responded
pragmatically, saying that all buildings are made of material elements
—so what's the difference? "As long as Krishna is worshiped," said
Prabhupada, "it doesn't matter what building one lives in."

John, who was sitting in the back, also asked a question, looking at
Prabhupada through his diamond-shaped, rose-colored glasses. With
his characteristic blinking and stammering, his question concerned
Kali-yuga, the current age of quarrel and hypocrisy, specifically about
when it would end. Prabhupada gave him the standard answer found
in all his books—that there is another 427,000 years to this age, at
which time a new epoch dawns.

The entire exchange was filmed and is today available on DVD.
The visual impact of seeing John in his early days as a devotee tells
us much about his mindset during this pivotal period. At the time,
which was the latter part of 1972, he had already shaved his head and
was wearing *tilak*, or the markings of a Vaishnava, on his forehead.
He wore a *dhoti*, the Indian dress adopted by Krishna Conscious
monks, and a Vaishnava bead-bag around his neck. But he sported
a beard as well, and a western shirt, noticeable when he prepares to
leave at the end of the meeting. These were physical symbols that
indicated conflicted allegiances—the beard was a vestige of his involvement in Moorish Science and Islamic orthodoxy, and the shirt
a statement about his individuality as a person living outside the
temple. He was a newcomer moving closer to Krishna. This meeting
with Prabhupada went a long way to consummate that closeness.

Prior to the meeting, John had had differences with Bhakti-jana.
He had objected to this devotee's Harlem project because of his Cau-

casian background and mindset. This was not, as some had claimed, racism in reverse. Rather, as already stated, it was a matter of practical concern—black people can speak to black people, as John put it. Otherwise, communication is too difficult; there are too many barriers to overcome.

Most of the black devotees agreed with John, in fact, and opened an alternate facility in Bedford Stuyvesant, Brooklyn. Rasikananda, Abhinanda, Shyamaka Ma, and Markendra Rishi, among others, frequented that establishment, as did John, who always, at that time, kept a separate dwelling as well. Bhakti-jana alone secured an apartment in Harlem at 115th and Lenox—working there for several years with little luck, gathering only one or two devotees to help him. Some hard feelings arose between the two groups, and even harder feelings between both groups and the established Krishna temple in Brooklyn, comprised mainly of white men and women. All of this led to the meeting with Srila Prabhupada described above.

Sometime during that same period, John had occasion to meet with Prabhupada again. This time he pointedly addressed the issue at hand: "Srila Prabhupada," he began, "there are prejudices in this movement." Prabhupada looked at him and said, "Ah. Someone is thinking you're the body? That is their nonsense. And if you're disturbed because they see you in this way, *then you are also nonsense.*" That was his reaction—that the bodily platform is sheer foolishness, whether one identifies a person with their body, or if the person so identified graces the foolishness with a response. Both perspectives show inferior consciousness, said Prabhupada, and should be avoided.

The subject was not a light one for Srila Prabhupada. His entire teaching begins with transcending the bodily concept of life and its concomitant racism, and it hurt him deeply that some of his disciples had not yet achieved this basic level of realization. Nonetheless, he saw it as prudent to emphasize a different point in this particular exchange with his fledgling disciple. He knew that John would eventually do great work for his mission, but he also knew that this work must be precipitated by a certain inner awareness. Yes, part of that awareness is the distinction between body and self. But, for John, it was also important that he bid adieu to his previous political and social concerns, at least in terms of the priority that he gave them. He needed to realize that their importance is secondary to Krishna Consciousness. Only then would he truly understand the ultimate spiritual message that Prabhupada was trying to bequeath to him.

Prabhupada's instruction to John was not unlike the instructions his own guru had given him some fifty years earlier. As a young man, Prabhupada was a part of India's Independence movement, and a staunch follower of Mahatma Gandhi. When he first met Srila Bhaktisiddhanta Sarasvati (1874–1937), the renowned saint of the Gaudiya Vaishnava tradition who would eventually become his guru, he questioned the legitimacy of focusing on spiritual life while under British rule. He emphasized India's prior need to free herself of foreign powers, pointing out that even China and Japan were independent while India still labored under political oppression.

Prabhupada gave his best arguments for nationalism and political freedom, but Bhaktisiddhanta dismissed them as superficial. He said that spiritual life shouldn't have to wait for a change in Indian politics, nor was it dependent upon who ruled. Rather, he asserted that it was the other way around—that spiritual maturity and purity of purpose would affect the external, political world for the better, and that what was really missing in the material world were spiritual leaders.

As a follower of Gandhi, Prabhupada was taken aback, not sure of how to react. And yet, as a born Vaishnava and as one who understood the importance of spiritual life, he also knew that Bhaktisiddhanta's words were true. He soon abandoned his Gandhian concerns in favor of a transcendent worldview, and he accepted Bhaktisiddhanta as his spiritual master.

Similarly, John had long been a follower of Martin Luther King, whose allegiance to Gandhi has been thoroughly documented. In 1959, eleven years after Gandhi's death, King had in fact journeyed to India just to see the land of the Mahatma and to imbibe its deep-seated spirituality. King was following in the footsteps of fellow African-American Mordecai Johnson, president of Howard University, who had earlier gone to India and actually met Gandhi. But King's regard for the Indian savant eventually came to surpass Johnson's, for he saw in Gandhi a model for his own life and work. As King said, "If humanity is to progress, Gandhi is inescapable. He lived, thought, and acted, inspired by the vision of humanity evolving toward a world of peace and harmony. We may ignore him at our own risk."

As a one-time follower of Gandhi, then, Prabhupada clearly understood the concerns and sensibilities of John Favors. In fact, in his own youth, as we have seen, Prabhupada was given to similar political and social interests. And just as his heart was changed by Bhakti-siddhanta Sarasvati, so, too, was John's changed by Prabhupada.

The Library Party

One day, while visiting the Henry Street temple in Brooklyn, John saw a notice on the bulletin board. It was an invitation to work with Satsvarupa Dasa Goswami at the Gurukula in Dallas, Texas. This was a major school for the children of Krishna devotees, and, having recently graduated from Princeton, John wanted to make good use of his educational skills. But more, he was intrigued by the idea of working with Satsvarupa Dasa Goswami, one of the first devotees he had ever met, and one that he deeply respected.

He immediately set off for Texas with the intention of giving his life to Krishna. Upon arriving there, he asked the temple president, whose name was Lakshmi Narayana, to engage him in the most humble service available. Says Sureshvara Dasa, a devotee who met John soon after his arrival in Texas:

I met him as he was cleaning the brahmacari *[celibate monks'] bathroom in Dallas in 1972. He was cleaning the only way he knew how: humbly and seriously. And that was his way—everything he did, he did with total determination.*

Rupa Vilasa, another devotee from the early days in Dallas, describes John's short stay there, too:

I first came to Dallas in the spring of 1972. We had just moved into the Dallas Temple on Gurley Avenue from another location. So, for months we were in the process of moving. Toward the end of that move, John arrived in Dallas. I remember him being there in the fall. And the first impression that really hit me right off was that he was black, because there weren't that many black-bodied devotees in the movement at that time. And then, as I remember, he had a shirt or a kurta *made out of some foreign material; it looked kind of African. This was the superficial memory. But more, I remember his determined spirit. He was always happy to do menial service, and he was immaculate in his personal habits. His sense of austerity, too, was unbelievable. Even as a new devotee, he was exceptional.*

His determined service attitude was brought to the attention of Satsvarupa Dasa Goswami, who invited him to join a small traveling party of particularly gifted devotees, a party that would bring Krishna Consciousness out into the streets. Sureshvara remembers:

Satsvarupa Maharaja took him on our traveling party, the party that eventually turned into "the Library Party." He was always enthusiastic, polite, friendly, and no matter what conditions we found ourselves in—freezing in a van at a KOA (Campgrounds of America) or whatever—he always emerged to chant in a fresh blaze of orange. I finally said to him one morning, "John, you're a great dresser." He smiled that smile: "Yes, if nothing else, at least I can dress nicely for Krishna."

From Day One, he never wasted a moment. He slept little and

often chanted intensely facing the wall, so he could concentrate.
John was grave, not fanatic. He was just praying his heart out.

Dhanurdhar Swami, a devotee for whom John had great admiration, also initially met him in Texas:

The first time I saw him, I was getting a ride with the Library
Party from Dallas to New York and so I traveled with them. One
of the things I remember of that trip is stopping in a campground.
. . . We got up in the morning to use the shower and I saw him in
the hallway. It was very early in the morning, and he was in the
hallway chanting very intensely.

At that time I heard among the Library Party that he was
chanting either forty-two or forty-eight rounds on his beads, on
his Vaishnava rosary, as opposed to most devotees, who chant only
sixteen. He was sleeping less, eating less. It was humbling to see—he
outdid everyone else.

His pronounced sense of austerity came from his early training
in yoga. It was also a determined effort to compensate for what he
perceived as fundamental deficits—his innate humility insisted that
he work harder than the other devotees, all of whom he respected as
his mentors and as leaders. He saw himself as low man on the totem
poll. But it was more than that. Spiritual life, to him, meant giving
your all—it was not something to be taken lightly. He would later
say, "We are all spiritual warriors, blessed by the best, and we have a
duty to reach out more, to help each other to pass the test."

More than anything else, however, his overwhelming resolve in relation to penance was inspired by Srila Prabhupada, who indicated early
on that this would be good for him. John himself tells the story:

We were walking with Srila Prabhupada, and at one point he
stopped and looked directly at me and quoted Bhagavad-gita *2.64.*
Afterwards the devotees were saying, "Prabhupada gave you such

a personal instruction; you're so fortunate!" That Bhagavad-gita verse has to do with renunciation, with controlling the senses, controlling the mind, and depending on Krishna's mercy. I took that to heart and started living an austere life. I would chant forty-two rounds every day, sleep about three hours getting up at 12:30, 1:00 AM, chant Japa before the morning services and do some reading. I was eating once a day, usually some fruit, or a little juice, or maybe some yogurt and a palm full of vegetables, and plenty of water. That instruction from Prabhupada was so piercing. He knocked me over with that instruction. At other times, other devotees got personal instructions, but different kinds of instruction. How much influence Prabhupada had on us, how he encouraged me in simplicity, in the life of renunciation!*

Satsvarupa Dasa Goswami talks about his initial impression of John, along with the origins of the Library Party and John's initiation:

He came to the Dallas Temple. I believe he had started up in Brooklyn, but they sent him down to Dallas, thinking he was kind of scholarly and should help out with the educational project there. I remember seeing him in the hallway—I have a visual image of him coming toward me, happy, friendly, smiling. And he was like really green, new to the movement. He began telling me about his material past, and that he worked in the prisons in New Jersey with the Public Defender's office, and that he went to Princeton University, and so on. And we took to each other as friends right away. I immediately liked him.

Pretty soon we started traveling, though he initially came to work with me in regard to the school, the Gurukula. I wasn't too connected to the Gurukula anymore, once I became a sannyasi, a monk in the renounced order of life. We went out in a van to spread Krishna Consciousness around the country. After a while we upgraded to a bus. Initially, though, I went out in a van with

Ghanashyam and Mahabuddhi and just maybe one or two others.
They weren't initiated yet. We were trying to get people to join us in
Krishna Consciousness.

We would stay maybe a month at a time in some city, going out
during the day and chanting in the streets, lecturing at some venue,
like a hall or something. We would advertise it, and then have some
place, like an apartment, or a room, where we would return in the
evenings. We'd try to rent an apartment for a month, and to draw
people to the apartment and get to know them. By the end of the
month, we'd make a couple of devotees.

It was just an easygoing program, singing and selling Back to
Godhead *magazine. It was a simple, blissful, God conscious life,*
but we made enough money to keep going. It was fun, and we all
became really close.

After just under one year, Satsvarupa Maharaja recommended John
for initiation. He wrote to Prabhupada on the young ascetic's behalf,
describing him as enthusiastic and determined to become Krishna
Conscious. And so two letters—one to Satsvarupa and the other to
John himself—soon arrived from Australia, where Prabhupada was
touring at the time, affirming that he had accepted John Favors as
his duly initiated disciple. The letters, only a day apart, brought great
happiness to the two devotees. The one to John reads as follows:

16 February, 1973
Sydney, Australia

My dear Son,
Please accept my blessings. On the recommendation of Satsvarupa
I am herein accepting you as my initiated disciple. Henceforth your
name will be GHANASHYAM DASA. Now you must agree to
very rigidly follow the rules and regulations, i.e., chanting sixteen
rounds of beads daily, rising early and attending Mangala Arati,
observing the four principles, attending the classes, eating only

bhagavata prasadam *as well as working under the instruction of my representatives, such as your GBC representative and Temple President, and if you follow this procedure very strictly then your life will be glorious and you will go back to Home, back to Godhead. This I can guarantee. I hope this meets you in good health.*
    Your ever well-wisher,
    A.C. Bhaktivedanta Swami (Prabhupada)

As mentioned in both letters, Prabhupada changed John's name to Ghanashyam Dasa, or "the servant of the beautiful dark cloud." This dark cloud, of course, refers to Krishna, God, whose dazzlingly radiant if also blackish complexion is described in India's scriptural texts and in the poetry of the Vaishnavas. Prabhupada had chosen the perfect name for his new African-American disciple. John was deeply touched.

Soon after the initiation, Satsvarupa Maharaja needed to tend to something immediately—it was an emergency phone call from Karandhar, who was then serving as Prabhupada's secretary. When Satsvarupa hung up the phone, the others waited with baited breath. They knew that this would be life altering, a message coming directly from their spiritual master. Sure enough, Satsvarupa reported that Prabhupada wanted him right away—he was to go to India to become Prabhupada's personal servant. This was an honor and something that Satsvarupa relished. At the same time, however, he would miss his little troupe of stalwart devotees. Says Satsvarupa:

> *Of course, I went at once, as soon as I could go. And the deal was that Hridyananda Maharaja, who was in Los Angeles, would come down and take care of the party—he'd take it over in his own way.*
>
> *So we switched and I went . . . I dove into all the myriad services of being Prabhupada's servant. And Hridyananda took over the party. I quickly found out that they weren't doing it the way I was doing it, with my low-key demeanor. Rather, they traveled quickly up to New England. And that's when the first Library Party was born.*

Hridayananda Maharaja had clear memories of those early days and of his founding of the Library Party:

Some background: In 1972, just about a month or two after I took sannyasa, *I was wondering what to do, and I thought I'd like to preach in colleges, to get Prabhupada's books into the hands of educated people. So I called Satsvarupa. At that time he had a party traveling through Boston. They had gotten a bus there and they had a few* brahmacharis, *celibate novices. I first met up with them in St. Louis, I believe. They were going to the main cities with their bus, chanting downtown and selling* Back to Godhead *magazines.*

And so I called him and we agreed we would work together, since we took sannyasa *together and were quite friendly at the time. So I met him in St. Louis and I convinced him that it was more important to preach to the college students. I remember that I specifically made the argument that books are more important than magazines, that they have staying power. Rather than just give out magazines to, you know, secretaries and various people downtown, why don't we preach in the colleges? So, after some preliminary conversation, he agreed. Once I had his support, I began booking the first programs at local universities. We were in St. Louis; so I went over to Illinois. Bir Krishna was my* brahmachari *assistant at the time, and you can ask him for specifics.*

Anyway, Bir Krishna and I had a little yellow Volkswagen bug. We drove to Illinois, got there late, walked in the Student Union, found an Indian professor and booked a program. It was that simple. No organization at all. And then we went up to Champagne, Havana, Bloomington, and did all these college towns in Illinois. It took us about a week to book them, and then we would come back to do the programs. That was our party. I was managing it, and we eventually bought some vans. And I think it was that same year, if my memory serves, that we were in Chicago and somehow John, Ghanashyam, was there. I actually don't remember if he'd been with the party origi-

nally or at what point he came, but he was in Chicago. The reason I remember is because I told him that we wanted to book programs in the colleges, and he was into it. So we sat down together for a couple of days and actually planned out our tactics for the Library Party.

He was a brahmachari. *And he was very good at Sankirtan, at distributing Prabhupada's books to anyone and everyone. He was always sort of elegant and persuasive, and people liked him.*

This all precipitated the Library Party proper. I'll tell you how it actually started. In 1973, I was with Prabhupada in his garden in Los Angeles. He asked me if his books were in the bookstores and libraries. I said they weren't, not really, and he wasn't pleased. To console him, I said people don't buy them so much in bookstores, anyway, even in those few bookstores that did carry them; they don't take them out of libraries that much, either. You see, I was trying to tell Prabhupada that it wasn't so important, that we could sell the books ourselves. But he insisted that it was important. So, at that point, I decided, well, we'll do it then. This is what Prabhupada wants. So, soon after that, we were in Iowa City and I decided to try to go and sell some books in libraries.

I went to a major library in that town. After awhile, I noticed a little bald guy coming after me, who finally said, "I know who you are and what you want." I thought he was going to throw me out, but he welcomed us in. He was the acquisitions guy. I went by myself. I was in my sannyasa *dress, robes and all, and I sold him a set of books. And not only was there not a library party, but there were no forms to fill out. That came later. At this point, we had nothing. And so I just called the Bhaktivedanta Book Trust (BBT) in L.A. and asked them what I should do. This hadn't been done before. I just sold a set of books, totally disorganized, but it happened.*

And so we started doing the same thing in other places. Now, at the time, Mahabuddhi and Ghanashyam weren't selling books to libraries. They were just doing their regular preaching. You know, just regular Sankirtan, selling the magazines, and inviting people to our programs. And so what Satsvarupa had turned over to me was not the Library Party—I turned it into the Library Party.

That was when I took over in '73, in San Antonio, Texas. We decided to go up to the Northeast and preach in the colleges in Boston. We went to Harvard and various other major institutions of learning. It was up there that I decided to train Mahabuddhi and Ghanashyam to do the library and professor work, to sell whole sets of books. I personally took them to the garment district in New York and bought them suits and wigs to cover their shaved heads. We got them respectable clothes, so they could go in and sell books to professors and acquisitions people at the libraries. Soon after that, Satsvarupa took over the party again.

This was the beginning of a major turning point in ISKCON's history. Prabhupada himself took notice of the devotees' tremendous results and gave them advice on how to effectively distribute books to colleges and libraries. John, now Ghanashyam Dasa, tells the story:

Once I joined Satsvarupa Maharaja and Hridayananda Maharaja on the Library Party, we started meeting with Srila Prabhupada more often. We were traveling around, distributing sets of books, and making standing orders. After we started this work, we had a wonderful encounter with Srila Prabhupada at Jayananda's apartment in San Francisco. Prabhupada wanted all of us to come. He talked to us so sweetly, and then we came up one by one, and he gave us a flower. We were asking him some questions about how to do the work, and he told us, "Try your best, and Krishna will help you." We realized that Srila Prabhupada was very pleased. Before he even wrote his books there was an audience waiting for them. That was the idea of "standing orders"—we would go to universities, professors, libraries and take orders and ship the books later. In other words, they agreed to take the books that were available now, as well as the books published in the future. For an author, there is nothing more wonderful than to know that "people are taking my books and are waiting for more."

Srila Prabhupada gave us a simple technique. He said that we should get an order from a prestigious professor, university, or institution and keep a copy of it. Then we should visit other universities or other persons connected in academia, and show them the order that we received. He was really telling us that everybody has a guru and everyone wants to be part of something that's successful or important. As important people do, so others will follow. We started doing that as we traveled through America, Europe, and India. We would go to the most prestigious place and then show other institutions, other professors, whatever we got from there.

One of the biggest sales we ever had in the history of the library party was at Brigham Young University. There I met the head of the Mormon Church, who was a linguist, historian, and philosopher, and who had been studying Vedic cosmology. When he saw the way Prabhupada's books were formatted and their detail, he was in ecstasy. He bought a complete set of Bhagavatams *and* Chaitanya-charitamritas *for himself, and he ordered them for his department library. He also wrote a note and told the librarian of the general library, "Buy these books. Buy everything this book salesman has." I took his letter to the librarian and then started visiting other departments. In most schools we would sell books to the history, philosophy, comparative literature, and religion departments. But this time I had a letter from the* acharya *of the institute. So every department I went to, I told them about the head of the church, and they would say, "I want the same thing." It was easy, and it was all based on the technique that Srila Prabhupada had given us. By the time I left I had almost twenty standing orders, just from that simple tactic.*

By applying such techniques and by using his own intellect and charisma, Ghanashyam became the preeminent book distributor on the Library Party, and in much of ISKCON as well. There were other sales virtuosos in the movement, dedicated devotees who gave their lives to the distribution of transcendental literature. People like Tripurari Swami, Pragosh, Sanjaya, Kavidhatta, Kashiram, Vaisheshika, Jadurani, Gauri—the list goes on. But Ghanashyam had something special. Mahabuddhi Prabhu was one of the early members of the Library Party, and he elaborates on some of that magic:

Ghanashyam was a mystic. I'll give you one anecdote to show you what I mean, but I could give you hundreds. I remember coming to this one place. I wonder if it was like Morehead State or some really offbeat little school out in the Midwest, Kentucky or Minnesota. I'm not sure. I don't even remember exactly where it was, but it was a small school, a small college. It almost looked like a prison. We happened to get there and, by my lack of organizational abilities, we ended up being there on a holiday. So everything was closed up tight. And I said, well, let's just go to the next place. We'll be ready for tomorrow.

And then Ghanashyam said, "No, no. I have to use the restroom." So I said, okay, but make it quick, because we had a long haul to the next place. So I'm sitting in the car for like twenty minutes, forty minutes, one hour, two hours. I'm starting to say, "Where the heck is this guy?"

So then he appears in the distance about two hours later. By this time, I'm curious, even angry. But then he comes walking up with his big Ghanashyam smile. No one can smile like him. He just captivated people like that. So while I was growling to myself just a moment earlier, I saw him and my heart melted.

So he gets in the car and I say, "Okay, what's up? What took so long?" He began explaining that while in the bathroom he ran into a person and they started to talk. Well, he started talking heart to heart with this guy as follows: "We're book-selling representatives for the Bhaktivedanta Book Trust, and we were looking for people who were basically in the Sanskrit Department and the Indian Religions Department—because we have the best books on the subject, bar none!" So anyway, by Krishna's arrangement, even though the place was entirely closed, the one person who was in the bathroom, who came to the bathroom at that exact same time, was the head of the Religion Department. And this man happened to be teaching Hinduism! I kid you not.

And do you know he not only sold this person standing orders for himself and for his department, but the professor signed slips to put the books in the library as well. Now, mind you, there was no one else on campus. I mean, there wasn't even another car in the parking lot. What were the odds of this happening?! But that was his potency. He was just amazing.

The Party Rages On

One might question the Hare Krishna emphasis on selling books. After all, Ghanashyam was a spiritual seeker for his entire early life, and his involvement in Krishna Consciousness was intended as more of the same, or even as an enhancement of his spiritual quest. And yet, here he was, traveling to parts unknown, selling books like a man possessed. To be sure, devotees were not motivated by entrepreneurial spirit, nor were they victims of one-upmanship, where one devotee tries to outdo the other. A sort of "transcendental competition" does indeed develop between those who sell books, but always with the high ideal of sharing spiritual knowledge. The whole point is that one feels grateful for receiving the gift of Krishna Consciousness and, as a result, wants to share that gift with others. This is called Sankirtan.

Originally, in the days of Lord Chaitanya some 500 years ago, Sankirtan referred to congregational chanting—to the phenomenon of taking Krishna Consciousness into the outer world, to engage others in the process of God realization. Kirtan refers to chanting the holy name or glorifying God. But when the Sanskrit affix "*san*" is added to the word, it implies a more complete, broader application of the concept. Thus, the associates of Lord Chaitanya would share Kirtan with others, making the process and the people who benefit from the process more whole.

In the modern age, book distribution is seen as a further extension of Sankirtan. Indeed, it is an alternate way of sharing the holy name with others; it is congregational chanting in the sense that it allows others to learn about Krishna, to hear about His name, form, and pastimes. It is especially Kirtan for Prabhupada, who wrote the books. In other words, chanting and writing coalesce for him in his service of glorifying God. And when his disciples distribute his books, they assist him in his Kirtan.

Since the main function of the Hare Krishna Movement is to help people understand their original, constitutional position as an eternal servant of God, Prabhupada's books serve a vital purpose. Therefore, he taught his disciples that "books are the basis." For devotees in ISKCON, this rallying cry has a threefold meaning: His books are his personal Kirtan, as described above; devotees can themselves learn about Krishna from reading these books; and they can help others by distributing them.

Before he left this world in 1977, Srila Prabhupada had written some fifty full-length books, largely translations and commentaries of the ancient Vedic scriptures. These books explain fundamental metaphysical truths as well as esoteric aspects of spiritual wisdom, and Prabhupada's purports, or explanations, make the meaning particularly clear and accessible.

The Bhaktivedanta Book Trust (BBT), founded by Srila Prabhupada in 1970, is the world's largest publisher of Vedic texts. It has produced all of his books in editions praised by scholars around the world. The BBT has for decades translated and printed these books in numerous modern languages to make Vedic knowledge available to all people. Prabhupada set up a system wherein devotees buy these books from the BBT and distribute large quantities of them in most countries of the world. An estimated 500,000,000 pieces of literature have been distributed by devotees in the last forty years, calculating from the time Prabhupada arrived in the United States. The Library party, of which Ghanashyam was an integral part, did much to initiate this worldwide distribution campaign.

To this day, Krishna devotees work hard to distribute books, but not at the expense of their personal practice—their goal is to *live* the books, not just to give them away. Ghanashyam excelled at both.

Kalakantha Prabhu, who probably traveled with Ghanashyam on the Library Party more than any other devotee, gives details about his day-to-day practice:

I joined the party in 1974, September, coming from the Portland temple. Ghanashyam and the Library Party arrived, and I was to be a trainee to work locally. So they took me out for a couple of visits. The party at that time consisted of Mahadyuti, Mahabuddhi, Shubhananda, Satsvarupa Maharaja and Bhakti Tirtha Maharaja, then Ghanashyam. So we were working together briefly, and subsequently they invited me to join the party, which my temple president allowed me to do. So in November of '74, I flew to Detroit and joined the party then and for the next two years. And I worked extensively with Ghanashyam. The party was organized around the vans and there were two or three van leaders. He was always one of them. And those of us who were not van leaders would rotate among the different vans, each week. So two of us would go out for a week to visit libraries in a given state or jurisdiction, and then meet again on the weekends to compare notes and have a weekend festival or attend the temple if it was a temple town. And this was a period in which we covered all the contiguous forty-eight states, so I spent many, many weeks in a van with Ghanashyam. He was twenty-five, and I was twenty. He had been through college and had been the president of certain human rights organizations there at Princeton. He told me a lot about his background. Here was a really fascinating person throughout his life.

And his example as a devotee, too, was something to behold! In those days, he would get up every morning at about 2 AM and chant his rounds, more rounds than the rest of us. We would then work all day and find a campground or a hotel in the evening, take rest, get up early, and do our practices. He'd get up at two o'clock and write a letter to Srila Prabhupada every morning. This was his practice for years. He never or rarely sent the letters, just kept them in a diary of sorts. And he'd be very quiet and every night he would go to bed listening to this particular tape of Prabhupada chanting "Hari Haraya Nama Krishna," the traditional song, in a very mystical and exotic melody. It was his unbreakable routine. And he would write his letter and then he would very gently call me at, say, four o'clock and I'd shower. Then we would chant our Japa together and have a Bhagavatam *class.*

Now, he had this rock-solid sadhana, *or practice, and he would chant in a way that kind of reminded me of a Southern Baptist revival, chanting Japa, softly but almost like singing. It's hard to describe—his left hand tucked behind his right elbow in his back and he would stand there just kind of shuffling and swinging with full absorption. Of course, we had no room to walk. But it was like a Gospel prayer, the way he chanted Japa. It was as if he were saying Hallelujah! With a big smile. It wasn't really singing, but speaking with that kind of exuberance. And somehow he worked in thirty-two rounds a day, sometimes more, and wrote his letter to Prabhupada. And we'd have a very focused class and prepare* prasadam, *our meal.*

He had a very austere diet most of the time. He seemed to want to stick to raw foods, very simple foods, very small quantities. Austere. And he never tried to impose that on anyone else. He would

always be very considerate. He'd often just eat once a day, but make
sure that you had your two meals a day without a problem—with-
out saying, "Oh, do you really have to do that? Can't you just be a
little more austere?" No. He never imposed his austerities on others.
One day I talked to him about why he was so austere and he said
that it was because he came from a disadvantaged background—he
felt he had to do more just to catch up to the other devotees.

But he wasn't always serious. He had a playful side, too. One
funny anecdote: He was in a professor's office in some university
in America in the 70s trying to sell a set of books. The guy had a
black light and some posters in his room. We all wore wigs and
Ghanashyam went in there with an afro wig, and in the black light
his afro wig glowed green.

So the professor said, "That's funny, I've never seen this happen
to anyone before." Ghanashyam replied without missing a beat:
"Yeah, it must be this new shampoo I'm using." [laughter] He was
unstoppable. And he was incredibly determined in his mission to
distribute the full sets of Prabhupada's books. He would go to a new
campus everyday and find professors who would sign these library
order cards for the books.

"Library order cards" were forms—sometimes they were small
slips or full sheets, depending on the institution, library, or university—that were filled out by professors to order books from various
publishers. These became an essential part of the full-set book distribution tactics of the Library Party. Amogha-lila Prabhu, who now
holds a prestigious teaching position in Pakistan, was on the Library
Party as well, and he remembers its methods:

I joined the Library Party in January, 1975, in Atlanta, Georgia.
It consisted, at that time, of Satsvarupa Maharaja, Mahabuddhi,
Ghanashyam, Mahadyuti, Kalakantha, and Vijaya, who I think
was Satsvarupa Maharaja's secretary or personal servant.

*Ghanashyam was assigned to train me in the art of book distri-
bution, because he was the best. No one could distribute books like
him. The main impression I have of him is that he was very, very
encouraging, and he was very strict with himself. He really pushed
himself incredibly—always ready to sleep less, eat less, chant more,
do more service. If there was an opportunity to squeeze in one more
professor at a college or to squeeze in one more college, he would take
the opportunity and do it, even though it would mean sacrificing
more time. But he was so kind and encouraging to me. He wouldn't
push me, but I would just get pulled along with him because he was
pushing himself so hard. His enthusiasm was contagious.*

*I think from Atlanta we went first to Alabama and Mississippi.
We were going to mostly small colleges, at first, where there weren't a
lot of faculty members who were likely to order the books. In some of
them, there weren't even really departments, but there was a professor who was in the area, in the field. So, he would just go through
the catalogue and get their names.*

*First, we would calculate which colleges we would go to and
then the first thing we'd do in the morning would be to go to the
library. Once there, we'd get the slips that professors use to order
books. They use these to order large quantity. We'd go to the library,
usually to meet the librarian and to ask for specifics. And invariably we would go to the catalogue of the college or the university and see which departments might order books, or which had
professors that might order. This was all done in the morning—it
was like the way we set things up. We would first see if they had
any department of South Asian Studies or something—the religion
department, the philosophy department, something that seemed to
resonate with what we were doing.*

*So we would go to the catalogue and try to find those professors
who were most likely to be in the field to order the books. And we'd
do these three things first—get those slips, meet the librarian, who*

was the ordering librarian, and then go and make a list, calculating which professors were most likely to order the books. And then we would go to meet them. Of course, the very first day, he just took me along with him and introduced me as a new book salesman who was coming along for training. But then very soon—I think it was actually the second day—he had me going out on my own. It was intimidating for me, even though I had some academic background. To go like a salesman and try to get these professors to order these full sets of books—it seemed impossible at first? But I went with him, and he did it. He got the order, and it was very easy because of his kindness, his enthusiasm, and his success; it was pretty easy to get into it. Without that it would have been really frightening to do something like this.

They had perfected the system, Mahabuddhi, Ghanashyam and Satsvarupa Maharaja, especially. I think Ghanashyam and Mahabuddhi were the people who refined it, who turned book distribution to colleges and to libraries into a science. They developed this system of getting the card from the library—this was a card that professors use when they want to order books. Then you fill them out—we would fill out the number of copies for the Bhagavatam set, the Chaitanya-charitamrita set, Bhagavad-gita, Nectar of Devotion, Teachings of Lord Chaitanya, *all of Prabhupada's books. You fill out the cards, find the appropriate professors or acquisitions people, and then you only had to get them to sign off on it. So we would have the cards all filled in when we went to the professors' offices. Once they signed the cards, the institution automatically ordered the books. Period.*

Kalakantha elaborates:

This was the whole accelerated process, and, yes, it was unique. Any professor could sign off on these cards, or slips, and when the religious and philosophy departments wouldn't sign them—or when the religion and philosophy people wouldn't—we'd go to English, Anthropology, whatever. Ghanashyam once went to "Nursing" and got the head of the Nursing Department to order eighty copies of the Krsna Book *for their students! He told them that it would be soothing for them to read the books to patients, which is, of course, true. Events like that were almost daily occurrences with him. It seemed that everyday he would go out in this tremendous mood of dependence on Krishna and with an enormous application of his intelligence, which was considerable. He seemed to have a mystic power to convey the urgency or the importance of the situation. He would tell the professors that he was a very important person who had been sent by even more important people to meet this very important professor to give him access to these very important books. And this would just leave people almost helpless—it became obvious that they just had to sign the order. I'm trying to paint a picture of Ghanashyam as a person with total focus and determination. That was from his* sadhana, *his personal practice, to his service, to his relationships. Everything was, "I want to do the very, very best I possibly can, and then some."*

Now, we were on the first team sent to Europe. He and I went to England in 1975, in the fall, and covered the whole country and also trained a number of devotees there. We were expecting a big field in England, but it turned out to be a bust. People were very prejudiced against anything Indian. After England, we went to the Scandinavian countries together—Denmark and Finland, for instance. We went to all of these new places for the first time together. We had many, many adventures. We also went to India together for the first time. I wanted to share that. It was the Mayapur Festival, 1975, and we were on a plane from New York—this famous chartered Air India jet that was full of devotees stopped in London and Frankfurt, and then went to Calcutta. This was our first time in India, his and mine. So it was exciting, life changing.

As the Library Party traveled around America, they stopped at various ISKCON temples along the way. This served as a battery, of sorts, recharging them for their many depleting nights on the road. Of course, they relished every exhausting moment, but it didn't hurt to arrive at a base where they could gather food, momentum, and devotional association, so they could then more effectively brave the austerities associated with traveling. Saudamani Ma, wife of ISKCON leader Ravindra Svarupa Prabhu, remembers when the boys pulled into Philadelphia, Pennsylvania:

We first met Ghanashyam as part of the Library Party in the mid-70s in Philadelphia. My husband told me that this young man is going to be a great devotee. This was his conclusion because, right from the beginning, Ghanashyam was totally dedicated, coming from the Library Party; he was so austere, selfless, exhibiting all good qualities. He didn't waste any time, always working so hard and doing exactly what he was supposed to be doing. My husband spoke with him at length while he was in our temple in Philly, because they had a similar background—they had both gone to Ivy League schools.

At that time, Ghanashyam expressed how he felt so indebted to Srila Prabhupada for saving him from all that. I'm sure he didn't mean to negate the value of an academic career. Far from it, Prabhupada was often proud of his disciples who had such credentials: "Oh, this is my disciple so and so, and he has a Ph.D." But Ghanashyam really had that sense of eternal gratitude to Prabhupada, for lifting him out of material life, and he expressed it by taking seriously his duties and responsibilities.

Now, I remember this period in Philly because Ghanashyam had just gotten Brahmin initiation—he received it in the winter of 1973 in Los Angeles. He was traveling, so he hadn't yet gotten a chance to offer arati, the worship ceremonies that are performed by Brahmins. He didn't have the opportunity to do any Deity worship,

because he was always on the road. So he came to me—I was the
pujari, the priest who took care of the deities—and had me teach
him. He did a breakfast offering and arati as his first Deity worship
as a newly initiated Brahmin. He worshiped Jagannath, Baladeva,
and Subhadra. These were forms of Krishna, his first expansion
and his internal potency—forms of God with whom Ghanashyam
would eventually develop a very personal relationship.

Krishna's form is seen as the pinnacle of beauty, with large lotus eyes, raven black hair, a mischievous smile, and a silver flute adorning His reddish lips. This form is the essence of beauty because it is the essence of truth, and truth is beauty. But Jagannath doesn't share those characteristics, at least not to the common eye. His appearance is almost crude. Here, even though He is Krishna Himself, He is abstract, stylized, appearing somewhat primitive. His body shows no legs and two arms dart out from His sides, His hands indicated merely by outline drawings of a discus and a conch, the symbols of the divine Vishnu. His large form is jet black, and so are His eyes, which are perfectly round, encircled, as they are, by red lining and by the whites of His divine oculus. It is interesting that Ghanashyam lovingly served this particular form of the Lord, and exactly why will be revealed in Chapter Five.

The idea of an iconic Deity (*murti*)—whether it be Krishna as commonly envisioned, or Jagannath, or any other manifestation of the Divine—is nowhere as developed as in Vaishnava thought. These plainly visible images of God, made of wood, brass, marble, or other "material" elements, are considered particularly merciful "incarnations" of the Lord. Before commenting on why this is so, the basic underlying philosophy should be understood: If all material nature comes from the Supreme Being, then, given the correct circumstances, He can certainly use this nature to manifest His original, spiritual form. In other words, material energy itself comes from Him—it is an extension of His essential being—and He would thus be able to utilize it, if He so desired, to reveal His actual self. He can do whatever He likes.

Regarding why the Deity form is considered to be among His most merciful incarnations: No other form of the Lord can be served, dressed, fed, or adored in quite the same way. You can't serve a form if you can't see it. Thus, the Deity allows Himself to be appreciated by those who do not have the ability to see spirit, to see His unmanifest form in the spiritual world. The Vaishnava tradition teaches that, when constructed and consecrated according to the scriptures, under the directions of an accomplished spiritual practitioner, the Deity affords a particular advantage to fledgling devotees, an advantage that cannot otherwise be obtained. In short, the Deity allows accessibility. Years of tradition reveal that those who utilize this advantage quickly progress on the spiritual path. This, indeed, is His mercy.

After a short stay in Philadelphia, having fully benefited from properly worshiping Lord Jagannath, Ghanashyam regrouped for more grueling but blissful days on Sankirtan. His book sales skyrocketed, and no one was more pleased than Srila Prabhupada:

9 November, 1975

My dear Ghanashyam Dasa,

Please accept my blessings. I am in due receipt of your letter dated October 5th, 1975 and was very glad to read the contents. You mention the well-renown psychologist at Harvard who is interested in finding about man's true nature. Man's true nature is to render service. Originally the living entity was meant for rendering service to Krishna and as soon as the living entity misuses this marginal position, he becomes conditioned by material nature. You are rendering first quality service to Krishna by your preaching success. Be blessed and continue your efforts and Krishna will recognize you very quickly. Anyone who preaches like this is very much appreciated by Krishna. I hope this meets you in good health.

Your ever well-wisher,

A. C. Bhaktivedanta Swami (Prabhupada)

Lila-smaranam, also known as Larry Holt, was a close friend of Ghanashyam's. One year, they found each other enjoying camaraderie in India, at a large ISKCON festival, when Lila-smaranam learned the difference between imitating Ghanashyam and following in his footsteps. He retells the story as follows:

> I went to the Mayapur Festival in 1976 and he was there. There was a little bit of dissension in the BBT Library Party, which I found disturbing. There was something going on between him and the rest of the devotees because he wouldn't chant with the rest of them. He would chant by himself in the morning, trying to concentrate without distraction. Some devotees were pointing to him and saying, "Why is he chanting by himself? He's not chanting with everyone else." I wondered about it, too. But what I did was that I started chanting with him. I wanted to see why he was avoiding the others. Well, he was getting up at 2 AM. That's the first thing—he didn't want to wake anybody, so he went to chant on his own. He would chant thirty-two rounds prior to Mangala-arati, the early devotional program that begins before dawn. And he would chant more rounds later in the day.
>
> Now, I figured if he could do it, why can't I? So, I woke up and I chanted thirty-two rounds with him. I did it the first day. The second day. I felt wonderful both those days. The third day after I chanted my rounds I was so tired that I actually passed out on the roof of the Mayapur Temple. The bad thing about it was that I passed out during the heat of the day. You can get roasted by the sun! It's India, remember. He came and woke me up and told me to go downstairs to take rest. I knew then that I shouldn't try to keep up with him. Follow in his footsteps, yes, but I shouldn't imitate him. He was on a whole other level.

Austerities in Eastern Europe

If Ghanashyam's determined book distribution efforts had conquered the States, his work in Eastern Europe was the stuff of legends. His good friend Guru Dasa was one of the few devotees to travel with him in that very risky area, where religion was considered illegal, particularly preaching, and devotees had to smuggle books in without the authorities catching them. They wore disguises, too, much as they had in the States, but here it was absolutely necessary, lest they be thrown in jail. Guru Dasa remembers:

> It was something like 1974. I had just come from some preaching tour in Northern Ireland and various places in Europe. I had been part of the traveling Krishna-Balaram Sankirtan party, but that was coming to an end. It was suggested that Ghanashyam and I team up and go to Eastern Europe. We had never met.
>
> In the Deutsche Republic, at the time, we were smuggling books in with Suhotra and Abhichandra. The authorities gave us a one-day visa. It was a time parameter—we had to reach the opposite border in a short period of time. It was unrealistic. We had to distribute the books at a certain spot, too, and only that spot. If you don't reach the border in time they start searching for you, and if you get there too fast they give you a speeding ticket.
>
> It was suggested that I meet Ghanashyam and that we work together. He was bringing the car from Frankfurt and I was meeting him at a station. I think it was in Sofia, the capital of Bosnia. It was a big station, cobblestone streets—it looked like the 1930s in the United States. It was a big area, and Ghanashyam was not there on time, so I just circled the station to make sure he wasn't waiting on the other side. No Ghanashyam. So I sat on the wall and chanted and read. He eventually arrived and we immediately felt comfortable together, although this was our first meeting. We got into the car, found a camping ground nearby and got settled. He had some letters of invitation from three or four universities in Eastern Europe. They were actually requesting to meet with him regarding purchasing sets of books for the university.

Anyway, to give you a gist, he was totally renounced. All the shops had the same dairy products and vegetables—they were small and there wasn't great variety. So, we purchased some foods and Ghanashyam said, "I'm not going to have any because I ate this morning." This really impressed me. I mean, food was scarce, but he was committed to one austere meal a day. I still offered him some, and he took a little out of kindness to me. Basically, he didn't eat very much, and food is a big enjoyment, a respite, of sorts, when you're on the road.

We were traveling quite a bit at the time—Czechoslovakia and all those places. Neither one of us could read a map. He was such an academic, and I was an artist type—so we had trouble reading maps. I'll tell you one incident. This is not to be glorified, but is an example of what I'm saying. We were very intellectual, it's true, but we should have had someone guiding us. At the border of Bulgaria, we had just come from the capital city of Sofia and I had gotten an exit visa to leave. We were going to Greece after our tour was over. Ghanashyam, for whatever reason, threw out his visa; he discarded it.

He seemed very nonchalant about it, too. Remember, we had both been activists, politically motivated, in our youth—that was something we talked about. We actually became close during this time. Okay, so he threw out his visa. I had mine. We were in this customs office that was practically devoid of any furniture and it was painted institutional green, if you know what I mean, and they had a television there that was just pure static. I remember that I could barely make out what was on. I think it was a dancing bear with balancing plates on a stick. Their television programs were not too sophisticated.

They were willing to let me out, but they had no idea how Ghanashyam got there because he had no visa. So they said that we had to go back to the capital, which was quite a ways away, to get his visa. Anyway, we came up with this idea that we would just wait and try explaining our case to someone else. What we did was we just slept in the area—we camped out and waited eight hours or so.

The next morning we tried a new customs official. I went along, to see what would happen. So we get there and there is this lane with customs walls on either side, and you have to go into the lane and wait there. We get there, and guess what? The same guy was there, and he had a 6:00 shadow. This is the same guy that told us to go back to the capital, okay? He sees us and we see him. Our eyes lock. At that point, we can't turn around. So, we're there and we still had no visa for Ghanashyam. But, believe it or not, the guard finally just said, "Go!" It was Krishna's mercy.

Another incident—we are once again in Bulgaria. We didn't have any funds and we wanted to contact Frankfurt, which was the ISKCON headquarters in that area, in Eastern Europe. We were in the Bulgarian embassy—we thought that we would go and meet different ambassadors and give them a Bhagavad-gita. *We were there to see if we could get an appointment with the ambassador, but we also wanted to telefax the Frankfurt temple. We got a man in the American embassy to send a telegram to their machine for us. Ghanashyam dictated the letter, and one of their officials was typing it for us.*

So Ghanashyam began to dictate. He said, "I have placed some books in the University here and we were successful in numerous ways. But we need a transfer of funds." That is why we were at the embassy, too, to find out how to do it. We had an arrangement to do this with the National Bank of Bulgaria. But here's what happened. Ghanashyam then continued dictating, saying, "...and after this we can preach in Poland." Well, the guy who was typing screeches to a stop—you could almost hear it, and he pulls the paper out of the typewriter. He quickly leaves the room in a huff, and then he returns seconds later with two marines. So they all take us and lead us to the ambassador, past people wanting to see him, in fact. We also wanted to see the ambassador. Now, this is a guy who looks like Carl Holbrook—he really looks like an ambassador. He had white hair and looked really good and competent. We come into the room and I had the Bhagavad-gita *in my hand. And—surprise of surprises—the ambassador says, "I like Bhakti-yoga."*

I said, "Do you know the distinction between Bhakti-yoga and other yogas?" He said, "Yes, I have studied yoga quite a bit." At that point I gave him the Bhagavad-gita, *which he graciously accepted. Okay, but then he brought us back to earth. He then said, "I hope that you guys are not planning to preach in the street." I said, "We're not. But, anyway, how do you know that we're Hare Krishnas?" He answered, "Because only you and the Jehovah's Witnesses—who are in jail right now—are courageous enough to do this in Bulgaria." He probably thought that we were going to chant or something. I said, "We're not preaching in the streets—we actually have invitations to universities." I then showed him the letters. He was satisfied, but he cautioned us that if we were caught while preaching in the streets, there would be nothing he could do. So, somehow, although we thought we were in deep trouble, Krishna bailed us out again.*

The significance of distributing religious books in Eastern Europe, particularly in the 1970s, will emerge only through the virtue of context. The risk was profound. To put it in perspective, Ghanashyam's work took him behind the "Iron Curtain," which refers to the former division between the communist nations of Eastern Europe—the Eastern Bloc—and the noncommunist nations of Western Europe. The term refers to the segregation that the Soviet Union imposed upon its subjugated nations in the Eastern Bloc and to the repressive measures of many Eastern Bloc governments.

Ghanashyam preached there at great personal risk. The Iron Curtain erected frightening border defenses between the countries of the Western and Eastern Blocs. These were among the most heavily militarized districts in the world, particularly the regions between East and West Germany. In some areas, the inner German border had intimidating double fences made of steel mesh with sharp edges, and, in others, a high concrete barrier similar to the Berlin Wall. The actual borderline was branded by ominous posts and signs and was guarded by numerous watchtowers set behind the barrier.

German border guards patrolled the area, with orders to shoot unauthorized persons on sight. Those who were lucky enough not to be killed were escorted to rough and unpredictable prison camps. This was the backdrop to Ghanashyam's service of book distribution in Eastern Europe.

In other words, he found himself in the midst of the "Cold War," a term used to describe the post-World War II struggle between the United States and the Union of Soviet Socialist Republics (USSR), along with their respective allies. During this period, which lasted from the mid-1940s until the end of the 1980s, international politics was virtually defined by these two great powers. The United States came to be known for its democracy and capitalism, while the Soviet Bloc became synonymous with communism. The countries of Eastern Europe—including Bulgaria, Czechoslovakia, Hungary, Poland, East Germany, and Romania—were dangerous for many, particularly for those who tried to promote religion of any kind.

It was into this arena that Ghanashyam foisted himself as a sacrifice for the mission of his spiritual master. The gravity of the situation cannot be overstated. He reminisces about his experiences in these most challenging of places:

There I was in this communist country, and communism was full on at that time. There was no way anyone could help me from the outside. And if you want to see horrible jails—in some of these countries it's just unbelievable. Even the hospitals, what to speak of the jails, were horrendous, and I've spent my time in both. Terrible food, sanitation, treatment—it was just unbelievable. But the part I wanted to mention is that a couple of times I escaped by the skin of my teeth. I mean, I had it down—James Bond didn't have anything on me. [laughter] I was able to sneak out without being noticed; I got the car and mapped out the best route, the different directions to the border.

But sometimes I was put in jail for distributing books, because we kept hidden books in the walls of our vans. While in jail I had nothing to do but to chant and to eat cabbage. I was eating cabbage and apples—that's what I lived on for quite some time. It was the only thing that was available. But I'll tell you—at that time, the cabbage was wonderful. And the apple was a great dessert. When you have nothing to eat and you're hungry, you begin to appreciate simple things.

One time, I was driving for the border and was stopped by the guards. Now, my license had blood on it from a small mishap that happened earlier that day. And when I handed it to them for them to check it, the guard looked and saw the blood. He immediately suspected something foul, of course, and called me into the station. Well, that was all they needed. I was temporarily arrested. But I got out. Krishna always protected me. It's actually amazing how I managed to maintain myself there. Sometimes I lived on public trains, going from one car to the other, narrowly escaping the authorities. Sometimes I would chant in public bathrooms—if I got caught chanting religious hymns or prayers, that would be it. I could end up in jail again. Or worse.

Prabhupada, of course, was overjoyed to hear of Ghanashyam's accomplishments in such risky terrain. But he was also worried about his brave disciple. Letters from Ghanashyam brought tears to Prabhupada's eyes. Once, in fact, while Ghanashyam was in India, he had had a very personal exchange with his guru, one that etched itself in his consciousness. Ghanashyam tells the story as follows:

One year the Library Party met up at Mayapur Festival; it must have been 1976. After some time there, at Mayapur, I realized that we were all going to have a meeting, and that the subject was me! You see, what happened is that most of the devotees on the party didn't want to go out with me anymore. They felt I was too extreme, too austere, or whatever. And I was oblivious to it. By the way, just a month or two prior to that, Srila Prabhupada had sent out these amazing letters, really encouraging the party and offering so many blessings to the devotees. So it was strange that now they all wanted to leave...and that I was the reason for it. But whatever the situation, when I found out, I was devastated, because these were serious devotees of Srila Prabhupada. I had actually become quite morose that I had caused such offenses.

Anyway, a few days later Prabhupada had this preaching engagement at a life member's house, and so many devotees went. I don't remember any of the details, but I also went—I just dragged my body there because I knew I was supposed to go. I was depressed, but, hey, this was Prabhupada, so I went. I was gloomy, frustrated, depressed, didn't know what to do. Just then, I was walking by Srila Prabhupada's room—I was going outside, maybe to chant. Hari-sauri Prabhu was Prabhupada's servant at the time, and he just happened to see me go by. And he called out to me. He said that there was some emergency and that he had to go some place. He further said that I should just stand outside and watch for a while, to make sure that someone was there when Prabhupada rang his bell—he would ring his bell if he wanted me to come in.

Before I had a chance to tell him that I was in no state of consciousness to do such an important service, he had already left. And so I had to stay there and act as a guard and a servant in front of Prabhupada's quarters. Within minutes, I was trying to look around to find somebody else to come and to do the service. But then Prabhupada rang the bell.

There were two rooms, and I went into the first room, looked around, and then I went into the room that Prabhupada was in. When I saw him, I immediately offered full dandavats, bowing down before him. The room was small, so just as I raised my head from bowing, I noticed Prabhupada's leg propped up on his little desk, close to the floor. He was sitting behind it and he took his leg, propped it up, and his foot was staring me in the face. So now I'm confronted with my guru, feeling foolish and a bit out of it, and I'm certain he is going to give me a big kick in the head or something.

Well, some background: a night or two before Prabhupada had an accident where he had rolled out of his bed and bruised his forearm, his shin, his leg, his elbow and also the insole of the foot. So he had some neem leaves on his desk, and he had placed his foot out in front of me like that suggesting that he needed a massage. He didn't say anything, but he just pointed. So he's pointing to his foot, and I'm just bewildered, thinking about all the things that had been going on in the past and that were going on in the present. But, most of all, I was thinking that I am in the presence of a pure devotee.

Understanding that he wanted me to take the neem leaf, and to put it on his foot, I grabbed a nearby cup, the neem leaf, and he started showing me what to do, how to make the medicinal mixture. And so I started trying to massage his insole with the neem leaf substance. But because of my prior anxiety, and my nervousness for being in Prabhupada's presence, I literally dropped this neem—a formula that stains like anything—all over Prabhupada's shirt, his dhoti, *and so on. Now I'm in total anxiety. I'm depressed and practically about to cry. But I look up at Prabhupada, and he is calmly pointing to his elbow, gesturing that I put some there. And so I tried to move it and put it on his elbow, but it started dropping on the other side of his* dhoti! *Now, I didn't know what to do, to run out, to cry, to scream, to beg forgiveness. I didn't know what to do; I couldn't even think! Just then, he pointed to a part of his leg.*

So while all this dropping is going on, messing up his clothes, he's acting like nothing happened! I mean, he could see all these heavy green stains on his light saffron cloth.

At one point, he looked up and I understood that my service there was finished. So, when I went down to offer obeisances, I had this amazing realization: It was very clear that Prabhupada was teaching me through this exchange. He was showing me that even though I was doing something wrong, he truly loved me and because of that, my mistakes were inconsequential. I should, of course, have labored to do it correctly, but he was showing me the love, letting me know that, yes, I was engaging in his service, and he recognized that I was really trying, that I at least wanted to do it right. Prabhupada was letting me know: Don't be depressed; don't leave the party. Just do your best—do the work in the right way, but even if you don't, don't give up. Continue your service. And so I rose to go out, and Prabhupada was just smiling as if I had done something really wonderful.

This incident gave Ghanashyam renewed enthusiasm, and he continued with his service, albeit with greater sensitivity for his Library Party comrades. Krishna-kshetra Prabhu, a scholarly devotee who had the good fortune to travel with him throughout Europe, even into the Eastern Bloc, fondly remembers those days:

I was lucky enough to meet Maharaja (at that time Ghanashyam Prabhu) in the late summer of 1977. He and a few other devotees, members of the BBT Library Party, were in Europe distributing complete sets of Bhagavatam *and* Chaitanya-charitamrita *to libraries, especially to university libraries and to professors. When they came to Germany, I was invited to accompany them and to particularly assist Ghanashyam with translation and whatever else he needed (driving, cooking, etc.) in Austria and East Germany (DDR).*

In a small car, I think it was a Renault, we set off to Austria, visiting universities in Vienna, Salzburg, and several other places. Ghanashyam would wear a dark three-piece suit and tie, and carry a black salesman's "sample case" full of Prabhupada's books, of which by that time we had a few published in the German language. As we met professors (making no appointments, just knocking on office doors and walking in), Ghanashyam would boldly yet humbly present the books, encouraging the person either to sign himself up for a "standing order" or at least write a note of recommendation for the university library. He was so charming, with such a big innocent smile, that many agreed, often to my complete surprise.

From the very start of our tour, he became my mentor, with all intention of training me to do the same service. Always encouraging, explaining his "method," always wanting to give confidence: "You can do it!" Within days he had me "go it alone" a few times. He explained his "secret," that I have always cherished: "Whatever situation I'm in, I always feel that Krishna has put me here for some reason. I don't know what He wants, but He wants something to happen, and he wants me to be His instrument. So I pray to Krishna, 'Please make me Your instrument.' And then, sure enough, something happens, and I understand, 'That was Krishna!'"

During those two or three weeks we were together, he maintained a very intense and strict sadhana: *He would get up in the morning at 2:30; he would eat only once in a day; and he would chant forty-two rounds of Maha-mantra everyday. I don't know how he arrived at the number forty-two, but that was his standard. He would say, chuckling, "I am so fallen, I have to make up for it by chanting so much."*

The most intense days were in the DDR, the Eastern Bloc. I reminded him again and again that the country is very restrictive, that actually we are not allowed to take our books into the country, and certainly we are not allowed to enter the university to sell them. He would simply smile and humbly say, "Okay, but anyway let's see what we can do." And I would be amazed at how Krishna would open doors, make customs officials too lazy to look carefully in our vehicle, and make university policemen forgiving when we were caught.

This last scenario refers to our visit to the University of Leipzig. Walking right by the reception desk of the main building (where as foreigners we certainly were expected to register and explain our purpose), we went up the elevator to the first floor. Then we just got out, knocked on the first office door we came to, were invited in, sat down, and he began his "pitch" to the friendly sociology professor. After a few minutes, the man said, "Oh, these are surely wonderful books, and although they are not for me, I know one professor who will definitely be interested," and he proceeded to give us directions where to find this other professor.

Very excited, we thanked him and made our way out of the main building (quickly rushing by reception) to an adjacent building, found the room, knocked, were invited in, sat down, and again he began his presentation. After one or two minutes, I began to understand where we were.

This was not a professor's office—this was the university police, and we had happily and foolishly entered a trap. When they started to explain the actual situation, I gulped hard, imagining what it must be like in a DDR prison in Leipzig and wondering how many years we would have to serve sentence there. Ghanashyam, however, didn't skip a beat or change his expression in the least. He simply began apologizing profusely (while they scrutinized our American passports). He explained that "we travel to so many different countries, all with different laws, all very confusing, you see, and, really, the last thing we would ever want to do is to go against the rules of your great country . . ." Before long, they were eating out of his hand.

In the end, of course, they simply let us go, with a rather polite manner and a smile. After that, I worried that Ghanashyam would say, "Okay, anyway, let's go try again in that big building, some other office!" He was like that—completely unstoppable. He was enthusiastic and fearless to serve Srila Prabhupada—but he was smart, with discrimination. To my relief, he didn't suggest that we go to the other building, so we moved on to the next city.

At the end of each week he would write a detailed report of the week's activities, which he would send to Satsvarupa Dasa Goswami, who managed the Library Party from America. Ghanashyam felt these reports were important, as they showed the program's success to the BBT, who were supporting (and funding) it.

After two weeks (one in Austria, one in the DDR) on the road we returned to Schloss Rettershof, the main German temple at the time, outside Frankfurt. This was in September, 1977. As soon as we walked in the door of the Schloss, someone exclaimed to us, "Srila Prabhupada is in London!" We were astonished. Prabhupada in London? How is it possible? We had been hearing how ill he was in Vrindavan, India. It was clear to everyone that he was preparing to depart from this world, and now he is in London?!

Within minutes we were back in the car, driving toward the UK. When we finally arrived, and when Prabhupada was told of Ghanashyam's presence, he immediately called for him. Satsvarupa Maharaja had been reporting to Prabhupada about Ghanashyam's great success in distributing full sets of his books, and now he was informed that he had just been in one of the communist countries of East Europe, so Prabhupada was eager to meet with him.

Somehow, I was allowed to accompany him, since I had been his assistant during the tour. Suddenly, I found myself at Prabhupada's feet in his room, together with Ghanashyam Prabhu, Upendra and Tamal Krishna Goswami (Prabhupada's servant and secretary, respectively), and Dvarakesh Prabhu (another pioneer of Eastern European preaching).

Ghanashyam had just finished writing his report for the DDR tour, so he sat cross-legged before Prabhupada and read it to him. Prabhupada, sitting in a chair (maybe a rocking chair—I don't remember), was by this time extremely thin and visibly ill. Upendra was lightly stroking Prabhupada's legs, to ease the pain. As Ghanashyam read his report, occasionally Prabhupada would make a short comment, and he told Tamal Krishna Maharaja to write down his comments.

At one point, Ghanashyam read from his report how we had observed people in the DDR standing in long lines before food stores, and how little was available in the markets in the way of vegetables and fruits. Suddenly, Srila Prabhupada's face was filled with tears. He interrupted, and spoke about the resulting suffering of people due to atheistic governments. He was crying out of compassion for these people's material situations and out of appreciation for Ghanashyam's work.

I was thoroughly surprised and amazed. Here was my spiritual master, himself about to leave his body, travelling thousands of miles to bid us, his Western disciples, farewell, and he is concerned about the material well-being of strangers in another part of the world!

It was at this point that I understood something about the depth of Prabhupada's compassion, and the good fortune of Ghanashyam Prabhu, for catching the spirit of Prabhupada's desire and therefore receiving the shower of his blessings, and my own good fortune to witness all of this.

But there is more to the story.

Blessed by the Best

It is important to understand the final part of Krishna-kshetra's story as described above. Ghanashyam had extended his spiritual master's mercy around the world by distributing his books. And this was particularly significant in Eastern Europe, where it took considerable determination to do so. Accordingly, Prabhupada showered his mercy on Ghanashyam.

Radhanath Swami, one of Ghanashyam's closest friends, explains the details:

The doctors had warned Srila Prabhupada that he might die if he traveled. Srila Prabhupada, however, reciprocated so lovingly with his disciples that despite his body giving way and only a thin layer of skin covering his bones, he decided to go to London and then America to inspire the devotees, and to express his gratitude for their loving service. He was taken on a wheelchair through customs and in the plane and finally to his room at Bhaktivedanta Manor in England. The devotees came from all over Europe to see him, even though their hearts were broken when they saw his condition. Yet they were simultaneously in ecstasy to see his unconditional spiritual love for them.

On receiving the news of Prabhupada's arrival, Ghanashyam Prabhu, Krishna-khsetra Prabhu and Bhakti Dayal Prabhu drove all the way from Eastern Europe to London. When Tamal Krishna Goswami Maharaja saw Ghanashyam, he rejoiced, knowing that his presence would make Srila Prabhupada happy. There is no greater happiness for devotees than to see Srila Prabhupada happy. Prabhupada's personal entourage knew that on seeing Ghanashyam Prabhu, Srila Prabhupada would be very happy, and therefore Tamal Krishna Goswami personally went down and brought Ghanashyam by the hand into Srila Prabhupada's quarters.

Ghanashyam offered his respects to his guru, at which point Srila Prabhupada smiled and called him near. Prabhupada then embraced him with tears of love and gratitude. Rubbing Ghanashyam's head, Srila Prabhupada said, "Your life is successful, thank you very much." Now crying, Prabhupada said, "This is the parampara system, or the system of disciplic succession, wherein a disciple follows in the mood of his teacher. My Guru Maharaja pushed me, and now, I am pushing you and you are pushing others to spread the mission of Chaitanya Mahaprabhu."

For Prabhupada to be crying and embracing and rubbing the head of his disciple was something very special. Soon, all the devotees around the world were hearing of Ghanashyam's good fortune and of the special mercy he had received from Srila Prabhupada.

But there is another part to this story that is not so well-known, and I was fortunate to hear it from Bhakti Tirtha Maharaja (Ghanashyam) himself a few months ago. Tamal Krishna Goswami was moved by Prabhupada's pleasure and, in an attempt to please Srila Prabhupada even more, he came upon a brilliant idea. He told Ghanashyam, "It will bring Prabhupada the greatest joy if you would please come and read the report of your work in Eastern Europe personally to Srila Prabhupada."

This was a great honor and pleasure for Ghanashyam Prabhu. Bringing him in front of Srila Prabhupada, Tamal Krishna Goswami said, "Today Ghanashyam will read a report to you of his preaching activities in Eastern Europe." Now, Ghanashyam was very reverential towards Prabhupada and quite nervous about doing this. But on the order of Goswami Maharaja he started to read.

As he began, Prabhupada looked totally disinterested, and was talking to someone here or there, looking around. Ghanashyam saw this and became nervous, feeling that perhaps he was disturbing Srila Prabhupada. At that moment, Prabhupada stopped him with a grave stare. Ghanashyam felt paralyzed. With a deep voice Srila Prabhupada chastised, "KRISHNA IS THE DOER." Ghanashyam Prabhu stood motionless.

Tamal Krishna Goswami, who was witness to the whole thing, said, "Ghanashyam Prabhu, I think it's time for you to leave now," at which point Ghanashyam offered his obeisances and quickly departed the room. Outside, he wept in gratitude—he knew he had received very special mercy.

He personally told me that this is one of the most intimate loving experiences he had had in his life. On this day, Srila Prabhupada had instructed him that he is not the doer and that one should never expect any credit for oneself. On the first day, Prabhupada had embraced him, cried tears of affection, stroked his head, and said, "Your life is successful and you are carrying on the parampara." It's not that Ghanashyam did anything wrong on that day. Yet the next day Prabhupada gave a more valuable instruction: He just ignored him and chastised him. Ghanashyam told me that these were also the last words that Prabhupada had personally spoken to him. Ghanashyam confessed that the world knows the first part of the story, but his favorite was this second part, "because through this Prabhupada showed his most intimate, special love towards me." Srila Prabhupada showed deep love and gratitude for Ghanashyam, but at the same time he wanted to protect him from egoism—a protection he would need for all the fame yet to come.

Soon, Prabhupada returned to Vrindavan, his illness taking its toll, and Ghanashyam returned to his service. The young disciple, enlivened by his encouraging exchange with his spiritual master, received a Bhakti-shastri award—an ISKCON degree conferred upon disciples who demonstrate exceptional learning and ability—on November 12, 1977, just two days before Prabhupada passed from this world. The degree was signed by Prabhupada himself and co-signed by ISKCON Governing Body Commissioner (GBC) Satsvarupa Dasa Goswami.

Back in the days when he was John Favors, Ghanashyam's Aunt Rose used to say, "I'm blessed by the best and too blessed to be distressed." Ghanashyam no doubt contemplated this aphorism in his last days with Srila Prabhupada. And he augmented it by saying, "I'm blessed by the best, and willing to pass all the tests."

CHAPTER FIVE

JAGANNATH PURI
AND THE
SAGA OF RENUNCIATION

"Lord Jagannath is an ocean of mercy and He is beautiful like a row of blackish rain clouds. He is the storehouse of bliss for Lakshmi and Saraswati, and His face is like a spotless full-blown lotus. He is worshiped by the best of demigods and sages, and His glories are sung by the Upanishads. May that Jagannath Swami be the object of my vision."

—TRADITIONAL POEM

WITH THE DEPARTURE of his spiritual master, Ghanashyam took solace in his service, traveling and distributing books, which he had now been doing for nearly five years. But at this juncture in his life he needed more—he wanted to increase his commitment in an unprecedented way. To this end, he contemplated taking *sannyasa*, the renounced order of life. During his time as a devotee, he had met many *sannyasis*, also called *swamis* ("controller of the senses"), and admired them greatly. Now he was seriously thinking about becoming one himself.

Sannyasa originated as part of "Varnashram," the socio-religious system mentioned in the Vedas and developed in later Hindu tradition. This system is comprised of four *varnas*, or social orders (priest, warrior, merchant, and laborer), and four *ashrams*, or spiritual orders (celibate student, married person, renounced married person, and full renunciant). The essential purpose of Varnashram is to accommodate a given person's material and spiritual inclinations, to acknowledge their distinct psychophysical makeup and to use this in God's service.

By taking into account one's psychosomatic dimensions, there is greater likelihood of their achieving realistic spiritual ends. Consequently, Varnashram has value in relation to one's reaching the ultimate goal of life. Otherwise, it is to be discarded. As the scriptures say, "Execution of one's duty in Varnashram is only so much useless labor if it does not give rise to love for Krishna." In other words, the system is useful only as long as it serves its ultimate goal, which is spiritual perfection.

The tradition of *sannyasa* is ancient, evoking images of austere ascetics with a penchant for renunciation, long revered in India. The word itself is traced to the Sanskrit root *sam*, meaning "together," or "complete," and *ni-as*, meaning "to reject," or "to resign from worldly life." In other words, a *sannyasi* is one who favors "complete renunciation." In Indian tradition this is associated with being a monk, or with the vows of a holy man, in which one becomes freed from all worldly obligations so that he can devote his life to the pursuit of the spirit.

Such renunciants are committed to the five "s's" of spiritual life, which, for the *sannyasi*, lead to ultimate liberation: (1) *Svadhyaya*. This means self-study. It requires that one look deeply at the nature of the self, who we are, what we are, and particularly in relation to God. It also refers to the systematic study of scripture. (2) *Seva*, or service. One must learn to serve both God and man. Although the *sannyasi* is a leader in society, he must come to see his leadership as a form of service; he must use it to help people and to bring them closer to God. (3) *Satsang.* A *sannyasi* must primarily associate with like-minded people, with others who are equally renounced; he also keeps company with souls who might not be committed to the spiritual path, but this he does mainly to give them a chance to move forward. (4) *Samarpan,* also called *Sharanagati,* or complete surrender—this defines a *sannyasi's* life, which is characterized by surrender to the will of God. Finally, (5) *Santosh* refers to inner peace, which is the natural result of nonattachment and renunciation. As Bob Dylan says, "When you ain't got nothing, you got nothing to lose." Thus, the truly renounced *sannyasi* lives a contented—even a blissful—life of divine service.

In the Vaishnava tradition to which Ghanashyam adhered, a *sannyasi* is one who dedicates full time to God's purposes in the world. He consecrates the three aspects of his being—body, mind, and words— to the service of the Lord. Accordingly, he carries a *tridanda,* or a staff with three sticks, symbolizing this triune consecration. He wears traditional saffron cloth, which, in India, is the color of renunciation, and commits to lifelong celibacy and religious scholarship, taking responsibility for guiding others. He is austere and dedicated.

Ghanashyam, clearly, had been inadvertently preparing for *sannyasa* for his entire life. His total absorption in service to God, his austere sense of diet, along with minimal sleep, and immoderate chanting were all profound indicators of his *sannyasa*-like inclinations.

One of Prabhupada's many descriptions of *sannaysa* bears this out: "This spiritual realization is obtained by *tapasya,* or undergoing the path of penance and abstinence from material pleasure voluntarily. Those who have been trained in abstinence from material pleasures are called *dhira,* or men undisturbed by the senses. Only these *dhiras* can accept the order of *sannyasa* . . ." With this in mind, Ghanashyam went to Mayapur for the yearly ISKCON festival, only four months after Prabhupada had returned to Krishna's abode.

Back to Lord Jagannath

It was March, 1978, and the young book distributor wanted to see the original form of Lord Jagannath in Puri, which is in the Indian State of Orissa. This is some 300 miles south of Calcutta, not far from the Mayapur Festival. He wanted to pray for the strength to remain celibate, the intelligence to be faithful to his Krishna Conscious vows—especially now that Prabhupada had recently departed—and he wanted confirmation that taking *sannyasa* would be appropriate for him. He reasoned that praying before Jagannath Himself would surely provide answers.

Jagannath is the unusual Deity of Krishna who reigns in Eastern India; His unfinished-looking form, with large, round eyes, black face, arms without hands, as described in the previous chapter, distinguishes Him from other images of the Lord. Ghanashyam, it might be remembered, had encountered this form—albeit a replica—while in Philadelphia, where he learned how to worship the Deity according to Brahminical rules. Now he was returning to this Deity, while in India, to ask for help, to bathe in His presence, to pray.

But it would not be easy. For centuries, the Puri temple has had a policy that shuns outsiders. This began as an attempt to preserve the temple's ritual purity but gained steam after the Mogul and British invasions of India. Precious gems and valuable jewels had been stolen from Deities throughout the subcontinent, until temple authorities simply said, "Stop!," deciding that foreigners should stay away altogether. The custodians of the Jagannath temple became particularly vehement about this, to the point that even Indira Gandhi, because she had married a non-Hindu, was denied entry.

Thus, today, only "Hindus" are allowed in. Worse still, the temple custodians hold a particularly conservative view of what exactly constitutes a Hindu. For them, belief is not enough—a true Hindu must be Indian, both racially and nationalistically. Ghanashyam, of course, looked askance at such prejudicial considerations, especially given his past in the Civil Rights Movement. But more, he disapproved of their policy because *Jagannath*, which literally means "Lord of the Universe," should in fact be accessible to everyone, as the name indicates, and because true spiritual life is a universal principle, nonsectarian and open to all.

But how would he override their long-standing rules? How would he get in?

Before telling his unique story of intrigue and good fortune, some background is in order. Jagannath Puri, a town of 75,000, is one of the world's most important pilgrimage centers and one of the four holiest cities in India, along with Badrinath in the north, Dvaraka in the west, and Rameshvaram in the south. The singular importance of Jagannath Puri, sometimes called Purushottama-Kshetra, is explained in the *Narada Purana*, one of Vaishnavism's early scriptures. Here we learn that simply by visiting Puri—a fortunate event that is rarely achieved, except by those who have performed many pious acts, for numerous lifetimes—and by seeing the Deity of Jagannath (Krishna), one can easily attain freedom from future births and, ultimately, reach the spiritual realm.

The current structure of the main temple was built in the twelfth century by King Chodaganga Deva, though the worship of the Deity goes back to antiquity. The temple is a huge complex—with numerous buildings, Deities, or manifestations of the divine, all centered on Lord Jagannath—housing as many as 5,000 priests and assistants. The entire compound is surrounded by a thick stone wall, more than twenty feet in height, enclosing a huge area the size of two football fields. The wall has four large gates, one on each side, and, for believers, these are entrances into the spiritual world. The main sanctum is the dwelling of the six-foot-tall Deities of Jagannath, Balarama, and the slightly shorter Subhadra, described in narrative traditions as Krishna, His brother, and His sister (or, in theological terms, God, His immediate expansion, and His spiritual energy).

The Deities stand on a colossal, regal throne, facing the many visitors who eagerly enter the temple in nonstop fashion. Specially trained priests conduct worship services six times a day—this service, called *arati*, is similar to the one that Ghanashyam had learned in Philadelphia. As many as 50,000 pilgrims, coming from all parts of the subcontinent, and from elsewhere as well, crowd in for each service, resulting in a diminished comfort level for everyone there. Pushing and sweating are not uncommon. But no one comes there for bodily consolation. Rather, one visits Jagannath to facilitate the spirit. And a trip to the temple is necessarily inspirational. Unfortunately, as already stated, foreigners are not allowed this asset, even if they can spy the Deities from the roof of the adjacent Raghunandan Library across the street, or when the divine forms are brought out of the temple for the yearly Ratha-yatra Festival.

The cautionary sign, "Non-Hindus not allowed," placed strategically on temple doors, is taken quite seriously—and this was particularly the case when Ghanashyam was there, in 1978—though changes in attitude are slowly emerging. It is not only foreigners who are shunned, either. The following groups of people are also traditionally banned from the temple: fishermen, leather workers, those who burn the dead, sweepers, distillers, brewers and wine sellers, potters, "fallen women" and prostitutes, members of non-Hindu tribes, and those belonging to other religions, such as Muslims or Christians. Besides these, other non-believers or atheists are not permitted beyond the temple gates.

Surprisingly, this restrictive administration has known little opposition. There have been exceptions, though. In 1958, for example, the Mukti Mandap Sabha, a political organization focusing on religious concerns, found itself reconsidering the admissions policy of the Jagannath Temple. As the story goes, four American women had been converted to Hinduism through the Ramakrishna Mission and wanted to enter the Temple while visiting Puri.

To obtain permission, they approached the local magistrate, who in turn placed the decision before the Mukti Mandap Sabha. The president of the Sabha, then Saccidananda Saraswati, decided that he should personally talk to the Americans, for only by doing so, he reasoned, might he arrive at an equitable decision. After a brief conversation with them, he found that he was sufficiently impressed, and he issued a positive statement that initially met with some resistance. Nonetheless, in due course his proclamation was fully accepted, largely because of his prominent position as a political leader, and the four Americans were allowed in. Part of his statement appears below:

The American ladies had put on saris and veils and they bowed their heads before their superiors just as Indian ladies do. They were reserved and respected their husbands as embodiments of the deity. They were not short tempered. They did not eat fish, mutton, beef, or any other meat. They were fully knowledgeable of Hindu principles of life. They took a morning and evening bath and prayed for the welfare of humanity. They were honest and very sympathetic towards the poor and the sick. . . . They had become truly Hindu.

This was the first time that a prominent Hindu organization had ever granted foreign converts permission to enter the Jagannath Temple. And it seemed to be a harbinger of things to come. However, this fledgling attempt at social reform ended in 1964 when the Mukti Mandap Sabha reversed its decision and denied temple entrance to other American members of the Ramakrishna Vedanta Society, mainly because of political pressure generated by caste-conscious Brahmins.

Since then, Srila Prabhupada's missionary efforts have resulted in large numbers of "non-Hindus" adopting the path of Vaishnavism. Predictably, many of these foreign devotees have tried to negotiate entry into the Jagannath temple. Most importantly, the celebrated spiritual master, Prabhupada himself, visited Puri on January 26, 1977, and although he, being Indian, was personally allowed to enter,

he came there only to implore temple authorities on behalf of his
Western followers. Prabhupada argued as follows:

> *This stumbling block should be dissolved. You want to pack Jagan-*
> *nath Swami up inside your home, and do not want to allow His*
> *mercy to expand. He is Jagannath, the Lord of the Universe, not*
> *only the lord of Puri, or the lord of Orissa. He is Jagannath. Krish-*
> *na declares in the* Bhagavad-gita *that He is Lord of all. That is the*
> *definition of Jagannath,* sarva-loka-maheshvaram. *So why should*
> *you deny the inhabitants of the world (*sarva-loka*)? Why not allow*
> *them the* darshan *[viewing] of Jagannath? Sri Chaitanya Mahap-*
> *rabhu never approved such denial. He said, "My name will be*
> *spread throughout every town and village in the world." Now this*
> *is being done and people from all over the world are eager to come*
> *here. So why do you restrict them?*
>
> *Of course, if you do not allow these foreigners to enter the temple,*
> *there is no loss for them, because Jagannath has already come to them,*
> *and they are worshiping Him. But it is the proper etiquette to show*
> *respect to the Vaishnavas. They are strictly observing the four prin-*
> *ciples of spiritual life: no illicit sex, no meat eating, no fish eating, no*
> *egg eating, no intoxication, no gambling. They are purified.*
>
> *Mahaprabhu has condemned offenses to the Vaishnavas. These*
> *European and American Vaishnavas are hankering after Jagan-*
> *nath's* darshan—jagannatha svami nayana-patha-gami bhavatu
> me. *["Lord Jagannath, please be visible unto me."] Through your*
> *intervention they may be able to see Jagannath Swami. Since these*
> *Vaishnavas are so eager to come to Jagannath Puri and to see Jag-*
> *annath, you should welcome them. I have thus come to specifically*
> *request that you remove this restriction and that you be friendly to*
> *the foreign devotees.*

While Prabhupada's words fell on deaf ears, he staged a personal
protest that was indeed heard by temple authorities—he refused

to go into the temple himself. When a renowned saintly person of his stature avoids a given temple, it has certain implications, and it is humiliating for those in charge. Thus, when the former chief minister of Orissa, Hare Krushna Mahatab—who was favorable to ISKCON—saw what Prabhupada did, he tried to intercede on behalf of the Western devotees. But he was unsuccessful. The tradition of banning nearly everyone not born to Hindu parents was deep-rooted, with few exceptions over the course of centuries. And then came Ghanashyam.

Mission Implausible

Ghanashyam knew of Prabhupada's journey to Puri just one year before his own, and he was aware that his spiritual master wanted the restrictions reversed. That was enough for him. So he devised a plan to get in. Says Ghanashyam:

A funny thing would happen when I would go to India. Many local people would laugh at me because they would try to speak to me in the local languages and not understand why I couldn't respond. They assumed that I would understand the languages due to my dark complexion, probably thinking I was from South India or some such. Once, due to my appearance and the mercy of the Lord, I had the most breathtaking experience in 1978, which was my first visit to India after Prabhupada had left. For this reason, I made special prayers to Lord Jagannath for the protection of the movement.

During that year, I had a personal chance to go to Jagannath Puri. I was touring South India and a few other places with a group of devotees who were all really wonderful, dedicated souls. For most of us, it was our first time visiting Puri. We had some classes by the sea and visited sacred places in the area. Of course, due to the fact that we were foreigners and ISKCON devotees, we were not allowed to go and see Lord Jagannath in the temple. Nevertheless, I had this passion to see the Lord. And I have a rather

*interesting history or, let's say, a certain ability that enables me to
get into different situations. Well, this time it got me into the presence of Lord Jagannath.*

As he approached the temple, it seemed daunting. How would he
defy countless years of tradition? And yet he knew that he had every
right to go before the Lord of all—his own spiritual master, as well as
simple logic, confirmed it.

For several hours, he stood outside, watching people come and
go. He took special notice of the guards—he had heard of the serious
dangers awaiting foreigners who were caught trying to get in. If the
guards could discern that a particular visitor was not a Hindu, that
person could be uncompromisingly brutalized. Stories of severe beat-
ings and torture permeate local legend. After some initial fear, however, Ghanashyam received inspiration, confidence, and he knew he
could accomplish what he had set out to do.

Slowly, he began to formulate a plan. ISKCON devotees, he noted,
tended to tie their robes in a particular way, inadvertently enabling
the temple guards to easily recognize them. Realizing that his own
dhoti was indeed wrapped in that peculiar ISKCON manner, which
exposed him not only as a member of Prabhupada's institution but as
a foreigner as well, he decided to put on Western clothes. The guards
might then think that he was a South Indian businessman rather
than an ISKCON convert. Danavir Goswami, who was rooming
with him at a nearby hotel in Puri, remembers the incident:

*It was early 1978, around the time of the Mayapur festival. He
didn't have any Western clothes with him and he asked if I did. For
some reason, I did have a pair of dark trousers and a dark shirt.
Since we were of similar size, the clothes fit him well. He went off
alone on his mission. When he returned he told me the entire story
of how he got in and how they gave him such a wonderful darshan,
or viewing, of the Deity. He said that he kind of intimated to them*

that he was from India but had gone to study in the West, as I recall. They accepted that.

In addition to wearing a dark suit and having the blackish complexion of a South Indian, he tied a cloth around his head to hide the texture of his hair. This enabled him to simulate the appearance of certain Brahmins who wear turbans—in those few hours he stood outside the temple, he had seen many such *pandits* going in and out. He waited until dark to further conceal his form.

As night arrived, he made his way into the outer courtyard, which was extremely crowded, bumping shoulders with excited visitors. Some appeared to be ordinary worshippers, others saints. Tourists, businessmen, women and children—everyone rushed by. And he wondered if anyone could tell that he was there on the sly. He tried to look casual, as if he belonged. Years of Sankirtan, especially the selling of books in restricted areas, had prepared him for this.

But the guards were milling about, watching for intruders, and this made him nervous. Although these sentinels tended to blend in—the regulars were accustomed to their presence—their clubs and military costumes looked particularly menacing to Ghanashyam, who realized he was taking a risk by being there.

The guards' duty, of course, was to stop unauthorized people from entering the inner sanctum. Ghanashyam, frightfully aware of this, didn't look up at them, nor did he draw any attention to himself by appearing intimidated or fearful. In fact, his ploy was highly successful, because, in minutes, he was virtually ushered through the main entrance area, his body pulled by a current of people, pushed by a river of bodies, with no guards acting as obstacles. Feeling like a small fish in a huge sea, with thousands of devotees all around him, he found himself face to face with Jagannath, Baladeva, and Subhadra.

Humbly, he stayed in the back, watching and thinking, his small dark eyes focusing on the divine form of similar hue. He was still mindful of local restrictions, aware that he could be asked to leave, or worse. But he was also ecstatic! Here he was with the Lord Himself. So he decided to pray, which is why he wanted to be there in the first place. The pushing persisted, however, minimizing his ability to focus. There was a positive side to this pushing, though. The crowd seemed to insist that he go to the front of the altar, not verbally but by bodies propelling him forward. So he accommodated them. And in due course he was right up front, in intimate association with Lord Jagannath. Ghanashyam shares details of that momentous event:

The altar is rather unusual. First, there is a big rail and then a long hallway in front of the Deities. The actual altar where the Deities reside is very high with this barrier in front as well. Every now and then, the pujaris, *or priests, open the barrier and allow a few people to go toward the Deities; they also give these lucky pilgrims a* tulasi *leaf or some* prasadam, *the food offered to the Lord.*

At first, I tried to stay back, because the closer you go, the more attention you draw. However, at the same time, I didn't want to fight against the current because that would also draw attention. Consequently, I was somehow pushed up to the rail. Now, I observed that some of the temple custodians, the priests, seemed to treat their service like a business. They would look into the crowd for Indian tourists who might appear wealthy—you could usually tell by their clothes or jewelry. The priests particularly looked for such wealthy tourists because they wanted to extract money from them. Perhaps not all of the priests had this mentality but this was definitely going on to a certain extent.

So, in this way, some people got called in through the barrier. Anyhow, I was pushed right up to the head pujari, who gave me some tulasi *and* charanamrita, *the leaves offered to Jagannath's lotus feet and the delicious liquid used to bathe His body. He then held out a tray for money and I offered a few rupees.*

When he started to speak to me, I thought, "Oh God, now I'm in trouble." He repeated the same words, and obviously I couldn't respond because I didn't understand his language. Then I got really nervous and started moving towards the back. I was trying to excuse myself, to find a way to run out. I figured that he might try to call one of the guards.

Then something strange happened. My nervousness subsided when I noticed all the priests gathering various foods to make an offering. I watched them scurrying about, running back and forth in the midst of thousands of voices, loud conch shells, bells, cymbals, drums, and other cacophonous sounds. The priests ran with these big pots of bhoga from the kitchen and tried to put as much on the altar as possible before it was time for the offering. All of this activity practically hypnotized me. I was astounded by the devotion, the determination, the hard work. I didn't really want to leave; I just had to observe this a little longer. I placed myself way in the back again and just watched.

With all this action, the doors of the altar began to close very slowly, almost closing in on the last pujari. *When the doors finally closed, the people were screaming and almost fainting, so intense was their perception of Lord Jagannath, so total was their devotion.*

Suddenly, I snapped out of it, realizing that I really needed to leave or who knows what would happen. I was waiting to find a way to move out, hoping the crowd would change directions, but it didn't. Then I saw one of the priests motioning to someone. I became really afraid when I realized that he was motioning in my direction. I thought, "How does he see me? There are so many people here." It was the same one who had tried to talk to me earlier, but I had merged way back in the midst of hundreds of people. I thought for sure that I had sufficiently hidden myself. I was just amazed that he was able to single me out.

I was in a dilemma. Do I go towards him, although he might call the guards on me, or do I run out? Running would be difficult, because there were so many people all around, and the exit was a far way off. So I decided to go up and find out what he wants, to plead with him, if need be, and to tell him that I'll be leaving right away.

I approached the gate slowly and I saw him still pointing at me. Then I thought maybe all he wanted was more money. But I wasn't sure. He said something again but just motioned that I should wait. Did that mean that he wanted me to wait while he calls someone to get me? Do I run away? Then I thought, "Maybe, if I act nicely, they'll have mercy on me. Even if they beat me, maybe they won't beat me so bad." I was actually thinking like that.

I waited for about five or ten minutes, although it seemed like much longer. The offering had stopped and the curtains opened. Then the priests again singled out some of the more wealthy pilgrims and maybe some who were also devotional. They then took these few people aside and escorted them down the hallway. In this hallway, there were at least five or six other priests at different intervals, and the initial priest brought the guests to where the other priests stood with trays. Each priest offered something to the visitors, who were then supposed to offer some money in return. Then they took these selected people close to the altar. I watched that for about two minutes before that same priest pulled me around the same gate. I then realized that he had wanted me to wait until the offering ended.

I thought that I should try something, anything, since my life could be at risk. In a situation like that, your mind starts to go off in ridiculous directions. So I started to speak English. At least I could try to minimize my beating. I said something like, "I feel so embarrassed that my family has kept me out in the West, and that I don't know my own language. I only know English." I was trying to think of something to elicit some sympathy. I don't know if he understood what I said, but he didn't seem anxious or worried. That made me feel a little better, thinking, "Well, he doesn't seem angry, so I don't have to worry right now."

Once he opened the gate and let in a few people, the main priest grabbed me and started taking me to the altar, which took about five long minutes, due to the crowd and my own imagination running wild. It was interesting because every time we would approach a person with a tray, he would push him out of the way, so I didn't have to give any money. Normally, when the tray comes up, you give money. But that was waved for me—he just pulled me right to the front. Wondering why he did this, I became really frightened.

At one point, we got up to the altar, to the Deities. The altar is very high, and Jagannath, Baladeva, and Subhadra are very big. He then grabbed me tightly by the hand, causing me to feel quite nervous, and started going around the altar with me. When he reached one corner of the altar, he grabbed my head. This was the high point; I almost freaked out. I was certain he was going to kill me, sacrifice me to the gods, or some such. I was practically about to cry because I was so scared. It was sort of mystical and fearful at the same time, because I was in this holy place and I didn't know what he was going to do. He pushed my head up against the altar and started to chant some mantras. Afterwards, he took me around to the other side and again pushed my head up against the altar. He took me to all four corners, pushed my head hard, and chanted these mantras. After the third time, I realized that he wasn't doing something bad. He was giving some blessings on the altar at Jagannath's feet while saying some prayers. Then we circumambulated the whole altar and came back out.

It was like a scary ride in an amusement park, but when it was over I thanked my Maker and realized what a blessing I had actually had. I offered my full dandavats, *falling down on the ground like a stick, and somehow I felt this internal realization, for lack of a better word, that I should pray. I started praying for the success of ISKCON and I felt that somehow Lord Jagannath had let me come there so that I could make that prayer. And, as a person contemplating* sannyasa, *I was also praying to be freed of sex desire.*

Before I left, the priest gave me a piece of Jagannath's cloth and, speaking broken English, he said, "Jagannath is very happy that you have come so far." Then, he gave me the cloth. I was awestruck—he seemed to know who I was and where I was from. This was Krishna's mercy. I walked out very carefully, cautiously, and looked up into the night sky, knowing that there is rhyme and reason to the universe.

Come Again?

But there is more to the story. Arriving back at the hotel, where he immediately told Danavir and the other devotees everything that had occurred earlier that evening, he eventually tried to sleep but just couldn't. Although it was late at night, he was wired, having just undergone one of the most intense experiences of his life. Later, he allowed the details to unfold:

I kept thinking about it, and my body felt so restless. I was tossing and turning. And then my eyes opened wide, and I knew what I had to do. I thought, "I should go back." It was kind of a greedy mentality. I thought of the risk, the excitement, the mercy.

It must have been 11 or 12 o'clock at night, but I decided to return. I wanted to find out what else went on in the courtyard of the Jagannath temple, because there were different sections. I thought, "It's dark and I'll just look around. I'll never get this chance again in this lifetime. So let me make the most of it." I went back and people were still there, but nothing like the numbers earlier that evening.

Then I guess I got a little too comfortable as I passed some of the same guards who hadn't bothered me before. The main temple was closed, so I just walked around. They have an area where they bury the earlier Jagannath Deities when they change Him, and they have an area where they make carts. So that's where I was staying. I guess I was being a little nosy, trying to get some more blessings, wanting to see these different places.

Since there were not as many people, I was more careless about concealing who I was, and some guards by the cart noticed me looking around rather inquisitively. Then one of them spoke to the other and then to me. He yelled over from a distance, again in the local language, which I didn't understand. Naturally, I couldn't respond, and so I just acted like I didn't hear him.

He came closer and started to address me again, at which point I started moving away, realizing that I might really be in trouble this time. I noticed out of the side of my eye that he was quickly moving toward me. So I started running, and, of course, he started running after me. Now, I used to be pretty athletic in school. At one point, I ran track, wrestled, and played a little football, so I really started running. And the guards started coming after me from all different places. I thought, "No one even knows I'm here. If these guys kill me, no one will ever know. I shouldn't have been so greedy. Now I'm being chastised for my greediness." So I just ran and prayed.

Somehow or other, I was able to dodge them and I actually made it away safely. I think one of them threw a club at me, but I got out.

It was interesting and exciting, in one sense, to see Jagannath, Baladeva, and Subhadra, and to have that experience. It was like going back to ancient times, to be in that environment. At the same time, it was somewhat sad to see their emphasis on consumerism outside the temple, or their attention to who is a foreigner and who is not. They seem to have moved so far from the original Krishna Conscious conception, the nonsectarian truth that lies at the heart of the Vaishnava tradition.

As I thought about it days and weeks later, I realized that somehow Jagannath had given me a chance to come there on behalf of the ISKCON devotees and to make a prayer to Him on behalf of the movement. Prabhupada had just left and of course all of ISKCON was going through a state of shock. I felt it as the special *mercy of Srila Prabhupada to be able to come and make such a prayer in front of Lord Jagannath, especially since I was not so clear about the situation. Remember, I was forcibly pushed against the altar, thinking that I might be risking my life. I was bewildered, but I persevered to see the Lord, and to pray in His presence.*

Preparing for *Sannyasa*

After returning from India, he continued to travel and distribute books. Divyanga, one of Ghanashyam's Godbrothers, i.e., a co-disciple of Srila Prabhupada, remembers this pre-*sannyasa* period:

Prabhupada had just left a few months ago. I was in Michigan— my parents live there, and I happened to be at the temple, where Tripurari Swami was giving a lecture. After the class they sent a brahmacari, a young monk, down to get me: "Prabhu, Tripurari Swami wants to see you." So I went up to the Swami, who said, "Divyanga, what are you doing? Don't you want to do Sankirtan—don't you want to distribute your spiritual master's books?" Naturally, I said yes, and Ghanashyam was there. He had recently returned from India. He said, "We have a new program. Instead of distributing single books at the airports, we go door to door and sell full sets, standing orders." Of course, he had been doing that for some time with the Library Party.

Anyway, I said, "Okay, I'll come." So I sold my car and got some suits from my dad, a suitcase, and I joined the party. It was Tripurari, Ghanashyam, Brahmananda and me. Of course, this was where Brahmananda, who had been preaching in Africa, planted seeds with Ghanashyam. Initially, Ghanashyam had some idea about preaching to black-bodied devotees, but he set it aside. He wasn't exactly anxious to start anything in Africa, but he had an idea that he might be effective in that situation, given his black identity and his past in the Civil Rights Movement. Anyway, Brahmananda fanned that spark.

After that, we went to Chicago, St. Louis, and several other places. One devotee would be on the phone making appointments for us. We would go out at 9 AM every day and come back around 8 PM. I always remember how kind Ghanashyam was. Almost every morning before Mangala Arotik he would wake me up, saying, "Divyanga Prabhu, if you get up now you can make it to the morning worship services." I'd say okay, and then I'd roll over. Then he would come back later on and say, "If you get up now, you can make it to Guru Puja." In this way, he would consistently return, giving me newer and newer opportunities to do what I knew I should have been doing anyway.

He always encouraged me. I never felt like he was envious or angry with me. He never treated me with disrespect. He was just sincerely trying to help me. He would get up at 2AM and chant 32 rounds before the early services—but he still took the time to come and try to help me. I was always dragging along behind him. I felt good being with him and fortunate to have such strong association. Just keeping the basic devotee schedule was practically impossible for me. Still, Ghanashyam was always patient and tolerant of me. That's just the kind of person he was.

Also his eating was kept to a minimum—I could see his high caliber as a devotee from that perspective too. I mean, he used to eat three carrots, three chapatis and some unsweetened dahi. That's it. Every day we were going out to these appointments, and selling sets of books. He would stop in the early afternoon at a grocery store, give me some money and say—go get lunch. I would get fruit, yogurt, whatever, and he would just chant extra Japa. This went on for the several weeks I was with him. He just didn't take much time, if any, to eat or sleep. It wasn't just for show, either. He was really absorbed. Another thing I remember—Mayapur Festivals. He was always serving prasadam. *He would be running around serving out chipped rice with a big smile: "Haribol Prabhu." That was another thing—he always called me "Divyanga Prabhu." I guess he did this to remind himself that we're all supposed to be servants of the devotees. You know, prabhu means "master." He was serious, humble, sincere and blissful. He is an example of a disciple who took Prabhupada's instructions to heart, and by looking at his life, we can see the virtue of following Prabhupada's teachings.*

Soon after his brief Sankirtan experiences with Tripurari Swami, Ghanashyam came to Los Angeles, California, to assist Rameshvar Maharaja and to prepare for *sannyasa*. His initial idea was to take *sannyasa* initiation from Satsvarupa Maharaja, who had trained him as a devotee and was the leader of the Library Party. But due to a misunderstanding, he eventually decided against it. In the interim, he thought it best to serve under Rameshvar, who was in charge of the BBT and who was rendering significant service to Prabhupada through book distribution. Sureshvar, his Godbrother and friend, remembers this period:

Soon after his time in India, Ghanashyam flew to Los Angeles to strategize with Rameshvar Maharaja, the then executive head of the BBT, about expanding book distribution behind the Iron Curtain. While there, he assisted Rameshvar as a secretary, preparing for sannyasa *by serving an established* sannyasi.

When he was in L.A.—this would have been in the first part of 1979—I asked him if every man was supposed to take sannyasa. *"At least in the heart," he smiled. As far as I know, he accepted* sannyasa *from Kirtanananda Maharaja instead of Satsvarupa. Years later, I told him I was surprised he didn't take* sannyasa *from Satsvarupa Maharaja. He said he thought he had been too familiar with Satsvarupa during the heat of the Library Party days and had offended him. When you read Satsvarupa Maharaja's posthumous letter about Ghanashyam now, he makes an indirect reference to this by saying that he and Ghanashyam were able to renew their friendship at the end, "Thank God."*

His Divine Grace A. C. Bhaktivedanta Swami Prabhupada (1896–1977), founder of ISKCON and spiritual master of Bhakti Tirtha Swami.

Sri Chaitanya Mahaprabhu (1486–1533), the dual Incarnation of Radha and Krishna who appeared as a devotee in Bengal, India.

God in both female and male forms, Sri-Sri Radha and Krishna are the eternal Divine Couple.

(From left to right:) Baladeva, the Lord's first expansion (His brother); Subhadra, His internal potency (His sister); and Jagannath (the Lord Himself). The original forms of these Deities are worshipped in Jagannath Puri, Orissa (India), and Bhakti Tirtha Swami was fortunate enough to visit them. (pp. 162-176)

Sri-Sri Radha-Damodara, the beautiful iconic manifestations of Radha and Krishna. Today located in Gita Nagari, they are lovingly cared for by the devotees who reside there.

Pearline Hill Favors Lard (1915–1998), mother of John Favors and guiding light for much of his early life.

Norman Anderson (1922–2000), affectionately known as "Uncle Nanda," was one of John's early mentors.

(Left:) Mother Pearline with John (on her lap), flanked by Paul (his brother) and Bernadette (his sister). (Right:) John and sibling on the lap of Santa.

Two photos (opposite page, top) from the Hawken Academy 1968 yearbook with accompanying quote:

"With his amazing strut, his flaming, irridescent, tapered, cuffless, beltless, sharkskin, electric, spray-paint, skin-tight, orange tubes (pants), his matching four-inch high-rolled-collar turtleneck, offset by contrasting sport coat (belted in the rear), and alligator pinstripe shoes, John Favors came to Hawken. Underneath that sartorial splendor was a real student. Favors' contribution to every class was always impressive. He was one of the few seniors who studied during the day (or studied at all for that matter) and he could be found anytime in his private carrel in the library . . . Hawken and John learned something from each other."

Two photos (opposite page, bottom) from the Princeton University 1972 yearbook with accompanying quote:

". . . John would like to be remembered at Princeton as a humanist who has chosen to dedicate his life to trying to play a part in "raising the level of humanity.""

In the mid-1960s, a teenage John Favors poses for a class photo (middle row, second from right) while at Rawlings Junior High School.

These are the many faces of John Favors, just prior to his metamorphosis into Ghanashyam Dasa and then into Bhakti Tirtha Swami.

Ghanashyam Dasa, not yet Bhakti Tirtha Swami, serves his beloved teacher, His Divine Grace A. C. Bhaktivedanta Swami Prabhupada (Toronto, 1975).

Always determined, ever resourceful, Bhakti Tirtha Swami lectures on behalf of his guru at colleges, talk shows, and festivals around the world.

Whether in a rural environment or in a city as rugged as New York (seen here), he boldly presents the timeless message of Krishna Consciousness.

In 1979, Ghanashyam Dasa takes sannyasa, *the renounced order of life, receiving the name "Bhakti Tirtha Swami."*

A portrait of those devotees who were instrumental in bringing Krishna Conscious-
ness to Africa. Seen here are Brahmananda Swami, Ekendra, Vraja-lila, Maha-
mantra, Bhutabhavana, Parameshvari, Ishvara, Omkara, Gopal, and others.
(Nigeria, circa, 1981)

He accepted numerous austerities in pursuance of his
spiritual mission, journeying from village to village.
He is seen here with Mother Hladini, his fearless
compatriot in Africa. (See pp. 226-229)

His exotic dress spoke of
both African and Indic
influences, but his heart
belonged to Krishna.

Travelling around the world and distributing free prasadam *(vegetarian food offered to Krishna) was among his most cherished activities.*

He rejoiced in bringing Krishna Consciousness to even the most remote of villages, as seen here in Nigeria (circa, 1981).

Bhakti Tirtha Swami meets Nana-Opuku-Ware II, the late King of the Ashanti people (in Ghana).

He is seen here marching in Warri, Nigeria, just after his coronation as an honorary High Chief.

In April, 1992, he travelled with friends and disciples to both Egypt and Dimona, Israel, to meet with Ben-Amin (embracing, center page), an important spiritual leader, and the African Hebrew Israelites, who have close ties with IFAST. (See pp. 285-294)

Giving advice to Muhammad Ali in the early 1980s. "Swami," the great boxer asked him in amazement, "how is it that you glow like that?"

Befriending Nelson Mandela in South Africa (circa, 1994). They discuss world peace and the prospect of working together in the future.

Bhakti Tirtha Swami and Nelson Mandela play their part during an ISKCON-sponsored cultural program for thousands of children in Africa.

Bhakti Tirtha Swami travelled around the world numerous times, making Bosnia, Russia, and Croatia special areas of interest. Above he is seen in Red Square, on "Good Morning Moscow," in an interfaith exchange with a Christian monk, and bringing the chanting of the holy name through the streets of the city.

In a prayerful mood, waiting to give one his countless lectures on the science of Krishna Consciousness.

Always ready to practice what he preaches, he gets his hands dirty working the land in Gita Nagari.

He was loved for his singing and especially his dancing, which inspired devotees in all parts of the world.

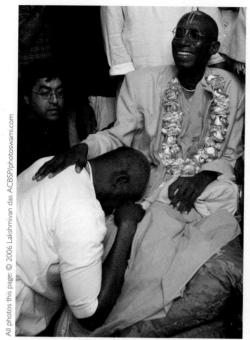

February, 2005: He is nearing the end of his earthly sojourn. Mahapurana Dasa, pictured here, says goodbye, as would many others in the months to come.

(Above:) Vraja-lila and Ekavirya, two of his most dedicated care-givers and disciples.

Chandramauli Swami, Dhanurdhar Swami, and Radhanath Swami, among others, offer prayers to their departed friend.

His Holiness Bhaki Tirtha Swami

Krishnapada Day

January 21, 2006

A PROCLAMATION BY THE MAYOR OF THE DISTRICT OF COLUMBIA

WHEREAS, His Holiness Bhakti Tirtha Swami Krishnapada was a spiritual leader, scholar, teacher, author and humanitarian; and

WHEREAS, His Holiness Bhakti Tirtha Swami Krishnapada will be honored at Howard University's Blackburn Center, by members of the Institute of Applied Spiritual Technology (IFAST) with workshops and panel discussion based upon his teachings; and

WHEREAS, His Holiness Bhakti Tirtha Swami Krishnapada founded IFAST and was the first person of African descent to become an initiating Guru in the ancient Brahma-Madhava-Gaudiya Vaishnava Sampradaya, Corronated High Chief in Warri, Nigeria, West Africa; and

WHEREAS, His Holiness Bhakti Tirtha Swami Krishnapada is a spiritual consultant, a specialist in international relations and conflict resolution, an esteemed graduate of Princeton University and the author of 16 books:

NOW, THEREFORE, I, THE MAYOR OF THE DISTRICT OF COLUMBIA, do hereby proclaim January 21, 2006, as **"HIS HOLINESS BHAKTI TIRTHA SWAMI KRISHNAPADA DAY"** in Washington, DC, and call upon all the residents of this great city to join me in recognizing this gentleman for his contributions to society.

Anthony A. Williams
Mayor, District of Columbia

Accolades and honors followed him in life and continue to follow him now. The above proclamation and others like it are testaments to his many accomplishments and to his ability to touch people on a deep level.

Ghanashyam grew restless serving as a secretary, and his talents demanded that he go back out on the road. "Preaching is life," his spiritual master had once said, and, remembering this, he wanted to live again, to share Krishna Consciousness with others. He consulted several senior devotees, including Jayadvaita Maharaja, who told him: "What are you doing here serving as a secretary? You should be a *sannyasi*, a leader, and you should travel and preach!" That was it. He decided to take *sannyasa* as soon as possible. But from whom, and where?

He had been corresponding with Kirtanananda Maharaja, who, at that time, was enjoying phenomenal success with his West Virginia project. It was called "*New* Vrindavan," after India's holiest town, where Lord Krishna had sported with His cowherd devotees some 5,000 years earlier. Many of the movement's senior devotees had either come to live in New Vrindavan, or would visit regularly, sensing that some major event was about to take place there.

New Vrindavan: Origins and Growth

In as early as 1968, the New Vrindavan project—which was meant to display the back-to-nature, ideal life of Krishna Consciousness in practice—was started by Kirtanananda Swami and Hayagriva Dasa, two of Srila Prabhupada's first disciples. They and a small group of devotees relocated to 130 acres, with the intention of caring for cows, tilling the land, and generally replicating the rural atmosphere of ancient India, when Lord Krishna's idyllic life as a cowherd once graced our planet.

Originally, only one 19th-century farmhouse dotted the New Vrindavan landscape, and that without electricity or running water. Although other cabins were soon built, the environment remained self-consciously "uncomplicated," in line with the spiritual master's motto: "Simple Living and High Thinking."

The idea was that modern urban life was leading to the degradation of the masses, and that a natural, back-to-basics outlook would be beneficial for people in general. A more holistic and wholesome life, taught Srila Prabhupada, is naturally healthful and nurturing, especially when combined with the "high thinking" of God-conscious ideals and spiritual awareness. This is a mindset that would serve humankind's economic, political, psychological, emotional, and religious goals, incorporating Varnashram and the teachings of Krishna Conscious masters past and present. One could see why the project was important for Prabhupada and for the entire Krishna Consciousness Movement.

The purpose of New Vrindavan, as stated by Srila Prabhupada himself, was "To erect for the members of ISKCON and for society at large a holy place of transcendental pastimes dedicated to the personality of Krishna." The establishment was meant to fulfill Prabhupada's vision of "seven temples on seven hills," for which he gave the devotees guidelines and directions. They were to establish a rural, self-sufficient community where they would learn to work the land with oxen, and to tend to cows, as stated above. He also wanted to establish "a school for educating Brahmins and Vaishnavas" there.

It wasn't long before neighboring property was purchased to expand the community. In due course, devotees were growing their own vegetables and fruits and getting their milk from mother cow. And speaking of cows, New Vrindavan became known in ISKCON for its loving treatment of them, along with oxen, horses, and even peacocks. In addition, the devotees attended normal morning worship services, as in any other ISKCON temple, and led the way in book distribution. New Vrindavan devotees were extraordinary. But more was yet to come.

By 1974, the community could hardly accommodate its growing dairy herd, and profitable business shot out from many an udder, with milk, butter, yogurt, and so on supporting the temple. Within three years, the community became known not only for its superexcellent dairy business but for its high level of spiritual attainment, with some of the movement's most important devotees living there. It was soon after this that Ghanashyam had contemplated going there and taking *sannyasa*.

It was only six months after his *sannyasa* ceremony, in fact, that New Vrindavan gave birth to "the Palace of Gold," which was a tribute to the then recently departed founder, Srila Prabhupada. The Palace complex was a massive accomplishment, utilizing the talents and abilities of numerous devotees, and constructed with substantial funding that seemed to appear out of nowhere. In the end, the Palace, its adjoining restaurant and landscaped grounds, was a feast for the eyes.

The beauty of the Palace contrasts with the original dilapidated barn, in Bahulaban, which is only two miles away. By the time the Palace opened in September, 1979, the New Vrindavan community had grown to almost 200 residents and over 1,200 acres of land. As a slight aside, the Palace eventually became one of the largest attractions in West Virginia, popularizing Krishna Consciousness throughout much of America. New Vrindavan, of course, would soon fall into ill repute, mainly because of Kirtanananda Swami's innovative if also questionable preaching tactics, as well as his illegitimate use of ISKCON's philosophy, leading to illegal activity. But that is another story, and New Vrindavan is now back in ISKCON as a viable asset to the movement.

"Have You Given Up Sex Desire?"

Before Kirtanananda's difficulty, he was acknowledged throughout the movement for his achievements in New Vrindavan. He was seen as a unique religious thinker, a quixotic spiritual adept whose charisma and devotional attainments had enabled him to do the impossible. The Palace was to be the first of numerous visionary projects, including a "City of God," interfaith communities around the world, and so on. These latter endeavors were never fully realized.

But Ghanashyam arrived there when the dream was palpable, and Kirtanananda was at the helm of a progressive spiritual mission.

It was a particularly cold winter in 1979, and *sannyasa*, Ghanashyam knew, was imminent. He had been arranging this for some time with Kirtanananda Swami, easily one of the most experienced and qualified *sannyasis* in ISKCON, and now it was about to actually take place. Radhanath Swami, one of Ghanashyam's most dear friends, remembers:

> *It was in Bahulaban in front of Sri Sri Radha Vrindavan Chandra, the presiding Deities of New Vrindavan. I was there. I noticed that Sri Galim tied on his* sannyasa *cloth and dhoti for him. Sri Galim had been Vishnujana Swami's assistant and sort of knew how to do it. Well, after the initiation there was a tremendously ecstatic Kirtan, and Ghanashyam, now Bhakti Tirtha Swami, was chanting and dancing like a madman. And now he was holding his danda above his head with one hand—you know, the way he would dance sometimes? It was really incredible.*
>
> *So he only had one arm that was free. This was significant because, in the midst of his dancing, his dhoti fell off. [laughter] You could see his kaupin [Brahmin underwear]! I guess Sri Galim didn't tie it very well. But everyone was so ecstatic that they simply laughed and continued with the ecstatic chanting. It was an embarrassing situation, no doubt, but he grabbed down and picked up his dhoti with lightning speed, holding it in place, chanting and dancing all the while, without losing a beat.*
>
> *Also, it was shocking when Kirtanananda Swami gave him the new name, because in ISKCON the custom had been to simply add "Swami" or "Goswami" to one's already existing name, with few exceptions. But Kirtanananda Swami changed it completely: "Bhakti Tirtha Swami." Of course, Ghanashyam accepted it graciously and always used it, from then on. But I knew how much he had loved the name that Prabhupada had given him: Ghanashyam. Anyway, who can understand these things?!*

Damodara Prabhu, another devotee who was initiated on that same day, remembers other details:

It was March 13, 1979, the auspicious day of Gaura Purnima, the birth anniversary of Sri Chaitanya Mahaprabhu. I was initiated at the same fire sacrifice, as was Mother Madri, Shikshashtaka, Jai Sri Krishna, Mother Sanat, Hrishikeshananda, and several others. Ghanashyam was the only sannyasi *being initiated on that day. He was positively effulgent—we knew he would be a gem in the Krishna Consciousness Movement.*

On that particular day, the dancing in the temple room shook the very foundation of the building—hundreds of devotees proclaimed the holy name with bang-up exuberance, and gyrated in wild, ecstatic Kirtan. And no one was more enthused than Ghanashyam, who had just been given his new *sannyasi* name, "Bhakti Tirtha Swami." Hrishikeshananda, who was also initiated on that day, emphasizes the impassioned dancing:

Bhakti Tirtha Swami has always been an inspiration to me. I first met him at his sannyasa *initiation at New Vrindavan in 1979, where he danced like a madman during the Kirtan following the initiation. I had never seen such energetic dancing before. His enthusiasm was contagious and the entire congregation of devotees erupted like a volcano shooting lava bombs into the sky. We were jumping so high into the air you would wonder if we would come down safely.*

Yet despite his powerful energy, Bhakti Tirtha Swami was also thoughtful, introspective, wise and kind. I had several exchanges with him during the years from 1979 to 2004 in which he exhibited a loving, elder-brotherly affection.

For those who knew him well, his wild dancing at the *sannyasa* initiation was something new. Although such ecstatic exhibitions became common in his later years as an experienced *sannyasi*, he was a rather quiet *brahmachari*; that is, as a novice he was rarely demonstrative or overtly expressive. Rather, he was known as low-key and gentle, soft-spoken and often in the background. The only time he moved to the forefront was in book distribution, or to serve out *prasadam*, as in the yearly Mayapur Festivals. Otherwise, he was demure and unassuming.

But Bhakti Tirtha Swami was no longer Ghanashyam. It was as if the mythical Phoenix had been burned to ashes and a new incarnation arose in its place. The veteran book distributor now experienced new life, and his ecstatic dancing was a symbol of this life: Somehow God's rain of mercy sprinkled down on him, allowing him to blossom in the forefront of the movement, as one of its most choice flowers.

In the mid-1980s, he reflected on his *sannyasa* initiation and his commitment to celibacy as a strategy for attaining ever-increasing heights of detachment and spiritual perfection. The following literary offering to his guru shows the direction and intensity of that contemplation:

Tomorrow I Must Meet Srila Prabhupada

By Bhakti Tirtha Swami

Today is the last day of my life. Tomorrow I must meet Srila Prabhupada. What will I say to him? What will he say to me?

I will say to Srila Prabhupada, "I am Ghanashyam Dasa, the one who distributed your sets of books to the academic communities."

Srila Prabhupada will say, "Very nice, but have you given up sex desire for me?"

I will say, "I have never broken any of the regulative principles, and I have faithfully chanted over sixteen rounds every single day since I joined the movement—never once missing."

Srila Prabhupada will say, "Very nice, but have you given up sex desire?"

I will say, "I have maintained a program of fasting all day on every Ekadashi—especially from liquids and all foods for most of my life as a devotee."

Srila Prabhupada will say, "Very nice, but have you given up sex desire for me?"

I will say, "I have also maintained a program of eating mainly once a day for most of my life as a devotee."

Srila Prabhupada will say, "Very nice, but have you given up sex desire for me?"

I will say, "I have for most of my devotional life maintained sleeping less than six hours each day."

Srila Prabhupada will say, "Very nice, but have you given up sex desire for me?"

I will say, "Srila Prabhupada, I have faithfully read all of your books, and I am trying now to distribute them in many countries where there is neither paper nor printing presses available."

Srila Prabhupada will say, "Very nice, my son, but have you given up sex desire?"

I will say, "I persevered as your GBC member responsible for the largest number of countries in the world, i.e., fifty, which happen to be the poorest in the world."

Srila Prabhupada will say, "Very nice, but how about the sex desire?"

I will speak about my cultivating a few heads of state and a few diplomats.

Srila Prabhupada will say, "Are you now free of sex desire?"

I will give Srila Prabhupada a report on the temple construction and farm projects in a few different countries.

Srila Prabhupada will say, "This is very good, but how about the sex desire?"

I will give a report on the number of temples I have opened and the number of devotees and new disciples I have made.

Then I will notice Srila Prabhupada's voice becoming even more penetrating as he chastises me (just as he did the very last time I was with him before he left the planet): "This is all by Krishna's mercy, and not ours." It is today that this chastisement has full meaning for me. You were telling me, Srila Prabhupada, then and even more so now, that I must give up this sex desire, subtle and gross.

We must first of all realize that any achievements we have accomplished internally, externally, individually or collectively, are simply by your mercy.

Secondly, we are to understand that as long as we still have such devastating sex desire, all of our offerings to you are tinged, having various degrees of contamination. The disciple can never repay the spiritual master for what he has given. Also, we understand that one must be careful not to think that the guru needs him or that he is doing something wonderful. Whatever we offer, it is so incomplete if we have not given up sex desire. You, dear Srila Prabhupada, preached up until your last breath, completely selfless, for the benefit of your disciples and the world. Now we must also give everything we have to you. As today I die, and tomorrow I have to meet you, it is today—right now—that I must give you the greatest offering a disciple can give his guru, while I still have a little more time. I must give up all remaining attachment to sex life, subtle and gross. I can understand that I have nothing really to give you, but if I can become totally free of all sex desire, then I can really become your puppet, so that you can do with me as you like. Now I am so much of an imperfect instrument.

In these days our Society is having many problems and varieties of understandings. These things are very small in contrast to our real problem, which is sex attachment. This attachment is obfuscating our vision tremendously and making big problems seem small and small problems appear big. While we are debating, the demons are getting more and more positioned to attack our movement and the global community in general. Most of us will not become really serious until major catastrophes hit us directly in the face. But how can I talk when I now hear you saying to me with deep compassion

and with sadness, "You cannot come with me. Still you are pos-
sessing sex desire." As you walk away, my pain is unbearable. As I
reflect on the pain I have and am giving you by my imperfect state,
my own pain increases that much more. I scream, crying out in
anguish, "Please forgive me, please help me, please don't leave me!"
   Then I remember I still have a few hours to surrender everything
to you, as today I die and tomorrow I must meet you.
   I am the insignificant beggar who is quickly running out of
time. But by your mercy I have this last chance to make the greatest
offering—to offer you myself in an uncontaminated state, free of all
sex desire, so as to be a perfect instrument for your mission.

This composition does not represent a morbid preoccupation with
sex, nor is it a way of denouncing the purpose of sex as ordained in
the scriptures. Coming from the Vaishnava tradition, Bhakti Tirtha
Swami was supportive of sexual intercourse in marriage, for procreation, which he saw as its God-given purpose. The love between a
man and a woman can be a beautiful thing, he felt, but it must go
beyond bodily appetites and have an underlying spiritual foundation. Along these lines, he would often encourage married couples to
express their love for each other and to have children.

But he was equally aware of the bastardization of sex, wherein it is
used for sense pleasure only, as a distraction from the real purpose of
life. According to the tenets of Vaishnavism, sex is among the most
intense of material pleasures, a seducing element that is able to sway
even stalwarts on the spiritual path, whether or not they were previously committed to celibacy. Vaishnava scriptures state, too, that sex
often wears an innocent-looking cloak, deluding people into thinking
it is something higher than it really is. Disguised as love, for example,
sex often hides behind romantic notions of life-long commitment
and happily-ever-after relationships. More often than not, however,
the masquerade is shattered when marriages end in divorce, or when
other intimate exchanges meet a similar end. This is because such

"love" is usually little more than the lightly veiled desire to titillate one's senses; it is the misuse—consciously or unconsciously—of a sacred rite. In other words, people consistently mistake lust for love.

Bhakti Tirtha Swami, as a *sannyasi*, would never again make this mistake. His commitment was now solely to developing love for God, bidding farewell to any potential distractions. His body and mind would never again be used for anything but the Lord's service. It had always been this way, but now it was formalized through the vow of *sannyasa*, an age-old scientific method—or, as he would call it, an "applied spiritual technology"—for gradually subduing the senses and redirecting them toward the Divine. This vow took hold of his life and wouldn't let go. His written offering, above, is meant to convey this sense of unremitting determination to love God, along with its attendant celibacy as a means to avoid distraction.

CHAPTER SIX

PASSAGE TO AFRICA

"Four hundred years ago, your ancestors were taken away from Africa as slaves, but now you have returned as masters."

—SRILA PRABHUPADA

H AVING RECENTLY ENTERED the renounced order of life, Bhakti Tirtha Swami thought long and hard about his new identity, a facility to be used in God's service. After all, *sannyasa* is just that—a facility. In ISKCON, as in India, the renounced order of life commands respect, with the mass of sincere practitioners anxious to attend *sannyasis'* lectures, to learn and to render service to them.

The Swami decided to return to his urban roots. He realized that his underprivileged past in a Cleveland ghetto afforded him something special: those who came from similar backgrounds would be able to relate to him, and he, for his part, was uniquely equipped to give these people Krishna Consciousness. With this in mind, he began to explore inner city venues, eventually founding The Committee for

189

Urban Spiritual Development in Washington D.C.

This was a world peace initiative focusing on the economic, social, educational, and spiritual betterment of humankind. The initial pamphlet for the organization, written by Bhakti Tirtha Swami himself, pointed out that true human development must accommodate material as well as spiritual needs. For world peace, he argued, a new community of human beings would have to emerge. This would be comprised of people who "use more of their dormant faculties," progressive individuals who see themselves as part of a global family. Indeed, such people would identify themselves as part of "an interplanetary family" as well, underlining the sense of cosmic "oneness" that such individuals necessarily feel. This community of exceptional beings, the pamphlet continues, truly loves its neighbors, without sexism or speciesism. Each of its members accomplishes this chiefly through recognizing a common father, God, and also by identifying with the spiritual spark within the body, sometimes called "the soul," thus rendering insignificant all bodily differences.

These souls who partake of Bhakti Tirtha Swami's vision would exhibit a willingness to "accept assorted technologies that are appropriate for progressive ends," such as meditation, yoga, and vegetarianism. Their lives would be governed by simplicity and they would revel in coexisting with nature, rather than in abusing or conquering her. "There can be no world peace without internal peace," concludes the pamphlet. "And there can be no internal peace without sense control and a higher level of self-realization."

This brief outline of a superior society contains the seeds of many of his later missionary strategies. Using the basic philosophy of Krishna Consciousness, he hoped to convey the idea that Vaishnavism might serve the world's many purposes, not only spiritually but in terms of her material needs. He presented it as a sort of panacea for all of the world's social ills. The pamphlet worked its way into the hands of important dignitaries in the international community, from whom he garnered much support. Gradually, he changed the name of his institution to "The International Committee for Urban Spiritual Development," with centers branching out from D.C. to Beachwood, Ohio, and eventually to West Africa. This institution, an offshoot from ISKCON, emphasized fifteen principles:

1. *Development of cottage industries and technical schools for simple but secure economic development.*

2. *Agricultural education, to encourage self-sufficiency.*

3. *Clinics specializing in natural and holistic medicine.*

4. *Free food initiatives, distributing* prasadam *(sacred vegetarian food) to the needy, particularly in poor urban areas and in the Third World.*

5. *Establishment of vegetarian restaurants, along with educating people in nutrition and in the science of offering food to God as a religious sacrifice.*

6. *Providing yoga workshops and treatment centers for prisoners and drug addicts.*

7. *Providing shelters for the homeless.*

8. *Conducting seminars and workshops on stress management.*

9. *Seminars for humanitarian educators who might wish to offer their services in the Third World.*

10. *"Books for Africa"—the distribution of spiritual classics to high schools, teacher training programs, libraries, hospitals, prisons, colleges and universities. Books would also be shipped to Africa for special distribution campaigns.*

11. *Sponsorship of academies especially designed for training in martial arts, meditation techniques, and sense control.*

12. *Holding conferences on the importance of world peace as well as on leadership roles to accomplish that end.*

192 / BLACK LOTUS

13. *Special classes on mantra meditation and on consciousness rais-ing—monastic orders are defined and encouraged.*

14. *The creation of AIDS treatment centers.*

15. *The establishment of "Cities of God," wherein people learn to work together despite differences in race, creed, and temperament.*

These would remain his long-term goals for the balance of his stay on Earth. Inner city missionary activity, combined with welfare work and *prasadam* distribution, usually through opening restaurants, became a focal point of his endeavors. His restaurant in Washington D.C. was particularly successful.

Meanwhile . . .

If Bhakti Tirtha Swami was, in America, beginning to propagate Krishna Consciousness in the above-mentioned ways, mainly among African Americans, much was already going on in Africa, and had been for many years. This was largely accomplished through the pros-elytizing efforts of Brahmananda Prabhu, formerly Bruce Scharf, who was one of Prabhupada's earliest disciples. Having joined ISKCON in 1966, shortly after it was formed in New York City, Brahmananda was among Prabhupada's most senior and trusted leaders.

The story of how the Hare Krishna Movement came to Africa begins in 1971 in the United States. At the time, Brahmananda was in Tallahassee, Florida, teaching an experimental course in Krishna Consciousness at the State University. Unexpectedly, Prabhupada contacted him and urged him to travel to a land of which he had little knowledge. A Jewish white male, Brahmananda knew little about Af-rican history, people, or culture, and he didn't know what to expect upon arriving there. A few hunting stories by Ernest Hemingway and American adventure films had led him to believe that Africa consisted of jungles, wild animals, and tribal peoples. Period. Still, faithful to his spiritual master, he gathered a few essentials—a drum, a pair of *kartalas* [hand cymbals for chanting], and a metal box full of Prabhupada's books—and prepared for the journey.

In fact, he was eventually rewarded with a certain modicum of success in East Africa, particularly in Mombassa, Kenya, where, in 1969, a woman named Shakti Mati Devi Dasi had established a preaching mission. His work there was chiefly confined to ministering to Indian life members, who already knew Krishna Conscious culture. He had little effect on the indigenous peoples, and had no connection with the large populations of South Africa or West Africa. One of his greatest accomplishments was that he had brought Prabhupada himself to Africa for a brief visit, blessing the land with the auspicious arrival of a pure devotee.

Srila Prabhupada returned to Africa—this time, South Africa—for one final visit in 1975, for he passed away only two years later in Vrindavan, India. During this last sojourn in Africa he expanded on the work that Brahmananda and others had been doing for almost four years. While there, Prabhupada addressed large groups of people, lecturing at major venues. His main approach was to explain the philosophy of Krishna Consciousness by focusing on the distinction between the body and the actual self, the animating spark in each person's heart of hearts. He explained that apartheid is based on a faulty premise—identification with the body. He further boldly claimed that it should be abolished, and that Krishna Consciousness could help people rise beyond such misconceptions.

A handful of his early disciples contributed to the mission in Africa as well, and their names should be known: Pushta Krishna Swami, Rishi Kumar Swami, Kishudhi Dasa, Janakaraja Dasa, Bhagavata Dasa, Jagat Guru Dasa, Chyavana Swami, and Riddha Dasa. As the years passed, other devotees would play their part, too. But it wasn't until 1979, only a few months after he took *sannyasa*, that Bhakti Tirtha Swami would revolutionize ISKCON's work in Africa. Indeed, he would eventually become the continent's most important preacher of Krishna Consciousness, second only to Srila Prabhupada.

The Seed of an Idea

It was around the time of the Washington restaurant's initial success that Bhakti Tirtha Swami had a dream in which Srila Prabhupada had asked him to "open the door." In the dream, he continued to tend to other services, leaving Prabhupada's request aside. Finally, after his guru had uttered the request for a second and then a third time, Bhakti Tirtha Swami opened the door, and a multitude of African people came running through. From this dream, he deduced that Srila Prabhupada wanted him to go to Africa. And so, without any particular inclination toward that part of the world—as a *sannyasi*, all living beings were now his family, and racial considerations had become a secondary concern, at best—and in the midst of a successful project in Washington, he left, suddenly, and with little planning. In the end, his African venture would prove immensely successful.

Of course, seeds had been planted through his earlier association with Brahmananda Prabhu, who had successfully begun missionary activity there almost a decade earlier, as explained above. And the Swami's background in the African-American community naturally pointed him in this direction. But the dream in which Prabhupada indicated that he should go to Africa—this was the artillery that shot him squarely into the land of his forefathers. And he was happy to be there, even if it had its challenges.

Of the many nations on the continent, there are numerous Hindu residents in South Africa (1.5 million), Tanzania (70,000), Kenya (70,000), Nigeria (40,000) and Zambia (30,000), with significant communities in Zimbabwe, Somalia and Botswana. As mentioned, Prabhupada had come to Africa some years earlier, and Brahmananda, Pushta Krishna Swami, and others had paved the way for Krishna Consciousness, too.

So when Bhakti Tirtha Swami first arrived, the Africans were not unfamiliar with Vaishnava customs and practices. The "Hinduism" already available there had given them a profound respect for Mahatma Gandhi, whose early history is inseparable from his stay in Africa, and a deep appreciation for Indian culture. Hinduism had long established in Africa the ideas of karma, reincarnation, vegetarianism, demigod worship, and the notion of a Supreme Godhead. Truth be told, these spiritual teachings didn't have to wait for Hinduism—they already existed in many indigenous African religions, too, giving scope to the theory that India and Africa had had a relationship in prehistoric times.

Bhakti Tirtha Swami took this connection quite seriously. He had even studied the theory of plate tectonics, which was developed in the 1960s, though its underlying premises go back some fifty years earlier. Here we learn about the movement of land mass, and how the Earth's plates shift according to natural occurrences. This causes earthquakes, volcanoes, oceanic trenches, mountain range formation, and other geological phenomena.

Some researchers, building on the idea of plate tectonics, claim that all of the world's continents were once joined in a single supercontinent called Pangaea, which was later divided into two smaller continents: Laurasia and Gondwana. Laurasia, according to this theory, was made up of what we today know as Europe, North America and Asia, while Gondwana consisted of Africa, South America, New Zealand, Madagascar, India, Antarctica, Arabia, Iran and Australia. Continental drift, along with similarities in rock types, fossils, flora and fauna provide additional evidence for the earlier position of the world's continents.

An example of this—one that was particularly interesting to Bhakti Tirtha Swami—is the Indian subcontinent, which, according to the theory, broke away from Antarctica and Africa about 100 million years ago. It drifted in a northward direction at about six inches per year, eventually arriving in Asia and forming the Himalayas. Part of the evidence for this is that India's living flora is more closely related to the flora of Africa than to that of the rest of Asia. The most likely way to explain this, say certain scholars, is by applying the theories of plate tectonics.

Bhakti Tirtha Swami noted that this theory could account for the many parallels found in Indian and African religion. For example, bodily markings resembling Indian *tilak* can be found in indigenous African religions, and specific demigods, exhibiting characteristics once thought peculiar to Indian deities, are apparent there as well. Both examples and others too numerous to mention can be traced to pre-Hindu habitation. Many experts thus agree that these lands must have shared common space in ancient epochs of world history. Naturally, the Swami appreciated these findings, since they coincide with the Krishna Conscious view that there was once a one-world culture based on Vedic principles in a distant past that time has all but forgotten.

Still, lest we travel too far adrift, like the Earth's plates themselves, let it at least be said that Africa already had much in common with India, even before Hinduism arrived on her shores.

Actually, Africans boast an amalgam of religious beliefs that derive from many sources. Christianity, for example, arrived through the efforts of traders and missionaries early in the second century CE, and it was adopted by many. Some time later, in the seventh century, Muslim conquerors came from the north, and many Africans welcomed Islam as their own. Thus, for those who do not adhere to native African religion, there are a number of alternatives. And then came the Indians, in the late nineteenth century. They were largely merchants and workers, primarily concerned with business as opposed to proselytizing on behalf of "Hinduism." Accordingly, a large percentage of diasporan Hindus in Africa today have lost touch with the religion and culture of their birth.

The Mission Begins

It was into this Africa that Bhakti Tirtha Swami thrust himself. Ishvara Dasa, one of the earliest African devotees, having joined ISKCON in 1980, explains the Swami's early days on the continent:

> By establishing The Committee for Urban Spiritual Development in Washington D.C., Bhakti Tirtha Maharaja was able to recruit many devotees who were ready to take a plunge into African preaching. With inspiration derived from Bhakti Tirtha Maharaja, and the general enthusiasm of those devotees, a contingent came and joined Brahmananda Prabhu, who was already in Nigeria establishing the movement in Africa. But, actually, Brahmananda Prabhu's preaching was limited to the Indians and Indian life membership, which basically consisted of getting monetary support from Indians. Remember, Brahmananda was white, and so he would only have occasional contact with the locals.
>
> The real momentum of local African preaching started when Bhakti Tirtha Maharaja came to Nigeria, and then to the other West African countries. It was a challenge, and Maharaja took it up with full enthusiasm. When he came to Nigeria, it was easy and natural for the people to identify with him, mainly because of his African-American body but also because of his profound purity and determined preaching spirit.
>
> Right from the beginning, Maharaja was establishing contacts with prominent people, such as ministers, educators, and so on. His idea, at that time, was that if intelligent and prominent people take to the philosophy of Krishna Consciousness, it would be easier to convince the general public. So when Maharaja came, and many African devotees started joining, they saw him as their natural leader.
>
> His major preaching in Africa started around 1981, and he became an initiating guru at the end of 1985. Even so, he started initiating disciples around 1986, taking a year to engage in prayer

and to contemplate the meaning of being a guru. Previous to that, he was representing Kirtanananda Swami. Yashoda Ma was one of his first disciples in Nigeria, which is in 1986, as she joined at that time. All devotees in West Africa previous to that time were initiated by Kirtanananda Swami. I was in one of Kirtanananda's first African initiation ceremonies in 1981.

The actual chronology is that Bhakti Tirtha Maharaja was actively preaching in Africa from 1981 to 1993, but maintaining a center in Washington D.C. as a base for coordinating fund-raising efforts to help the African temple, of which I was initially in charge. After 1993, he started his focus more in the USA among the professionals, and started to concentrate less on Africa. I guess he wanted to broaden his concerns, to make a shift from primarily African preaching. By the twenty-first century, he had expanded his efforts to Europe, South America, and so on, with less emphasis on Africa. But that's another story.

The actual seeds of the African mission were planted soon after Bhakti Tirtha Swami had taken *sannyasa* in 1979. He was always naturally concerned with the African-American community, and he closely observed Brahmananda's efforts in Africa. He and Brahmananda, had, in fact, corresponded on a couple of occasions, and plans were in the works for the two of them to develop Africa together. They had met in New York to discuss the future, and young Ekendra Dasa was privy to some of those meetings.

As a young African American himself, Ekendra was keenly interested in Bhakti Tirtha Maharaja and the potential for African preaching, but, for the time being, they limited themselves to related work in New York. Ekendra, a musician, had many contacts in the greater Metropolitan area, and he arranged for the Swami to speak at various bookstores and hip youth venues, particularly in Harlem. This led to the preaching center and restaurant in Washington D.C., mentioned earlier, where Ekendra and his then wife Vraja-lila came to help out.

But the actual move to Africa originated as follows: One morning in *Srimad-Bhagavatam* class, to everyone's surprise, Bhakti Tirtha Swami casually mentioned that Ekendra, along with Papastaya and Sanat, two local devotees, would soon be going to India, to the Mayapur festival. His idea was that they would become enriched in Krishna Consciousness by going to Mayapur, and then they would join Brahmananda in Africa. He mentioned it briefly in class, and then didn't broach the subject again for a couple of weeks.

At that time, he gave another morning *Bhagavatam* class in which he said, "So, Ekendra and Papastaya, I've arranged for you to go—I have tickets for you, and you'll be leaving for Africa." They were stunned. And this time, there was no talk of going to India, either. He just said, "You're going to Africa." Finished.

Ekendra, it should be remembered, was married to Vraja-lila at the time, and there was no mention of her accompanying them to Africa. Naturally, this inspired curiosity, and so the devotees spoke to Bhakti Tirtha Swami afterwards. It was at this time that he informed them that there was really no temple in Africa, no facility. Brahmananda was just staying in a small apartment and he wasn't even sure if he'd kept that. In other words, he felt that it wasn't safe for Vraja-lila to go right away, but that as soon as the three male devotees, along with Brahmananda, could get something established, he would send her to meet them there. Ultimately, Ekendra ended up going by himself.

Some background might be in order about Vraja-lila, who would eventually become one of Bhakti Tirtha Maharaja's closest disciples. She was born Gilda Garcia in Belize, Central America, though she grew up in New York City, arriving there when she was just twelve years old. Soon she found herself attending college in Berkeley, California, with a desire to accrue a certain amount of material success. But she was also a disciple of Swami Muktananda, a teacher of the impersonal school who emphasizes the worship of Shiva, the demigod in charge of universal destruction. And so she developed a knack for juggling two different worlds at once.

In 1979, her former husband, Ekendra Dasa, mentioned above, brought her to Govinda's Restaurant, the ISKCON vegetarian establishment in New York, and she became a devotee of Krishna. This she saw as a natural development from her former practice as a devotee of Shiva.

Still, she was pursuing a career in international marketing, and this initially kept her from becoming a full-time devotee. It was the same two worlds she had encountered earlier. But Krishna was deep in her heart, and this would eventually help her resolve the dilemma. This she knew from her first visit to the temple. At that time, she saw Radha Govinda, the Deities in New York, and broke into tears. A few moments later, she saw Lord Jagannath, who, at the time, shared the altar with Radha Govinda. Seeing His large, piercing eyes and beautiful face, as she puts it, she fell in love. This was a major turning point in her spiritual life. She tells the rest of the story with added details:

Some devotees invited me to a Ratha-yatra Festival in Philadelphia, and I asked Ekendra if we could go together. I told him I really wanted to go. Anyway, he had a gig—he's a percussionist—and couldn't get away at that time. So I just went. And after I went to Ratha-yatra, Lakshmi Nrisimha Prabhu, the New York temple president, was really kind to me, inviting me to check out the temple, to stay a little while. I wanted to do that . . .

And so I asked Ekendra, telling him that I wanted to stay at the temple for a week. It was okay with him—he had lived as a devotee for some time in Los Angeles, and was still into Krishna Consciousness—and so I packed some essentials and went to stay at the New York temple. But then, after a week, I wanted to check it out a little longer. Ekendra was like, "I don't think so. At least not in New York." So I said, "Okay." He was into it, but he wanted to go to L.A., because he knew the devotees there.

So we went cross-country, and when we first arrived, I was in-

troduced to Jadurani—she was a really senior devotee, totally dedicated to painting pictures for Prabhupada's books and also to going
out on book distribution. Well, she thought that I might be a good
person to train for Sankirtan. Turns out, she was correct, and I did
pretty well distributing books.

One day, I went to the airport to sell books, as usual. But on
this particular day, Bhakti Tirtha Maharaja had apparently come
through L.A. This was still 1979, and I had never met him. Ekendra had told me about him in New York, but I never actually
saw him. Anyway, when I came back from the airport that evening, Ekendra said that the Swami had just left. I just missed him.
Still, Ekendra mentioned that the Swami wanted us to join him in
D.C., because he wants us to help him with inner city preaching
and to work with him in Africa.

Now, I had been to Africa and had done some work there, so
I was somewhat enthused. I actually like to travel. I thought that
when the Swami comes back, we could talk about it. Ekendra was
shaking his head, like I didn't understand what he was saying. The
Swami, he said, wanted us to come to D.C. right away. We needed
to leave, like, tomorrow. So, remember, we dropped everything and
moved to L.A., and now we were expected to do the same by dropping everything and moving to D.C.

The next day, in fact, we were on a bus going to Washington
D.C. A devotee picked us up at the station and brought us right to
the restaurant, which was then Govinda's on 8th Street, Washington, D.C., Southeast.

When I walked in, Bhakti Tirtha Maharaja was sitting on a
small, special seat, sort of like a Vyasasana [a chair used exclusively
for gurus], but not quite. Anyway he was sitting up high, looking
regal and stately. But I couldn't make him out. Well, one reason is
that as soon as we walked in, we bowed down, which is the custom,
out of respect for sannyasis. At first I didn't really see him. Ekendra

and I both offered obeisances. When I finally raised my head and looked at him, for the first time, I was surprised—and I said it out loud: "I know you!" I knew that we had never actually met, but there was this intense familiarity—I knew that face, that presence, that energy. And he just looked at me calmly, and said, "Yes, we've known each other for many lifetimes."

Soon after Ekendra and Vraja-lila arrived in D.C.—toward the end of 1979—they took their place among the first dedicated followers of Bhakti Tirtha Swami, who quickly sent Ekendra to work with Brahmananda Prabhu in Nigeria, as already mentioned.

Brahmananda, for his part, was staying in a run-down apartment in Surulere, which is both a residential and commercial area in Lagos, and it is today known as the film Mecca of Nigeria. His apartment was a small, bare dwelling, but it served as a base from which he would daily go out on Hari-nama, chanting in the streets, and cultivating people in Krishna Consciousness. His main audience was the Indian community, particularly those of Sindhi extraction. At the time, they were among Africa's wealthy elite. And they had given him the apartment. It was to this address that Ekendra was sent.

Once there, due to a Western predisposition and a dislike for Third World conditions, Ekendra quickly determined to turn around and go home.

But Brahmananda encouraged him, showing him the potential for the humble facility that would initiate Krishna Consciousness in Africa. He took Ekendra upstairs, revealing a little makeshift altar and temple room. The apartment consisted of two bedrooms, a kitchen, a bathroom, and a sizeable living room, piled with boxes of books. This provoked a smile, since Ekendra had long heard about Bhakti Tirtha Swami's "Books for Africa" program, which he had inaugurated along with Brahmananda. This was a program in which devotees would travel to temples, homes, libraries, bookstores, and other locales throughout the world canvassing for books—particularly

Prabhupada's books—for Third World countries. These books were especially meant for Africa, so that literally tons of books were eventually shipped to Brahmananda's apartment. The Bhaktivedanta Book Trust, too, would donate books, and Brahmananda's living room was thus filled with transcendental literature.

This allowed him to distribute books rather freely—whole sets of *Srimad-Bhagavatam*, *Chaitanya-charitamrita*, and so on—not only to people in general but to schools and public libraries throughout Nigeria. As a result, many Africans became familiar with Prabhupada's teachings. Ekendra resolved to stay on to see what he could do.

Unfortunately, Brahmananda soon lost the apartment in Surulere, forcing the devotees to store all the remaining literature in a van. They envisioned themselves as taking the books to all parts of Africa—and having lost their temple, they didn't have many alternatives. Even so, they didn't get very far.

A wealthy Indian gentleman became concerned about their plight. He was a doctor, and he and his daughter were planning to open a clinic in the nearby area of Ilupeju. It was on a prominent road in Nigeria in a particularly upper class section of Palm Grove. As fate would have it, the Indian gentleman offered the devotees a small part of the hospital facility to use as a temple. Brahmananda and Ekendra, to put it bluntly, were overjoyed.

When the doctor first brought them to the new facility, they explored only the downstairs area and its surrounding compound—huge though it was. As a former mini-hospital, it was overrun with operating tables, gurneys, medicines, and all associated equipment.

The devotees took possession of the facility and continued their program of book distribution and public chanting. And things were going well. Bhakti Tirtha Maharaja and Brahmananda were still campaigning for books—Maharaja from America and Brahmananda from within Africa—and numerous boxes would regularly arrive from the States and other parts of the world.

The devotees in Nigeria received the books, distributed them, and sustained themselves in that way. New devotees began to join. Soon, encouraging reports made their way to Bhakti Tirtha Maharaja, who wrote to Ekendra to say that he would now be coming to visit them. This would have been his second or third trip to Africa in general—though he would now be greeted by a newly established temple and a successful preaching program. The devotees saw all this as a significant development.

And so it was that, in late 1980, Bhakti Tirtha Swami and Vrajalila came to Africa, as did a few others, such as Parameshvari and Sri Natha Prabhu—important devotees who, along with Madhava and several stalwarts who joined locally, were responsible for establishing the African mission of the International Society for Krishna Consciousness. Says Ekendra:

> Prior to the arrival of Bhakti Tirtha Swami, we never really ventured into the upstairs area of the hospital building—believe it or not—even though we were living there for some time. We were given the downstairs and we were told not to wander into the other areas. So that's what we did. We had the whole downstairs as a temple room and there were sleeping rooms downstairs as well. I stayed down there, and Brahmananda stayed down there. But now we had women who would need separate living arrangements. So we were going to venture upstairs—we thought maybe we would start using that facility.
>
> So once Bhakti Tirtha Swami arrived, he had the room downstairs sort of next to Brahmananda's room, and myself, my wife, Parameshvari and Sri Natha took rooms upstairs. As I said, we had not been upstairs previous to that. So we got some buckets and some water and prepared to go up to clean those rooms upstairs.
>
> Now, listen to this: When we first got up there, it smelled really funny. We thought, okay, this is some kind of hospital smell. It's old hospital equipment, and we're also in a Third World country. But when

we opened the door, we found that there was blood all over the walls. I'm not sure, but I think the place had been an abortion clinic.

Long story short, there was no alternative but to just clean it and work with it. So we cleaned everything, made it nice, burned incense; we actually went through the place with a Kirtan party, too, to purify the atmosphere. Then the families, married couples, had those rooms upstairs. A couple of newcomers moved in too—Ishvara Prabhu, who is in Vrindavan now, and another devotee named Omkara, who's currently staying in London. Bhakti Tirtha Swami really liked it and saw tremendous potential.

Starting to Snowball

As of 1980, ISKCON had no official guru in Africa. Bhakti Tirtha Maharaja was a *sannyasi*, but he was not yet recognized as a spiritual master. At that point, Africa did not warrant one, at least not until Bhakti Tirtha Swami arrived. It wasn't until then that large numbers of Africans began taking Krishna Consciousness seriously—which is the prerequisite for initiation. Only then does an initiating guru become necessary.

This is not to say that there were no initiated devotees in Africa. A handful of Prabhupada's disciples were already there, including movement elders, like Brahmananda. But there was no one of guru status. The only exception was Jayatirtha Maharaja, one of Prabhupada's leading devotees, who had several disciples of his own in East Africa, especially in Kenya. Because of this, he became Bhakti Tirtha Maharaja's first choice as a guru for the African people. The reasoning was simple: If Jayatirtha was already frequenting the Eastern part of Africa, he'll naturally be able to go to West Africa as well.

But he declined. Bhakti Tirtha Swami then asked Bhagavan Maharaja, another one of Prabhupada's leading men who sometimes worked in Africa. He wasn't interested, either. As it turned out, none of ISKCON's leaders wanted to take it on. In one sense, their reluctance was understandable. Most of them were already engaged beyond normal capacity. And, besides, this was difficult terrain, beleaguered by Third World conditions and a foreign cultural setting.

When the more obvious options were exhausted, Bhakti Tirtha Maharaja settled on Kirtanananda Swami. In actuality, Kirtanananda's guruship in Africa made sense. He was the *sannyasa* guru of Bhakti Tirtha, who was beginning to win over the African people, resulting in numerous followers for ISKCON. Moreover, Kirtanananda's close relationship with him would serve the African devotees well. Their initiating guru would be able to communicate with them through the person who was actually facilitating their Krishna Consciousness.

Kirtanananda Swami agreed to take on responsibility for Africa. He was, at the time, one of the most successful devotees in the movement, with worldwide preaching establishments from America to India, a successful restaurant, and the Palace of Gold in West Virginia. Because of his then recent achievements, he felt unstoppable, and so Africa, though unfamiliar to him in every way, seemed entirely doable.

The team of Kirtanananda Swami and Bhakti Tirtha Maharaja worked well. And preaching in Africa started to snowball. Bhakti Tirtha Maharaja was traveling back and forth—making devotees that were then taking initiation from Kirtanananda. At this point, Brahmananda receded into the background, at least as far as Africa was concerned. He traveled to Mumbai (then Bombay) and began serving there.

Kirtanananda Swami didn't come to Africa with any frequency. He was more or less a guru figure from afar. It was Bhakti Tirtha Maharaja who cultivated the African devotees, nurturing them and helping them in Krishna Consciousness. New Vrindavan was Kirtanananda's primary concern, which was consistently growing and expanding as well.

Consequently, Bhakti Tirtha Maharaja started taking more of a prominent role in Africa. He would come back and forth more often. People started to realize that even though they were taking formal initiation from Kirtanananda, Bhakti Tirtha Swami was their real guru. This worked well, since Bhakti Tirtha Maharaja was African-American, and his visual appearance made the local people feel more comfortable. In this way, Africa started to open up to Krishna Consciousness more than ever before.

In fact, Ekendra and Vraja-lila, who were enormously pleased by the results, were now thinking about preaching elsewhere in Africa. It was clear that, in this particular area, their work was already done— people were taking shelter of Krishna Consciousness through Kirtananananda and Bhakti Tirtha Swami. But Africa was a big place, and they knew they had to recreate this phenomenon in other quarters.

Apropos of this, Bhakti Tirtha Maharaja soon confirmed that his comrades should indeed strike while the iron was hot. He asked them to go to Ghana right away. So Ekendra and wife, along with two other devotees—Martin, who would become Maha-mantra Prabhu, and Lakshmi-pati Prabhu, who was the son of one of the former presidents of Ghana—packing only a few necessities, made their way to another African land. It didn't hurt having the former president's son with them.

After a musky drive through Benin, Togo, and other difficult terrain, they finally arrived in Ghana. A beautiful and important nation in West Africa, it borders Cote d'Ivoire to the west, Burkina Faso to the north, Togo to the east, and boasts the Gulf of Guinea on its southern coastline. This would be an important preaching field for Bhakti Tirtha Maharaja—"Ghana"shyam Dasa—who eventually made this area a central concern.

Ekendra, Vraja-lila, and the others began by getting a small house in a place called Alajo. There, they repeated the successful formula begun in Nigeria. Taking it to the streets with a box of books and the holy name, they attracted all who passed by with their intense Vaishnava spirituality. A particularly good spot was in front of the Ghana Electric Company. Ekendra or one of the others would give a little speech and then people would gather around; the devotees would field questions, debate with people who had opposing views—especially Born Again Christians—and reveal the depth and profundity of Krishna Consciousness.

After six to eight months at their initial location, the devotees moved to Odoko, which is on the outskirts of Accra, the capital of the country. A much more picturesque location, the new building had two levels and its own compound. At the top of the temple structure, there was a long balcony, overlooking the town. It was on a hill, and so the balcony afforded a brilliant view of all of Odoko. The temple environment was simply beautiful.

This perhaps acted as a catalyst for an interesting phenomenon: Whereas, in Nigeria, the devotees were able to attract people to Krishna Consciousness but weren't able to get them to come back to the temple, in Ghana they were also able to do both. And seeing the way in which devotees lived—the simplicity, the sincerity, the devotion—was important, inspiring others to do the same. Thus, many gave their lives to Krishna after just a few visits, and because of this, the movement in Ghana grew rapidly.

People especially loved the Kirtan. In some ways, it was like being in sixteenth-century India, with large crowds swelling along with the chant. The devotees in Ghana had a special relationship with the local people, such that when they went out chanting, everyone would want to join in. These big Kirtan sessions would start in the early evening and, as they built in momentum, you could see people shut down their businesses for the day—earlier than usual—just to follow along. They had little sweet shops, bread shops, savory shops. All would close early as the devotees led chanting processions through the town of Odoko, making a big circle and coming around again toward the temple area. By the time they got back to the temple, there would be a good couple hundred people with them, singing and dancing.

The first time Bhakti Tirtha Swami came to Ghana, which was soon after the devotees had relocated to Odoko, he arrived unannounced. The devotees were out on one of these huge Hari-nama festivals, with townspeople joining in, numbering in the hundreds. After they had circled the town, returning to the temple gates, they noticed a taxi pull up at just the same time. Lo and behold: Bhakti Tirtha Swami emerged from the vehicle.

He didn't say he was coming because his arrival was precipitated by a sudden change in plans—*he* didn't even know he'd be going to Ghana until the last minute.

As he exited the car, his huge smile brought new life to the Kirtan. And upon seeing him, the excitement intensified for all who were there. The Hari-nama started up again. This time, Bhakti Tirtha Swami led it—in his own inimitable way—and the crowd became euphoric. The frenzy harkened back to the massive, ecstatic Hari-nama festivals held by Sri Chaitanya and His associates, as suggested above.

Shrivasa Dasa, one of ISKCON Africa's premier regional secretaries, sums up Bhakti Tirtha Swami's work in Ghana:

> *His preaching in Africa and specifically in Ghana has many chapters, but for the sake of space I will highlight the important areas. When he came to Ghana, there was not a single Krishna devotee, what to speak of a temple. However, as of today, the story is different. There are many devotees of the Lord throughout Ghana by the singular effort of His Holiness. Furthermore, a Vedic temple has been built in Accra, the capital of Ghana, and five other centers—our own properties—are located in five other big cities.*
>
> *Over three hundred acres of land has been acquired for farming purposes, to fulfill his overwhelming desire to establish self-sufficient farming communities throughout the world. A school has been established in Accra and a clinic is there as well. It provides free health care for devotees and the community in which we live. The inspiration, guidance, and ability of his disciples to do all this, considering the impoverished situation in Africa, clearly came from him.*
>
> *By his powerful presentations of the philosophy and practice*

of *Krishna Consciousness* on national TV and radio, he reached many distinguished citizens, including the former head of state, Mr. J. J. Rawlings, who viewed one of His Holiness' TV programs and demanded a video of the program to keep at home—he also gave Bhakti Tirtha Maharaja an unprecedented private audience, spending several hours listening to Maharaja discuss the intricacies of Krishna Consciousness.

Royals of great cultural heritage, the Asantehene of the Ashanti kingdom, eagerly received him, anxious to hear his enlightening words. Many kings and chiefs have become disciples of Bhakti Tirtha Maharaja. National directors of sensitive state organizations sought his association in order to nourish their souls. Pressmen and women who by some good fortune managed to interview His Holiness were always so impressed that they wanted to have him again appear on their programs. His message of love, peace, and unity in the midst of diversity appeals to everyone irrespective of religious differences. He was such an empowered preacher that prominent Christian leaders avoided meeting him on TV and radio programs, fearing that he, like them, would want to debate, not understanding his true, nonsectarian spiritual message.

Shastra Dasa, another early disciple of Bhakti Tirtha Maharaja, reiterates the snowball analogy, illustrating how Maharaja's work spread from Ghana to other African nations:

> My first contact with His Holiness Bhakti Tirtha Swami was in 1980 in Lagos, Nigeria, just a year after he took sannyasa. Initially, he was playing the role of our "big brother" in the sense that ISKCON was divided into "zones" with various gurus in charge of a given area. Kirtanananda Swami was then the guru for West Africa, and Brahmananda Prabhu and Bhakti Tirtha Swami were ISKCON's Governing Body Commissioners (GBCs), which is a kind of managerial post, working with him.

Anyway, under Bhakti Tirtha Swami's guidance and inspiration, Port Harcourt temple was the second temple to be opened, followed by one in Benin. After that, Abeokuta temple, Ibadan temple, Kaduna temple, Calabar temple, Warri temple, Owerri temple and Enuga temple. It was expanding in an incredible way. Also, Bhakti Tirtha Swami was often on television programs all over Nigeria, and well-wishers were inviting devotees to open temples in their cities.

It seemed like Krishna Consciousness was taking over Africa, and Bhakti Tirtha Swami was leading the way. He was like a powerful snowball, entering one country, moving fast and picking up momentum. This would lead right into another one. So, you see, his contribution will always be remembered, because he established over twenty temples in seven countries. And two farm communities and two public schools are also in his list of achievements in the West African region. But more than all of this, he gave his soul to Africa. This is why he is so dear to us.

"Ain't No Stopping us Now"

Bhakti Tirtha Swami's enthusiasm and charisma brought the Holy Name of Krishna throughout the continent. From Ghana, the movement spread to Zimbabwe, which is Central Africa, and then to Zambia, in the south, where the movement made tremendous inroads. The Republic of Zambia takes its name from the Zambezi River, known for its many rapids and waterfalls, especially Victoria Falls, famous throughout the world. The river arises in the northwest corner of the country and forms its southern boundary. Sometimes known as "the real Africa," Zambia's neighbors are Congo DR to the north and northwest, Tanzania to the northeast, Malawi to the East, Mozambique to the southeast, Zimbabwe to the south, Botswana and Namibia to the Southwest and Angola to the West. All felt the power of the Hare Krishna Movement.

Zambia's terrain is unusually beautiful, with a highland plateau
that covers much of the country. Here, one cannot help but marvel
at her numerous exquisite mountain chains, such as the Muchinga
in the northeast. Most of the country has savanna-type vegetation,
including grasslands interspersed with exotic trees. Teak forests in the
southwest are home to various animals, such as elephants, lions, rhi-
noceroses, and several varieties of antelope. In many ways, Zambia
is stereotypical Africa, with an emphasis on its beautiful and striking
environment. Ekendra briefly describes Bhakti Tirtha Swami's accomplishments in this most special place:

*Bhakti Tirtha Swami came to Zambia and we started doing our
thing—big time. In Zambia, he really developed his international
preaching, especially among celebrities. Here, we met one influen-
tial High Court judge named Aiyadurai Shivanandan. He was
extremely favorable to begin with, but Bhakti Tirtha Maharaja
really took time with him, and conveyed the truths of Krishna Consciousness. And so, after some time, this judge would even wear
tilak [sacred Vaishnava bodily markings] to the bench. Amazing
person. He arranged for us to meet all the ministers of the Justice
Department and the Communications Minister.*

*We were staying in a little house that belonged to one Indian
family, just outside the city in Lusaka, Zambia. It was really, really
ecstatic, because we were reaching extremely high-level people. And
Bhakti Tirtha Swami fit right in. He was in his element. While
we were there, we only had a small room with two double beds.
So Bhakti Tirtha and I had to sleep right next to each other, and
Vraja-lila had to sleep on the other one, across the room. But we
were so happy with what was going on that throughout the night
we kept calling back and forth to each other.*

I would say, "Maharaja, are you asleep?"

"No," he'd answer.

"And wasn't that amazing? I mean, I can't believe it. We're

working with the Justice Minister, and he's wearing tilak *to court! This is just amazing." And he wasn't wearing* tilak *because he came from a Vaishnava family. No. After Bhakti Tirtha Maharaja spent some time with him, he really got involved and started to understand what Krishna Consciousness was all about; that's when he started wearing* tilak. *He would take pictures with the* tilak *on, and his curly wig—the hairpiece that those old time judges used to wear. It was in national newspapers.*

For me, it brings to mind the lyrics to that pop song, "Ain't no stopping us now . . ." Anyway, while we were staying there, Maharaja would tap me at night and say, "Did you fall asleep yet? It's a possibility that we're going to meet the president." It was actually very exciting.

Sure enough, the next thing was that an arrangement was made for us to meet the President of Zambia, who, at that time, was President Kaunda. He was a special person. He was known as the Gandhi of Africa. Kenneth David Kaunda—he served as the first President of the Republic of Zambia from 1964 to 1991. At that time, in the early '80s, Bhakti Tirtha Swami, Vraja-lila, Navayogendra Swami [a disciple of Srila Prabhupada who was visiting at that time], and I went to see him. In fact, we were invited to an official presidential dinner. Also, President Kaunda was a vegetarian. So he was really excited to host this vegetarian affair, and we were excited to be there.

It was an amazing dinner with the President—a dream come true. The whole time the President was trying to talk to Bhakti Tirtha Maharaja on a more personal level, but at that dinner there were many ministers, and other important political figures, presidential aides and top people in the government. They were also at the table. Then, when the dinner was over, the presidential aides came in and thanked us for coming. We thought it was time to go. But, at that moment, as we were about to leave, the President grabbed Bhakti Tirtha Maharaja by the arm and said, "Oh, I just want to show you something." And he showed us some art piece or something like that. But it seemed as if this was just an excuse; it was really about holding Maharaja there a little longer, to talk to him more privately. And, sure enough, as he was walking with him, he made sure that they walked up a little ahead of everybody. The next thing you know they walked outside of a door and into a garden, a little separate from the rest of us. However, we all piled in after them. At this point, the aides looked a little concerned, naturally. They're supposed to watch out for the president.

We were walking in the president's garden, and I'm walking a little behind with Vraja-lila, and Navayogendra is walking in between both of us. Maharaja is with the president, up front, and they're having some dialogue. Of course, when we got back to our room, we stayed up all night talking. Maharaja told us how the president was genuinely interested in spiritual life—he asked Maharaja one question after the next, really curious.

The president confided in Maharaja about his aides and about his co-workers in government. He said that he was surrounded by people who were non-spiritual, so to speak, and that they couldn't relate to his philosophy about governing, which was grounded in spiritual principles. So he and Maharaja had some pretty amazing conversations. This is in 1984 or '85. Preaching in West Africa was booming, mainly because of immense sacrifices made by Bhakti Tirtha Swami.

ISKCON soon acknowledged Bhakti Tirtha Maharaja's considerable conquests in Africa, with hundreds and eventually thousands of local people clamoring for initiation. In 1984, he was made full Governing Body Commissioner (GBC) for all of West Africa and co-GBC, with Bhagavan Maharaja, for East Africa.

By 1985 he was made an initiating guru, both because ISKCON management began to recognize his exceptional qualities as a spiritual leader and because they knew that Africans would feel more at home with an African-American teacher. Still, as Ishvara Dasa mentions above, he took one full year to meditate on the meaning of his new role as a guru, and to perform austerities that might help him fulfill his mandate properly. When he returned and started initiating in 1986, he was unstoppable, like a proverbial *juggernaut*. (The word itself, incidentally, is traceable to the name of his worshipable Jagannath Deity.)

Nonetheless, his accomplishments in Africa, as we have seen, reach back to 1980, anticipating his acceptance of guruship. That being said, below is a summary list of those accomplishments, from both before and after he adopted his new role. Some of these spiritual victories are directly attributable to him; others come from the inspiration he instilled in his followers. In both cases, he was unquestionably at the helm.

1983:

Zimbabwe's president Canaan Banana and prime minister R. B. Mugabe received ISKCON books, and expressed deep appreciation for them. The Herald and ZBC TV, major media networks, covered the African Food for Life program, an ISKCON free food initiative.

1985:

First Ratha-yatra in Nairobi, Kenya, held on August 10th of that year. Lord Jagannath strolled down a main thoroughfare on a massive cart, as in India and around the world. A local newspaper estimated that 70–80,000 people participated in the festival.

In that same year, 100,000 attended the ISKCON temple opening in Natal, South Africa, even though the area was ablaze with racial tension. Despite summer-long violence, leaders of the Afrikaans, English, Black, and Asian communities came together for the new ISKCON temple dedication in Natal. The three-day festival in October attracted more than 100,000 visitors, including several major political figures.

1987:

Devotees fed flood victims in Natal. After one of the heaviest rains in recorded history, many thousands faced homelessness, poverty, disease, and starvation. Hare Krishna Food For Life responded to by cooking hot, nutritious meals daily and providing blankets and clothing.

1988:

Food for Life in Kwazulu, South Africa. Devotees traveled deep into the homeland of the Zulu nation to relieve people from the effects of massive flooding. An important Ciskei Chieftain advised citizens to replace meat eating with *prasadam*, sacred vegetarian food.

1989:

Durban Ratha-yatra drew 50,000 locals. South Africa's first large-scale Ratha-yatra rolled along Durban's Marine Parade. At the two-day festival Durban Mayor Derek Watterson delivered the opening address, thanking the devotees for "prompting love and peace among all races of people in South Africa."

1994:

"Everything you eat, grow. Everything you use, make." These are the words of Bhakti Tirtha Swami that devotees in West Africa immediately took to heart—so much so that the kinds of items devotees have traditionally traveled to India to purchase have for the past decade been manufactured by the devotees themselves. Through various cottage industries they are now producing incense, *kartals* [hand cymbals], *mridanga* drums, devotee clothing, bead bags, and even Deities.

In Ibadan, Nigeria, the ISKCON ceramics factory, which employs a number of local people, won second prize and national recognition in a government-sponsored nationwide competition to find the best use of natural resources in Nigeria (population 90 million). Overall, ISKCON industries and farm projects have contributed greatly to furnishing the needs of the masses—food, clothing, and other accouterments of life.

We are the Children

As one of his most determined efforts in Africa, Bhakti Tirtha Maharaja worked hard on behalf of the children. He felt—as has often been said—that children are our future, and he exerted considerable effort to free them from unnecessary disease, to feed and clothe them, and to educate them.

In Ghana, for example, where a large part of the population is either hungry or uneducated or both, ISKCON is fulfilling both basic needs as well as spiritual ones through temples, Food for Life programs, farm projects, and schools—all initiated under Bhakti Tirtha Swami's supervision. After the success of Lord Krishna's Academy, a primary school situated next to the main temple near Nsawam village, ISKCON now supports:

- Approximately 100 children who attend temple functions every day, and many others who use the facilities regularly
- A daily *prasadam* lunch program—free food for all children
- A children's Hari-nama, street chanting, and preaching team
- A new government-approved class subject: Krishna Consciousness. It is taught in the school alongside other official subjects.

The school has been in existence for many years now. It was conceived by Bhakti Tirtha Maharaja in response to several letters that Srila Prabhupada had written in which he talks about the importance of not only getting courses on Krishna Consciousness in public schools but also on the importance of education in general.

According to UNESCO statistics, in the year 2000, the education enrollment in Ghana, primary level, was 58.2 percent, which can be significantly compared to South Africa's 88.9 percent and the U.K.'s 98.9 percent. The United Nations declared an official Literacy Decade between the years 2003 and 2012, during which it aims to extend literacy to the more than 800 million adults who are functionally illiterate worldwide, and the roughly 113 million children who have no access to school. The lowest literacy rates worldwide are in Sub-Saharan Africa (where Ghana is located) as well as South and West Asia. Thus, Bhakti Tirtha Swami thought that this is an ideal time—and place—for ISKCON to play its role.

And it has. In 2003, Shastra Dasa, a disciple of Bhakti Tirtha Swami, gave a full report on one of the several successful Krishna Conscious schools of Ghana:

> *The day begins with the school pledge, as follows:*
>
> > *I, a soul eternal,*
> > *Who fell from Krishnaloka*
> > *Am ready to return home*
> > *Via Lord Krishna's shloka:*
> > *"One who is fully conscious of Me*
> > *Can enter the Kingdom of God."*
> > *So eager am I*
> > *To depart for home*
> > *That I bow to God's instruction*
> > *And vow to follow His direction*
> > *Sinning and offending no more,*
> > *Serving and loving ever more.*
> > *May I be guided by devotion*
> > *As I head for Krishnaloka*
> > *Resolved to reach the spiritual sky*
> > *Of harmony and happiness*
> > *To the land of love—Krishnaloka!*
> > *To the place of peace—Krishnaloka!*
> > *To the abode of bliss—Krishnaloka!*
> > *For this free flight back home*
> > *I do sincerely pledge to please Krishna*
> > *Now and forever . . .*
> > > *—(Composed by Nrsimhadeva Dasa, Ghana)*

Classes then include six examination subjects: Math, English, Environmental Studies, Moral Education, Local Language, and Krishna Consciousness. The children watch educational DVDs in the small school library, or color in their "Krishna Rhymes Book," which is a treat for village kids who live in bamboo and mud houses without electricity. Sometimes they have drama practice and always enjoy good, nutritious vegetarian meals, offered to Krishna, of course.

Along similar lines, one devotee, Prasada Dasi, writes about several of Bhakti Tirtha Swami's projects in South Africa. For example, he inaugurated the "Selfless Love Project," organized by the Hare Krishna Food for Life team, as well as the "Stop Raping Our Children" Campaign at the Snake Park Informal Settlement in Soweto.

The Selfless Love project, which operates from the South African Broadcasting Corporation (SABC) premises in Auckland Park, is a humanitarian activity that focuses on the feeding of underprivileged children who attend the conducted tours of the SABC. The Higher Taste Restaurant in the SABC, managed by the Hare Krishna Movement, offers freshly cooked meals for the children on a daily basis. Plans are presently underway to expand the project in order to distribute free meals to schools that are not presently touring the SABC.

Bhakti Tirtha Swami, while at the SABC himself, addressed those present on "Media, Ethics and Morality in the Year 2000 and Beyond." His lecture was met with thunderous applause, and many became devotees as a result of that talk.

The Stop Raping Our Children Campaign, functioning in conjunction with Rand Afrikaans University (RAU), is presently working in the Snake Park Informal Settlement in Soweto, where the highest number of child rapes in Gauteng has been reported. The campaign aims to bring to the attention of the relevant authorities the seriousness of child rapes in South Africa. According to some reports, children as young as three months old are being raped in various parts of the country.

RAU has joined the Selfless Love project in its fight against child hunger and molestation in the Soweto area. More, RAU's social welfare department is offering its counseling services to the victims of child rape and to the parents of the children as well.

Bhakti Tirtha Swami, who was aware and concerned about the plight of these children, addressed numerous local communities and leaders on this issue, spending countless hours ministering to the victims of these crimes, both the children and their parents. The Food for Life project, under his direction, fed the 10,000 residents at the settlement and began many other initiatives in due course.

High Chief of the Spiritual World

Because of his humanitarian and spiritual work in the African nations, Bhakti Tirtha Maharaja was bestowed the highest honor known to Africans: He was coronated as a high chief in a time-honored and significant African nation in the city of Warri. The Ohroje (king) of Okpe (Warri), also known as the "Erhumuakpo of Okpe," which means, "The man who stands for the good of the world," is considered one of Nigeria's greatest kings of all time. It is he who granted Bhakti Tirtha Swami special chieftaincy in November of 1990, a distinguished honor conferred on few souls.

The Okpe Kingdom is located on the Niger Delta, or the southern tip of Nigeria, and has a population of about 2.2 million people. Areas such as Sapele, Warri, Agbaror, Ororokpe, Adaje, Oha, Okuodete, and so on, are integral parts of the Kingdom. Thus, Bhakti Tirtha Swami's coronation was no small affair, but rather it affected the lives of millions.

Prior to the coronation, the Ohroje (King) of Okpe was a regular guest at the Warri ISKCON temple. Under the direction of Bhakti Tirtha Swami, whenever he visited he always bowed down before the resident Deities—Jagannath, Baladeva, and Subhadra, who, as readers of this book already know, were dear to Maharaja's heart.

Devotees started cultivating the Ohroje in 1989; this was initially the work of the then temple president, Jagannath Mishra Dasa. After that, however, Bhakti Tirtha Swami made sure that whenever the king visited, he was nicely cared for and offered sumptuous *prasadam*. Interestingly, on one of his visits, he brought another prominent king with him. When they were offered *prasadam*, he accepted it but the other king refused—traditionally, a king never eats outside of his own palace. But the Ohroje encouraged him to eat, pointing out that the food was highly spiritual.

In the course of his regular visits, the Ohroje acquired chanting beads and started regularly chanting the Hare Krishna Maha-mantra. After almost one year of chanting, he told Bhakti Tirtha Maharaja of his desire to crown him as a High Chief (second only to the Ohroje himself) because of his monumental work in Africa.

Elated by the implications for the Krishna Consciousness Movement, Bhakti Tirtha Maharaja informed the then temple presidents of Benin (Ganga Dasa) and Warri (Haridham Dasa) of the Ohroje's desire. He instructed them to broadcast the news to all the devotees in the area, and to those of adjacent countries—this was to be an event of colossal significance. He wanted all nearby well-wishers of ISKCON to prepare for the upcoming function at the king's palace.

And then the day came. Normally, the tradition holds that the person to be coronated must reside at the palace for one full week, thus allowing for ritual purification by the chief priests of various deities in the kingdom. But the Ohroje waived these for Bhakti Tirtha Swami. Also he waived other traditional commitments attached to the crown.

All the devotees at Warri gathered at the temple; fifty devotees came from nearby Benin, including prominent chiefs and professors, individuals who either had close ties with Bhakti Tirtha Swami or else had some intimate connection with the temple. In all, some 150 devotees converged at the palace in buses and cars, all waiting for Maharaja's arrival.

The function was supposed to commence at about nine in the morning; but it was as late as eleven, with no sign of Bhakti Tirtha

Swami. Such tardiness was uncommon for him; he always made it a point to be on time, if not early. The Ohroje and his cabinet chiefs—as well as thousands of his subjects, who had gathered for the coronation—were starting to wonder what had happened to the Swami.

About three hours later, Bhakti Tirtha Maharaja arrived with one of his disciples from Port Harcourt. The two of them informed the curious attendees of a terrible accident involving Maharaja's car. Apparently, he had left Port Harcourt temple that morning with his entourage in two cars, as planned. He was seated in the front of one of them, en route to Warri. Then, on the Warri-Port Harcourt Highway, his vehicle crashed into another car.

By Krishna's arrangement, he was wearing his seat belt, and he emerged with only light wounds on his hand and several scratches on his body. Other devotees were injured as well, but no deaths. The car was totaled. Madhurya-lila Dasi (Lucy Eboigbodin), one of Maharaja's earliest African disciples, was one of the few devotees in the car with him; she suffered a head injury necessitating thirty stitches. Her memories of that day and of the momentousness coronation are vivid:

Maharaja considered the coronation to be a great honor. Such a thing is never awarded to outsiders, but they were giving it to him. Even though he was from America, he was made chief. This was really not possible. It was a first. You had to be an insider. But that's how much the king admired him. Actually, he considered him part of his family. He called Maharaja a warrior, because he worked tirelessly to help the African people, as only a true African king can. The word he used was erhumuakpo, *which means that Maharaja was a "conqueror," or a "hero."*

So this was really huge, and the last thing we needed was to get into an accident. Maharaja didn't want to be late—this was such an incredible honor. Being a chief in Africa gives one a lot of access to the people and it would be a great facility for spreading Krishna Consciousness. But what can you do? It happened—a complete car wreck. The amazing thing, though, is that he made sure we all got to the hospital for care. Just imagine: He's on his way to this historic event, and he gets there late, not only because of the accident, but to make sure that his disciples are properly cared for in the hospital. That's the kind of loving, compassionate person he was.

After Maharaja arranged for the treatment of those who were seriously wounded, he and the disciple from Port Harcourt proceeded to Warri in the second vehicle, and then to the palace.

Once there, he was personally received by the Ohroje and his chiefs at the gate of the palace and then taken into the palace auditorium, which was to be the actual site of the coronation. On the way, the Ohroje and his men informed Maharaja that they were not surprised by the car accident—many powerful leaders were vying for the position of High Chief in Warri, and they had no doubt placed a curse on him, using magical incantations and various spells, hoping that they might become High Chief instead. But Bhakti Tirtha Swami showed little concern: "I have Prabhupada and Krishna, who will always protect me."

The Ohroje and Bhakti Tirtha Swami walked to the palace auditorium, where hundreds of people were seated and waiting for the function to begin. When the two dignitaries entered, everyone stood up in respect. The Ohroje seated Maharaja on a nicely decorated throne near his, on the same level. This, of course, was quite unusual, since no one ever sits on same level as the Ohroje, except the Otato, who, this time, had to sit on a lower throne near Bhakti Tirtha Swami. The local people, observing this break in tradition, were shocked. Nonetheless, it helped them to see the high regard in which the Ohroje held the Swami.

The Ohroje then expressed his profound happiness and gratitude for Bhakti Tirtha Swami's visit, and for his gracious acceptance of the chieftaincy. The Ohroje told him that with this coronation he is now considered an integral part of the kingdom, entitled to all the benefits of a very high chief. He should also, the Ohroje told him, attend all traditional functions and cabinet meetings, at least whenever it might be convenient for him.

Bhakti Tirtha Swami, visibly moved, expressed his appreciation for receiving the honor. He further explained that he was actually accepting the crown on behalf of Srila Prabhupada, his spiritual master, whom he sees as the true High Chief. He explained how Prabhupada took Vedic knowledge to the West at an old age. After briefly recounting his revered teacher's story, he said that Vedic knowledge is very similar to ancient African traditions and that these traditions are deeply related. But now, he said, they are brothers more than ever before.

He encouraged everyone present to follow the good example of their king by investigating the knowledge of the Vedas. He thanked senior members of the community for their warm reception, and especially the Ohroje and his cabinet chiefs for the honor. He also offered a gift of several sets of Srila Prabhupada's books to the Ohroje and his chiefs, and he encouraged them to spend some minutes chanting the Maha-mantra with him.

After the coronation, the Ohroje's traditional singers, playing African drums, situated themselves in front of the Ohroje and Bhakti Tirtha Swami, offering customary obeisance to the Ohroje and the new high chief (Bhakti Tirtha Swami). Then they broke into royal melodies, inviting the Swami, as required by tradition, to dance. Thinking he was shy, that he might not get up and accommodate them, they were going to respectfully move on to the next part of their performance.

But they didn't know who they were dealing with. Bhakti Tirtha Swami elegantly arose from his seat, surrounded by the local chiefs, in traditional dress, and started dancing—but unlike they had ever seen before. He moved outside the palace auditorium to the adjoining grounds, as required, with the musicians and other dancers following along. At first, he simulated the traditional royal dancing steps as much as possible, following the chiefs at his side. But then he broke into "the Swami step," with his routinely massive smile and arms upraised in distinct Hare Krishna fashion. Many of the locals had never seen such dancing before, but they would now pray that they could see it again.

At the end of the dance, Bhakti Tirtha Swami invited everyone to join in a tumultuous Kirtan on the palace grounds, an event that was particularly relished by the Ohroje and his chiefs. Meanwhile, devotees started distributing *prasadam* to everyone present, and people were rushing to devour the plates of delicious vegetarian food and the books that came along with them. The entire area was set alight by thousands of blissful faces, their bodies reverberating to the sounds of the holy name. The Ohroje could see that he had no doubt just given great facility to a man who truly deserved it. Indeed, the Ohroje noted that the Swami was not only the High Chief of Warri but quite possibly of the spiritual world as well.

As an addendum to this story, Bhakti Tirtha Swami's initial coronation made him one of the top ten chiefs in the ancient kingdom of Warri. However, a recent reconsideration of high chief status, based on humanitarian work and popularity among the people, saw the Okpe Kingdom Traditional Council elect Bhakti Tirtha Swami as one of the top five high chiefs of the empire. This is a distinct honor, and even more so because he was given the new title Olorogun, meaning, "chief among high chiefs." His new position situates him in a prominent place in the Warri people's hearts, such that his picture now sits alongside those of prominent personalities such as presidential candidate Senator Dafinone in the homes of many members of the Okpe kingdom, which, again, amounts to millions of people.

When Bhakti Tirtha Swami returned to America, he would use his crown, regal African dress, and high chief status itself as a foil to share Krishna Consciousness with newcomers, particularly with young African Americans. His flair for dress, a characteristic that dates back to his childhood, would now be imbued with deep meaning, as he combined saffron and Indic-style motifs with Afro-centric fabrics and patterns. Eventually, he would also carry a lion-headed cane, prepared for him by Uncle Nanda, adding to the exotic nature of his attire.

Mother Hladini: The Emblem of Devotion

It is difficult to assess Bhakti Tirtha Swami's African sojourn without acknowledging that several devotees made sacrifices on a par with his own. One such person, in particular, was Mother Hladini, a dedicated disciple of Srila Prabhupada who literally gave her life for the African preaching mission.

She and her husband, Mahananda Prabhu, were initiated in Detroit on March 29, 1970. Eventually, she became associated with New Vrindavan and dedicated her life to the Deities there, especially Lord Jagannath. In keeping with standards set at that specific temple, she inevitably adopted the *sannyasa* order of life. But as time went on, she felt a bit uncomfortable with a role traditionally assigned to men, and she wrote to Bhakti Tirtha Swami, who guided and consoled her. The two devotees came to feel like kindred spirits, with mutual admiration and respect for each other. Maharaja would say that she was his mentor, and she would claim that he was hers.

After several years, she became dedicated to the idea of spreading Krishna Consciousness around the world, and, by the Swami's grace, ended up in Africa. She traveled around the continent with an intense desire to genuinely help people. She had the energy and demeanor of a young Mother Teresa and the Vaishnava wisdom and charisma of a Bhakti Tirtha Swami. Consequently, people loved her almost as much as she loved them.

Her work took her to the most needy parts of the continent. Unfortunately, this included Monrovia, the capital of Liberia, West Africa. In recent history, Liberia is chiefly remembered for its two civil wars—the Liberian Civil War (1989–1996) and the Second Liberian Civil War (1999–2003), the former of which would bring an end to Mother Hladini's life.

Some background is in order: By the time she arrived in Monrovia, the war had reached absurd proportions, with civilians killing each other in the streets and children being trampled underfoot. Many fought while under the influence of drugs, with a surreal callousness in regard to human life.

The devotees worked in the capital, Monrovia, under the auspices of the Economic Community of West African States Monitoring Group (ECOMOG). The Freeport area, which is some five miles outside the capital, was controlled by the troops of the Independent National Patriotic Front of Liberia (INPFL), led by Prince Yormei Johnson, a dishonorable assassin who had tortured and killed the former President Samual Doe. Johnson, it is said, killed his own men at a faster rate than he did his enemy.

At the time, the devotees were engaged in *prasadam* distribution: two out of every three Liberians had been made homeless through the horrors of war, and starvation was not uncommon. With nowhere else to go, ISKCON's tireless members approached Johnson, who controlled a good deal of the commerce and raw materials of the region, and made a proposal to him, asking for food and the facility to distribute it. By some miracle, the tyrant agreed and gave them food that was meant for others. The devotees then offered it to Krishna and distributed it as *prasadam*.

But Johnson's homicidal reputation did not sit well with the devotees, and so they innocently wrote him a letter, saying, "You are a great personality, and as such you should stop conducting yourself in such a demonic manner—please stop killing people. This will benefit you and all of humanity." Perhaps because he had accommodated them by giving them food, they thought that he might be able to hear their message.

Quite the contrary. Instead, Johnson and his troops arrived late one September evening in 1990, and he meant business. There was banging on the door, and then a crash. Two brothers in the house saw him from the window and decided to hide. Because of this, they escaped with their lives and were later able to tell the story. All the other devotees—seven African men and one African woman, along with Mother Hladini—were assembled downstairs. The situation looked bleak.

Johnson viciously ranted while holding up the letter, shaking it in their faces. "How dare you send this to me!" His men then pushed the devotees out of the house and into a waiting vehicle. They were driven over a low bridge that crosses the muddy St. Paul River and stopped by an adjacent beach. At gunpoint, the nine devotees were forced out of the car and lined up on the cold, dark sand.

Johnson claimed that only the men would be killed. One can only imagine what he was planning to do with the women. Whatever the case, it was at that moment that Hladini showed the utmost bravery, befitting a disciple of Srila Prabhupada. As Johnson raised his weapon to execute the men, she leapt forward and attacked the madman with her own hands, crying, "How dare you kill the devotees of Krishna!" For this, she was instantly shot. So were all the rest, except the African girl, whose whereabouts are now unknown. The devotees chanted as they met their end.

According to Jalakar Dasa, a Prabhupada disciple who researched the subject and wrote an eloquent article on Hladini's passing:

> *The bodies were left on the beach. When the tide came in they were washed out, but as the river is tidal at that point, the bodies were carried back into the town with the tide. The bodies of some of the men could be seen drifting in and out in the St. Paul River for days, their dead hands stiff with rigor mortis holding their beads within their bead-bags. Hladini's body also drifted in. Her* sari *became entangled with the structure of the bridge and remained there for several days, rising and falling with the tide.*

Radhanath Swami, her good friend and a senior Vaishnava, says:

At times she was boldly preaching to heads of state in Africa. At other times she was lovingly teaching garland making to the small child Sonia in Cincinnati. Hladini Devi was always the same humble, gentle soul, selflessly giving all of her heart. In her glorious passing from this world she personified the perfection of renunciation. She graciously gave up her life in the service of the Lord's beloved devotees.

Hladini Ma's story is significant for many reasons, not least because it shows the caliber of devotee needed to preach in Africa and in war torn countries around the world. It shows the importance of sacrifice, compassion, love. These were qualities prized by Bhakti Tirtha Swami, and this is why he counted Hladini among his most cherished friends and mentors.

He was genuinely thrilled when she decided to come to Africa, and he made all arrangements to facilitate her service there. She, in turn, was excited to serve with him, for he embodied the same qualities that they both cherished, that they both *needed*, to preach in Africa. Indeed, trying to spread a spiritual movement is a challenge in any part of the world, but this is especially the case when Third World conditions tend to limit what one is able to do. Bhakti Tirtha Maharaja, and Mother Hladini as well, tried to show that such limitations are primarily in the mind, and that with a strict spiritual regimen, combined with a heart full of devotion, anything is possible.

Bhakti Tirtha Swami's friend and Godbrother, Radhanath Swami, offers an overview of Maharaja's accomplishments in Africa:

African preaching expanded like nowhere else in the world. Soon Bhakti Tirtha Swami was on television stations and featured in all of the major newspapers, magazines and radio shows. Prime ministers, presidents, and heads of state were approaching him for spiritual guidance. His compassion, love and determined preaching fetched him the highest civilian honor. He was made the honorary chief of the Warri people in Nigeria. In a grand ceremony, they coronated him as the king of their tribe. He had immense influence, and he became a spiritual counselor for many celebrities.

Leading world magazines had at one time voted Muhammad Ali, the famous boxer, the most popular man on the entire planet. He was another success story. Born in the ghettos of Louisville, Kentucky, he had to learn how to fight just to survive, and he made it into an art and a science, eventually becoming a world champion boxer. During the Vietnam War, he was drafted, but he filed as a conscientious objector, saying that according to his religion, Islam, he was supposed to be nonviolent. It is difficult to meet somebody so popular and well regarded in the public eye, but Bhakti Tirtha Swami not only met him but was regularly going to his house to give him spiritual guidance. Muhammad Ali was confiding in Maharaja, revealing his problems and seeking help to overcome his weaknesses. The United Nations, heads of countries and celebrities were calling on him for counseling, guidance and advice.

During the grand opening of the magnificent Radha-Radhanath temple in Durban, South Africa, the leaders of ISKCON requested Bhakti Tirtha Maharaja to come to South Africa to give the opening address. This is one of the most significant speeches ever given in ISKCON—it was historic—and it was attended by prominent religious and political leaders. Maharaja's address was enthralling, capturing everyone's heart. He spoke so powerfully, convincingly, and so charmingly. During the Food for Life inauguration in South Africa, Nelson Mandela was the chief guest. Bhakti Tirtha Maharaja gave the opening address. When he introduced Nelson Mandela, Mr. Mandela walked onto the stage and embraced him. From then on, they met on many occasions, and Mr. Mandela received spiritual guidance from him.

Concluding words appropriately come from Pushta Krishna Dasa, who was one of ISKCON's early preachers in South Africa:

When I look back at my own short time of under three years in South Africa, working and serving Srila Prabhupada during the era of apartheid, I never would have imagined that what would be ignited would be anything so beautiful or large as has come to pass in South Africa today. It is a miracle indeed. Hence, we do not know what role we might play, and we don't know what potential role any other person might play, in Sri Chaitanya Mahaprabhu's divine activity of Sankirtan. We must be cognizant that any and all people we encounter could become of great service as an instrument to this divine mission.

Such was the case of Srila Bhakti Tirtha Maharaja. Inspired as he was to first take up Krishna Consciousness, and then to pursue a life of complete sacrifice, we can see how he ignited the fire of Krishna Consciousness in so many individuals, in so many places. Especially, he boldly presented Krishna Consciousness in Africa with the sensibilities of appropriateness for the time, place, and circumstances there. With obvious style and full faith, His Grace Bhakti Tirtha Maharaja, only one man, performed the miraculous function of helping to transform the consciousness in many African countries. His determination undoubtedly gave strength to many others to persevere, even risking their lives, to present the teachings of Sri Krishna. He remained a humble servant of his Gurudeva, Srila Prabhupada, from start to completion during his incarnation as a devotee in this lifetime. We must therefore be reminded what one person can do or facilitate, if he or she only sincerely wants to. There are none more dear to Krishna in this world. Those who help the devotees surrender to Sri Krishna by teaching and nourishing their spiritual aspirations are the most beloved of the Lord.

We can thus recall the beautiful life of selfless service of Srila Bhakti Tirtha Maharaja with inspiration to one and all. He

232 / BLACK LOTUS

helped to transform both the leaders of countries and of large ethnic groups, and the most humble of people, with his example and with his dedication to teaching what he had learned and realized from Srila Prabhupada's books and teachings. We may never be able to fully digest all of this, and that is good for us. We must have those to whom we can look upon as beacons and caretakers of the true path that leads to love of God. Hare Krishna.

CHAPTER SEVEN

APPLIED
SPIRITUAL TECHNOLOGY

"The Institute for Applied Spiritual Technology (IFAST) was illustrative of Srila Prabhupada's peace formula. When a leader is able to bring people together on the common ground of the soul, the secondary really does become secondary. Not that concerns of race, sex, culture, age, etc., are not relevant or don't need to be addressed; Bhakti Tirtha Swami Krishnapada was well-known for fearlessly addressing these issues. They just become understood and experienced as what they really are: secondary."

—CHINTAMANI DASI

BHAKTI TIRTHA MAHARAJA did not spend all of his time in Africa. Rather, he traveled the world and pursued his work in other countries, too. This chapter will briefly explore the initiatory phase of those global triumphs, which centers around the founding of the Institute for Applied Spiritual Technology in America's capital, Washington D.C. This began with deep contemplation, looking for the right words, the right environment, the right approach for bringing Krishna Consciousness into a new era.

234 / BLACK LOTUS

He perceived the movement's need for a "face-lift," if you will, in which the traditions of Vedic culture could be more easily accessed by contemporary peoples, many of whom were no longer looking for alternative lifestyles or total spiritual commitment. When ISKCON was founded in the late-60s, the youth of America and Europe, especially, were rebelling against conservatism of all kinds and were questioning established religious norms. But times were now different, and Maharaja knew that this warranted a different approach. His main meditation thus gradually focused on how to present Krishna Consciousness in the modern world.

Swami Krishnapada

Meanwhile, he traveled extensively, for it was important to see how ISKCON was flourishing, and to consider both the successes and failures that devotees were experiencing worldwide. This would help him devise new means for spreading Krishna Consciousness. While in South India, which was part of an extensive tour undergone for just these purposes, Bhakti Tirtha Swami was privileged with a new title: Swami Krishnapada. Such an esteemed honorific, or its closely related variants, were traditionally assigned to the most important Vaishnava teachers in history: "Prabhupada," "Vishnupada," "Bhaktipada," and so on. These were names used by perfected masters of antiquity.

ISKCON Sanskritist and Prabhupada disciple Gaura Keshava Dasa, a burly Australian with a contagious sense of humor, knew India well, and he gave Maharaja a thorough tour of the south, which was his specialty. It was Gaura Keshava, in fact, who was largely responsible for conceiving the name Krishnapada in relation to Bhakti Tirtha Swami. Here, he explains how it came about:

I took Bhakti Tirtha Maharaja, Jagat Purusha, and Rohini Nandana on a South Indian tour one time, perhaps in the mid-1980s. I remember that on that trip, Maharaja ate very little. He had a small bag of trail mix and he would eat a few handfuls of dried fruit and nuts everyday. I don't remember him eating much more than that. I was impressed with his sense of austerity; he seemed like an especially qualified sannyasi. We toured the major places that Lord Chaitanya had visited in South India about 500 years ago.

Once on the train, Bhakti Tirtha Maharaja told me that since he was now a guru, he needed a "pada" designation, that this was the standard in ISKCON—all of his guru Godbrothers had adopted a "pada" title and so, he thought, he should as well. And so, since I know Sanskrit, he wanted to know if I had any ideas. I told him that it wasn't necessary and that the usual nomenclature of the guru is "Vishnupada," or "one who takes shelter at the lotus feet of Vishnu." But he didn't want to use that name because several other ISKCON gurus were already using it. So I said that the obvious thing would be to use "Tirthapada," because his name ended in "Tirtha" and because this is also a traditional "pada" name. He also rejected this idea because the name was used by Jayatirtha, another guru who had by that time left ISKCON.

Finally, I suggested "Krishnapada." He asked me if this was a "bona fide" title in our tradition. I responded by saying, "Well, why not? If the guru can be called Vishnupada, then he can also be called Krishnapada." I also pointed out that Krishnapada was even better, since, in Gaudiya Vaishnava theology, Krishna is the original Personality of Godhead, the source of all Vishnu expansions. Besides, it's a more specific name for a devotee of Krishna than Vishnupada.

Then he asked me what it actually meant. I said, "Well, Vishnupada means 'one who is situated at Vishnu's feet,' i.e., His servant, and so Krishnapada would mean 'one situated at Krishna's feet.'" He was very satisfied with this meaning. Then, knowing that Sanskrit words have multiple meanings, he asked me if there was any other meaning to Krishnapada. So I said "Well, krishna also means 'black' and pada, *of course, means 'foot.' So, I guess it can also be interpreted as someone with a black foot."* We both laughed out loud at this. *Interestingly, he had a black birthmark on his left foot.*

Bhakti Tirtha Swami "Krishnapada" continued his conversation with Gaura Keshava, inquiring from him about *pranam mantras,* which are traditional prayers that are tailor-made for individual spiritual masters. It enables disciples to recite personally relevant glorification for their guru. As a newly ordained spiritual master, Krishnapada did not yet have such a prayer to give to his students.

Gaura Keshava told him that the usual custom was that a given guru's disciples will write *pranam mantras* for their own spiritual master, to which he responded that his disciples didn't know Sanskrit. At that point, Gaura Keshava said that one could just take the *pranam mantra* of one of the previous gurus—of any stalwart in the lineage—and modify it so that it is germane to the guru in question. Maharaja liked this idea, and so they discussed several possible mantras. Finally, they came up with the one that is now used by all of Bhakti Tirtha Swami's disciples. The first line is a modified form of the mantra used for Prabhupada, and the second line is specifically about Krishnapada:

nama om vishnu-padaya krishna-preshthaya bhutale
shrimate bhakti-tirtha swamin iti namine
"I offer my humble obeisances to Bhakti Tirtha Swami, who is very dear to Lord Krishna, having taken shelter at His lotus feet."

namas te krishnapadaya prabhupadashritatmane
shri-gaura-karuna-shakti bhakti-tirtha iti namine
"Obeisance unto you, Swami Krishnapada! You have taken full shelter of Srila Prabhupada and are therefore a conduit for the merciful energy of Lord Chaitanya."

The mantras are explained by Gaura Keshava:

After asking me about the pranam mantra, *he said that later on, perhaps, some of his disciples would learn Sanskrit and write something more specific. But for right now he needed something for them to use, like for offering food, obeisances, and so on. So he asked me if I would help him. Initially, I just told him that he could use Srila Prabhupada's first mantra and substitute his name in the third line, which would be,* namah om vishnupadaya krishna preshthaya bhutale shrimate bhakti-tirtha swamin iti namine. *But he rejected this when I offered him a literal translation. You see, he didn't want to use the word* preshthaya *about himself, because it indicates that he is "best" amongst the devotees. And we had already decided on Krishnapada, so the* vishnupadaya *in the first line was out.*

I told him that my Sanskrit was pretty rudimentary, but that if he wanted, I could suggest some mantras based on other standard pranams. *He then asked me to recite numerous such mantras and we sort of picked out the stuff that he liked. I remember that he wanted something to remind people of Srila Prabhupada. So I told him that it is not uncommon to mention the name of one's own guru in one's* pranam. *I gave some examples: Some people mention that they are the best son, or best devotee, of such and such a person, etc. He thought that that was a bit much.*

At that point, I offered this: What about saying that you are just the servant of His Divine Grace, or a soul surrendered to Srila Prabhupada. He felt that this was much more appropriate. So instead of using a word like preshthaya, *which means "best," he opted for* prabhupada ashritatmane, *which simply means having taken shelter of Srila Prabhupada. Shri* gaura karuna shakti *is straight out of Srila Bhaktisiddhanta Sarasvati's third* pranam *shloka. He liked the idea of "the personification of Lord Chaitanya's mercy potency."*

However, it's interesting that shri gaura karuna shakti *can be an adjectival phrase, describing either* prabhupada *or* bhakti-tirtha. *So it works out both ways. In other words, it could mean, "I offer*

*my respectful obeisances unto Srila Krishnapada, who has taken
shelter of Srila Prabhupada, who is the embodiment of Lord Chaitanya's mercy." Or it could mean: "I offer my respectful obeisances
unto Srila Krishnapada, who has taken shelter of Srila Prabhupada, and Srila Krishnapada is the embodiment of Lord Chaitanya's
mercy." The double meaning is something that we especially liked,
since it allows the subject of the mantra to take a humble position,
if interpreted in the former way, but yet highly praised at the same
time, if seen in the latter way. He ended up using the first line of
the Prabhupada mantra, slightly modified, and then the new one
as a second* pranam *specifically about him.*

*I remember that he wanted to get as many divine personalities
as possible mentioned in one* shloka. *For example, by using* krishnapadaya *there was an allusion to Lord Krishna,* karuna shakti
can also indicate Radha, the divine feminine Godhead, gaura *indicates Lord Chaitanya,* prabhupada *indicates Prabhupada, and
of course his name fittingly comes last. Bhakti Tirtha Maharaja
seemed very happy with these ideas, as were the Godbrothers and
the disciples.*

He was now a fully recognized guru in ISKCON—with a "pada"
name of his own. He was also a Governing Body Commissioner,
which is the highest managerial authority in the movement, and one
of the movement's most respected devotees. With these successes
under his belt, he decided to return to his hometown—the proverbial triumphant return—and to help the loved ones of his past in
Krishna Consciousness.

Cleveland hadn't changed much, and yet it had changed immea-
surably. His mother was still there, as well as much of his family and
friends. Many of these people had not seen him for a number of
years. They were so proud of him, feeling that their "Johnny Boy had
made good." He was a world traveler, friend of the poor, master of
spiritual science, and so on. But he was still the same person they had

always known, with that same smile. But they all sensed that he now had something special, too. And now he would be there for them, to guide them in spiritual life, showing his character yet again—this was not someone who would ever forget his roots or the people who loved him. Parvati Fair, one of his early disciples, talks about his frequent visits to Cleveland:

Srila Krishnapada would often come back to Cleveland, to visit family and friends, and to tend to our Krishna Consciousness. In fact, as a celebrated guru and world preacher, he was often honored here—and around the world—in a ceremony known as Vyasa-puja, which is a traditional festival, usually held on the teacher's birthday. On Vyasa-puja, disciples show appreciation with offerings of gifts and prayers. Actually, his first official Vyasa-puja ceremony was in Lagos, Nigeria in March, 1986. Several months later, in Atlanta, Georgia, devotees honored his first Vyasa-puja celebration on American soil. There were also numerous such celebrations in West Africa during the following year, as well as in America and elsewhere.

But one of the most important Vyasa-puja events for him was in 1988, held in my home in Shaker Heights, Ohio—it was a sort of "coming home" celebration. This is when his mother, father, aunts, and other relatives came and joined in. He loved it, and it made us really happy. We were always putting on festivals in Cleveland. For example, we were regularly going to Mother Pearline's Senior Citizen Apartment Complex and engaging in chanting and feasting. The elderly people there, her friends, were so pleased with the ways of the devotees and with the tasty prasadam, too. Srila Krishnapada asked us to watch out for her, and also for his other family members and friends. So we did so many activities with Mother Pearline that she became like a local celebrity. She and her friends loved this special prasadam preparation, made from fried cabbage, more than any other. I think that's why they kept inviting us back.

Another major event was The Love Supreme Reception and

*Fundraiser, which occurred at Cleveland State University. Swamini
Turiyasangitananda (Alice Coltrane) came to Cleveland for the purpose of doing a fundraiser for Swami Krishnapada and his work. In
that same weekend, the two of them were special guests on my radio
show, called "Path of Devotion" at WABQ, Cleveland, Ohio. They
became quick friends and would periodically do events together.
He did plenty of TV and radio here, too, really big time stuff.
He was expert at what we call "bridge preaching"—that is, he was
able to help people outside the Krishna Conscious tradition work
their way in. He gave them points of similarity, points of interest,
allowing them to more fully appreciate the Krishna Consciousness
tradition. The results speak for themselves. We now see him being
appreciated all over the world.*

Institute for Applied Spiritual Technology

While in America, after a brief visit to Cleveland, Bhakti Tirtha
Swami Krishnapada established "The Institute for Applied Spiritual
Technology" (IFAST), even if his focus was clearly Africa. The Insti-
tute arose organically, as Swami Krishnapada himself recollects:

*We started the Institute for two or three basic reasons. At one point,
we had all these temples in Africa, including a couple of farms, and
we even started some boutiques and clinics. We had ten or twelve
temples just in Nigeria alone. Five or six in Ghana, Ivory Coast,
Sierra Leone, Liberia—land, temples, projects, on and on. We were
meeting many presidents, giving them books, talking to them, networking. So we got to a point where things were really happening.
And eventually we were thinking that, "Okay, we've established
things in Africa, but what have we done in America? I would come
back to America for regular visits and then I would go to different
parts of the world. But nothing was really organized in the States.*

*I was chiefly concerned with Africa at that point, but since I
was born in America, I felt some obligation there, obviously. But*

I was especially thinking that I would like to find more ways to reach the many people who, for various reasons, were not coming to Krishna Consciousness. I was thinking that we didn't have so many professional people in America—at least not on a massive scale. And I noticed that we didn't have so many minorities in our movement, either. So I started to think about forming the Institute, and Washington D.C. seemed to be a natural place. Washington is a place where at least 75 or 80 percent of the people are African American. I thought Washington would be a good place to start, and we already had a restaurant and a boutique. A few things were already going on.

We started off very small because we didn't have anything. It was just Yashoda, Ekendra, Vraja-lila, and Maha-mantra, who had come later. We were living in a basement of somebody's house, not far from Walter Reed Hospital. It had one window that you hold up, like a basement window, and we did everything from those humble beginnings. It was our temple, our kitchen, our living quarters. Women just had a little sheet separating their area, and we all just slept on the floor. And you could only come in from the back. This is how the Institute started.

The name for the Institute was casually conceived during a momentous cab ride in 1989. Ekendra remembers:

Here's how the name came about. We're getting this preaching going and we realize we have to move, because we were living out of a basement on Butternut Street. So we decided to work with the devotees on 16th Street—a really nice place. And it's in an area that's like a spiritual haven. You've got the Ba'hai right there, the Buddhist temples, everything. Really progressive. And we had a sort of inter-religious vibe, what with our Vaishnava sense of non-sectarianism and the African cultural phenomenon.

And so we really fit in; this is when the preaching really started flourishing. But right before we moved there, we did a preaching program at Howard University. This is when IFAST really got started. The program was arranged by one of the students there—her name is Chintamani. You'll hear more about her later. She and her husband, Jagannath, now live in Gita Nagari. But back then she had arranged a preaching program at Howard.

So we went. Myself, Vraja-lila, and Bhakti Tirtha Maharaja—we were all staying in that one basement apartment at the time. We just had blankets dividing one section from another. It was a difficult situation but also somehow simple and heart-warming. Anyway, we were riding back from Howard University in a taxi, and we were talking about cultivating a more sophisticated group of people, like the kind of people we had just witnessed at Howard, because these people were all professionals. They would get a lot out of Krishna Consciousness, and they could also put a lot into spreading Krishna Consciousness, too. These are people who were working on their doctorates or had respectable jobs.

Now, we were talking about how it would be really far out to create something like an Institute. This was the popular concept at the time. Deepak Chopra had an institute; there were so many. Maharaja was going on and on about it. These people are busy, he was saying. They don't want to become monks, but they could use a facility, and they could certainly use the knowledge of Krishna Consciousness and related sciences, too. So I mentioned this name. I just sort of blurted it out: Institute for Applied Spiritual Technology. And the acronym was IFAST. It sounded good, but I wasn't sure at the time if it just went in one ear and out of the other.

Clearly, Swami Krishnapada had retained both the concept *and* the name of IFAST, for soon after the crucial taxi conversation mentioned above, he made quick reference to it on the Cathy Hughes Show, a local but popular TV program in Washington. No one was more surprised than young Courtney Bullard (Chintamani Dasi before initiation), who met the devotees in 1988, soon before the Institute's formation. A graduate student from Howard University's psychology department, she received her masters degree in developmental psychology and was working on her doctorate.

By the time she saw the TV show in 1990, she was learning about Krishna Consciousness under the guidance of Vraja-lila and her then husband, Ekendra. When Krishnapada was in the D.C. area, she would also have personal audience with him, to ask questions, help cook for him, and so on. Before joining his mission, she was part of an organization called the Divine Universal Sisterhood (DUS), an interfaith society of women that was started by the African Hebrew Israelites. She was, in fact, one of the leaders of the sisterhood, part of a board called the "Vision Management Committee." Their role was to keep the spiritual vision of the organization in the forefront, emphasizing their spiritual integrity. Still, she didn't really consider herself part of any religious or spiritual organization at the time. Rather, she was "shopping," visiting assorted New Age events, African cultural presentations, and spiritual festivals in the D.C. area.

When she met Vraja-lila at a "Metaphysical Conference" sponsored by the devotees, the two women developed a natural relationship of spiritual camaraderie. In fact, Vraja-lila gradually started attending DUS activities out of respect for their friendship, if also to network on behalf of Swami Krishnapada. Here Courtney—soon to become Chintamani Dasi—talks about seeing him on TV. She refers to him here as Gurudeva, for by this time he was long accepting disciples, and, to them, this is how he was (and is) known:

> Vraja-lila and I were in my apartment, which was on Sixth Street in the Southwest section of D.C., and we were watching Gurudeva on this popular TV program—the Cathy Hughes Show. He was talking about his preaching activities and his various accomplishments. And then he said it, "We now have this Institute—The Institute for Applied Spiritual Technology."

I was shocked! The Institute for Applied Spiritual Technology! What Institute? The Institute at that time did not formally exist! He was in the interview expressing his vision as if it already happened. He was talking about our many programs, seminars, and activities—but they were yet to come! He saw it all as clear as day, but it hadn't actually manifested yet.

I remember that Vraja-lila and I were looking at the TV, and then we looked at each other, and then at the TV again. We were in shock. We felt: "Oh, my goodness! Gurudeva just announced that we have this fully functioning institute. Well, now we have to make it happen."

For ISKCON devotees, the story brings to mind an incident in the life of Srila Prabhupada, who was Swami Krishnapada's spiritual master. Soon after Prabhupada arrived in America, he was sitting on a park bench on New York's Lower East Side. An elderly gentleman sat down next to him, and the two men engaged in casual conversation. As their interaction wore on, Prabhupada told his friendly interlocutor about his many disciples, as well as about his beautiful centers and farm communities around the world. He mentioned his special schools for training children in Krishna Consciousness, and his posh vegetarian restaurants that served only food that was first offered to Krishna in sacrifice. Prabhupada mentioned all of this, but, in fact, none of it had yet occurred.

The man listened intently but wondered why he had not previously heard of these wonderful accomplishments. The answer, of course, is that Prabhupada was expressing his vision for the future as if it had already come to pass. In the spiritual world, he taught his disciples, time is conspicuous by its absence. Prabhupada often seemed to exist in this realm beyond time.

But back to the bench. Eventually, the old gentleman asked him outright: "Where *are* all of these disciples and establishments?" The wizened guru looked the man straight in his eyes and said: "Only time separates." And, indeed, all of these things eventually came to pass.

IFAST Develops

Initially, Swami Krishnapada conceived of IFAST as an extension of his "Urban Spiritual Development" program, but as it became more clearly formulated, it took on new meaning, new direction.

The mission of IFAST, as he defined it, was to conduct seminars and offer services wherein members of both ISKCON and the larger global community could support and assist each other's spiritual development. The specific "technologies" involved would include those propagated by ISKCON, drawing from the ancient Vedic system of learning, as well as on related sciences that support this system. The goal was to train "interested seekers who might thereby become God-awakened spiritual warriors."

To hear Swami Krishnapada explain it, being a "spiritual warrior" is not about military training or expertise in combative arts. It is not the "physical jihad," to use Islamic terminology. Rather, it refers to the primary jihad—the battle that individuals are fighting within themselves. Thus, a true spiritual warrior, by Krishnapada's standards, will:

• *learn the art of combating and overcoming negativity through the application of time-tested knowledge*

• *utilize techniques for spiritual awakening and survival, thus battling spiritual sluggishness*

• *implement devotional practices centered on the Lord, thereby conquering demoniac forces in one's own heart*

All of the Institute's workshops, seminars, and services were intended to promote a central theme consistent with the universal principles of love and service to God contained within the world's great spiritual traditions. Jagannath Pandit, a close disciple of Swami Krishnapada, remembers various ways that the IFAST acronym was understood in the early days:

Srila Krishnapada often used the term "emergency consciousness." He explained that spiritual life was an urgent necessity for all living beings. So IFAST kind of hinted at that. He said that people should be aware that this could be their last day on Earth, and so they shouldn't waste any time. Don't go slowly—go fast. So, IFAST. He also used the phrase: "We're on borrowed time." Of course, he personally lived his life in this way to the max, which is a symptom of spiritual advancement.

Another way to look at IFAST, and I know some of us saw it this way: "I FAST." In other words, I fast, or abstain, from material sense pleasure—I seek out the higher spiritual variety of pleasure. The Institute was about living a holistic lifestyle. We had vegetarian cooking classes, meditation, Ayurveda, health on all levels, fasting on special days, and so on. Either literally fasting or fasting in terms of performing austerities in Krishna's service for deepening spiritual growth and enlightenment.

Soon, in spring 1990, the Institute for Applied Spiritual Technology issued its "Statement of Purpose":

The time for spiritual rejuvenation is at hand and the key to success in this endeavor is for each of us to continuously apply the divine principles contained in whatever scriptures we hold dear. In that light, the Institute for Applied Spiritual Technology has been created as an outreach project of the International Committee for Urban Spiritual Development, directed by Swami Krishnapada. The purpose of the Institute is to conduct seminars wherein members of our community can assist in each other's spiritual development by sharing God-centered techniques and principles that we can use in our daily lives.

The Institute is a nonsectarian effort whose staff members represent a variety of spiritual paths, and whose foremost aim is to fan the flames of love for and service to God. In pursuit of this goal, the

Institute's seminars and workshops address such issues as:
  --Conflict Resolution
  --Psychic Defense (evaluation of mind control)
  --Stress and Time Management
  --Vision Management
  --Healing and Music
  --Death and Dying (law of reincarnation)
  --Spiritual Empowerment
  --Yoga (science of God-communion)
  --Tai Chi (and other martial arts therapies)
  --Holistic Health Care (homeopathy and herbology)
  --Vegetarian Cooking (vegan/non-vegan)
  --Consciousness Transformation
  --Male-Female Relationships
  --Youth Organizations

The Institute also sponsors an African exchange program, an India exchange program, a Central American exchange program, and settlement in Africa for those who are so interested.

With this as a backdrop, the first IFAST lecture was held on April 25, 1990 at the Howard Plaza Towers, two newly built dorms on Howard University's elaborate campus, in a community room on the first floor. Ekendra Prabhu gave that first lecture, focusing on "Consciousness Transformation." The next four lectures were given by other respected members of the Institute: Shelley Graham, who was associated with the Institute through the Divine Universal Sisterhood (DUS); Kibwe Bey, a well-connected and deeply religious person in Washington's African-American community—he also owned a health food store/cafe down the street from Howard University; Courtney Parks (Chintamani Dasi), whose connection with IFAST was ever deepening; and Dr. Cleeretta Henderson Smiley, who was also part of DUS, mentioned above.

Swami Krishnapada himself gave the next lecture on May 30 of that year. He spoke on conflict resolution, particularly on its psychological dimensions and how it can lead to spiritual awareness. The people who attended these sessions had been hearing him on radio and television in the D.C. area for some time. They were also attending the programs at the new center on Ingraham Street in Northeast, D.C. These functions were well advertised. Public service announcements were made on radio stations and fliers were circulated weeks in advance. Chintamani Dasi here explains the overall importance of the Institute:

I feel that the Institute for Applied Spiritual Technology was a significant event in American history, especially in three respects. (1) It was a successful expression of unity in diversity. That is to say, on religious, cultural, and racial levels, it helped people transcend their limitations and boundaries, enabling them to align based on the commonality of their spiritual essence while appreciating their functional differences in the material world. Closely related to this, it (2) brought people very high, transcendental teachings in a way that was accessible and appealing; and (3) it gave them a unique facility for adopting principles that are diametrically opposed to materialistic society (e.g., surrender to a personal God, vegetarianism, celibacy, sobriety, and so on).

Interestingly, IFAST really did attract people from all different religions: New Age, Buddhist, Christian, Muslim, Hindu, and others. People were given transcendental themes and were encouraged to utilize these eternal truths to go deeper into their own religions or, if interested, to explore within the faith of Krishna Consciousness. This approach honored anyone's prior spiritual experience and all time-tested approaches to serving the Supreme Lord while introducing one to the principles and practices of Vaishnavism. Everyone was challenged to become a serious and dedicated practitioner—no matter what his or her professed faith.

He made the approach very personal, and because of his broad knowledge of different religions, he was able to quote passages from the Bible, Koran, ancient Egyptian texts, and so on, to make the transcendental teachings relevant, to help them come to life. When he spoke, the audience was often astounded with the way he was able to take a topic and put a unique spin on it. This was something they had never been exposed to before, and they liked it.

Even though Institute participants were exposed to new and/or different ways of seeing and doing things (e.g., chanting on prayer beads, Sanskrit language, etc.), Srila Krishnapada trained them to utilize the new knowledge and skills that they were gaining in ways that brought meaning and positive results in their daily lives. He offered them established spiritual technologies with a distinct emphasis on practice. Hence, the name: The Institute for Applied Spiritual Technology.

He was training those who were ready to become dedicated devotees of the Krishna Conscious tradition while simultaneously training everyone to become better devotees of their tradition of choice—evidencing, as always, how he was a master of unity in diversity.

The Institute for Applied Spiritual Technology, therefore, can be seen as a module of the International Society for Krishna Consciousness. True, when it was conceived, it was not officially affiliated with ISKCON, nor was it packaged in exactly the same way. But the philosophical foundation was the same: love and service to the Supreme Personality of Godhead and to His parts and parcels, the innumerable living entities.

Other relevant components of the Institute's approach included rigorous education in Vaishnava philosophy, etiquette and practices, which is also characteristic of ISKCON temples. And just as Srila Prabhupada only gradually exposed the early devotees to these principles, Swami Krishnapada and his senior disciples—Vraja-lila, Ekendra, Maha-mantra and Yashodamayi, among others—trained newcomers in a step-wise fashion. Sometimes this necessitated adjusting details in favor of conveying the essence. For example, Srila Krishnapada emphasized glorifying God and engaging in prayer just as much as focusing on Sanskrit mantras. He also encouraged people to dress in ways they were accustomed to, and to wear *dhotis* and *saris* only when they were so inclined.

Of course, he gradually led his disciples toward Krishna and the nonsectarian cultural milieu associated with ISKCON, for, ultimately, he was representing the ancient Vedic tradition and the eternal principles of Krishna Consciousness. But had he adamantly insisted on the full Indian-flavored program right from the start, he would not have attracted many of his initial followers. This was particularly true of his predominantly African-American following in Washington, D.C. For them, he extended his compassion by implementing a process of gradual transformation, and to this end he wore African attire, participated in kwanzaa programs, and supported the African cultural movement. That is to say, for those who were not ready to embrace Vaishnava spirituality as such, the Institute still offered a surcharged, challenging and ever-fresh environment for spiritual growth.

Howard University and the Cathy Hughes Show

IFAST had certain venues or forums that served as initial springboards for its ultimate success. These were, first and foremost, the series of lectures at Howard University and his appearances on the Cathy Hughes Show, as the foregoing has clearly shown.

Howard, for its part, was founded as a historically black university, though in recent years Caucasians, Asians, and others have infiltrated its halls. Established by a congressional charter in 1867, the school is situated on Seventh Street in the Northwest section of D.C. Much of its early funding came from the Freedmen's Bureau, which was formed to assist downtrodden refugees of the Civil War, including former slaves and down-and-out white farmers. From its outset, it was supposed to be nonsectarian and open to people of both sexes and all races. It thus seemed like the perfect environment for Swami Krishnapada to inaugurate his IFAST lecture series, especially because young African-American professionals, like Chintamani, were in majority there. And they worked hard to arrange regular programs for him.

When Howard University was coupled with the visibility that came from appearances on the Cathy Hughes Show, the Institute seemed inescapable, especially in the D.C. area. Hughes, an articulate, nononsense African-American woman, was born in Omaha, Nebraska in 1947. Beginning her radio career in 1969, her first major position was with KOWH, a black radio station in Omaha. But her successes there soon won for her a position at the Howard University School of Communications, where she served as a lecturer and as Assistant to the Dean of Communications. Eventually she was dubbed "the voice of the community," because she wasn't afraid to challenge prejudicial points of view and to ask penetrating questions about national policy and established norms. As a result, she was also the center of numerous controversies and sparked vehement criticism. But all of that was good for business.

Today, Radio One, her own enterprise, owns sixty-five radio stations throughout the country, making it the largest black-owned radio chain in the nation. And, in 2004, she launched TV One, a cable television channel targeting the African-American community. TV is a business she had flirted with in the past, hosting Swami Krishnapada, among others, as already mentioned. But now, with experience and considerable funding behind her, her work with cable TV is likely to go the triumphant route of her radio franchise. Cathy Hughes is a success story without a doubt, but, in many ways, her greatest success can be seen in her rapport with Swami Krishnapada. Here, she talks about her experiences with the Swami:

I met him in the mid-1980s. He was booked on my morning talk show as a guest. And I had never, ever had the occasion or the blessing to talk to a real live swami. So this was a real treat. And, particularly, I didn't know African-American swamis even existed. I was thoroughly intrigued.

I had many spiritual leaders who were regular guests on the show. And usually when there is someone who supports good health and spirituality, especially if they're not in the mainstream media, we wanted them on the show. And they kind of found us, too.

Regarding how Swami Krishnapada specifically, initially, came on the show: I don't know if my assistant became aware of him, since he has such a large following in the D.C. area, and called him, or if his people contacted us. But I had fulltime producers who were always on the look out for interesting topics and individuals to come in and share my airway. It was WOL, 1450 AM, in Washington, D.C. It was the first talk radio station—all talk, news radio—from an African-American perspective in the entire United States.

I personally interviewed everyone who came on my show. And my first impression of Swami Krishnapada was that he was clearly a man of God. I know it sounds like a cliché, but he had a certain spiritual aura about him. I was very taken by his incredible peace, which really seemed to vibrate throughout my entire studio. It was like he brought something tangible in with him . . .

There seemed to be a deep, deep, deep—and I mean deep—understanding of life and God. It was something that went far beyond the usual guests that I had, who, again, were often highly evolved spiritual people. So that's saying a lot.

It surprised me, quite frankly, to see the genuine article, so to speak. And the first time I met him, there in the studio, I think that perhaps I might not have been as respectful as I should have been, even despite this intense spirituality. Well, let me explain. You see, I was fascinated that a tall, good-looking, well-educated brother, a black man of this caliber, was making this type of sacrifice—taking on celibacy, giving up all worldly possessions. With some people, you think, "Okay, they couldn't make it in the material world. So they adopt a rigorous spiritual path." But not him. He could have had it all. So his spiritual life was completely voluntary, and I really admired that.

I was like, "Yo, bro. Do you know you could be whatever you want to be? You can have whatever you want to have?"

But as I grew to know him, I became more respectful. He would often do my morning show, anytime he was in town. They made it a habit; his people would call me and tell me Swami Krishnapada will be here in two weeks or two months, whatever. They would notify us like that, and so I would just automatically reserve a block of time for him.

He went from the first visit, which was just an hour, to staying on the air with me for three or four hours each time. You see, I was on for four hours every morning. And he was interesting, so he could fill up that time slot quite easily. Sometimes we'd have on-air counseling sessions, where he would patiently answer questions for anyone who called in. Now, the people calling in were not always that conscious, if you know what I mean. They had no heightened sense of awareness, and maybe they weren't ready for his answers. But he would still give them his time, his heart. There were Baptists and Catholics and atheists and everyone—people would call in seeking his advice. And he could in fact give advice covering a wide area of concerns. Now that fascinated me also—his influence and his knowledge were not limited to his own tradition. He was well-versed in so many areas, from so many perspectives.

He was universal. He was—I have to honestly say—the first universal, truly universal, teacher I have ever had the pleasure of knowing. I mean, you hear this phrase, "Citizen of the world." Well, that was him. He was a citizen of the world. Not only did his knowledge, his compassion, and his love for his fellow man and woman transcend any type of religious boundaries, but they also transcended cultural boundaries. He was able to embrace all of God's creation. And he was able, I think, to touch a person spiritually without proselytizing. So that was pretty remarkable.

To be honest with you, he touched my soul, and there's not a lot more I can say about it.

Eureka!

In fact, Swami Krishnapada's work at Howard University and his stints on Cathy Hughes' radio and cable TV shows touched a lot of people, who began joining IFAST in great numbers. Usually, highly qualified and slightly older individuals were drawn from these two sources. One example was Charlesetta H. Griffin, a professional woman from the D.C. area:

I first learned of Swami Krishnapada in the early '90s through a black-owned radio station in Washington, D.C. He was interviewed by Cathy Hughes, the owner of Radio One, on her then current morning show. I was immediately impressed, not only by his knowledge of spiritual matters, but also by the fact that he appeared to be so approachable. At that time, my concept of a "swami" was that of someone who is mystical and whose message is veiled and could only be discerned by those with an advanced level of spiritual development. Not so with Swami Krishnapada! He was direct and made his message accessible to all. When he mentioned the Institute for Applied Spiritual Technology, I was very much drawn to the notion of "Applied Spiritual Technology." It reinforced to me that, through his teachings, the Swami was providing all the technical tools necessary to apply his teachings to our lives in a way that would be meaningful in our daily lives and on our quests for spiritual enlightenment.

I had many "light bulb" moments through the Swami's teach-

ings, through the Institute, his books and, most importantly, through those precious opportunities that I had to sit in his presence and hear him teach. One that I will recount is the Swami's teaching about our relationship with God. He said that if you take a drop of water from the ocean, that drop will have all the properties of the entire ocean. In the same way, we are a part of God, taken from God for our sojourn here on earth. Because of who we are, then, we have all the properties of God, if in smaller quantity. This message resonated with me in a way that was very powerful and challenged me to keep this truth in the forefront of my consciousness.

Over the years, the Institute, led by Swami Krishnapada, has created a spiritual community not bound by its physical location. It is truly a worldwide community, with devotees and supporters all over the world. I treasure all of the people I have met who are associated with the Institute, their never-ending industriousness, all of the wonderful social and spiritual activities sponsored by the Institute, and, of course, I treasure the memory of the Swami. His calm and loving countenance and warm sense of humor put all at ease immediately, and, most significantly, he lived his teachings and showed me how to see God within him, and within me as well.

Another example is Sharon McCabe Baukman, who went on to become a noted sociologist:

I first learned of Swami Krishnapada in 1990 when my youngest son, David, invited me to meet him at the Blackburn Center at Howard University, and to hear the Swami speak. David had heard Swami on the radio and knew somehow that hearing him would give me the spiritual lift that I needed. I was not affiliated with any orthodox religious group at that time, but I knew that something had to give as I was totally outdone by the first George Bush having started the Gulf War. I knew that there had to be some people somewhere who were grounded in something other than the materialistic world that was presented to us on the TV and various news media.

By the Grace of God we were led to Blackburn Center and heard Swami speak on several occasions. I remember that one of those times, Swami invited anyone who was interested in hearing more to come and visit the Institute up on Ingraham Street in Northwest Washington, D.C. It was not until after visiting the Institute that I realized that Swami and the devotees were part of the Hare Krishna Movement.

I believe that it must have been around the spring or summer of 1991 when I started visiting the Institute (a small row house) in the mornings (two or three days a week) before going to work. I remember being so impressed that Swami was truly a holy man and fully deserving of the reverence with which the devotees treated him. His countenance was full of love and peace, and he treated the devotees and all with whom he came in contact with gentle tenderness, caring and concern. At the same time, His Holiness exuded personal strength, intelligence, power and tremendous fervor for Krishna Consciousness.

Over time, I observed that Swami and the devotees practiced a strict regimen of vegetarianism, meditation, fasting and prayer. It was through the teachings of Swami Krishnapada, in fact, that I was first able to become a vegetarian. Swami taught reverence and compassion for all life, and that the Creator had provided us with wonderful vegetables and fruits to sustain life. Thus, it is unnecessary for us to sacrifice animals to satisfy our hunger. He also explained to us that due to all the negative energy and activity during the night time hours, it was most advantageous for us to begin our meditations and prayers around 4:00 AM, when negative energies had quieted down.

I continued to come to the Institute while it was on Ingraham Street to the prayer service in the mornings and sometimes to the more formal classes in the evenings. Most often, Swami gave the lessons and led the prayer songs and chanting. However, senior devotees such as Vraja-lila, Maha-mantra, Yashodamayi, and others would sometimes give the service or class. Sunday afternoons were the most well attended events and they always included a magnificent vegetarian feast.

Most importantly, however, the principles that Swami taught resonated so strongly in my heart that I truly felt as though I was being fed spiritually when I was in his presence. It seemed as if he was reminding me with his teachings of things that I already knew but had somehow forgotten. He made the distinction between material and spiritual consciousness. He taught us that our spirit-soul was the true essence of our being, and that we are not our bodies. He taught us that the purpose of returning to Earth, time after time, was to learn about God and, more than learning about God, to know God, to love God, to see God, to be God's agents in this world, and finally to return to God and to be with God through all eternity.

Swami Krishnapada taught his disciples that the aim was to embrace love-in-action; that we should learn to be detached from the results of our actions, but that we should perform our actions all the same. He taught that we should realize that service to God is evidenced in our service to others with whom we come in contact.

His Holiness was the example of what he taught. He followed the strict practices of celibacy, vegetarianism, fasting, prayer, meditation, and endurance of physical hardship. He developed and nurtured many groups of devotees to Krishna within the United States, many countries in Africa, Asia, Europe, and South America. From the depths of our hearts, we will miss his presence here on this physical plane. On the other hand, we know, in the depths of our hearts that he is an eternal spirit-soul, and that, like all of us, he is enjoying pastimes with Krishna and he is with us for all eternity.

One of Swami Krishnapada's most prominent disciples, Madh-vacharya Dasa, epitomizes the results coming from the programs at both Howard University and the Cathy Hughes Show. He also explains some of Krishnapada's methods and his general character of love and affection:

In the fall of 1990 I was driving around Washington, D.C. when I heard a "swami" being interviewed on the radio. He was talking about relationships and spirituality and seemed to be so sensible. At the end of the program a phone number was given. I was at a point in my life where I was looking for direction, especially spiritually. One week later I was in a meeting in a small classroom with a variegated group of people from all types of religious and cultural backgrounds. Among them were a few disciples of Bhakti Tirtha Swami Krishnapada.

The next week he himself was there speaking and he continued to speak weekly, Wednesdays, at Howard University. Each week the crowd grew larger so the venue had to change. After six weeks we were filling up an auditorium that seated more that three hundred people—this was on a Wednesday, in the middle of the workweek. His lectures were compelling as he gave us Krishna Conscious philosophy without actually mentioning the term "Krishna Consciousness." Within a year IFAST had grown dramatically.

In the summer of 1991 I took initiation and got married. My wife was immediately attracted to the philosophy and took initiation a few years later, receiving the name Kunti Devi Dasi. People from all walks of life were attracted to IFAST and were coming in droves to hear Maharaja speak—doctors, lawyers, engineers, new-agers, the afro-centric community, etc. Eventually, ISKCON sannyasis from all over the world would stop in to see for themselves the dynamic and dramatically successful urban preaching of Bhakti Tirtha Swami. After hearing him speak many people became his disciples and loyal supporters, who were then organized into various "cells" (the business cell, health cell, farming cell, and so on) to promote self-sufficiency. This is how Gurudeva expertly engaged everyone in realizing his vision.

The building where the Institute was housed became a place of spiritual and emotional nourishment. There were classes or meetings every evening and even throughout the day people would come by for lunch and conversation. It was a wonderful family atmosphere. Bhakti Tirtha Swami would even take us on different excursions, such as picnics, boat rides, and even abroad to help bring people together and to promote this family atmosphere. These excursions and gatherings were a powerful way of providing strong relationships and a social support system in which to facilitate our spiritual growth. He did not just give philosophy; he gave a setting in which the philosophy could flourish and be practically applied.

The IFAST story would not be complete without the Mother Indrani story. In her own words:

I was born at home in Harlem, New York, on October 31, 1926. It was now May 1990. I was walking on the Howard University campus in Washington, D.C., and I was handed a flyer. All I remember seeing was the word, "Spiritual," and the address for a meeting. I went to the meeting on time, expecting an answer to my prayers. It was the first meeting of The Institute for Applied Spiritual Technology, under the directorship of Bhakti Tirtha Swami.

Two Institute staff members conducted the meeting. They spoke of consciousness and the spirit-soul in a way that held my attention. It was a pleasant, informative evening, and I knew I would return. I attended every meeting after that.

A few weeks later, I heard that Bhakti Tirtha Swami himself would conduct the meeting. He spoke on stress management with a marvelous spiritual flair. The subject was so intriguing that I began to get a taste of "the something more." The next week he spoke about *conflict resolution, again with a spiritual flair. I was intrigued because years ago when I lived in New York I tried to give workshops on personal growth and development with a spiritual basis. Here was something to fill my empty cup.*

I found each meeting more informative than the last. I also found the meetings to be presenting something higher than any other lecture or workshop I had attended. Bhakti Tirtha Swami answered all questions with knowledge and understanding. After a few weeks, he left to travel to Africa and his staff members again conducted the meetings.

One evening one of his staff said, "God is a person." I was taken aback. A person? God? But because I had already opened myself to learning from these people, I took in the information. At the next meeting, someone in the audience asked if the meeting's facilitator was a Hare Krishna, and he said he was. Well, my mind jumped. What is a Hare Krishna? What was I getting myself into? I questioned myself all the way home. What had God brought me to? I found I trusted God, and I decided to keep attending the lectures.

Eventually, one of the staff members recommended I have a meeting with Bhakti Tirtha Swami himself. I was surprised that someone so knowledgeable and busy would take time to speak to me. When we met, I felt I could speak openly with him. I told him of my experience in the community in Uganda and of other spiritual pursuits. He listened attentively. As the meeting came to a close he said, "God knows what is in your heart." I cherished those words, because I knew I wanted to know God. He also suggested that instead of thinking that my experience in Uganda was incomplete, I should think of it as being all that I needed at that time. I should now look forward to the next experience. Then he informed me that the plans for the Institute in Washington, D.C. were being formed and that he thought I had a role to play in them. I could be of some service.

Bhakti Tirtha Swami kept an open-door policy at the Institute. That was helpful for me. I was still letting go of so many old ideas I had gathered from my various paths. He made it easy for me to understand the concepts a little at a time. Through that time I realized that my search had brought me to the Swami and to Krishna Consciousness. Now I began to learn how to serve. There was always some service to do. I enjoyed meeting the people who came to visit Bhakti Tirtha Swami after attending his lectures or hearing him speak on radio or television, and I was beginning to enjoy discussing the concepts taught in the Krishna Consciousness philosophy.

On October 3, 1990, Bhakti Tirtha Swami left for West Africa. At the departure gate he handed me a rose and said that I was the mother figure for the Institute. At the end of that month I celebrated my sixty-fourth birthday. I was beginning a new life with a new family and a loving family leader, and I was thankful.

After initiation my services increased fantastically. The Institute for Applied Spiritual Technology was growing at a tremendous rate. Bhakti Tirtha Swami was giving lectures in Washington, D.C., Maryland, and Virginia. People were crowding into our temple on Sunday afternoons. They came to Bhagavad-gita *classes, meditation classes, and training classes. Endeavoring to understand devotional service, I transcribed tapes of Bhakti Tirtha Swami's lectures. I put out a newsletter and set up the Institute mailing list. I was meeting, greeting, encouraging, and counseling. I found that many of the mature professionals who were coming because Bhakti Tirtha Swami had touched their souls had been on the spiritual search for many years, as I had been. So I could understand, encourage, and share with them.*

In 1992, IFAST moved to the corner of 9th and F streets in Northeast D.C. The new location was along a bus route and just a few blocks from Union Station. This move marked a significant development in IFAST's history. The building itself was initially discovered by a woman named Maskeelah, a member of the African Hebrew

Israelites. She was extremely supportive of Swami Krishnapada's endeavors and wanted to help in the expansion of his movement.

She brought the IFAST team to the impressive three-story complex, where they immediately noticed that the building would be ideal for their purposes, with its living space for numerous devotees and a sizeable hall that could easily be used as a large temple room. More, it was situated in a bustling up-and-coming neighborhood, where many new souls would have access to IFAST activities. At first, the devotees thought the building too expensive, suggesting a project too ambitious to maintain. They were hesitant to get involved. But Swami Krishnapada, always exuberant and optimistic, affirmed that, by God's grace, anything is possible, and that both the structure itself and the location would be ideal for expansion.

Frankly, since IFAST was now growing rapidly, the new building would be just what the doctor ordered. Apropos of this, Swami Krishnapada inspired three devotees, Ekavira, Sadachara, and Bali Maharaja Dasa, to take on the project. After all, they were young disciples who worked normal jobs and had the income to maintain such a huge endeavor. In due course, they moved in, paying rent and various other expenses, and IFAST continued to grow as a result. It was here, in fact, that Swami Krishnapada introduced full scale Deity worship. He and Murari Hari, a Godbrother from Mayapur, India, had searched the length and breadth of Calcutta for the most beautiful Deities of Radha and Krishna, to properly grace the new IFAST headquarters.

The two Godbrothers eventually found the Deities that would be called Sri Sri Radha-Gopinath, the compassionate Lord and His divine consort, who were mesmerizing in their otherworldly beauty. Swami Krishnapada, taken by their transcendental effulgence, carried them back from India himself, eventually presiding over the now historic installation ceremony in the 9th Street Center. For the festivities, Ekavira, Bali Maharaja, and Rantideva labored incessantly to construct a beautiful cabinet in which the Divine Couple would now be housed. The cabinet had to be completed in short order to meet the installation date—the elegant sliding doors alone made it unlikely that they would be able to finish the piece on time. Still, empowered by their Guru, Swami Krishnapada, they managed to do the impossible, and, in conjunction with the scheduled date, Sri Sri Radha-Gopinath were installed for all to see in the new 9th Street Center. These Deities are today cared for in the loving home of Madhvacharya and Kunti, two of Srila Krishnapada's disciples.

It was at this 9th Street location, too, where, for the first time in many years, a number of Krishnapada's Godbrothers and Godsisters visited and saw what he had accomplished. Specifically, Ravindra Svarupa Prabhu, one of the leading ISKCON devotees at that time, came there and met with him, as did many others. All were impressed. And it wasn't easy to impress ISKCON leaders, for they had all achieved numerous conquests and successes throughout the world. But few, if any, did anything comparable to what he did.

Swami Krishnapada's disciple, Jagannath Pandit, remembers that Kirtan, singing and dancing in glorification of the Lord, specifically expanded in IFAST when the mission moved to 9th Street. Such singing and dancing, of course, is a hallmark sign of ISKCON spirituality, and so its implementation by IFAST members made it clear that the two groups were really one. The Ingraham temple, to be sure, always included elements of this, with the beautiful Nimai-Nitai Deities, and even images of Jagannath, Baladeva, and Subhadra, so dear to Srila Krishnapada. But at 9th Street it was taken to new heights. Says Jagannath Pandit:

> *After a while, we outgrew the Ingraham house and found the wonderful facility in Capitol Hill on 9th Street. Now that we had a spacious temple room, stand-up Kirtan became a regular event and it was so ecstatic! Srila Krishnapada was often there leading and dancing ecstatically with us. This singing, music, and dancing was and is completely unlike its mundane counterpart. The purpose was*

for the glorification of God, singing His holy names, and having spiritual fun in the process. It was something for the whole family. Srila Krishnapada would involve the kids, dance in a circle, and form lines facing each other and moving back and forth. Then he would form a circle and have each of us individually get "on the floor" in the center of the circle and do our spontaneous styles of dancing while the others surrounding the circle would cheer them on.

Srila Krishnapada would lead us in all kinds of dance steps and formations. The singing and chanting was performed in call and response format: the leader would sing a line or a phrase, and then everyone else would sing the same. Each Kirtan was a new, spontaneous experience due to the flavor or the mood of the leader at the time. There were so many melodious tunes, and we used Indian and African djembe drums, cymbals, tambourines, and other instruments, so each Kirtan was an ever-fresh experience.

Sometimes the tempo would increase to an intense, feverish pitch, and we'd dance more ecstatically in accord with the tempo. Sometimes we would form one big circle, circumambulating together as one big family, and most of the time, the men would dance together as would the women, and the kids would join in everywhere. After more than an hour, we would be soaked with sweat. These Kirtans, depending on the program, were sometimes before or after an interactive discourse. Then of course we would all enjoy the most delectable vegetarian prasadam feasts. One time, a friend of mine was visiting from California and experienced this program. He later told me that he didn't understand some of the words that were being chanted during the Kirtan, but that it didn't matter. He said he felt the high vibrations and found himself participating and enjoying the dancing as much as we were.

Everywhere Srila Krishnapada traveled around the world, his Kirtans were a trademark and something that people would look forward to. When he led the Kirtan, he had so many spontane-

ous ways of involving everyone, even those who would not usually dance. He was always so surcharged with spiritual energy that he would have us dancing for hours, especially during our holidays and festivals. His dancing was another expression of his love and his desire to create a devotional family and community atmosphere wherever he went. Every aspect of his life exemplified these aims, through his seminars, his books and tapes, his dancing, his austerities and selflessness, making time for people, and first and foremost, by his personal example. He lived everything he taught, which made his words and his actions more powerful, because it was all coming from a profound level of self-realization, compassion, and love.

Giriraja Swami, a senior ISKCON leader, was among the many Godbrothers who came to see Krishnapada's work. His favorable impressions, reproduced here, were again not uncommon among ISKCON leaders:

I remember some years later I came to America to visit. That was probably late 1994. I visited IFAST, the Institute for Applied Spiritual Technology, in Washington, D.C., and I was very impressed by the caliber of people that he had attracted and trained. They were all so well trained, well-behaved, and competent. He explained his technique, and I was really impressed. He said that he had people chanting sixteen rounds and following the four regulative principles—no illicit sex, no intoxication, no meat eating, and no gambling—who didn't even know that there was such a thing as the Hare Krishna Movement. He just attracted them by his personality and his principles and gradually induced them to chant and follow the rules and regulations without reference to the Hare Krishna Movement.

I was very impressed, and then I realized that his novel ways of dressing and presenting himself and presenting the philosophy of Krishna Consciousness were actually potent and effective. Oth-

erwise, having lived in India and being conservative by nature, I was somewhat doubtful. But when I saw the results, I understood. As Srila Prabhupada said, "Judge by the results: phalena parichiyate." I had not seen that caliber of recruit in America. I had hardly seen that caliber of recruit anywhere outside of Chowpatty in Bombay—so many professionals, so sincere, so dedicated, so competent. It was really something to see.

Eventually, in the spring of 1995, the Institute moved from 9th St. to Harwood, Maryland. There they attracted a large, new gathering, having secured the elegant, newly built home of Madhvacharya and Kunti, a married couple dedicated to the work of Srila Krishnapada. Soon after, with the expansion of the project, many of the devotees relocated to the Gita Nagari farm community, as described in the next chapter.

Hari-Nama Press: Books for the Soul

"With the children asleep and the basement apartment finally quiet for the night, I sat at the computer screen into the early hours of the morning typing in the handwritten words scrawled across the pages of a battered exercise book. Slowly, after many years, *The Beggar, Meditations and Prayers on the Supreme Lord*, the first book by His Holiness Swami Krishnapada was beginning to manifest on the physical plane."

So writes Yashodamayi Dasi, one of Swami Krishnapada's earliest disciples. She is remembering the beginning days of Hari-Nama Press, the publishing arm of IFAST. After all, what is an educational institute without books? And what is the value of a swami, who has considerable knowledge, both realized and from study, if he does not share it with others? For this reason, Swami Krishnapada established Hari-Nama Press.

"The year was 1994," continues Yashodamayi, "and I was working in the basement of 118 W Street in N.W. D.C." She tells the story with clarity and insight:

I was working on an offering to my spiritual master for his upcoming Vyasa-puja. For at least thirteen years the Swami had expressed a desire to see his teachings in print. He saw it as a way to do even more service for Srila Prabhupada in that he would be able to be in more places at once spreading the message of Bhakti [spiritual devotion] to an even greater audience than he was reaching via television, radio or newspaper articles. He also knew he would carry more credibility among intellectuals and scholars—people with whom he was frequently interacting. In addition, he would be able to leave valuable tools with the numerous heads of state and diplomats he was counseling.

We brainstormed on the name of the company. I had presented three possible ideas, and personally liked the name "Pilgrims Press," with the idea of a footprint as the logo. Srila Krishnapada liked the idea of using the holy name in the title, so that there would be blessings on anyone who simply said the name of the company. That's how we landed on Hari-Nama Press. Hari, you see, is another name for Krishna. To me, "Hari-Nama" conjured images of Lord Chaitanya dancing and chanting. I especially liked the painting of Lord Nityananda and Lord Chaitanya—the divine brothers, manifestations of Balaram and Krishna—depicting the passage in the Chaitanya-charitamrita, which referred to them as the "Sun and Moon simultaneously rising over Nadia." So I gave the idea of a sun and moon logo to Madan Mohan Dasa, who was a graphics expert and the leading cover designer for Gita Nagari Press, the sole publisher for Satsvarupa Maharaja's books. He created the Hari-Nama logo as it is seen today.

So many devotees, disciples and Godbrothers stepped forward to answer the constant calls for help and guidance, from Archita Prabhu in Los Angeles securing a diacritic font for us, to Madhvacharya's going on a photographic assignment to produce photos for the book. Bali Maharaja posed as the model for the hands on the cover beautifully designed by Madan Mohan Dasa. Kaishori Devi Dasi, then senior editor of Gita Nagari Press, was an invaluable resource in this beginning phase, as was Aja Dasa the computer expert, along with Imar Nkeba, who had arranged for the computer and printer we were using.

After the release of his initial book, which garnered considerable accolades from professionals as well as from spiritual and political leaders around the world, Hari-Nama Press started to prepare for future publishing endeavors.

However, some ISKCON devotees had concerns about the book, as they did with the several that followed. Swami Krishnapada's vision was focused on his audience, whom he knew well. Some ISKCON devotees may not have understood his approach, which involved a certain trend toward metaphysics, psychology, community building, alien encounters, and personal dialogue with the Lord. Others, of course, loved it, and Swami Krishnapada was encouraged to produce other volumes. Yashodamayi continues:

It was full steam ahead for the production of Spiritual Warrior: Uncovering Spiritual Truths in Psychic Phenomena *and* Leadership for an Age of Higher Consciousness: Administration from a Metaphysical Perspective. *IFAST now had transcribed volumes of Swami Krishnapada's lectures, books that would help support the Institute, both financially and in terms of the prestige that comes from having published works.*

After the second and third books were published in 1996, I moved from producing the books to promoting them. Before IFAST's expansion to the Gita Nagari Community in central Pennsylvania, I helped to coordinate and produce the International Holistic Health and Psychic Fair held in Silver Spring, Maryland, at which Spiritual Warrior *and the* Leadership *book were officially launched.*

Ultimately, Swami Krishnapada would produce four series of books. In no special order, these are the *Leadership* series, *Spiritual Warrior*, the *Beggar*, and *Reflections*.

The *Leadership* series was conceived to give modern leaders—whether in the workplace, at home, or at the head of an institution, spiritual or otherwise—a new paradigm of leadership, one that is centered on love, appreciation, compassion and giving. It had begun as a series of lectures. Swami Krishnapada had been meeting presidents of countries, heads of State, and leaders in various capacities. He was concerned that many of them lacked principle-centered leadership qualities, as well as the integrity that separates a true leader from someone who merely attained their position as a matter of good fortune. He argued that leaders could and should incorporate a softer approach to good effect, and that militant autocracy would have only short-term value, if any. He had hoped his brothers and sisters who managed ISKCON might take advantage of these ideas, as well as others. Some did.

The *Spiritual Warrior* series focuses on human interaction, helping readers to deepen their relationships. It is a "how-to" series, delineating methods by which loving exchanges can come into being and eventually prosper.

At first glance, the phrase "spiritual warrior" seems paradoxical, for how can a warrior be spiritual? And yet, if we think about it for a moment, we realize that warriors fight and often sacrifice their lives to preserve what they believe in, protecting family and country. With this in mind, we can understand why those who attempt to advance on the spiritual path are often analogized as warriors. In the *Bhaga-vad-gita*, for example, Krishna encouraged Arjuna, who was, literally, a warrior, to take up arms against the forces of ignorance and fear. In the West, the heroic adventures of knights in shining armor still inspire us. So, too, does the heroism of courageous men and women who, armed with virtue and determination, set out to vanquish oppression, protect the weak, and restore righteousness. Their "weapons"—charity, patience, austerity, integrity, and an unfailing zeal not only to win their high purpose but to rescue others no matter the risks to themselves—were acquired by conquering their own weaknesses and by developing their higher spiritual qualities. These were the "warriors" that Swami Krishnapada sought to train.

Interestingly, the idea of a "spiritual warrior" goes back to his study of the Moorish Sciences, wherein the Islamic doctrine of jihad, or "holy war," is explained in depth. Swami Krishnapada believed in the "holy war" concept—even in terms of an external, physical battle—but only in the most extreme conditions. His focus, instead, was on the subtle jihad, or the battle to be an authentic spiritual practitioner in the midst of materialistic temptations. This, as stated earlier, is known as the primary jihad, even in the Islamic tradition.

His involvement with Sri Chinmoy, prior to coming to Krishna Consciousness, brought his Spiritual Warrior concept even further. Sri Chinmoy's metaphor of spiritual seekers as "divine warriors" was something that always enchanted Swami Krishnapada. The Bengali guru would always say, "Never give up!" This was his way of indicating that one must be persistent in spiritual life, determined to develop the qualities necessary for developing love of God. He would sometimes use the phrases "Peaceful Warrior" or "Warriors of the Inner World." These left a deep impression on Swami Krishnapada, and he incorporated them into his *Spiritual Warrior* series. As Krishnapada himself says:

The Spiritual Warrior conception came out of realizing that every day we are all on a battlefield—that there are constant challenges and attacks that manifest in so many different ways. One must be very careful to not become a casualty and even when one becomes wounded, they should be able to pick themselves up and to continue accelerating toward victory, i.e., self-realization.

Just as in a battle, one must not only be good at what one does, know the proper things and the proper people to associate or form alliances with, one must be just as expert at understanding what is to be avoided, and who and what the adversaries are.

Spiritual warriorship, of course, emphasizes that the biggest battle is taking place on the battlefield of consciousness. And the emphasis is that the weapons to fight this battle are such weapons as love, compassion, selflessness, and my entire list of the twelve qualities of a spiritual warrior:

-sense control and mastery of the mind
-humility
-fearlessness
-truthfulness
-compassion and pridelessness
-material exhaustion and disinterest in material rewards
-avoid idle time
-patience and selflessness
-firm faith
-perseverance
-curiosity and enthusiasm to learn and grow
-surrender to divine will

In the *Beggar* series, the reader becomes privy to Swami Krishnapada's personal prayers, wherein he cries out to God in numerous heartfelt ways. These books give witness to his internal mood of devotion, mainly for disciples but also for anyone who wants to see a determined soul in action. It might be said that the *Spiritual Warrior* books represent his external mood, his guidance on how to interact with the world outside ourselves, while the *Beggar* books allow us inside, to see what underlies the consciousness of one who surrenders to God.

The *Reflections* series, on another level, shows where his heart really lies: Here he takes traditional Gaudiya Vaishnava scriptures and teachings and makes them accessible, readable for a contemporary audience, explaining their implications for modern man (and woman).

Lila-katha Devi Dasi, one of the editors of these books, spoke about how he approached the writing process and how the work reached completed form:

In 2001, when I returned from India, Vraja-lila had mentioned to Srila Krishnapada that I had majored in English when I studied at the University of Michigan. When he heard that, he immediately sent me several manuscripts, and he asked me to engage in editing services.

In the beginning, I didn't receive too many instructions. He simply said, "Start editing." Over the course of that year, however, we exchanged many emails in which he gave more detailed instructions in relation to what he wanted. He was always open and encouraging, allowing us to do what we felt necessary to improve his books. The main instruction was to not change the essential meaning and yet to make it sound as good as possible. And that is what I did for the next four years straight. He kept sending manuscripts, one after another.

Now, most of them came from his lectures, except the Beggar *books; he wrote those separately. Therefore, the material was not new to me. As a disciple I often listened to his lectures and attended his classes. It was an extension of my existing relationship with him. I thought that the books addressed a lot of practical issues that many other ISKCON books hadn't, and I found that to be quite beneficial. For example, he often addressed the day-to-day issues that most people have to deal with, like anger, depression, and fear.*

Sometimes, for those of us not yet at the highest level of realization, we cannot always understand or apply the highly philosophical topics of scripture. We cannot always connect to them, at least not in an applicable way. We hear, "be detached," for instance. But what does that really mean? How can we take it in and really process it? So Maharaja's books would demonstrate how to work through particular issues that are keeping us, say, from chanting

Hare Krishna with attention. In other words, they would tell us how to be detached in a way that actually pertained to us on a basic human level.

Thus, when Swami Krishnapada contemplated publishing books, "practical application" was his catchphrase. He wasn't interested in dry philosophy or abstract theory. Rather, he was concerned with actually making a change in the world. To that end, he wanted to direct people to Srila Prabhupada's books, where they could find the philosophical basis for leading a godly life. He saw his own books as an addendum, as facilitating a practical, contemporary understanding of all that Prabhupada had taught. Murari Gupta Dasa, president of Hari-Nama Press, indicates that Swami Krishnapada's goals were largely realized, and continue to be further realized, as he shares some of the Swami's publishing conquests:

Bhakti Tirtha Maharaja Srila Krishnapada, following in the footsteps of his spiritual master, was determined to spread Krishna Consciousness to as many people as possible and thus presented workshops, seminars, and lectures to community groups, churches, and interfaith gatherings, along with the traditional Vaishnava programs. The outreach endeavors were enhanced by his lectures, which were converted to tapes and later into books. Hari-Nama Press was set up as a nonprofit corporation to publish his books and was entirely composed of devotees who did the service on a voluntary basis.

Swami Krishnapada traveled extensively and did many ten-city book tours assisted by devotees in the various areas who would arrange book signings, radio interviews, newspaper articles, lectures, interfaith appearances and also home programs and ISKCON temple functions. Swami Krishnapada had the ability to speak to and influence people of varying ethnic, economic, educational and cultural backgrounds. An example of this was the Psychic Fair New

Age Program sponsored by the Institute in August 1996 at the Silver Spring Armory in downtown Silver Spring, Maryland, a very large facility. Seminars and workshops went on all day, 1,000 plates of prasadam *were sold, and* bhajans, *devotional chanting, could be heard at the entrance, compliments of the ISKCON devotees from the Potomac temple. Swami Krishnapada's evening lecture was the highlight of the event, with an estimated 2,000 people attending the day's activities. Bottom line: literally hundreds of books were sold on that day alone.*

My service as a bookseller, and with Hari-Nama Press, gave me the opportunity to observe Swami Krishnapada in various settings, such as an Islamic community program in Philadelphia, a Nation of Islam get-together in New York, visiting university professors' homes, book-signings at Barnes and Noble, Borders, and also small book stores. He had the amazing ability to relate to and be accepted by people from a wide range of establishments and outlooks, and his books have this same effect.

Some examples: He was able to give a course at Montgomery Community College with the result of having his Leadership *book accepted as the text for the course. His* Spiritual Warrior II *book was used in a Christian church as the text for a Bible study group. These kinds of things were not uncommon. His new books, as they came out, were introduced by carefully planned lectures and book-signings at bookstores and colleges, at New Age centers and various venues around the world.*

Swami Krishnapada attended the large Book Expo in Chicago on two occasions and was able to do book signings and meet other well-known authors there. A full-page article appeared in the Washington Post *in 1998 entitled "Love not Lust," as well as major articles in* The Gainesville Sun *[Florida],* The Cleveland Plain Dealer *[Ohio],* The South China Morning Post *[Hong Kong],* Today *[Ukraine],* The Natal Mercury *[South Africa], and* The

Beacon *[Nigeria]. All as a result of his lectures and books. In the past few years, he has done world tours with speaking engagements at universities, where he promotes his books among students, and they sell in huge numbers—the same with interfaith conferences, business and governmental meetings, and at ISKCON centers worldwide. Also, his books make devotees all over the world.*

Bhakti Tirtha Swami Krishnapada has sixteen books in print and, as of this writing, three more ready for press. His international book team consists of translators working on the following: German, French, Spanish, Portuguese, Macedonian, Croatian, Russian, Hebrew, Slovenian, Balinese, and Italian, for he has disciples and friends in the many countries that utilize these languages. Many of the books have already been printed in these many tongues, and a few are still in the process of being translated.

To conclude, let it be said that there are certain principles by which he lived his life, and he wanted to convey these to people around the world, especially to those who would be known as his disciples. Those same principles lay at the basis of IFAST and are also echoed on every page of his books:

Four Principles for Community Building

1. Treat everyone you encounter as if the success of your spiritual life depends upon the quality of your interactions with them.

2. Reflect upon the person you love the most, and aspire to treat everyone with that same quality of love.

3. View all conflicts as your own fault first. See conflicts as a chance for growth, to clarify perceptions, and to create synergy.

4. Realize that the people in your present environment might very well be the people with whom you will live out your life, and who will be with you at the time of death.

Four Expectations of Disciples

1. Have a healthy balance between material and spiritual concerns.

2. Have strong Vaishnava relationships.

3. Be chaste to Srila Prabhupada but not sectarian.

4. Protect children, women, and the elderly.

Swami Krishnapada instilled these principles in the hearts of his disciples, not just by words but by personal example. As a result, people came from all parts of the world to join IFAST. Often, initiations were held in Anuttama's house in Maryland. This was one of Swami Krishnapada's Godbrothers who had become successful in the automobile business, and who had a huge home that he generously offered for IFAST activities and functions. Swami Krishnapada used this facility for bringing members of his community together—holding elaborate wedding ceremonies, where as many as nine couples (in one instance) would get married according to Vedic ritual, and numerous souls would become initiated into the principles of Gaudiya Vaishnavism. Truly, Swami Krishnapada pleased his Guru and Lord Krishna by these activities, and that pleasure was palpable to all who came into his association.

CHAPTER EIGHT

GLOBAL LEADER
AND CHAMPION
OF THE DOWNTRODDEN

"True heroism is remarkably sober, very undramatic.
It is not the urge to surpass all others at whatever cost,
but the urge to serve others at whatever cost."

—ARTHUR ASHE

S IMPORTANT AS SWAMI KRISHNAPADA'S BOOKS were for his
disciples, there were four in-house enterprises that were argu-
ably even more important, at least for internal purposes: the
Tour Report, the Tape Ministry, the Video Ministry and the IFAST
Newsletter. These strengthened his disciples' sense of community, for
being able to regularly hear and see their guru and to read synopses of
his worldwide preaching activities became their lifeblood, a bond that
connected them in a meaningful way. And, as Swami Krishnapada and
his followers worked more closely with ISKCON in the mid-1990s,
it was important for them to maintain a sense of solidarity, a sense of
unity within the larger superstructure of the parent organization.

Out of respect for ISKCON policy, IFAST underwent certain changes, most of them superficial. For example, ISKCON gurus gradually became disinclined to use the "pada" names, and so Krishnapada, for all intents and purposes, went back to using his prior *sannyasa* name, "Bhakti Tirtha Swami." Alternately, disciples also referred to him as "Gurudeva" or "Guru Maharaja," the prerogative of those who accept him as mentor. Overall, ISKCON and IFAST blended well, and few were happier than the Swami.

The Tour Reports and the various ministries mentioned above also served to impress ISKCON leaders, who at that time were largely unaware of just how successful their Bhakti Tirtha Swami had become. A small sampling of the many places he visited and the work he performed in those places appears below. First, several excerpts from Tour Reports will give the general flavor of his accomplishments around the world. This will be followed by testimonies from various devotees and from onlookers who were affected by his presence in their respective countries.

Though the official Tour Reports seem endless, as do his travels, the few excerpted here should give the reader a general idea of how all-consuming his activities were and how relentless he was as a preacher. Indeed, he gave precious little time to his own needs, always emphasizing the greater mission of serving God's children and sharing spiritual knowledge.

The Spiritual Globetrotter

From the year 2000 through 2004, while upholding all his former responsibilities, Bhakti Tirtha Maharaja reached out to devotees and to the outside world in dozens of countries, and that with the enthusiasm of a forest fire. Under strenuous travel conditions, and with minimal sleep, he conducted as many as six programs each day, vigorously sharing Krishna Consciousness with all those who would hear him. Observing the suffering of humanity around the world, he extended himself as an agent of change in long-standing arenas as well as in places he had never previously visited. Thus, the first four years of the twenty-first century saw him expand his global traveling as never before—he tirelessly lectured and addressed audiences throughout the world, covering between twenty to twenty-five countries in five months time, an impressive schedule that he reenacted repeatedly.

A typical Tour Report, edited only for brevity and clarity, reads as follows. As an aside, it is important to bear in mind that these reports were written by disciples. Thus, the basic language is here kept intact, so that the reader might absorb the mood and tenor of his disciples' devotion:

Tour Reports
July - August 2000

His itinerary included an important stop in Belgium, where he would teach various seminars. He would also be going to France, Austria, Germany, and Switzerland in this short time. His group arrived in Belgium and was driven to the Radhadesh Temple, which is one of the nicest temples in Europe. It is basically a wonderful, ancient-looking castle, with an attached museum, bakery, and large restaurant; the devotees are in the process of building many guest rooms and conference facilities as well. As it is, devotees have been having conferences there for over ten years. It is thus one of the most active temples in ISKCON. This is one of the best places in the movement for holding seminars, especially. The guests come from many different countries throughout Europe.

His Holiness Bhakti Tirtha Swami gave a seminar on forgiveness and on coping with depression, which, once again, commanded the highest attendance—and many other prominent and talented devotee leaders gave seminars as well.

Some of these courses lasted for five days. Maharaja's was one of them. The first day of His Holiness' discussion was similar to the one he gave in Malaysia. The special feature of this seminar was that he touched upon various altered states of consciousness: Beta, Alpha, Theta, and Delta. He explained what happens in each of these states, the problems that could arise when one is too absorbed in any of them, and what benefits are connected with being in them as well. He compared them to states of consciousness given in the Vedic scriptures: Jagat, Swapana, Susupiti, and Turiya; Jagat is the waking state. Swapana is the dream state; Susupiti is the deep dream state; and Turiya is the transcendental state. He went into detail describing how to connect with these different states as well as why one should or should not do so. Later in the week, His Holiness gave a powerful "forgiveness" workshop, where he took devotees on a guided meditation. He put them in a deep alpha state, allowing them to visualize someone they had a grudge against or ill will towards. He gave them techniques to release their anxieties and to allow themselves to forgive the person.

In the forgiveness workshop, His Holiness started by asking the devotees to share their conceptions of forgiveness and emotional pain. Maharaja helped them to use various emotional pains in a positive way. When discussing abandonment, for example, he helped devotees to see that being abandoned could allow one to become more independent, and that negative feelings could be converted to a positive outcome or seen in a positive way. He had devotees gather in small groups, wherein they were encouraged to share those times in their lives when they may have experienced great pain or disturbance. They were then asked to discuss forgiveness—to ask themselves if they were able to forgive the people who may have caused their discomfort. After this, His Holiness read quotes from the scriptures on depression and forgiveness. He made it clear to devotees that forgiveness frees one from the debilitating act of holding on to pain. It frees one to let go of hurt. It frees one to feel better and to find love.

Bhagavad-gita, he mentioned, teaches us that one should not be *one's enemy's enemy. Rather, we should see all living beings as part and parcel of Krishna, and we should love them accordingly. Additionally, the duty of the devotee is not to be overly attached or to see themselves as proprietors. Krishna is the only real proprietor. His Holiness explained that seeing oneself as a proprietor of anything plays a big role in creating depression. One aspect of this false proprietorship is the holding of grudges—we should not even consider ourselves proprietors of our own grudges!*

As devotees shared their realizations, they had tremendous breakthroughs. Some shed tears as they related their stories. His Holiness explained that the purpose of giving this kind of workshop is not only to inform people about certain spiritual technologies, but to also help them combat certain negative karmic patterns. Once again, his workshop was the most popular of the conference, no doubt partially due to the timeliness of the topic, especially in ISKCON, and it was his first time giving the workshop in Belgium. He was also a new face, many devotees had been reading his books, and so they now had an opportunity to meet with him in person. The several cases of Spiritual Warrior III *he had with him were quickly depleted.*

The devotees were so pleased with his discussions and interactive activities that they requested him to come every year. His Holiness said he was quite impressed with the quality of the audience and has agreed to include it as a part of his yearly schedule.

Paris, France

After leaving Belgium, His Holiness and most of the devotees went to the Paris Ratha-yatra festival. The Ambassador from Nepal, the Ambassador from Mauritius, the Ambassador from India, and some officials from the French government spoke, as did several other dignitaries. The weather was problematic; it began to rain at the commencement of the parade, and the rain gradually increased as the procession gained steam. His Holiness led the chanting for the first hour-and-a-half during the heaviest part of the storm. The heavier it rained, the more he would speed up the Kirtan, inevitably making it more ecstatic. His Holiness said that he was delighted by the many hundreds of people who attended. And despite the weather, very few dropped out of the Kirtan. At various points, the devotees were soaked, totally drenched, but few were bothered by it. Rather, it was such an ecstatic experience that all the devotees continued on, even though it was pouring.

That evening, His Holiness was driven to the New Mayapur project, which is about three hours away from the festival site. It is a big castle in a rural area. He stayed there for two days with some of the devotees and gave classes. He returned to England, stayed overnight, and prepared to return to America so that he could attend the Gurukula reunion in New Vrindavan.

European Tour: August-October 2003

Below are highlights of Bhakti Tirtha Swami's tour of Europe. He addressed the media almost daily on ways to minimize social degradation, increase authentic spirituality, business ethics, principle-centered leadership and strategies for world peace. He engaged in about one hundred interviews on radio, TV, newspapers and magazines. Many times he appeared on the most popular national TV stations and was covered by the leading newspapers. Several times he was the subject of full-page interviews and even front-page coverage.

Some of the TV programs aired all over CIS, which boasts a population of 300 million people. In most cities, he visited with leaders in business, education, religion, politics and social services. Maharaja was generally received as an African king, a scholar of international relationships, a Vaishnava guru and an author of sixteen books, now being translated into thirteen different languages.

While doing all of these engagements, often five programs a day, he gave classes at the local ISKCON temples, met with large groups of his disciples, and gave private audience to as many devotees in each area as he could. He gave almost twenty seminars and workshops to the devotee community and often led life-altering Kirtans. As usual, he compiled much of the media coverage for his own cable TV show in the States and some of the seminar material for his next book. After this, he began a tour in Africa and, later, Australia.

Italy

1. One week festival for Pandava Sena, the youth of ISKCON in the UK. He gave seminars for 200 students on:

    a) "Choosing Love over Fear"

    b) "Reflecting on the Agenda of Non-devotees"

Ireland

1. TV interviews:

    a) BBC Interview on arrival

    b) BBC coverage of Initiation ceremony

2. Taught a three-day workshop for sixty students on "Transforming Anger"

3. Met with Gurukulis, or ISKCON's younger generation, from all parts of Ireland.

United Kingdom

1. Three day seminar at Soho Street ISKCON temple for 150 students: "Transforming Fear to Love"

2. Course at Bhaktivedanta Manor: "Servant Leadership"

3. Class in East London for young professionals: "The Paranormal in Connection with Spirituality"

4. Workshop at six-day Krishna camp retreat: "Creating and Identifying Miracles in Our Lives"

5. Initiations

Bosnia

1. *Class on "Mission and Vision for the Devotee Community"*

2. *Public lecture on "Dreams" in connection with a drama on the same topic, 300 guests*

3. *Public book-signing program featuring the Croatian editions of his books*

Croatia

1. *Krishna Appearance Day celebration (public program) as well as Srila Prabhupada's Appearance Day celebration. Gives lectures*

2. *Workshop at yearly one-week summer camp and festival—"Conquering over anger." 350 students*

3. *20th anniversary celebration for ISKCON in ex-Yugoslavia—class on his earlier visit to the former communist Yugoslavia some twenty-six years prior*

4. *Interfaith conference in Lika—Croatia*

5. *Visit to rural community in Lubena—Lecture on "Rural development"*

6. *Meeting with politicians*

7. *Met with Croatian former ambassador to India, UK and Italy, Dr. Drago Stambuk—Maharaja encouraged him to enter again into politics but as "servant leader" with a spiritual emphasis. Gave him a copy of the* Leadership *book.*

8. *Assistant to the president was given* Leadership *book*

9. *Met with head of the Seventh-Day Adventists as well as leader of Buddhism for the country*

10. *Met with delegation from Indian embassy*

11. *Interview for Women's magazine, "Gloria"*

The first of the above reports emphasizes Bhakti Tirtha Maharaja's meetings with devotees and his mission to help ISKCON heal. That is to say, for those devotees who had difficulty maintaining vows, and those leaders who couldn't live up to ISKCON's high standard of purity and spirituality, he gave lectures and extended a special form of compassion. The latter reports show how his travels incorporated much to benefit the outside world as well. As the reader can see, his itinerary invariably included book-signings, meetings with political figures, dignitaries, media people, celebrities, as well as radio talk shows and, often, television. His demanding schedule left little time for personal concerns.

For the final twelve years of his life, it should be noted, two of his disciples, Madhvacharya and Kunti, the married couple mentioned earlier, opened their home to him, giving him much needed relief from his international trekking. Whenever he was in America, he would make their home in the Washington area his shelter. These two devotees, in particular, showed tremendous care and love. Being a *sannyasi*, he really had no home of his own, but he had many homes all over the world provided by his loving disciples.

Sometimes he would take disciples with him on educational tours, allowing them to assist him while visiting regions that both possessed rich heritages of their own but remained unaware of the intricacies of Krishna Consciousness. Such was the case when he and a small group of disciples visited Northern Africa and its surrounding areas in 1992.

Northern Africa and Israel

Bhakti Tirtha Maharaja was interested in a religious group commonly known as the "Black Hebrews." They seemed to have much in common with IFAST, and the two groups related well. In fact, members of their group repeatedly invited the Swami to visit their main center in Dimona, Israel. But due to the intensity of his schedule, he had to set aside any thought of accommodating their request.

The Black Hebrews, whose full name is "The Original African Hebrew Israelite Nation of Jerusalem," have two primary centers of worship, in Chicago and in Dimona. About 2,500 members live in

Israel—most of them in Dimona, while the rest are in Arad and Mitzpe Ramon, with insignificant numbers in other parts of the country.

The group was founded in Chicago by Ben Carter, a former steel worker who changed his name to Ben-Amin Ben Israel upon his arrival in the holy land. Carter said he had a "vision" in which he was told that African Americans were descended from the "lost tribe of Judah," Israelites who were expelled from Jerusalem in 70 C.E. After wandering for 1,000 years, they settled in West Africa and were later transported to America as slaves. Carter first established his sect in Liberia, and, in 1969, began moving his people to Israel, entering the country on temporary visas that were periodically renewed.

Significantly, Ben Amin's people founded the Divine Universal Sisterhood and the Divine Universal Brotherhood in Washington D.C., and had had a favorable relationship with IFAST. Some of the Institute's members, in fact, were originally associated with Ben Amin's group. He had even visited the 9th Street center, and Bhakti Tirtha Maharaja honored him with reverence, offering him the same exalted seat he would any guru from an ISKCON temple. So, in 1992, when the foreign minister of Ben Amin's community, Dr. Yuriel Ben Yahuda, personally approached Bhakti Tirtha Maharaja and asked him to attend their 25th anniversary and Passover celebrations in Israel, offering to pay his ticket, it was clearly time for the Swami to make the trip. He gathered several disciples and friends and prepared for what would turn out to be an extremely gratifying journey.

The plane left from Washington National Airport on April 27th without incident. But the connecting flight to Romania was delayed for almost three hours, after which it would take another eight hours to get there. After that, there was a ten-hour stopover before connecting with the plane that would take them to Egypt, affording the devotees an intermediate adventure before moving on to Israel. The time was well spent, though. Maharaja caught up on some reading and also spoke at length with the fortunate devotees who were traveling with him: Ekendra, Vraja-lila, Ekavira, Jambavati, Indrani, Sadachara, Achyuta, Nandini, Jadurani, and several others. Naturally, these were already memorable moments for the devotees, and the trip hadn't even really begun. As they waited to board the plane to Bucharest, the Swami told them of his past experiences in Romania, when he was distributing books with the Library Party, more than a decade earlier.

Finally, they boarded the plane for Cairo. It was a two-hour flight, and they were all quite exhausted by the time they arrived. Descending in Cairo was like flying into New York City. The ground below was glittering with lights, and as the plane zeroed in for landing they could see the many skyscrapers and what looked like a massive western metropolis. The old Cairo airport seemed somewhat modern compared to Bucharest, and the devotees were ushered through the immigration line in timely fashion. The devotees' tour director, Munir, was on time and escorted them to their hotel.

Driving through the city of Cairo, Bhakti Tirtha Maharaja noted how the architecture, the people, and their attire resembled those of India and black Africa, and he spoke briefly about ancient parallels between these rich cultures. During the forty-five-minute ride to the hotel, he also spoke casually with the tour guide, befriending him in his own unique way.

They arrived at the hotel by 1:00 AM, but even then there was one more chore before taking shelter of a good night's sleep—they needed to be briefed on their itinerary for their first day in Cairo. Excitement and exhaustion mingled in their bodies, as they braced themselves for another hour of attentiveness before giving way to much needed rest.

The hotel was directly opposite the Nile River, which winds its way 6,500 kilometers from its origin in the Great African Lake to the Mediterranean. In ancient Egypt (Kemet), the Nile was glorified for bringing life to the whole country. Accordingly, a few of the devotees decided to walk around the Nile before going to sleep, chanting the holy names of Krishna in honor of His creation.

The first day started with much chanting and a brief visit to the necropolis of Sakara and the pyramids, along with a guided tour of the Great Pyramid of Gizeh and finally the Sphinx. As they took in these historic sights, Bhakti Tirtha Swami reminded them that their purpose in this part of the world was to see and understand the overlap and similarities between all prehistoric cultures—how Vedic culture had at one time permeated the entire ancient world.

He began to tell his followers about the pyramids, how they served as funeral compounds for the pharaohs, kings and queens of ancient Kemet. Engraved in the walls of those magnificent structures were hieroglyphic writings describing the activities and pastimes of those great leaders. Maharaja's small troupe looked carefully, realizing that they were touring an important site connecting the modern world with the distant past. Most importantly, he told them, the pyramids were believed to house the souls of the dead. From there, the ancient Egyptians believed, the souls would go to their next incarnation. Thus, like India's sacred texts, the people of Kemet believed in the immortality of the living being inside the body, or in the principle of life after death. These hieroglyphic writings cried out these truths in numerous ways, and the devotees listened with ears wide open.

Next, Bhakti Tirtha Swami pointed out the extent to which ancient Egyptians worshiped demigods, or the angelic beings who are actually servants of Krishna from higher planetary systems. Most of the pictures on the papyrus paper, set before the tour group, indeed indicated the worship of higher entities, though they were referred to by names alien to the Vedic scriptures, the sacred literature with which the devotees were familiar. A predominant god shown in the papyrus was the sun, along with its three attributes: shape, light and heat. The sun's essence was called Amon or Amon-Ra, a name that means "hidden sun." Various representations of the sun can be found throughout Egyptian culture, in the tombs and in the pyramids. For the Egyptians, the sun was the symbol of the afterlife.

The drive from Cairo to El Minga gave the devotees an opportunity to view the countryside of Kemet. As they passed through many small villages, they were again reminded of those in India and Africa—the small fruit stands with flies landing on the edibles, and the proprietors hawking their merchandise; children begging when the buses and cars pull to the roadside; and the small houses along the landscape, looking as though they had been there for centuries.

In Safaga, the devotees finally rested, and then swam in the Red Sea. Following this refreshing interlude, Bhakti Tirtha Maharaja gave them a formal class, lasting over three hours. Here he spoke on the three most significant elements of the pilgrimage thus far:

1. The importance of devotional camaraderie. He discussed how the devotees came together to participate in the trip and he addressed their various challenges in coming along, such as raising the required amount of money for tickets and travel expenses, and arranging for someone to cover their responsibilities back home, and so on.

2. He pointed out that Egypt was now populated by Christians and Muslims, but that few if any of them were aware of the ancient knowledge of the soul, which, as the devotees had already discussed, was an integral part of Kemet's philosophical system. So far, except for their guide in Abydos, the devotees did not meet anyone who understood or practiced the ancient knowledge of the pharaohs.

3. He also noted that this small Vaishnava tour group was important because it had the ability to draw parallels between the ancient teachings of Israel, Kemet, Central and West Africa, and India. The devotees might then inform others of these connections, thus establishing the eternal truths of Vedic culture, the missing links that could harmonize the essence of each.

A short two-hour flight landed the devotees in Tel Aviv, and they immediately noticed a difference in how they were treated. Going through customs, for example, was quite an ordeal—even then, in 1992—as the officials mechanically and vehemently enacted security procedures.

Still, as Bhakti Tirtha Swami and his followers rolled their luggage outside the airport, they were greeted by the sweet smell of jasmine flowers, supplied by Dr. Yuriel and one of the princes from the Hebrew community, who brought garlands and warmth. This was a welcomed contrast to the harshness of the airport's inner chamber.

The Swami enthusiastically greeted the few Hebrew representatives who met them there, and he and his exhausted disciples filed into two vans for the two-hour drive to the Hebrew settlement known as the "Kingdom of God." Along the way, those who were still awake were informed as to why the roads were virtually devoid of street lights: to make it difficult to bomb the cities. Upon arriving in the "Kingdom," the Swami and his entourage were greeted by some of the leading patriarchs of the community. This is significant, because it was about 3 AM—they were eager to meet the young guru about whom they had heard so much. Now they could see him in person.

After a brief night's sleep, the first day started with Maharaja giving an insightful lecture about the importance of seeing Krishna Consciousness in other cultures. He spoke about its universal and non-sectarian message, and that it is not the property of any one religious tradition. During their week-long stay, the devotees received royal treatment; all members of the community were extremely attentive to their needs. Twice daily, in fact, they were offered the most magnificently prepared meals—the Black Hebrews are strict vegans—and would, in turn, offer the food to the Supreme Lord, transforming it into *prasadam*. They then feasted on the remnants.

Maharaja met with Ben Amin, and they discussed the universality of spiritual knowledge. The Hebrew leader also recommended important places to visit in the general area. Accordingly, the next few days were full of activity: King Solomon's pools, Mount of Olives (where Jesus was betrayed with a kiss from Judas), the Garden of Gethsemane (where Christ prayed just prior to being betrayed), the Dome of the Rock (where Abraham attempted to offer his son Isaac to the Lord as a sacrifice), the Valley of the Dead, and, after all of this, they arrived in the city of Jericho.

Jericho is celebrated as one of the oldest cities in the world. Today, it is mainly occupied by Palestinians and Muslims. This is the place, the devotees were told, where Joshua marched with his people and broke down the walls with their intense sound vibrations. Maharaja used this story to emphasize the power of sound. A few properly chosen words can change a person's whole outlook on life, and powerful mantras can change one's consciousness. Externally, the name of God appears like just another word—but it can transport a person to the spiritual world.

The devotees also made stops at the Church of Ascension (where Christ ascended into Heaven) and the Mount of Temptation (where he was tested by Satan and fasted for forty days and forty nights). Maharaja spoke on each of these events, using analogies and teachings from the Bible and from Vedic texts.

The devotees were next brought up into the hills and found an ancient African village. The Prince of the Black Israelites explained that this village has a population of 5,500 indigenous African people who never left their land. They are northeastern African people, mostly farmers, and are largely observant Muslims. They support themselves by raising goats, from which they get milk and cheese, and also with sheep, providing wool. They also engage in vegetable farming. The natives in this village looked like they could have come from anywhere in West Africa—but they were here, in Israel. Maharaja affectionately interacted with the northern Africans, and was fascinated by the implications of their very existence.

Jambavati Dasi, a disciple who was fortunate enough to have traveled with him on this trip, offers her own reflections:

What stands out for me was Swami's spiritual commentary on the places we visited. The most significant thing I recall was that he was always contrasting the spiritual significance with the material, pointing out that unlike India and a few other places around the world, many Egyptian landmarks and places of worship had been lost. The contrast being that age-old religious practices and places of worship in India were still intact.

During this trip Vraja-lila would arrange for Swami's vegetarian diet. She would personally instruct the cooks on our spiritual diet restrictions and oversee the cooking. Sometimes she was allowed access to the kitchen to help prepare the food. En route to Israel there were several adventurous stopovers. Once, while in the Hebrew Israelite community, during morning services, Swami was leading the Vaishnava prayers and just before the ending we noticed tears streaming from his face. We were puzzled but nobody questioned his emotional mood until we returned to the U.S. He later told us that Srila Prabhupada had shown him a vision of so many people suffering in the material world. We realized that they were tears of global compassion.

When we returned to Washington, D.C., we were greeted by a welcoming party of senior and aspiring devotees and friends from the Institute. Upon exiting the gate, each returning traveler was presented with a fresh flower garland. We were equally elated to discover that Bill (now Bali Dasa), had secured a multi-passenger vehicle that accommodated all the travelers and their luggage from the airport back to the Institute, where we were welcomed by a huge prasadam *feast! Not more than two weeks later, on May 19, 1992, I was officially initiated by Maharaja and given the spiritual name Jambavati Devi Dasi.*

The journey to Egypt and Israel was especially gratifying for Bhakti Tirtha Swami, who used the trip to learn more about plate tectonics, a theory already mentioned in a previous chapter. It was on this excursion that he confirmed several prehistoric connections between India and Africa, including Egypt. Hladini Shakti Dasa, a disciple of Tamal Krishna Goswami and a scholar of African religions, talks about the implications of the Swami's travels:

Scholars have uncovered clear connections between India's ancient Vedic culture and the highly developed cultures of ancient Egypt (Kemet), Ethiopia (Abyssinia), Meroe, Punt, Cush, and Somalia. For example, it has been noted that in ancient times, many royal lineages in Africa have had notable figures bearing names identical to those found in the Vedic culture of India, names such as Manu, Surya, and Soma, kings of ancient Africa. The Egyptian culture attributes its origin to a descent from the solar deity Aton, whom they worshipped as "the God of Gods" and "Father and Mother of all." They considered the sun to be the eye of God, a conception not unlike the Vedic conception of the sun and moon as God's eyes. It's notable that in Orissa the temple to the solar deity is called Konnark, remarkably similar to the name of the ancient African temple at Karnak, wherein was worshipped the solar deity Amen-Ra of the Egyptians. Note, too, that in the Vedas, Vishnu is known as a solar Deity.

Also, there is speculation that the name Somalia derives from the Vedic moon god, Soma. Dr. C. Hromnick has demonstrated that the Near Eastern kingdom of Mittani was culturally Vedic, much akin to that of India. Members of its royal lineage married members of the Egyptian royal lineage and in some cases ruled in ancient Egypt, propitiating the same gods, with the same names, and the same functions as was traditionally done in India. Research suggests that the two civilizations held other cultural phenomena in common: vegetarianism among the higher classes (especially the priests); claims that the kings and queens descended from either the solar or lunar planets; the priest's tonsure (shaven head with a single, prominent lock of hair, much like Vaishnavas of India); rites of initiation; worship of ancestors (extended family included deceased relatives who were venerated and depended upon to ensure the family's well-being, and whose well-being, including needs such as food, drink, and raiment, it was the responsibility of the living to provide); a pantheon of demigods and demigoddesses (servants of the one God); belief in reincarnation and concomitant laws of karma, immutable except for divine or magical intervention.

During his many years in Africa, Bhakti Tirtha Swami knew and developed a rapport with many African priests and holy men. Much of their wisdom is passed down through oral tradition. Because he was trusted and held in such high regard by these persons, he was often made privy to the knowledge ordinarily reserved only for their duly qualified initiates. For example, representatives of the Akan priesthood in Ghana told Bhakti Tirtha Swami that their deities, sacred rituals, rites of initiation, and even their sacred words of power were an inheritance from ancient Egypt. He was further told that these had been carefully preserved in an unbroken, oral lineage from that great civilization. During his sojourn in Northern Africa, he learned that much of this was true. He noted many similarities at that time. The use by African priests of the ceremonial whisk, the fire-bearing lamp, the incense, and various other items in their worship were similar to or identical with practices he was familiar with from the Vedic tradition.

The Black Hebrew Israelite experience was not uncommon, at least in terms of IFAST having meaningful interaction with other religions. Bhakti Tirtha Maharaja had long had a penchant for interfaith activity. To this end, he had numerous exchanges with Reverend Frederick Massey (of the Galbraith AME Zion Church), Tariq Saleem Ziyad (of the Al-Warith Deen Islamic Center), Shekhem Tepraim Saa (of the Ausar Auset Society), Reverend Carolyn Boyd (of the Spirit of Truth Center), the Buddhist Society in Potomac, Maryland—the list goes on and on. The Swami developed deep relations with members of these groups and others like them, lecturing to their congregations and showing the harmony that exists between all genuine spiritual revelations.

He also expanded his interfaith preaching into corporate leadership, networking with motivational speakers and New Age gurus such as Stephen Covey, Marianne Williamson, Ken Blanchard, and others. In fact, Ken Shelton, founder of Executive Excellence, a nearly two-decade-old training and publishing firm that features the best in values-based personal and team development, ethical management, and principle-centered leadership, says that the Swami's "work on leadership sets a new standard, expressly because it explores the spiritual dimension in ways that popular gurus like Stephen R. Covey, Kevin Cashman, and Ken Blanchard have not done."

Equally important, an endless stream of devotees would find themselves traveling with Bhakti Tirtha Maharaja, or inviting him into their home or temple, and they would benefit greatly from his association. Wherever he went, he would both absorb and convey the truths of Krishna Consciousness. Whether this occurred in an ISKCON environment, while preparing some media event, or when visiting an alternate religious community, his company kept everyone in proximity enlivened in Krishna Consciousness, and theirs kept him enthused as well.

Loved Around the World

Bhakti Tirtha Maharaja favorably influenced people throughout the world. Though a plethora of anecdotes could be quoted to show his positive, wide-reaching affect on numerous souls, a few representative stories will have to do, given the space constraints of the present volume. To begin with but one example, Bhagavatananda Dasa, a disciple of Srila Satsvarupa Dasa Goswami, remembers when Maharaja visited Jamaica:

In January of 1997, Bhakti Tirtha Swami was conducting a preaching tour in the Caribbean. He was moving through Trinidad, Surinama, and Guyana, all of which have long-standing es-

tablished ISKCON temples, with many initiated devotees, large congregations, etc. As usual, he was very well received by the respective devotees, to the extent that Maharaja was flown in someone's private jet from Surinama to Guyana.

Around the end of January, Maharaja's secretary phoned to tell us that the Swami wanted to come to Jamaica for a three-day preaching trip. With five days to prepare, the Jamaican devotees (all five of them) moved into high gear like I'd never seen them do before. Louie, a wealthy businessman, transformed overnight one of his homes into a first-class temple, complete with Krishna-lila paintings and transplanted sacred tulasi bushes (they grow wild in Jamaica). We all took up residence there, awaiting the Swami's arrival.

On February 3rd, we drove to the Kingston Airport to receive him. Normally, I was accustomed to seeing him always surrounded by servants and well-wishers, so I was quite surprised and touched to see him crossing the tarmac solo, pulling his little suitcase behind, coming to meet the people of Jamaica. We drove back to the "temple" and discussed the preaching activities, after which the Swami took rest. We had gotten a very nice picture of him, along with a short biographical sketch, into the main newspaper of the area, so the word was out—an "African swami" had come to Jamaica!

The next morning (Mon.) at 7 AM, the Good Morning Jamaica TV crew arrived and conducted a very lively interview with Maharaja. That evening Maharaja attended two home engagements, one at the home of Dr. Mansingh, an Indian gentleman and leading figure at the University of the West Indies (UWI), followed by a very sweet meeting with Mr. Duncan Hughes (an elderly Jamaican who met Srila Prabhupada in Miami in 1975) and family. On Tuesday, we drove across the island for a live radio broadcast in the afternoon. The call-in "Questions and Answers" session was very provocative, with some Christians trying to belittle the Swami's philosophical outlook. But he very tactfully fielded their questions *and surprised them by using various biblical passages to support his overall presentation.*

The interview completed, we then drove back to Kingston for a presentation at UWI, with just over 100 people attending. As Maharaja concluded and rose to leave, many of them walked with him to his car, unwilling to break the connection until the last moment. For our concluding program on Wednesday, we had rented a reception room in a very nice Kingston hotel called the Terra-Nova. Because everything was happening with practically no advance notice, we did not expect more than seventy-five people to come that evening. But we soon had to shift to a larger, outdoor space for the more than 200 people who gradually arrived.

It was a very diversified group, with many lawyers, doctors, and other professionals attending (the wife of the prime-minister was there), as well as many different spiritualists (yoga societies, Rastafarians, and so on). With the completion of Maharaja's talk, as the people filed out, they bought every single book and ate every bit of prasadam *on our table. Come Thursday morning, we drove Maharaja back to the airport, and off he went, leaving the Hare Krishna mantra buzzing all across Jamaica.*

Kaishori Devi Dasi, one of his disciples in Mexico, remembers the impact he had on several of his visits to her hometown:

The most wonderful thing was to see him preaching on the "battlefield." He came to Mexico City in 2002, and he was giving a Bhagavad-gita *class. The temple was packed because everybody knew that Bhakti Tirtha Swami would be there. Suddenly, there was an earthquake. The lights were moving profusely, and the devotees became afraid. Mothers were anxious and children were crying. Guru Maharaja just remained seated and continued speaking to comfort the devotees. Suddenly the lights went out, and we couldn't see a thing. But we never stopped hearing Guru Maharaja soothing*

298 / BLACK LOTUS

us with his voice and reminding us to always think of Krishna and never forget Him. Normally when there is an earthquake in Mexico, we have been trained to get out of the building as fast as possible. But this time, we felt so protected just listening to Gurudeva that nobody left the room and the curtains of the Deities remained open.

The exchanges of love between Guru Maharaja and his disciples were always very sweet. Every time he would leave for another country, all his disciples (non-disciples and well-wishers as well) would accompany him to the airport. Before leaving you would see tears in many devotees' eyes. We would all be standing in a sort of informal line, and he would go to each disciple and give him or her a flower from the garland he was wearing. Later he would remind us that the guru comes with a particular message and that when he leaves, separation allows us to think about his message, to try to advance more, so that next time we see each other, it's on another, higher level. The next time we reunite, he would tell us, we should be in a higher state of consciousness. Then, after saying these words, he would catch his plane as we stood by, watching him leave for his next preaching engagement. But before disappearing from our sight, he would turn around and send us all a kiss with his hand.

I had an especially memorable time with Guru Maharaja in 2001. I had come to America from Mexico to stay in Gita Nagari during my summer break from University, and also to travel to the different temples and Ratha-yatras in the area. Guru Maharaja invited Paramdhama and me to go to Cleveland with him. So we did, but we could have never imagined that we would be receiving so much mercy. Gurudeva is originally from Cleveland, and he took us on a tour of all the important places in his life—like the place where he was born, his sister's house, the first place where he chanted Japa, the area where he lived as a child (the house was being torn down), the place where he would preach as a child evangelist, his primary and middle school. He even took us to Hawken Academy, the prestigious school he attended before being accepted to Princeton. He felt that, as his disciples, we would appreciate seeing these things, and we did. For us, these were places of pilgrimage.

The Gurukulis, or "*kulis*," as they're sometimes called, were quite dear to Bhakti Tirtha Maharaja, and they loved him as well. These were the children of Prabhupada's disciples, the "second generation," as it were. They had gone to Gurukula, or the ISKCON schools around the world. Gaura-vani Dasa, a leader amongst the Gurukulis, has fond memories of Maharaja:

I remember Bhakti Tirtha Swami walking into the Gurukula re-union in Los Angeles and he was shining. Honestly, he was always shining, wasn't he? He was wearing a mix of African and sannyasa dress, and was followed by a disciple and a god-brother or two. He was leading the little group. He always seemed to be rushing ahead of everyone as if his stride was just a little bit wider. This was the first year that the Gurukula reunion was held at "the hill," a public park in Culver City—years before the court case and years before most devotees were focusing on the role of the second generation.

Anyway, he sat down and started chatting with the kids, just trying to do what they call in the film biz, "a recky"—research to figure out what was going on with the kids for himself. I saw all of the oldest, coolest and most jaded kulis giving him deference and respect, and talking with him from their hearts. I remember that when I first saw him he seemed like someone I had known for a very long time, and that he knew me really well. I can't explain it, as I had never really seen him. But every time after that, I had the same feeling, like he knew much about me that I didn't. I was too young and in my own world at the time to want to be involved in the discussions, but I took special notice of this shining black swami. Very cool.

A couple of times Bhakti Tirtha Maharaja attended the Srila Prabhupada Vyasa Puja in the temple in Potomac. He was often traveling so it was a treat to see him. During Kirtan he played a round drum that was light enough so he could hold it in his left hand while striking it with a mallet held in his other hand. He would dance like an athlete. During one Kirtan he was feeling so ecstatic. The Kirtan leader built to a crescendo and reached the breaking point of the Kirtan and then stopped. Not Bhakti Tirtha Maharaja. He continued banging his drum and dancing, his head bouncing back and forth. I was playing the mridanga *drum and when I saw Maharaja's mood I joined him and just kept dancing and playing the drum. The whole temple room was silent watching Maharaja dance. It only lasted a few extra moments, but we played and danced together, lifting our knees high and hopping around the temple room. Someone snapped a picture of us dancing, too. We are both in midair, smiles stretching our faces. I can't explain how honored I was to get caught in his ecstatic mood, even for that moment. That moment still exists for me.*

Vakreshvara Pandit, renowned throughout ISKCON for his melodious singing voice and his enthusiasm for Kirtan, reflects on his relationship with Maharaja as well as Maharaja's absorption in the holy name:

There was an incident when he came to Puerto Rico. That was an extremely special visit because he was always promising to come, but he never seemed to be able to make it. He'd always say, "I'm coming now. Oh, Vakresh, I'm coming down." After awhile, I'd just say, "Yeah, sure." He said it so many times that I just became sarcastic in my response every time he called me. But, one day, he said, "You know what? Since you don't believe me, I'm just going to show up one day at the airport. That's right. One day, when you least expect it, you're just going to have to come pick me up at the airport." So I said, "Okay, Maharaja. Alright. Whatever you say."

So, one day in 2003, I got this phone call out of the blue. He would call me at least every couple of months and play this game with me. So he calls up. "Alright Vakresh, alright. You didn't think I would come, huh?"

"Sure, Maharaja. How are you doing?"

"No, no, no," he said. "I'm really here. I'm at the airport. I'm really here." I didn't believe him, and I kept answering him like I knew it was all just a joke. Well, this went on for about five minutes and he really got upset. He was like, "Look, I'm in the airport. Are you going to come get me, or not?" Apparently, there was one of our Puerto Rican devotees there at the airport. He got him on the phone and said, "Hey, come tell him I'm here." And then all of a sudden I find out that he's really at the San Juan airport. I said, "Oh my God, you're really here."

We rushed down and got him, and brought him up to the temple. Now, I had always told him about this great rainforest here, in Yunkue, and that I would take him up there. It's really an incredible place. Beautiful waterfalls cascading off of these huge rocks into crystal clear pools. Some of them would squeeze between waters and then jut out. It was like a natural jacuzzi spray, and there were beautiful parrots, coconuts, and all kinds of fruit trees, mango trees, coconut trees, papaya trees. So he was anxious to go. But it's not a simple task to get there, and I told him that. It's not like going to the beach and running into the water. You have to climb.

Anyway, to make a long story short, we climbed these rocks and went down into this one particular area. It had just rained a few days prior, so the current was strong. The water runs right off the rocks. It's really pretty powerful; you have to be very careful. The rocks are slippery and you could fall or get swept away. So, I went out there and climbed across the rocks, and then gestured to Maharaja that he should follow me.

Now, we get half way out into this area where we are at a point in which we have to go into the water, and you've got to be really *careful. You have to swim kind of strongly against the current to catch on to the next rock to get across. So, we're already out there and Maharaja says, "Hey, Vakresh, I need to tell you something. This is something that might be kind of important right now." So I said, "Well, alright, okay, Maharaja. No problem. What's up?" And then he lays it on me, "You remember I once told you I was kind of a mama's boy? Well, you're about to find out what that means: I can't swim."*

I said, "Damn, Maharaja. We're in the middle of this heavy-duty situation here, and now you tell me you can't swim?"

At that point, we couldn't turn back; we were in a predicament where I had no choice. So he grabbed onto my shoulders and I got him across. But while we were there, getting across this difficult rockslide and body of water, he said, "You know, actually, if we don't make it, we'll just go down together, chanting the holy name." And he had this huge smile on his face.

And speaking of the holy name, here's another story: Part of his nature was total absorption in Kirtan. And we would compete in a sweet way: who can dance the longest? Who could just really get more into it? That kind of thing. Now, when one becomes so absorbed in the holy name, he's blessed by Krishna in a particular way; he worships Krishna in a particular form, and he becomes a madman, not caring for public opinion.

Well, Maharaja was really a victim of that. He had it really bad. And so when we would meet in Kirtans—Ratha-yatra, largely at Ratha-yatra festivals, but at other big events, too—we would always hook up and get into it together. Well, there was a recent Kirtan at a Ratha-yatra. I think it was 2004 or maybe 2003. Maharaja was singing and dancing, and he was kicking his feet so high in the Kirtan; it was actually amazing. After the completion of the Ratha-yatra, we were in the park and I think Vaiyasaki was leading the Kirtan. They were on the stage. And so all the devotees had filed into the park and were dancing like mad. And something happened. The Kirtan went into that special zone of no return. You know what I mean—that ecstatic place that only devotees know about. There are these certain levels experienced in Kirtan where one really become almost like totally egoless—just gone. The holy name takes over.

I was watching Maharaja and something happened to him. He looked like he was having a heart attack. He was stunned and his eyes were wide, wide, wide open. And he just kind of froze, and no one knew what to make of it. But everyone kind of stopped looking at him after awhile and just went on with this uncontrollable Kirtan. He kind of stumbled back against the stage. I kept looking at him, though. And I noticed something. I watched him for about ten minutes. He was standing there as if he didn't know where he was. But the look on his face—I realized that he was experiencing a high level of ecstasy.

He was looking around like he was seeing the world for the first time, like he was given a special vision. Finally, he looked like he was just trying to gather himself, trying to regroup and come back to the external world. And then he came right back into the Kirtan and started dancing like a madman again. I asked him later what it was all about and he was embarrassed by it. He said, "Well, you know, I'm sorry you had to see that." But I wasn't sorry. It was one of the most beautiful things I had ever seen.

Working for the Disenfranchised

Bhakti Tirtha Maharaja's greatest accomplishments, both inside and outside of ISKCON, were on behalf of the misunderstood or the ostracized. He disliked chauvinism and fought against the charge of inequality, even in its most subtle manifestations. This included mounting strong defenses for people who were viewed as second-class citizens—the disenfranchised. There are numerous examples of this, and, in a previous chapter, his work for underprivileged children—feeding, schooling, clothing, and protecting them—was briefly mentioned. His work for African Americans, of course, has been a focus throughout. There are two other categories that would have significance here as well: homosexuals and women. Both are groups that are often misunderstood if not considerably demeaned in traditional cultural milieus.

Sexuality is a complex subject in general but even more so in the Vaishnava tradition with which Bhakti Tirtha Maharaja aligned himself. The tradition lauds celibacy as a way to break free of material attachment, to gain mastery over the body and mind, to overcome the illusions associated with irrational passions. Still, the tradition acknowledges that most practitioners will not be able to accommodate this high ideal. And so it gives allowances and concessions for individuals, according to their level of consciousness and their station in life, ranging from conservative to liberal.

Bhakti Tirtha Maharaja, like any discerning guru, thought deeply about how to accommodate devotees who might live slightly "outside the box." And so we begin with a brief discussion of his compassion for homosexuals, the first of the two groups under consideration. While they are often shunned in traditional religious settings, he saw them as spirit-souls, in the same way that heterosexuals are spirit-souls. Indeed, Bhakti Tirtha Maharaja taught that whatever one's sexual orientation, the real chore of existence is to become free from the bodily concept of life. It is this fundamental misconception—thinking the body to be the actual self—that needs to be addressed, not one's sexual preference. If a person can overcome this illusory view of their underlying identity, then sexuality becomes less important.

He often told his disciples that, overall, sex is the main binding principle in the material world, and that the intoxication associated with its many pleasures tends to keep us here lifetime after lifetime. Thus, whether one is a heterosexual or a homosexual, sex, as stated previously, should be utilized only for one specific purpose: procreation. Animals, on the other hand, are free to engage in sex whenever they like. But humans can control the sex urge, using their energy and intelligence for higher purposes. If they don't, they have missed the special prerogative of human life.

Homosexuals, therefore, should not be singled out. If heterosexuals misuse their sexual organs for purposes other than procreation, taught Bhakti Tirtha Swami, they are guilty of abuse, plain and simple. Rather, it is better to be a chaste homosexual, with one partner, than to be a promiscuous heterosexual. "What about sex as an expression of love?" one might ask. The Swami believed that such a thing is rare—more rare than most are ready to believe. But if two people genuinely felt such love for each other, and wanted to pursue spiritual life together, they could then certainly engage in sexual relations without harm.

But *would* they? Because there are numerous ways for two people to show love and affection, and because the bulk of one's energy is meant to be used in the service of God, sex would naturally be de-emphasized in favor of devotional service. This was Bhakti Tirtha Swami's main point.

His support of gay devotees bore this out, and was especially noticeable in his interaction with the Gay and Lesbian Vaishnava Association (GALVA). The president of that organization wrote the following letter in appreciation of the Swami's work and attitude. He received the letter just a few months before his illness took his life:

February 2, 2005

Dear respected Bhakti Tirtha Maharaja,
Please accept my humble obeisances. All glories to Srila Prabhupada and all Vaishnavas!
I have been following your health situation over the past few months with much concern and empathy. Your situation is no doubt one we will all pass through. However, I must say, after read-

ing all of your beautiful letters full of realization and detachment, I'm confident that your life and soul are directly in the hands of Srila Prabhupada and Krishna.

I was disappointed that I did not get to see you while you were in Hawaii. Your disciples told me that you were undergoing treatment and were not well enough to see visitors. My hope is that you may return to the Islands; however, if you are unable, I thought it important that I write you this letter.

Maharaja, you have been an inspiration to so many people and devotees all over the world! I will present my own story here. I first met you in the late 70s and early 80s when you had a small preaching center in D.C. At that time I was a head priest at the Potomac temple, and I always remember how especially ecstatic the Sunday feast Kirtans were when you and your disciples would arrive. The dancing and chanting of Hare Krishna were simply out of this world!

The next time I met you was many years later on the Big Island, where you gave a lecture at the University of Hawaii (Hilo). In that lecture you made an enormous impact on my life and planted an important seed within my heart. You challenged the audience to preach Krishna Consciousness in innovative and effective ways to all members of society. You specifically requested that we should preach to the gay and lesbian community, try to understand them, and find out how to inspire their Krishna Consciousness in the most effective way possible. That request had a big impact on me and I thought about it for a long time, years actually. In reality, it was the beginning of GALVA (The Gay and Lesbian Vaishnava Association). I was very impressed you had the compassion and magnanimity to include this up-until-then ignored social class within your call.

Later that night (or was it the second time you came to the Big Island, when we went down into Waipio Valley?), you happily joined in dancing with the devotees. It was an ecstatic Kirtan and we danced together for quite a while in the celebration of Krishna Consciousness and the holy names. How wonderful that time was! I felt a deep, spiritual connection with you.

After contemplating your instruction, I eventually began jotting down ideas on how to present the third gender to the devotees and remind them of Srila Prabhupada's example of all-inclusiveness. That inspiration went from a few notes, to an article, to a website, to an e-group, to the incorporation of GALVA, to even a book, and so on. I have personally witnessed many devotees made, revived, renewed, resuscitated, etc., from that first simple instruction you planted within my heart so many years ago. I thank you for that inspiration and will always be eternally grateful and indebted.

Your unique and insightful style of preaching has always been much needed within our movement. When I first heard of your illness, I must admit I was quite despondent after contemplating the special void your departure would leave in its wake. Nevertheless, I am certain that your contribution to ISKCON has had such an impact that your presence will be felt far into the future. I'm also certain that your disciples will continue to spread Krishna Consciousness with the same love, compassion, care, innovation and enthusiasm you have always demonstrated.

Therefore, with the deepest, heartfelt gratitude, all of the members of GALVA send our love and thanks to you. We have truly been blessed to have your association here on earth. You have been a wonderful Godbrother, guru, teacher, friend, and servant to the world.

With much love and affection,
Amara Dasa,
Gay and Lesbian Vaishnava Association

His support of women in ISKCON is in some ways even more complicated than his support of homosexuals. Traditional Vaishnava culture reveres feminine energy as a powerful force, able to penetrate the essence of Krishna Consciousness or to distract one from pursuing it, depending on how the energy is channeled. Thus, women are traditionally seen as goddesses, but also as temptresses. Overall, however, they are respected as mothers of humankind, the first guru a child sees when coming into the material world. And so they should be honored as one would honor the spiritual master. As the Vedas say, "Where women are esteemed, the demigods rejoice."

ISKCON, to be sure, always accepted this positive view of womanhood, at least intellectually. In Prabhupada's commentary to *Bhagavad-gita* 9.32, he emphatically states, " . . . in devotional service there is no discrimination between lower and higher classes of people. In the material conception of life there are such divisions, but for a person engaged in the transcendental service of the Lord, there are not." He also specifically addressed the notion of women devotees, claiming that, in Krishna's eyes, they are equal to their Vaishnava brothers.

Many in Prabhupada's movement, however, unfortunately harbored sexist views as well. They belittled women, often holding them back from meeting their potential. The result was that nearly half the movement felt under-appreciated, at best, or terribly abused, at worst. Clearly, the seeds for this behavior were already there in ISKCON, even if Prabhupada's own treatment of women reflected his highly developed sense of love and compassion; he was naturally unbiased, viewing the world from the embracing perspective of a pure devotee.

But he had established an institution that favored *sannyasis*, a monastic order characterized by total commitment, without the distractions usually associated with marriage and family. This created an imbalance that made life in ISKCON difficult for women. His reasoning, however, was sound: In Vaishnava culture, *sannyasis* are the leaders of society, and he wanted to make sure that ISKCON would have the benefit of such leaders after his demise. All movements need leaders, and he knew that his own time was short—he had founded ISKCON at the advanced age of seventy.

For this reason, among others, he emphasized renunciation and the *sannyasa* order of life, hoping that this would secure the future of his movement. In doing this, he was also following the precedent set by his spiritual master, Srila Bhaktisiddhanta Sarasvati, who founded the Gaudiya Math, too, with an emphasis on monasticism. The overall vision of these two masters, of course, was not limited to the solitarian lifestyle, and they avidly endorsed Varnashram, a system that accommodates women, children, students, married people, and so on. More, they propounded Bhakti philosophy, which broke through all social restrictions and established heartfelt devotion as the only important quality for attaining perfection. Apparently, this latter subtlety was lost on some of Prabhupada's disciples, and the monastic emphasis, coupled with Western, youthful extremism, gave way to the abuse of women.

Bhakti Tirtha Maharaja found it ironic that the body/soul distinction, which is not only taught but emphasized in ISKCON, often falls flat when male devotees interact with their female counterparts. The lofty philosophy of "you're not that body" is sometimes overshadowed by discrimination toward the opposite sex. The Swami acknowledged that bodies are, in fact, different, and that these differences might effectively be used in the service of Krishna. But to overemphasize these bodily distinctions, he said, would miss the point, allowing Maya, or illusion personified, to get the upper hand.

Bhakti Tirtha Maharaja would not let this rest. As a champion of the downtrodden, he spoke out against such hypocrisy and actively fought against it. He and several other ISKCON leaders were vocal about their indignation, and ISKCON has consequently come a long way in its equitable treatment of women. Rukmini Devi Dasi, a female disciple of Srila Prabhupada, remembers how Bhakti Tirtha Swami would often defend them. Here she cites one of many such incidents:

> *I believe it was 2002 when a group of senior women disciples of Srila Prabhupada addressed the Governing Body Commission*

during their annual meeting in Sridham Mayapur. They spoke articulately and feelingly about the inappropriate treatment of female devotees over the past many years in ISKCON. Of course, in an international body there are significant cultural differences between the members—both men and women. But the general mood was one of contrition and regret, although some more conservative members appeared to be quietly disgruntled. As always, Bhakti Tirtha Swami expressed compassion and concern for those who had been treated unfairly. The majority then voted to institute changes to long-standing policies that were found to be sexist, or at least unfair toward the women devotees.

The Governing Body agreed that women devotees should be allowed to give class, lead Kirtan, and accept leadership roles if they are qualified, as they had in previous years in the presence of our Founder-Acharya, Srila Prabhupada. In addition, all women devotees must be treated respectfully as sincere and dedicated members of our society. It was further decided that Vishaka Devi Dasi, a learned and respected Godsister, should give the Srimad-Bhagavatam class the following morning. This would initiate the new policies.

Naturally, then, upon arising the next day, we sat in the temple room, excitedly anticipating the rare opportunity to hear from our revered Godsister. Some of us noticed that there were many fewer devotees than usual in the room—there were more women than men. There were whispers that some of the local brahmacaris, *celibate monks, in protest, had organized a separate class elsewhere. As Vishaka Prabhu tried to begin to chant the traditional prayers as invocation, it became apparent that someone had taken the microphone, the cymbals, and the book from which she was supposed to speak. They were nowhere to be found, and the class could not be conducted without them.*

At that point, Bhakti Tirtha Swami jumped up and, in a mood of fierce compassion, spoke vehemently to a resident sannyasi:

"Listen," he said, "you'd better get that book, microphone, and cymbals! And you'd better get them NOW!" In full force he ordered different resident devotees who were present, adamant that they correct the situation immediately. Seeing him in this bold mood, I was reminded of the description of Chaitanya Mahaprabhu as He danced at the Ratha-yatra Festival some 500 years earlier. Like a whirling firebrand, it is said, He appeared to be everywhere at once. This same effect was brought to bear by Bhakti Tirtha Swami. I was stunned with admiration for him, for his righteous anger, from one who had known discrimination all his life. I felt blessed to see his loving care for everyone, his fearless compassion. Within moments, someone brought the Bhagavatam, *the cymbals, and the microphone. Vishaka proceeded to give a lucid, erudite, sublime class, with no political agenda, that was deeply appreciated by the devotees who were present.*

Women in ISKCON have come a long way. Prior to the incident described above, Sudharma Dasi, a female Prabhupada disciple who is active in both animal rights circles and in ISKCON politics, was elected as an executive officer for ISKCON North America. That position entitled her to attend GBC conferences around the world. Eventually, with the help of several male GBC members, she formed the International Women's Ministry, which was approved as an official ISKCON entity in 1996. In due course, Malati Dasi, a senior female Prabhupada disciple, became a GBC member in ISKCON. Together the two female devotees began attending the International GBC meetings in Mayapur and a new day in ISKCON dawned.

The Women's Ministry began holding conferences in the United States and in Europe. These conferences afforded women the opportunity for training, positive association within ISKCON, and the respect of their Godbrothers. Today, Women's Ministry conferences are held annually in America with an average of more than 150 participants at each one. These conferences are attended and deeply appreciated by male and female leaders of ISKCON, as well as by professional counselors and professors of religious history. In many ways, Bhakti Tirtha Swami was one of catalysts through which such progressive changes took place.

Mother Vegavati, a senior Prabhupada disciple, tells of her personal interaction with Maharaja, how he encouraged her in spiritual life. This is one of many such testimonies from women throughout the movement:

> *It is the mark of a great person that he makes others feel special. Maharaja surely did that with so many, many people. I am no exception. I remember early on during Maharaja's time at Gita Nagari, when there were a lot of devotees visiting, maybe for the Vrindavan Institute of Higher Education (VIHE), Maharaja personally called my name and asked me to lead the Kirtan at Tulasi-puja. I felt grateful for the honor and happy to do it, as I love to sing Kirtan.*
>
> *He always treated me with respect and affection, as a real God-sister, yet a younger one. Once, when I was having some real difficulties with authority figures in Gita Nagari, he heard me out with genuine compassion and openness, and I know he strongly desired the well-being of all parties concerned. He did as much as he was able to try to bring healing. Such a wealth of caring he had!*
>
> *I have to say that I am grateful more than anything for his friendly, affectionate dealings. Not only with me, but with the children, with his disciples, his Godbrothers, his family members, and with whomever he came in contact. But I personally am grateful that he reached out to me and pulled the love out from my heart, even though it can be quite stone-like. I tell you, I get happy just thinking about him.*

Moving to Gita Nagari

Bhakti Tirtha Swami, global spiritual leader and champion of the downtrodden, had a vision for the future, too. He saw self-sufficiency, community living, cottage industries and a "small is beautiful" sensibility, as essential for the sustenance of the planet. It was not insignificant, therefore, when his IFAST community in Washington D.C. relocated to Gita Nagari in Central Pennsylvania—a beautiful, 350-acre farm community nestled in the scenic countryside of Port Royal, where devotees manage a farm and care for cows and oxen. It is the home of Sri Sri Radha Damodara, Sri Sri Radha Kalachandji, Jagannath, Baladeva and Subhadra—the various forms of Krishna and His eternal associates worshiped by the devotees there.

The community's prior history in ISKCON is noteworthy: In 1974, the devotees purchased some acreage for a farm project. Srila Prabhupada soon dubbed it Gita Nagari, "the village where the *Bhagavad-gita* is sung." Accordingly, the devotees wanted to use the facility to demonstrate the natural relationship between the land, the animals, humanity, and God—a relationship that becomes increasing obscured as people move away from spiritual pursuits. A similar project was already underway in West Virginia (New Vrindavan), and devotees were excited about the implications of expansion.

Gita Nagari's approach included animal protection, natural farming, and a back-to-the-land way of being. By the late '60s, certain groups of people in the Western world began to recognize a disturbing fact: modern urban life was separating them from God and nature. They realized how removed they were from basic, God-given responsibilities, such as milking a cow or tilling the land—they felt out of touch with their environment, and they didn't like it. This perception was exacerbated by other downsides of modern life: rampant consumerism, the failings of government and society, including the Vietnam War, and a growing public concern about environmental pollution. All of this was anticipated by the Vedic scriptures, which not only mentions "simple living and high thinking"—the way of life preferred by the Vaishnava sages—but prophesies the urban plight of modern man.

Practical application of Gita Nagari's ideals would embrace many of the principles of permaculture, organic agriculture, renewable energy, vegetarianism, enlightened cow protection, animal draft and alternative housing, to name a few. Make no mistake, devotees do not reject technology. In fact, they make good use of it, acknowledging the virtues of computers, printing presses, and so on. But living simply necessitates reconsidering when and where technological advances would be appropriate. Hi-tech methods require a complex industrial base and knowledge of physics and material sciences, which are currently part of a military-industrial complex, making it difficult to apply simple living ideology.

On the other hand, technology can allow greater productivity and communications between communities, for example, providing information on effective lifestyles for those who wish to simplify. But these can be run on renewable sources of energy as well, and Gita Nagari's researchers were looking into this. It was for such a balanced approach to life, coupled with worship of God as elaborated upon in the Vedic literature, that Gita Nagari was founded.

In 1985, as the community came into its own, it established "Adopt A Cow," a program intended to bring the "cruelty-free" and "back-to-basics" message to others, enabling even non-devotees to take part in cow protection. Participants could "adopt a cow" by giving donations to ensure feed and care for cows or oxen. This was a huge success, with coverage in national newspapers, television, and hundreds if not thousands of adoptive "parents."

One of Gita Nagari's goals was to show a living example of ideal human/ bovine interaction, as described in the Vedas. This begins by allowing cows to provide milk and oxen to plow the fields. In return, the devotees protect the cow and the ox so they can live out their natural life and avoid the slaughterhouse. Gita Nagari also wanted to educate the global community about cow protection, ox power, and vegetarianism; they accomplished this through travel, lectures and newsletters. Gita Nagari, in fact, met these goals—and continues to meet them—even if the community sporadically ran into hard times throughout the years.

Bhakti Tirtha Swami, too, was interested in self-sufficient farm communities. He had looked at some land in Virginia with just such a project in mind. His vision of self-sufficiency, community building, and cottage industries required an outlet in the United States, and soon Gita Nagari would fill that role. He had established similar projects in Africa, and it was high time, he felt, to do the same in America. He was especially interested in cottage industries, for this would be a major component if devotees were to become self-sufficient and less dependent on materialistic society.

By cottage industry, he primarily meant land-based manufacturing—the kind that operated en masse before the Industrial Revolution. Cottage industries were common when a large proportion of the population engaged in agriculture, because the farmers (and their families) often had both the time and the desire to earn additional income during the winter, when there was little farming work to do. Big businesses and multinational companies have seriously diminished such cottage industries. But Bhakti Tirtha Maharaja saw that Gita Nagari could bring them back to life. So he decided to take over the project, especially because it was going through a rough time and could use someone like him to rejuvenate it. Mother Vegavati recalls how it all began:

> It was 1994. My home phone rang; I answered it. A devotee by the name of Vraja-lila was on the other end, asking for directions to Gita Nagari. She said that she and her husband were coming, along with Bhakti Tirtha Maharaja, from D.C. I gave the road directions and hung up.
>
> Minutes later the phone rang again. This time it was Ekavira Prabhu, who introduced himself as Vraja-lila's husband, and explained that Bhakti Tirtha Maharaja was considering moving

to Gita Nagari, coming as the GBC. This information brought a wildly enthusiastic exclamation of approval from me, as I had long been attached to Gita Nagari, had seen it in its prime, and had been sad to see the gradual dwindling that had taken place over the last years. My previous association with Bhakti Tirtha Maharaja was limited—amounting to one Sunday feast lecture in Cleveland when I'd been on traveling "Sankirtan" for Gita Nagari, plus a Vyasa-puja homage he'd written for Srila Prabhupada. These, and a report from my Godsister, Yamuna Devi, about the wonderful devotees at the Institute in Washington, DC, who were so nicely trained by him, led me to hope that here was the person who could revitalize Gita Nagari.

I'm sure it was simply because of this phone call and my spontaneous and vocal response that Maharaja always gave me the credit for welcoming him to Gita Nagari. In truth, it was Krishna's plan, Prabhupada's desire, and the invitation of Tamal Krishna Maharaja, as I understand it, which got the ball rolling, and I was only one among many residents of Gita Nagari who were glad he had come. But somehow there was always a strong bond of affection between us, beginning from that day.

In early 1994, ISKCON had held its annual temple presidents and GBC meeting in Dallas, Texas. It was at that time that Bhakti Tirtha Maharaja was nominated Chairman of the North American GBC. Although much of his work in Africa and IFAST seemed, externally, to be "outside" of ISKCON, and so he seemed to be "away" for a number years, he was immediately asked to be the chairman—the most important managerial position in ISKCON! At that time, he also agreed to assist as co-GBC for South Africa, Detroit, and Pennsylvania, which includes the Gita Nagari farm.

Actually, it was Jayadvaita Maharaja, his longtime Godbrother and friend—and a senior ISKCON leader—who asked him to accept the position of North American GBC Chairperson. Some time later,

Tamal Krishna Goswami, as Mother Vegavati says, visited Bhakti Tirtha Maharaja at his IFAST headquarters in D.C. and asked him to resuscitate Gita Nagari. After deeply considering how important this would be to Srila Prabhupada's overall mission, and how much it coalesced with his own vision for community development and cottage industries, he agreed to explore the possibilities there. Vraja-lila recollects more specifically how his involvement emerged:

> In the early 1990s, in the midst of our urban preaching, Gurudeva encouraged us to become more competent in self-sufficient skills, emphasizing community development, loving relationships and lifestyles that would exemplify "simple living and high thinking," which was one of Srila Prabhupada's mottos. Guru Maharaja especially emphasized developing self-sufficient skills. We knew he was preparing us for something big, but we had no idea what would unfold.
>
> To expand our consciousness in these areas, it was our practice to visit other communities to learn more about their successes and failures. So in the fall of 1994, Gurudeva asked Ekavira, Lila Avatar and me to accompany him on a visit to the Gita Nagari Farm in Pennsylvania. It appeared, at the time, that we were visiting this farm community simply as part of our attempt to research various farm communities. Not for a moment could any of us foresee the magnitude of commitment that would follow from this simple one-day tour of the farm.
>
> Within a few months of that visit, at the request of Tamal Krishna Maharaja, one of his very dear Godbrothers, Gurudeva accepted the responsibility of care-taking and developing Gita Nagari Village. He assumed the role of co-GBC for the area. This service added to his already existing responsibilities as International Chairman of the Society, co-GBC of West Africa, South Africa, Mexico City, New Vrindavan, and Detroit. He was also one of the coordinators for Srila Prabhupada's Centennial, in 1996, and of course, the Director for the Institute for Applied Spiritual Technol-

ogy in Washington, D.C., which at that time was in Harwood, Maryland. Gurudeva told us that he could show his gratitude to his spiritual master, Srila Prabhupada, by committing himself to Gita Nagari, and working for its betterment. Along these lines, one of his favorite quotes from Srila Prabhupada was: "If you really want to honor someone, don't just build some statue or memorial building. The most potent way to honor someone is to build a community that exemplifies the values that person taught."

On our ride back to Maryland, after our second visit to Gita Nagari, Gurudeva discussed with Ekavira and me the importance of commitment and of fulfilling the desires of the Guru. Before we arrived back in Maryland, he had hinted at least three times about us going to Gita Nagari in a leadership capacity to assist the community. The next thing we knew, within a few days of our return to Maryland, Ekavira and I were packing all our belongings to move to Gita Nagari. Gurudeva had convinced us of the importance of exemplifying "simple living and high thinking." To us, Gita Nagari was beautiful but austere—there wasn't much in the way of accommodations for those who wanted to live there.

On a subsequent visit, Gurudeva brought along one of his disciples from Maryland, Loka Dasi, to look at a house that the temple president owned. His desire was for Loka to purchase the house, and then we would come along and live in it. Without hesitation, Loka agreed, and she bought the house to assist Gurudeva with his service. Thus, in May, 1995, with mixed eagerness and sadness—we were, after all, leaving our Godbrothers, Godsisters and close friends in the Maryland/ Washington area—we left the Institute and the excitement of urban teaching to move to Gita Nagari for a new frontier in Krishna Consciousness. Prior to our arrival in Gita Nagari, Gurudeva had sent Bali Maharaj, Pariksit, and Anasuya, and so we were happy to have the association of our God-family there. Shortly after we moved to Gita Nagari, we were joined by Kartamisha, the present head priest for Sri Sri Radha Damodara at the temple. A year later, under the instruction of our Gurudeva, three families from the Institute also came to assist with the project.

Pariksit Dasa, one of the Swami's disciples, remembers the actual move to Gita Nagari, which came in early 1995:

There were four devotees that came with His Holiness Bhakti Tirtha Maharaja to Gita Nagari that day; Garuda Dasa, Ekavira Dasa, Bali Maharaja Dasa and I—we were all disciples. The twenty-four-foot rented U-Haul truck was loaded with mostly Maharaja's belongings, which consisted of furniture and some clothes. Earlier in the day the truck was loaded at the IFAST house at the corner of 9th and F Streets in Northeast D.C.

We left at around six o'clock in the evening. When we got to Gita Nagari, Maharaja mildly chastised me for driving too fast. Garuda was also frustrated and complained a little bit. Maharaja's residence was on top of a hill facing "Govardhana hill" (one of the small hills on the Gita Nagari property where the cows would often graze). The residence had been bought by one of Maharaja's disciples, Nisha Dasi, from Shamika Rishi Prabhu, currently the temple president at the ISKCON temple in Towaco, New Jersey.

The house was very close to the Gita Nagari property but not part of it. It was a rambler (one floor and a basement). It also had a village-style split rail fence bordering the lawn, and a circular driveway. The first floor had two decks on either side of the front of the house, and an enclosed porch in the back. There was one decent-sized room (about fourteen feet by sixteen feet) with a spacious bathroom connected to it. This was on the right end of the main floor. Maharaja would later use that as his private quarters. The living room was quite long (about twenty-five feet long and about sixteen feet wide). It turned at right angles (90°) to a small dining area, and connected to that was the kitchen.

Three of the four walls of the living room had glass windows from the top to about two feet from the floor so when the sun was setting, a lot of light and heat would fill that room. Maharaja's private residence and the adjoining living room were carpeted. Maharaja's bathroom was tiled, and the kitchen and dining area had nicely polished wood floors. The basement consisted of three carpeted rooms, a small kitchen area with a linoleum floor, a tiled bathroom and a small room with concrete floor at the left end of the house. That room served as the laundry and utility room. Next to the house was a smaller building, which now serves as a manufacturing facility for all-natural health and beauty products (soap, massage oils, bath oils, hair cream and hair oils). It is also used as Maharaja's audio ministry. The description of the house is significant, because this is where Maharaja would spend his final days.

We got to the residence at about 9:30 that evening and parked the truck at the back of the house, which had already been cleaned. Bali, Ekavira and Garuda started moving in the furniture. I helped a little bit but I was tired from the driving. Maharaja was also in the house. As each piece of furniture was brought in, Maharaja would immediately direct the men as to where to put it. Normally, one would just load everything into a new house and then later decide where things would go, but in Maharaja's case, he was thinking of where to put the furniture as the pieces were being brought in. After awhile, I fell asleep.

At seven o'clock the next morning, I awoke. At that point, Maharaja came down and announced that the house had been fully decorated. I went upstairs and was amazed at what I saw! It was clearly an expert job done by Maharaja himself! One half-hour later, some devotees from the Gita Nagari farm came up to the residence to visit Maharaja. None of us knew that they were coming. Later, one of them expressed to me how surprised he was that the place had been decorated and was ready for "spiritual business" that quickly.

He was expecting boxes all over the place and expecting to talk with Maharaja on the back porch or something like that. The devotee visitors knew that we had arrived only the night before. I said to myself quietly, "Only he (Maharaja) can do things like that."

Chandramauli Swami, one of Bhakti Tirtha Maharaja's Godbrothers, remembers the early days of IFAST's presence in Gita Nagari. He especially notes Maharaja's wisdom in regard to Vaishnava relationships and community building—that before actually working the farm it was important to establish strong, loving interactions between the Vaishnavas. Maharaja talks about this himself in *Spiritual Warrior III*: "A community gains its strength from the quality of its relationships. Indeed, every aspect of creation is involved in relationship, and, as spiritual warriors, we should view all interactions in terms of the kinds of relationships we want to achieve. Relationships within communities must be strong, or anything the community builds will be temporary and cosmetic." Here, Chandramauli Swami specifically talks about this principle in relation to Gita Nagari:

From 1994 to 1996, Bhakti Tirtha Maharaja moved his operation from D.C. to Gita Nagari. The Gita Nagari community had been having difficulty, although there were more than sixty families there at the time. I know this because he asked me to do some research and find out how many families were actually there.

The devotees who were there were overburdened with responsibility. Bhakti Tirtha Maharaja decided to move his devotees in and establish self-sufficiency based on Prabhupada's original desire for Gita Nagari. It was a major undertaking and very few of the residents were eager to get involved with Maharaja's plan for self-sufficiency. It would mean a lot of work, a lot of reassessing people's services, and so on. At the same time, none of his disciples, who had been living in D.C. and had become devotees in the city, had any training or experience in farm life. I can clearly remember that

Bhakti Tirtha Maharaja organized, practically every day, seminars on how to implement self-sufficiency. He asked many of his leading devotees to do research in various areas of farm life and modern approaches to living close to the land, with cows, and working the earth. A lot of information was compiled, but Maharaja realized that before he could implement a self-sufficiency program, he would first have to build community and establish devotee relationships.

Gradually, the devotees gave up their occupations and took up residency at the farm. Then, Maharaja embarked on a very bold program to build a community. Unfortunately, Maharaja was counting on the present residents of Gita Nagari to help out and to cooperate. This did not manifest, except in very specific cases. So, with a few Gita Nagari devotees and a group of devotee professionals from D.C. (none of them accustomed to rural life), he worked hard to build devotee relationships and at the same time maintain and expand the present situation at Gita Nagari. It was practically an impossible task, but Maharaja was determined. We can see today what a wonderful community has developed.

Achyuta Dasi, one of Bhakti Tirtha Swami's early disciples from Gita Nagari, talks about her guru's methods there:

In 1995, he began talking about the need for us to prepare ourselves to become self-sufficient. He encouraged us to read books that taught practical skills for developing self-sufficiency. At the same time he organized us into "cells" based on our acquired talents and skills and those that we needed to develop in a self-sufficient community, including health, farm, counseling, self-defense, food storage, water, alternative energy, clothing, land/building, research, etc.

I joined the health and farm cell. The health cell interviewed every member of the Institute to collect detailed health histories in the event that this information was ever needed to assist someone in an emergency situation. We took classes in first aid; prepared first

aid kits; and equipped ourselves with stethoscopes and blood pres-
sure cuffs to monitor those with special health concerns. In the farm
cell we nurtured seedlings and planted them in a plot at ISKCON's
Potomac temple. We experimented with intensive growing methods
to maximize the small garden's yield potential.

When we first arrived in Gita Nagari, we lived in the temple in
a small room for three months before we moved to a one-bedroom
apartment, not much bigger than the room. A few of Gurudeva's
senior disciples from IFAST had already moved to Gita Nagari,
paving the way for others who would come later. My husband
Sadachara and I, and Kalpa-vriksha and Laghima Siddhi, also
disciples of Gurudeva, were his first disciples to be married in the
Vedic tradition in Gita Nagari. This was an important part of
establishing community—he wanted us to use the samskaras, *or*
"rites of passage" found in Vedic writings. This would go a long way
in forming the foundation for a genuine Vedic village.

Gurudeva was involved in the planning of the momentous occa-
sion, which included the bride's riding on an ox-driven cart—this
was his idea. Such wedding ceremonies became an annual event
at Gita Nagari. Gurudeva always enjoyed planning these kinds of
activities to keep the devotees enlivened in Krishna Consciousness,
including biking, sleighing, and racing at a nearby park. I have
had some of the best times of my life on these occasions in the as-
sociation of my Gurudeva and God-family in Gita Nagari.

We conclude with Bhakti Tirtha Swami's own words about community. He here muses on the implications of a true community-
centered project, the kind he began to establish in Gita Nagari. After
this, his disciple, Jagannath Pandit, summarizes some of the teachings that his guru spread around the world:

Many people today realize that spiritual culture is related to a strong
sense of community. One great ploy of the negative forces in this age is

to divide us by means of personal ambition and the desire to distinguish ourselves from others. Yet, the most God conscious people have been modest and have belonged to an organized group or order.

Many indigenous peoples still live in closely-nit communities, where their strong ties can be seen in their manner of speech, dress, work, and worship. They receive strength to withstand cultural and spiritual erosion through this unity of will and action. Together, they penetrate many artificial expressions of individuality and reach a more profound intimacy, understanding more subtle aspects of existence.

Members of a tightly knit community have interests of the whole at heart and become their brothers' and sisters' keepers. Being our brothers' and sisters' keepers means loving one another as we love ourselves. We cannot muster the faith to care for anyone but ourselves if we fear resource shortage or do not understand who supplies these resources. Nothing material lasts forever, but the love we give to one another and the sacrifices we make for something greater than ourselves endure because they come from a higher source. A strong community can give us wonderful guidance and security to help us cope with our daily challenges.

The natural and innocent love that we imbibe in a close community burns away behaviors that are unnatural and unhealthy. Thus, we grow spiritually in such an environment. At one time, it was openly acknowledged that some persons died from heartbreak, and even today, medical science understands that people who receive fewer hugs and less affection are more prone to degenerative diseases. In this way, too, community life can be good for our health.

Community is not simply a system or set of concepts, it is a living organism whose personality is the aggregate of individual consciousness. Community has unlimited potential, yet must be protected and nourished to develop fully.

We can create community by crisis, by accident, or by design. People come together in crisis when, for example, their relation-

ships might not last because they based it on something temporary or external. Community can be formed accidentally as well, but there will be no clue or purpose and plan for coming together. At the root of the word community is the idea of communion meaning wholeness, communication, co-operation, and commonality. Without these elements, there is only pseudo-community, where people come together to discover what they can take, use, or exploit rather than what they can share and how they can serve.

Community is about relationships. A sense of community only emerges as a result of honest communication, cooperation, and fellowship. Community with nothing to communicate is simply an artificial grouping without life. When a community has genuine validity, the members have something to communicate and to share with each other. Each member is straightforward while at the same time being sensitive to the feelings of others. Real community is never exclusive. When the nucleus of a community is strong, it becomes flexible enough to balance, adjust, expand, and include the new. Real community is never exclusive or ambiguous. Ultimately, real community facilitates closeness with God.

His preaching around the world focused on the following broad messages, which are here summarized for his disciples:

(1) Let us remember that the Bhagavad-gita *was spoken on a battlefield, and as spiritual warriors, we each have our own battlefield to deal with on a day to day basis. Whether we're in a festival, at work, at home, at school, at a festival, in the temple, or even on the altar, Krishna is there and Maya, or illusion, is there, too. This battle is always in the background, as we attempt to annihilate our lust, anger, greed, and the other enemies of the mind. The battlefield is designed for both defeat and for victory. No other arena is more provocative and intense than a battlefield—it brings out the best and the worst in people. In a war, we have casualties, traitors,*

and spies. We also have victims, survivors, and high achievers. In war, we depend on association, strategy, and mentors. But each individual person is held responsible for certain duties, and one person's failure can often bring disaster to many. Also, one person's success can often bring victory to many.

(2) Take a daily personal inventory, in the morning or the evening, to see how you are progressing spiritually. Look at each day as if it could be your last. Take inventory and cry out directly to your Deity, to the pictures of your gurus. Let them know your heart and mind, and beg for their help, guidance and chastisement. Tell them what you have offered to them that day for the mission of Srila Prabhupada and the mission of your gurus. The more we are personal with Krishna and with our spiritual masters, the more we will get that kind of reciprocation in our lives.

(3) Look at your life and distinctly see if you are helping to relieve the miseries of others. Our lives as Vaishnavas have as much value as we touch the life of another. Most of our thoughts and arrangements are about what isn't working in our own lives. That is not transcendental. Yes, problems will be there and many of them will stay there. But we are all bigger than our own little problems. These experiences, problems, and challenges are part of our particular battlefield, and we have to deal with them to meet Krishna on the other side. That's why Krishna says that one who is dear to Him will be unaffected by happiness and distress. They're not seeing themselves as the center. As we think, act, plan, and strategize more in that way, we will correspondingly see so many issues, problems, and even stagnation in our own lives becoming minimized or removed.

(4) Remember this prayer: "Dear Lord, whatever we need to be better servants for Srila Prabhupada's mission, let it happen or come to us. Whatever we need to have taken away to become pure in Srila Prabhupada's service, let it be taken away."

CHAPTER NINE

THE LONG JOURNEY HOME

"He reasons ill who tells that Vaishnavas die,
When thou art still living in sound!
The Vaishnavas die to live, and living try
To spread a holy life around!"

—BHAKTIVINODA THAKUR

AS BHAKTI TIRTHA MAHARAJA became something of a well-known international spiritual leader, with numerous college lectures, TV and radio talk shows, and inter-religious conferences lined up for years to come, the ravages of time manifested in an unexpected way, changing his plans forever.

In 2004, he was diagnosed with fourth-stage melanoma on his left foot. Ten years earlier, he had been told of a suspicious lump there, just beneath the birthmark that had given special meaning to his title, "Krishnapada." But it was benign, and removal would have meant losing the use of his foot entirely. He therefore opted to leave it alone. In a later examination, however, doctors found that it was malignant, and a further diagnosis of diabetes would limit his medical options.

All of his well-wishers and disciples will remember where they were when they received the news on August 11, 2004, via a letter from one of his representatives:

> *Dear Devotees*
>
> *Please accept my humble obeisances. All glories to Guru and Gauranga! All glories to Srila Prabhupada.*
>
> *I just got off the phone with Gurudeva following his post operative review with his doctor. It seems that the tumor that was removed from Gurudeva's foot was cancer. He will be going back to the hospital later today to have a CAT scan of his entire body to assess the extent of the spread. To put it simply, the best case scenario is that the cancer is only in his left foot and if so this will mean he will have to have his left foot amputated. However, the worst case scenario is that the cancer has spread to other parts of his body, which means that he will probably require chemotherapy and even then the outcome is uncertain.*
>
> *This email is not meant to frighten anyone, but Gurudeva was very clear on the phone that devotees should know the situation as it is, so that nothing comes as a shock. He was very grave and introspective about the whole situation. He is totally surrendered to whatever Srila Prabhupada wants—whether it means staying here and continuing his service here or leaving and joining Srila Prabhupada somewhere else to serve him directly.*
>
> *He is continuing to imbibe the mood of Vasudeva Datta and is continuing his prayers to be the carrier of so much of the karmic burden of the devotees. Gurudeva often stresses the importance of strengthening our relationships with each another and also strengthening our internal relationship with him—there is no time like the present. I would like to invite each and every one of you to not just work on these aspects of our spiritual life but also really reflect on what we as individuals can do to reduce this burden that Gurudeva is choosing to carry.*

Let's all try and accelerate and go deeper in our prayers and in the quality of our service. Let's all please come together to give Srila Prabhupada a reason to let Gurudeva stay.

Yours in the service of Guru and Gauranga,

With love,

Your aspiring servant,

Chiti-Shakti Devi Dasi

Praying for Calamity

It's not that his ailment came as a surprise. He had long been praying to take on the pains of the movement, to bear the karma of those who were working hard to make ISKCON successful, and this is alluded to in Chit-Shakti's letter, quoted above. Vaishnava philosophy asserts that karma—"for every action there is an equal and commensurate reaction"—accrues with each action we perform, and that its laws are binding. Moreover, it tells us that everyone is responsible for his or her own actions. Thus, only God's intervention, or the grace of one's guru, can help one bypass the results of previous activities. Vaishnava adepts thus feel compassion for fallen souls, who seem hopelessly entangled in karma's intricate web.

Chit-Shakti also mentions Vasudeva Datta, an extraordinary devotee from the time of Lord Chaitanya, some 500 years ago. Datta is traditionally viewed as a Vaishnava counterpart to Jesus Christ, for he is remembered as the magnanimous soul who wanted to take the karmic reactions of all living beings on his own head; he wanted permission to assuage each living entity's pain by suffering on their behalf. Lord Chaitanya assured him that by the intensity of his desire, all living things—man, beast, aquatic, plant, germ—would experience liberation from worldly affliction.

The main teaching brought forward by this exchange is the profound empathy of the Vaishnavas, that they feel the pain of all living beings, and that they are willing to sacrifice on behalf of others, to alleviate the burden of souls who are trapped in the material world. Bhakti Tirtha Maharaja was particularly moved by the Vasudeva Datta story, and his desire to evoke the spirit of this great soul in his own life was something the devotees had been hearing about for several years.

In his personal diary, for example, he had penned many prayers in the mood of Vasudeva Datta, periodically mentioning this great soul by name. Similarly, his Vyasa-puja offering to Srila Prabhupada in 2003 finds him begging to be "a 'change agent' who can help tremendously to remove or minimize" the suffering of others. In 2004, his Vyasa-puja essay specifically mentions Vasudeva Datta directly: "So, in the mood of Vasudeva Datta, I would like to ask you, 'Can you arrange that their sufferings come to me so that many can be freed from their anguish and thus joyfully serve you and return to Krishna with fewer encumbrances?'" Also, in that same year—just months before his diagnosis—he asked devotees throughout the world to pray with him as follows: "Whatever we need to become better servants for Srila Prabhupada's mission, let it happen or come to us. Whatever we need to have taken away to become pure in Srila Prabhupada's service, let it be taken away."

And then it came. In his own words: "So here in like ten days I have this accelerated tumor, I have sugar diabetes, prostate problems, I get the operation, and then I have cancer. The MRI didn't suggest this, nor did the previous blood work. So my intuitive understanding or reflection is that Prabhupada seems to be calling me back, and then again, maybe not. The prayer has been heard; the prayer has been accepted. Now, whatever He does with it, I am okay."

Others watched in amazement. Satsvarupa Dasa Goswami, for example, in an essay entitled, "The Letter He Asked Me to Write," addressed the Vasudeva Datta phenomenon head on:

But I was surprised that he made such a sudden change in the momentum of his outward preaching to make a prayer to take away the world's sins by an act of petition to the Lord, an intercessionary prayer, or prayer that all the world's karma be put upon himself. It was a very different kind of thing than he had been doing. When I asked him about it, one answer he gave was that he thought that his present preaching had not been effective enough. He wanted to do something more dramatic because the world's corruption was so great and there was also a need for purification even in ISKCON. So he was willing to put his body on the line completely for total purification of himself (so that he could become a pure actor on behalf of Krishna) and—provided Krishna would take the karma from others in return for Bhakti Tirtha Swami's sacrifice—he would increase his work in this world.

Some have doubted his prayer. But I accept it as sincere and also as efficacious. Bhakti Tirtha Swami has shown the proof of its working in the many good things that have happened as a result of his prayer. He did not expect to get hit so fast with a terminal illness. But neither did he expect to get so many good results in terms of people reforming their ways. Many, many people wrote him letters that they were inspired by his sacrifice and that they themselves were now reforming their acts and purifying themselves. He said that in particular many ex-Gurukulis wrote to him of their change for the better and also many errant ISKCON adults appreciated what he was doing and were returning to the field—many, many. So he could not help but think that his intercessionary prayer on behalf of karmic-laden souls was doing good. And he felt it was doing good for himself also. So this is one thing I am writing in my letter as my own personal faith in the spiritual warrior.

Ultimately, then, Bhakti Tirtha Swami saw his cancer as a result of his prayer. In the months that followed, he would greet it with mixed feelings of pain and pleasure. He was distraught that he would prematurely leave his loved ones, particularly his disciples, and experience an abrupt end to his many services, from book publishing to world tours on behalf of his spiritual master. But he was relieved, even enlivened, to know that his prayers were answered, that he would return to the spiritual world—or go to whichever realm needed him the most—in the service of guru and Krishna.

At first, he responded with some measure of ambivalence. Should he fight to stay, or should he go, accepting the disease as Krishna's will—as the answer to his prayers? Both would be legitimate reactions: He was still relatively young and could potentially do more service while in his current incarnation, and his friends and loved ones wanted him to stay. But his commitment to his prayer, and his original intent while making the prayer, remained a reality. He had prayed to suffer for others' sins, particularly to help ISKCON emerge from its recent woes. Should he, then, view the cancer as an enemy, to be defeated by a determined spiritual warrior, or as a comrade, who was helping him purge ISKCON and others of the reaction to their poor choices? Tamal Krishna Goswami, when afflicted with prostate cancer himself, eloquently expressed this tension of seeing the disease as friend or foe:

> Cancer, *Latin for "crab"* (karkata *in Sanskrit) was flourishing malignantly in my prostate, threatening to infiltrate and metastasize; in the absence of treatment, it would terminate my life. In Hindu culture,* atithi, *an uninvited guest, is entitled to hospitality, even welcomed as God. An* atithi *is considered auspicious, but my "guest" was clearly the bearer of vicious ill will. Or, was I mistaken? Was this seemingly malevolent visitor, this feisty crab-like possessor of my prostate, a providential blessing in disguise? How was I to be certain, and more to the point, had I the requisite faith to find out? Theoretical questions seemed to multiply as quickly as the cancer they sought to explore.*

Again, both—fighting the cancer, or relenting, giving way to death—would be justifiable. In fact, the famous story of Pariksit Maharaja, a king from ancient India who was cursed to die within seven days, embodies this same tension, confirming that, according to the

Vaishnava tradition, one could, indeed, go either way. In the more popular version of the story, as found in the *Srimad-Bhagavatam*, Pariksit does nothing to avert his mortality. He is cursed to die by a young Brahmin, and he accepts his destiny as the will of the Lord. To prepare for his untimely demise, he renounces his kingdom and possessions and goes to the sacred Ganges River, where he fasts and hears the glories of the Lord until his time arrives.

In the *Mahabharata* version, however, Pariksit tries to circumvent his fate with the aid of ministers and priests. He has an impenetrable palace constructed on a huge pillar, surrounded by physicians, ritual experts, and healing herbs. He hopes to thereby avoid the horrible snake-bird that is destined to take his life. In the end, of course, he dies the same glorious death depicted in the *Bhagavatam*. But what are we to learn from these interesting variants? Each rendering shows an alternate approach to death. The king, like Bhakti Tirtha Swami, had abundant reason to live, as well as the desire to do so, and the *Mahabharata* epic reflects those facts. The *Srimad-Bhagavatam*, on the other hand, shows that, when death comes, she can be greeted gracefully, with enthusiasm and with full dependence on the Lord.

The Battle Begins

Ultimately, Bhakti Tirtha Maharaja opted for the *Bhagavatam* approach, even if there was a short period in which his mood seemed more in line with the *Mahabharata*. At first, he tried naturopathic cures and an extended stay in medical facilities in both Mexico and Hawaii, to try to get well. Vraja-lila and Ekavira, two of his dedicated disciples and determined caregivers, talk about the beginning stages of what would turn out to be a long ordeal:

Ekavira: *In the spring of 2004, soon after he submitted his Vyasa-puja offering to the BBT for the 2004 Vyasa-puja book in honor of Srila Prabhupada, he started experiencing more discomfort in what we called "the lump" in his left foot. He sought acupuncture* *therapy from a well-known acupuncturist in Washington D.C. The treatments alleviated some of the pain, but there were some noticeable changes in the lump's physical appearance—it had decreased in circumference but increased in height.*

He was also experiencing pain from one of his teeth. On the day of the New York Ratha-yatra, I drove him and Vraja-lila to New Jersey, where he received dental care. He wanted to continue on to New York even though his mouth was sore and he wasn't feeling fit to dance in the parade. As we got nearer to 5th Avenue, he saw many devotees running to meet Lord Jagannath's cart, and he immediately asked us to drop him off, so he could take part in it. He had decided that he wanted to dance with Lord Jagannath and the devotees. As soon as Lord Jagannath pulled into Washington Square Park, Gurudeva asked us to drive him to his Kalpa-vriksha and Lagima's house—these are two of his disciples who lived in the general area. I remember he spoke with Yogeshvara Prabhu and another devotee and then we left the festival site.

On the way to Kalpa's house, Gurudeva expressed that he really wasn't feeling well, and he wanted us to drive him back to Gita Nagari. He was experiencing pain in his foot and, he said, he had never felt so much fatigue after dancing in Kirtan. We all agreed that this fatigue was possibly the result of the anesthesia administered during the dental procedure done earlier that day. During this general time period, he continued receiving acupuncture treatments for the pain in his foot and maintained his active preaching schedule.

Vraja-lila: *In that same year, only one month later, Gurudeva was invited, and agreed to attend, the yearly celebration of the "Festival of the Chariots," Lord Jagannath's Ratha-yatra in Toronto, Canada. I remember the day before he left for Canada, he revealed to Ekavira and me that he was experiencing slight pain and twitches in his foot. Even though Gurudeva was receiving acupuncture treatments, the height of "the lump" had grown significantly. He rarely* *shared information about his physical condition with anyone, but his disciple, Nimai Chaitanya, a health care practitioner, would visit him regularly to care for the foot, and so information about his condition leaked out.*

Gurudeva asked us to call Nimai to come to Gita Nagari when he returned from his extended trip. I remember Ekavira asking him to cancel the trip, but he refused. He said he could not disappoint the devotees. He also planned to facilitate workshops arranged by his disciples in Detroit, Cleveland, Maryland and then back in Gita Nagari.

Before Gurudeva left for Toronto, he instructed Ekavira and me to attend the yearly "Lord Have Mercy Festival" in Cleveland, and to meet him in Detroit with Bhutabhavana Das, one of his disciples visiting from England. The morning after the festival we received a phone call informing us that Gurudeva was experiencing severe pain in his foot after dancing ecstatically at Ratha-yatra, and that he needed immediate medical care. Gurudeva was then driven from Toronto to Detroit, which is quite a trip.

The evening he arrived in Detroit, he facilitated the program for the devotees who were in deep anxiety, waiting to hear about his condition. The next morning he was taken to see the doctor, who arranged several tests.

Ekavira: *The doctor informed us that the results of the tests couldn't exactly determine what was wrong with the foot. However, he strongly recommended that Gurudeva see a foot specialist right away. As Vraja-lila mentioned, the tumor was continuously increasing in size. Gurudeva did not give much attention to the tumor because he was always more focused on his responsibilities for his Guru's mission, which kept him on a nonstop traveling schedule.*

He cancelled all his programs in Detroit, and the next day we drove to Cleveland, where Gurudeva again facilitated a program at the home of his disciples, Avadutha Das and Agnihotra Dasi. The next day we left for Maryland. Once in Maryland, a foot specialist examined the tumor and recommended an operation, to extract the tumor altogether. After the operation, a biopsy on the tissue would finally determine what the problem was in exacting detail. Hearing this, Gurudeva agreed to do it.

The doctor then ordered pre-operation exams and scheduled an operation to take place only two days later. Gurudeva received the pre-operation exams and we went back to the Institute, which is at Madhvacharya's house. The next day, Gurudeva received a call from the doctor's office with the test results. Gurudeva's blood test results were almost "off the charts"! His blood pressure was well above normal and glucose level was at a dangerous level of 475! He was told that the operation must be postponed and could not be performed until his blood test results were within normal range. At that time he was prescribed a medication to reduce his blood glucose level. We also modified his diet and made sure that his body was well hydrated—he drank at least three liters of water per day. A few days later his blood test results were in the normal range and a tumor extraction and biopsy were performed.

Vraja-lila: *Madhvacharya had taken Gurudeva to the hospital to see the doctors; they were supposed to give him the results of the biopsy. I remember Ekavira and me waiting at Madhva and Kunti's house in Gurudeva's room, anxiously waiting for him to return. He was smiling when he walked in the room and sat in his chair. We were both relieved when we saw his smile. Then he started to speak, "It looks like cancer—and they want to cut my foot off; that's what the experts say."*

We were stunned, looking at him in disbelief! And he was joking about it. He was joking, laughing; he said, "Yeah, I'm outta here! I'm outta here!" Like that. So, because of his light-heartedness, we were thinking that maybe it's not real, you know, because he wasn't very serious about it. I thought maybe the doctors had made a mistake, that it was just not possible. How could he have cancer? He was just dancing at Ratha-yatra. He is never seriously sick—my mind was reeling; I sat down and could not speak for quite some time. This was definitely the biggest shock I had ever experienced in my life.

Ekavira: *Soon after, his lighthearted mood changed. He became grave. He spoke in a more serious manner, and we understood that it was time to inquire about cancer therapy. Murari Gupta, Dhruva Maharaja, Devarishi and I acted as a research team. We talked to many different physicians throughout the world to try to figure out the best approach, the best method, that could possibly lead to recovery. That's what we were hoping for, at least at that point.*

After compiling the information, we reported the results to Gurudeva. While the team was investigating various cancer clinics, Murari Gupta scheduled appointments to get a second and third opinion. He was referred to an oncologist who specialized in melanoma, and was one of the most successful and experienced oncologists in the country. The third appointment was scheduled at the National Institute of Health (NIH). Murari Gupta also scheduled an appointment at the Laurel Health Clinic. This is where we met Dr. Sevieri, an allopathic and naturopathic doctor.

Gurudeva liked this particular doctor, who worked with several cancer clinics in Mexico, which was a bonus. He was also extremely helpful with Gurudeva's therapy and acted as one of his primary physicians. Whenever there was a need, wherever we were, if we contacted Dr. Sevieri he was anxious to assist us. He recommended the "Hope for Cancer Clinic" and provided a reference. After researching the Clinic's cancer therapies, Gurudeva had an extensive conversation with its Director, Dr. Antonio Jimenez. After the consultation, Gurudeva called Vraja-lila and the team into his room and informed us of his decision to go to this clinic. Then he told Vraja-lila and I that he wanted to leave the following day. And so, the next day we were on our way to Mexico.

Vraja-lila: *This journey with Gurudeva would only begin in Mexico; it would continue to California, Hawaii, Maryland, and finally Gita Nagari. For over twenty-five years, Gurudeva had been teaching me many spiritual lessons. However, I was to learn some of the most valuable lessons on this journey. Was I ready for this? No, I wasn't, but Gurudeva gave me strength—his will to please his Guru Maharaja was an inspiration.*

Dr. Antonio Jimenez, or Dr. Tony, as he was affectionately referred to by his patients, arranged for us to have an apartment in a residential hotel close to the clinic. Our apartment in the hotel had one bedroom, a small kitchen area, and a living room. Gurudeva stayed in the bedroom, Ekavira and I in the living room. This was not the first time we had to live with Guru Maharaja in such close quarters, and traveling with him often meant staying in austere situations. His focus was always to expand Srila Prabhupada's mission, never his own comfort.

This time, however, was a little different. While it was still somewhat austere, we were not here planning and developing a teaching strategy; we were living together to assist our Gurudeva battle a deadly disease—cancer.

Aware how stressful this was for us, Gurudeva was extremely gentle with Ekavira and me. He often openly expressed so much gratitude for everything he was experiencing. In the mornings before we left for the clinic, he would rise early to chant his rounds. We would leave the hotel every morning by at 7:15 AM to start his first treatment at 8:00 AM. We rarely left the clinic before 8:00 PM. Gurudeva strictly followed the protocol given by the doctors, and he also maintained a disciplined daily schedule writing his book, recording his life events, having Ekavira read to him from books by both Srila Prabhupada and Shivaram Maharaja, and he was also dictating e-mail letters to me.

He was in constant communication with some Godbrothers—I

*particularly remember Bhurijan Prabhu. He wrote often and Gu-
rudeva relished reading his letters. He also wrote regularly to some
members of his book team. It was during this time that I more clearly
understood how much he depended on the disciples who worked on his
books. At night, when we returned to the hotel, he would read whatever replies he could not read during the day. Some evenings Ekavira
would complete Gurudeva's treatment at the hotel, because the last
vehicle to the hotel left the clinic at 8:00 PM. We were always the first
to arrive at the clinic and the last to leave. It was intense, but he was
determined to do his part if it would help him heal. The meals were
austere—salt free, sugar free, oil free, everything steamed or raw.*

*Even with the intensity of this situation, and with the open
wound, his tumor, not healing properly, Gurudeva always remained steadfast, sometimes grave, but always with a caring mood.
We always looked forward to our evenings back at the hotel because
he would share many realizations from his experiences before we
retired for the night. We tried our best to accept his condition, even
if it was all a little surreal. On good days, when his treatments
seemed to be helping, we felt as though we were on another teaching
adventure, as we had been so many times before.*

Ekavira: *The employees at the clinic were amazed with Gurudeva's
attitude. They said that they had never had a patient with such a
positive mood. And the physicians there, like Dr. Jimenez, had been
treating cancer patients for eighteen years or so—some had been
treating cancer patients for thirty-five years. When Dr. Jimenez
saw Gurudeva's tumor, he said that it was the largest concentration of melanoma he'd ever seen. But Gurudeva was fine. He was
diagnosed with one of the most intense forms of cancer, and he just
chanted, spoke about Krishna, and wrote meditations.*

*The doctors were very attentive to Gurudeva. The senior-most
physician would spend as much time as possible with him. Every
day he would sit and ask spiritual questions. Dr. Jimenez would*

also speak to him every day and arranged for various colleagues to have discussions every few days. Dr. Jimenez also arranged for Gurudeva to speak to a group of healthcare practitioners. Gurudeva in fact spoke most compassionately to this group, reminding them of the God factor in health care. The audience was inspired, and, after his speech, they lined up to greet him and to speak to him about his life experience as well as his experience with the Hope for Cancer Clinic.

The physicians, nurses, staff, and patients loved him. During the three weeks he was there, they all used to care for him, and talk to him, as much as possible. When his treatment at the Hope for Cancer Clinic was complete, everyone there saw him off with eyes full of tears.

Vraja-lila: *The staff at the Hope for Cancer Clinic always encouraged their patients to focus on how "hope" played a role in surviving cancer. Of course, the staff had never met an advanced spiritual person who imbibed the mood of "hope" unlike anyone else—and who simultaneously taught everyone around him how to surrender to the arrangements of the Supreme Lord. Gurudeva was seen as a living saint in the clinic. He inspired everyone to think more about the Lord in their daily activities.*

The patients, as well as the staff, would lovingly call him "The Swami." Often, they would have in-depth discussions with him to learn more about his beliefs. News traveled fast about Gurudeva's stay in the clinic, and of course many devotees wanted to visit him. Gurudeva would always ask us to discourage anyone that wanted to come, because he wanted to stay focused on his daily routine.

Just before the end of our stay in Mexico, Gurudeva agreed that a Godbrother, Yamuna Das, and two disciples of his Godbrothers, Yudhishthira Prabhu and Radha Dasi, both very dear friends of Ekavira and I, could visit him. They were eager to serve Gurudeva. These devotees were instrumental in arranging for Gurudeva's care at our next stop, which was in Palm Springs, California.

After three weeks of intensive treatments in Mexico, Radha Dasi, the wife of Yudhishthira, and Radha's mother, too, arranged for us to stay at an exclusive townhouse in Palm Springs, California. Radha and Yudhisthira made this arrangement to facilitate Gurudeva's treatments. Dr. Tony had suggested that we stay in the area for another two weeks, so that Ekavira could administer the treatments and still be near the doctors' offices in case of complications. Ekavira was now trained by the doctors to administer the different therapies and to care for the large open wound on Gurudeva's foot.

A treasured memory of our experience in Palm Springs was a home program arranged by Yudhishthira and Radha Dasi in their home. That day, Gurudeva was extremely nauseous and could not retain any food or water in his stomach. Ekavira suggested that we cancel the program, but, of course, Gurudeva refused. Yudhishthira and Radha had invited many people, mostly from outside the movement, and Gurudeva was excited to meet with them.

During the ride to the home of Yudhishthira and Radha, Gurudeva was still nauseous, but he was determined to go to the program. When we walked into their home, there was a room full of people waiting for him; we were surprised that among the guests were many devotees who had driven from as far as Los Angeles and Sacramento, just to hear Gurudeva speak. He was especially happy to see his Godbrother, Archita Prabhu, and also Divyambar. I remember how Gurudeva hopped with his cane on one foot, offering his compassionate smile to all who were present, and he sat on a chair arranged specially for him.

When he started to speak, he shared one of the meditations from his book, Beggar IV, *and elaborated on his many realizations about being ill. Driving back to our apartment, I asked Gurudeva about his nauseous condition. He had actually forgotten that he was nauseous all the way up until the program had begun. As was his custom, when we accompanied him to preaching programs, he ecstatically shared highlights of the evening on the entire ride back to the apartment. He was so happy to see and speak with the devotees who came to the program as well as to meet all the friends of Yudhishthira and Radha. We were both—Ekavira and I—so happy to have this moment with our Gurudeva.*

As the time got near for us to leave Palm Springs, Gurudeva contemplated where we would go next. He wanted solitude, a place where he could concentrate on his writing, his treatments, and, hopefully, his healing. He had several offers for quiet places, and we discussed the pros and cons of each one. Gurudeva decided that we should accept the offer of his Godbrother, Dasharath Prabhu in Hawaii. And so, once again, we packed everything and left.

This time we flew to Maryland to Madhvacharya and Kunti's home for a short visit. Gurudeva had us call disciples, friends, and well-wishers so that he could meet with them and share his then-present health status. Of course, we ended up having a house full of devotees and well-wishers, and he lovingly brought everyone up to date, informing them that we were leaving for Hawaii in a few days.

His doctor in Mexico had suggested that he remain at one location for at least six months, minimizing his frequent travels. But this was not possible at the time. Within a few days, we flew out of Dulles Airport to Big Island Hawaii. We arrived at Dasharath's house the day before Kartik 2004.

During this most auspicious month living in Hawaii, Gurudeva, Ekavira and I had to face the horrors of how cancer can quickly attack the entire body. Unlike the clinic in Mexico and the apartment in Palm Springs, our Hawaiian residence was especially austere and extremely quiet. Gurudeva wanted solitude. He wanted to concentrate on writing, and on his daily treatments. Ekavira resumed his daily services administering Gurudeva's medicines. I resumed my service as the secretary, cook, and pujari. On occasion, a few devotees would visit Gurudeva to offer service. I remember his Godbrother Pariksit Prabhu, one of the first artists in ISKCON, and his wife, came by. Mahesh and Brihan, from New Vrindavan, and Vidugya and his wife Radha, who served with Gurudeva at the restaurant in Washington D.C., were there too. A few disciples that lived in Honolulu also came to offer their services. Gurudeva was extremely pleased when the devotees came to visit, but he rarely spoke to them about all the physical challenges he was facing. Rather, he spoke about Krishna Consciousness.

On two occasions he was invited to speak to different gatherings of devotees. He was invited to speak on Govardhan Puja at the temple in Honakaa. The other invitation came from his Godbrother, Gopavrindapal Prabhu, who invited him to speak to the devotees on Srila Prabhupada's disappearance day at his preaching center in Hilo. Gurudeva went on both occasions, complying with the wishes of the devotees, even though he was extremely weak. The devotees were eager to hear from him, and he was just as eager to reciprocate.

He always encouraged the devotees to stay committed on the path of Krishna Consciousness, regardless of the challenges they might be facing. This principle came to life while we were in Hawaii. The entire time we were there, we felt like we were riding a roller coaster with Gurudeva's health. Some days he was strong, and on others, he was weak, with his illness experiencing so many complications. And each time, we would rush him to the emergency hospital. First, his tooth became infected and had to be extracted, and then the port in his chest had to be removed and replaced. After that, the wound on his foot became infected.

In addition to these emergency visits, Gurudeva was admitted in the hospital at least twice. We called Dr. Tony in Mexico to explain what was happening with Gurudeva. As a result, Dr. Tony informed us that he would come to Hawaii to meet with the doctors. When he arrived, he came straight from the airport and met us at the hospital.

He examined Gurudeva's foot and he and the other doctors agreed that Gurudeva should consider amputation. This was because the tumor was growing rapidly, and Gurudeva's energy level had decreased significantly, which was a sign that the tumor was depleting his body. Remember, Gurudeva had refused to get the foot amputated when the doctors made the suggestion in Washington D.C. This time, he was faced with again having to make that decision.

I remember the night Ekavira brought him back from the hospital after he had been there for a few days—he couldn't walk. Ekavira carried him to bed. That night, he asked Ekavira for me to come to his room with a pen and writing pad. I was really frightened, not knowing what to expect. He looked tired and weak, but he was determined to dictate what he called his "last instructions." These were a few particulars about how things should go on in his physical absence. He told us he might leave his body that night, because he didn't want to go on with the physical suffering any more. I remember saying to him, "Gurudeva, please don't leave tonight; we are far away from all the devotees. Please let us take you back to those who love you."

I never slept that night. We just kept praying that he would not leave his body in Hawaii. It was after that night that Ekavira and I suggested to Gurudeva that we must leave Hawaii. I was sending daily correspondence to devotees all over the world, so when his God-family learned that he had made a decision, at least at that time, to not undergo the amputation, they started calling to speak with him. I remember giving Malati Prabhu, Bir Krishna Maharaja and Radhanath Swami his phone number in the hospital. I do believe it was the love that he felt from his God-family that helped him to make the big decision to amputate his foot.

Within thirty-six hours of his saying "yes," Ekavira, Vidugya, Radha and I packed as much as we could take on a plane and prepared to go. Chintamani and Anasuya arranged our tickets and we were on our way back to Maryland. We contacted Madhvacarya before leaving Hawaii and he made all the arrangements in the hospital for Gurudeva's amputation. Murari and Padma were to meet us at the airport with a wheelchair. Gurudeva had a first class seat on the airplane. However, when we went to seat him, he asked us to have the person sitting next to us in the coach section exchange seats with him. He wanted to sit with us. Of course, that person in coach readily agreed. Once we were all seated, Gurudeva placed his foot on Ekavira's lap and went to sleep. We thanked Krishna on the plane for allowing us to bring our Gurudeva—still alive—to the devotees on the East Coast.

Chintamani Dasi tells us her firsthand memories of the amputation episode, which took place on December 23, 2004:

When Bhakti Tirtha Swami went to the hospital for the amputation, a number of devotees went to be with him. He was in a room getting some tests before the surgery. Jagannath Pandit, my husband, was in the room talking to him and I was outside the door, feeling conflicted about whether to go in or not. Gurudeva asked where I was and told Jagannath to tell me to come in. I slowly entered the room. He was lying down and looked very, very sick and weak. The whites of his eyes were dark yellow. I said, "Gurudeva, we're praying for you." He said, "Your prayers are received. They're in storage." Then he winked at us. It was such a loving gesture, particularly when he was so ill but still getting us to smile.

He was speaking very slowly, almost in a whisper and was closing his eyes frequently. He told me how he had dictated details to Vraja-lila about the Health Fund and that I should "study them carefully." His thoughts were on how to make sure that devotees' health needs would be taken care of; this is the purpose of the Health Fund. He was commenting on how this Fund might be financed in the future and I offered a way that I might be able to help. He said, "You buy a house and get your family situated. That would make me more happy." (We had been displaced from our home since 2001 due to mold problems and recently had started renting a small trailer.) Jagannath responded, "We can do both."

Gurudeva's comments almost brought me to tears. He was so sick and still he was thinking of the other devotees' welfare in terms of the future of the Health Fund. And then, even though that project was so important to him, when I mentioned a sacrifice I could make to help financially, his concern was for our family. The amount of love I felt coming from him was so overwhelming it was almost painful.

By the end of December, his pain was minimal, because his body was not burdened by the cancerous foot. He was soon moved to a rehabilitation clinic, so he could learn how to maneuver his body and to take care of his basic needs now that he was missing a limb. He was there for three weeks, as 2004 turned into 2005. Vraja-lila and Ekavira cooked his meals, dutifully taking *prasadam* to him every day. His niece (Renita) had flown in from Cleveland the day of the operation, just to be with him. His oldest sister's daughter, she stayed at the hospital during the initial ordeal. When she returned to Cleveland, other devotees came to assist while he recuperated.

In early January, 2005, Bhakti Tirtha Maharaja was discharged from the hospital, at which time he went to stay at the home of Murari Prabhu and Padma Devi. The quiet atmosphere there was healing, and he took the time to regroup—to get used to having one leg, and to become accustomed to his prosthesis. He needed to regain strength and to continue learning how to tend to basic needs, like going to the bathroom. To do all of this properly would call for physical therapy, and he was enthusiastic to begin, to learn how to move around in his new debilitated condition. He seemed to get stronger with each passing day, and his breathing returned to normal, as did his appetite. Still, a prostate problem complicated matters, especially during the night, when he was forced to wake up every hour or so to urinate.

For the next couple of months, his health seemed to fluctuate, but, overall, it was deteriorating.

By the end of March he was taking medications via a catheter, inserted directly into the left side of his heart. Earlier that month, he had noticed a throbbing sensation and tenderness in his chest, just above the catheter. This eventually gave rise to a swollen and painful area over his left collarbone. Thinking that the catheter might have caused an infection, he journeyed yet again to the hospital, hoping to assess the damage.

The attending doctor ordered a scan to see what was going on inside Maharaja's body, and then, if necessary, he would order that the catheter be removed. While waiting for blood tests prior to the scan, Maharaja went to lift his briefcase with his left hand and suddenly heard a "crack," which was accompanied by immense pain. Afterwards, he had difficulty moving his left arm, and, because of this, a rush was put on the scan.

As it turned out, the swelling and pain was in fact a tumor on the left collarbone—a result of the cancer having now spread to the bones. The tumor had eaten away so much of the collarbone that only a thin layer of normal tissue remained, causing it to crack under the minor pressure of lifting his briefcase. The doctor's report: the cancer was now in the lymph nodes, muscles, and bones. This meant that the amputation did not accomplish its intended purpose—to stop the spread of the cancer.

His left arm was now in a sling, and it was unlikely, said the doctors, that it would ever heal. The entire left side of his body, in fact, was severely compromised, both due to the fracture of the collarbone and the amputation of the lower portion of his leg. For a spiritual warrior such as he, who was accustomed to moving quickly, world travel, and ecstatic dance, limited movement was as good as death. Though optimistic and Krishna conscious, he was now certain that he was going to leave the world much sooner than previously expected.

In fact, by April, 2005, he would come to Gita Nagari and stay there for the rest of his life—which lasted another two months.

Going Inward

On May 31, Bhakti Tirtha Swami's disciples issued the following letter to all devotees. It was an attempt to summarize his last public appearance, which had taken place the prior day, and to reconcile his decision to leave this world. He no longer wanted to do battle with cancer but instead wanted to set an example of how a devotee could leave the material world as an honorable spiritual warrior. The letter reads as follows:

> *Dear Maharajas and Prabhus,*
>
> *Please accept my humble obeisances. All glories to Srila Prabhupada. Yesterday afternoon in Gita Nagari, His Holiness Bhakti Tirtha Swami made his final public appearance. He was joined by Radhanath Swami, Gunagrahi Swami, Bhaktivaibhava Swami, Bhakti Vishrambha Madhava Swami and Chandramauli Swami. Bhakti Tirtha Swami spoke with great love and compassion to the devotees as he embarked on sixty minutes of honest and open sharing, explaining why this would be his last public appearance. "The time has now come to enter into* nirjana-bhajan," *Maharaja revealed, sharing his decision to focus on his internal life by engaging in* mana-scva *(service in the mind). His desire now is only to speak, hear and think about Krishna. Maharaja went on to say that although a devotee is traditionally not meant to reveal his or her internal* bhajan, *it is also important at this time to consider* priti, *which involves revealing the mind in confidence and hearing others reveal their minds. In this mood, Maharaja desired to share some of his experiences involving the separation of the body, mind and soul that devotees undergo when they leave their bodies.*
>
> *He went on to say that his perception of dying on the battlefield was to leave this world like Grandfather Bhishmadeva, to preach*

until his very last breath. At the same time, he realizes that his service to Srila Prabhupada in this body, plane and institution is now over. As a result of his prayer in the mood of Vasudeva Datta, Maharaja has opened himself up to being used as a puppet by Srila Prabhupada, publicly undergoing the death experience in such a way that he can share it with us, leaving his example as a legacy to assist in preparing us for when we, too, must one day leave the body. So in many ways he is still dying on the battlefield.

Maharaja acknowledged that his service to Srila Prabhupada was unorthodox, and that this was both a blessing and a curse. A large part of his preaching involved being attentive to secular happenings on the planet, requiring him to acquire information through which he could relate to people involved in corporate leadership and politics. This was his sacrifice. By extending himself to preach, he fortunately received many blessings, but at the same time, immersing himself in secular subject matter did not supply the deep nourishment necessary for his soul. Now it was time for him to give his complete attention to the pastimes of Lord Krishna in Vraja, to compensate for that deficit.

From now on, Bhakti Tirtha Swami explained, the only devotees who would be seeing him personally would be his caregivers and Radhanath Swami, who will be staying in Gita Nagari until Bhakti Tirtha Swami departs. Bhakti Tirtha Swami expressed his deep thanks to Radhanath Swami, whom he views as a very special caregiver sent by Srila Prabhupada to assist him with the transition. If anyone else gets to see him, Maharaja said, it would be as a result of their services—as they bring something into his room, or read Krishna's pastimes to him. Only hearing, speaking and thinking of Krishna and Vrindavan from now on, Maharaja cautioned devotees that he would more than likely not respond if any other topic is brought up in his presence. The twice-daily Kirtan outside his room will continue: although the devotees who come to sing for him may not see Maharaja in person, they should know that he really appreciates their services.

Before closing with three quotes regarding nirjana-bhajan, *Bhakti Tirtha Swami emphasized the need for us to understand this process properly. Under no circumstances should it be undertaken prematurely. Here are those quotes:*

"While Sri Chaitanya Mahaprabhu thus resided at Jagannath Puri (Nilachala), he was continuously overwhelmed, night and day, by separation from Krishna. Day and night He tasted transcendental blissful songs and verses with two associates, namely Svarup Damodara and Ramananda Raya. He relished the symptoms of various transcendental emotions such as jubilation, lamentation, anger, humility, anxiety, grief, eagerness and satisfaction. He would recite His own verses, expressing their meanings and emotions, and thus enjoy tasting them with these two friends. Sometimes the Lord would be absorbed in a particular emotion and would stay awake all night reciting verses and relishing their taste." (Chaitanya-charitamrita, Antya *20.3-7)*

"Thus Bhaktisiddhanta Sarasvati Thakur advocated that every devotee, under the guidance of an expert spiritual master, preach the Bhakti movement, Krishna Consciousness, all over the world. Only when one is mature can he sit in a solitary place and retire from preaching all over the world. Following this example, the devotees of the International Society for Krishna Consciousness now render service as preachers in various parts of the world. Now they can allow the spiritual master to retire from active preaching work. In the last stage of the spiritual master's life, the devotees of the spiritual master should take the preaching activities into their own hands. In this way the spiritual master can sit down in a solitary place and render nirjana-bhajan.*" (Srila Prabhupada,* Srimad-Bhagavatam *4.28.33, commentary)*

"In 1977, A. C. Bhaktivedanta Swami Prabhupada, at the

age of 82, suffered illness repeatedly and became in a physically weakened state. He decided to discontinue his travelling around the world and take shelter of Vrindavan, the sacred place of Lord Krishna's pastimes. He listened and chanted 'Hare Krishna' and meditated on the transcendental pastimes of the Lord, throughout the day and night. However, Srila Prabhupada remained in the association of his loving disciples, who assisted him during his final pastime by chanting, very softly and sweetly, the Hare Krishna mantra twenty-four hours a day. Srila Prabhupada said that this was his 'nirjana-bhajan,' *and that his* sannyasi *disciples . . . had to take over the responsibility of travelling and preaching all over the world, as he would not be able to travel anymore. This great spiritual master had taken shelter of Lord Krishna in Vrindavan during the last days of this life. (Jayapataka Swami, Commentary on Srila Bhaktisiddhanta's* Vaishnava Ke?, *Verse 19)*

The idea behind *nirjana-bhajan*—"solitary worship, becoming absorbed in higher meditations"—is to focus on Krishna. The *Bhagavad-gita* (8.5) states that a person's focal point at the time of death determines where they will go upon leaving the body. For this reason, practitioners attempt to absorb their consciousness on God's essence throughout their life—so that focusing on Him can become almost second nature when it is time to leave the body. Though Bhakti Tirtha Swami had dedicated his life to God, the vast majority of his time was spent "on the battlefield," distributing books, preaching to others, helping them to walk the spiritual path. Now it was time to focus his own consciousness on the Supreme, on Krishna, specifically, and by such absorption to transfer his soul to Krishna's realm.

Srila Prabhupada states in his book, *Krsna*:

It is essential for persons who are actually liberated to hear about the pastimes of Krishna. That is the supreme relishable subject matter for one in the liberated state. Also, if persons who are trying to be liberated hear such narrations . . . then their path of liberation becomes very clear.

While Bhakti Tirtha Swami's decision to enter into the state of *nirjana-bhajan* is certainly sanctioned by his esteemed predecessors, one might wonder why he chose to do so in Gita Nagari. After all, the great teachers in his lineage place great importance on the holy environment known as Vrindavan, and part of this higher *bhajan* specifically recommends residence there, especially if one hopes to reach ultimate perfection.

There are many reasons for his choice, and they are all in line with the philosophy of his Vaishnava tradition. First of all, he wanted his disciples to have access to his final lesson—how to die on the battlefield. If he had chosen to breathe his last in Vrindavan, India, precious few would be able to follow him there, thus missing this most crucial of all instructions. In addition, he wanted to show that the holy places established by Srila Prabhupada and his disciples were not different from their counterparts in India. Indeed, this is why they were named "New Vrindavan," "New Varshana," "New Talavan," and even "Gita Nagari," among others.

"Vrindavan" is ultimately a state of mind—it is a place of dedication, where love of Krishna blossoms and is fully embraced. It is a transcendental world where God's inner nature can be absorbed and understood. As Prabhupada says, "Actually, going to Vrindavan involves taking shelter of the Six Goswamis [great teachers of the tradition] by reading the *Bhakti-rasamrita-sindhu, Vidagdha-madhava, Lalita-madhava* and the other books that they have given. In this way one can understand the transcendental loving affairs between Radha and Krishna." In other words, Vrindavan is not so much a place but a mood, a course of action, a meditation.

Absorption in the esoteric truths of Radha and Krishna is ultimately absorption in Vrindavan, for by such absorption one eagerly anticipates achieving the Lord. As Sanatana Goswami, one of the senior patriarchs of the tradition, writes, "Wherever one develops an intense desire to achieve the Supreme Lord, there one can obtain Him. But the Lord's merely residing in a certain place does not grant one His association." (*Brihat Bhagavatamrita*, 1.4.34)

Still, it should be clear that geographical Vrindavan, where the Lord always resides, is special, and that residence there is an advantage in spiritual life. In fact, Vrindavan is a magical place, with uniquely transformative abilities. It can bestow spiritual consciousness on those who even briefly visit its sacred precincts. But not everyone can go there, and, in such cases, its special fruit can be derived from other soil.

The Horrors (and Bliss) of War

And so, during Bhakti Tirtha Swami's final months, he stayed at his chosen departure portal: Gita Nagari. Here, he was assisted by a team of dedicated disciples from around the world, who acted as his caregivers until his final days. They tended to his every need around the clock. Several of them—specifically the men, given the restrictions of a *sannyasi*—literally slept in the same room. This way, there would never be a single moment in which he was alone, in case he needed someone for any purpose whatsoever. Every week the caregivers would send out reports to the Swami's website. The caregivers were Ekavira and Vraja-lila, who were among his leading disciples from America, along with Brahma Muhurta Dasa and Mangal Aratik Dasi. Dhruva Maharaja and Parijata Dasi, from South Africa, were there as well, as was Chiti-Shakti Dasi, from England, and Mahajana Dasa, from Argentina. Closer to the time of his departure, Kalpa-vriksha Dasa, Gopal Dasa, and Vrindavan Dasa joined the team, too. Purusha-sukta kept an elaborate journal of day-to-day developments, and Radhanath Swami, Bhakti Tirtha Maharaja's dearest friend and most transcendental associate, was always at his side. Other devotees would come and go frequently.

By early June, Bhakti Tirtha Maharaja was ensconced in *nirjana-*

bhajan. His absorption was as total as possible under the circumstances, but he still had to tend to disciples and dear ones, who would often come to visit him.

His body was now experiencing intense pain. Sangita Dasi and others assisted Ekavira Prabhu in administering pills for pain management. Sangita's presence was particularly appreciated. She was a highly qualified healthcare practitioner, and had founded, along with her Godsister, Jushaniya Dasi, "Vaishnavas C.A.R.E." (Counseling, Assistance, Resource, and Education for the Terminally ill and Their Families), a project fully supported by Bhakti Tirtha Maharaja. She writes:

> *During my visits to the Gita Nagari farm to see him, I watched in awe as he used his last bit of strength and energy to teach others about what he was experiencing. Every Sunday he willingly accepted much personal discomfort to travel from his house down a rocky road in order to give class to the large crowd of devotees who assembled weekly in the temple room. He began each class with a Kirtan and within minutes his voice would choke up and tears would flow from his eyes as he sang the holy names of Radha-Damodara, the presiding Deities in Gita Nagari.*
>
> *Watching him, I could not imagine the level of intense physical pain he was feeling, but like the "spiritual warrior" he was, he simply tolerated it in order to speak one more time to his devoted disciples and loving Godbrothers and Godsisters. Just as Maharaja lived his entire life thinking about the welfare of others, he spent his last days in this same mood.*
>
> *He never cared for himself or the pain it would bring him to give yet another dynamic lecture that touched the hearts of all who were present. The one class that stands out the most in my memory (and I am simply paraphrasing this) is when he asked for a show of hands from everyone who had ever suffered in any way and had asked, "Why me? Why not someone else?" He then asked for a raise of hands from those who had ever watched another's suffering and*

thought, "I'm glad it's not me." Finally, he asked who in the room had ever watched another's pain and suffering and thought, "Why them? Why not me?" This is the mood of a Vaishnava.

What can be said of such a rare soul?

After some time, of course, he did not make those regular trips down the rocky road to the temple. He remained, instead, at the nearby Institute house, lovingly tended to by his friends and caretakers.

The beginning of June also saw erratic sleep patterns. He would often stay up throughout the night. During those periods, Brahma Muhurta read to him, for he hungered for Krishna's pastimes, and Dhruva fanned him—he was sweating profusely. His eating was sparse and his voice was soft.

Vraja-lila: *The last few nights the men had been bringing him out of his room into the sitting room for a few hours to get a change of scenery. Usually he chanted, or watched a DVD on the holy temples in Vrindavan. He wanted to absorb himself in the Vrindavan mood, and this was obvious from his every gesture.*

Most importantly, he was completely absorbed in hearing and chanting. Each day he seemed more reconciled to his fate, happy about the prospects of returning home to the spiritual world. The devotees around him were also endeavoring to become more absorbed in focusing their consciousness on hearing and chanting. Even though they were keenly aware that they will grieve when their guru departs, there was a certain sweetness in the air, a certain intimacy, and the soothing knowledge that he will soon move out of his deteriorating body. From this point on, his close disciples, especially Purusha-sukta Prabhu, documented the final events of their guru's life. Below, we reproduce the most heart-rending segments of this documentation, and although heavily edited it is generally kept in its original present-tense format. The goal here is to assist readers in experiencing his last month as if it were taking place today.

June 6, 2005: He is getting noticeably weaker, and the cancer is spreading. His body shows more and more signs of stress. Still, his demeanor is strong and his thoughts clear. He continues to lose weight, though he is noticeably effulgent.

He tells the few disciples in his room, who were eager to hear him speak, what a relief it was to actually rest, since, for so many years, he had been a traveling preacher, without pause.

Although his appetite is minimal, he still honors his favorite dishes, sporadically prepared for him by his loving aides. Today, Radha Vallabha Dasa, a New York disciple of Radhanath Swami, came to Gita Nagari and prepared his specialty, pizza, for everyone in the house. Bhakti Tirtha Maharaja thanked Radha Vallabha for his mouth-watering offering, and the evening ended with Radhanath Swami personally serving pizza to all the caregivers.

June 9: Last night and early this morning Guru Maharaja's vital signs were very low. This means his blood pressure was very low, his pulse high, and his temperature high. This vital level could not maintain a physical body for very long, and is usually a sign that the body is shutting down. As the day progressed, Guru Maharaja's vitals improved and are currently stable. He is weak and has eaten very little (which is common these days). Still, he ate his tofu ice cream.

Guru Maharaja has been joking a lot. His mood is peaceful and happy, as he remarked today, "I am waiting for my chariot to come."

The sweet Krishna magic came forth in such a special way today, with the unexpected appearance of some very unique and exalted Brajabasis, that is, residents of Vrindavan. This group of devotees is specifically from Varshana, Sri Radha's village, in India, and Radhanath Swami had known them from his time in Vraja before he joined ISKCON. Of all the possible places in the world and all the possible times to be there, these rare devotees happened to be in Harrisburg,

Pennsylvania, only forty-five minutes away from Guru Maharaja!

Somehow, Radhanath Swami found out about their presence in the area, and arranged for them to come to the Institute house to chant for Guru Maharaja—a sign of Krishna's blessing on him.

These Vrindavan devotees came with Radhanath Swami into Gurudeva's quarters and began to chant *bhajans* about Sri Radha. Their group included a flute player, and when Maharaja heard the flute, he began to cry. This continued for around twenty minutes. Guru Maharaja was ecstatic. He said, "Today, Vrindavan has come to me."

There are so many special instances where the spiritual world becomes more overt in the Institute house. The other day, for example, Guru Maharaja requested more pictures of Vrindavan and of its residents, so that he could be engulfed with memories of the transcendental kingdom as per his *nirjana-bhajan*. Attempting to cater to this wish, the caregivers began meditating on how to cover up the large bookshelf that he is forced to look at throughout the day. Just then, our Godbrother, Ishana Gaura, brought in a large canvas picture of Radha and Krishna, just big enough to cover the bookshelf. Here was Vrindavan, situating itself right in front of Maharaja!

June 11: Basically, Guru Maharaja is anticipating his return home, his spiritual journey to Vrindavan.

It is taking him a much longer time to chant his rounds. Radhanath Maharaja extolled him as a modern-day example of Haridasa Thakur, the great teacher of the holy name. Ekavira Prabhu remarked, "For me, the thing that stood out the most was the example he sets by chanting his rounds. He is doing it for us, to set an example. He is not just sick—he is dying. Yet in this condition he is chanting his prescribed rounds just to set an example for us." Up until recently, Gurudeva was chanting twenty rounds daily on his beads, in addition to continuous hearing of *lila*, or the Vrindavan pastimes of the Lord. Now he is continuing with sixteen rounds.

Today, also, a twenty-four hour Kirtan began at the Institute house. In the living room, select *bhajaneers*, usually duets, chanted very softly for Gurudeva throughout the day and into the night, a short distance from his bedroom. He could hear it and would periodically smile approvingly.

The mysterious visit from the inhabitants of Vrindavan (who just happened to be in Harrisburg at the time), incessant hearing of Krishna's pastimes, the Radha-Krishna canvas covering his bookshelf, the soft but persistent Kirtan outside his bedroom door, the devotees surrounding him with love, and his determination to chant the holy names of the Lord—this is Vrindavan. But not just any aspect of Vrindavan. Brahma-muhurta Dasa reveals that he was absorbed in a high level of Krishna Consciousness:

> As Guru Maharaja always encouraged me to study our philosophy and culture, I had access to and presented Maharaja with texts written by our various acharyas. Right before he went into nirjana-bhajan, he stopped reading emails so he could start to identify himself less and less with the "Bhakti-tirtha Swami" persona. Although that persona was still connected to Krishna, it wasn't his eternal identity, which he wanted to remember and start to embrace as he left that particular body.
>
> I started putting together the summary verses of Govinda Lilamrita, the eight verses of Krishna's daily pastimes, so that Maharaja could meditate on them and remember what is happening in Vrindavan—in the spiritual world. It was at this point that he named me the "time keeper." He said that he would ask me the time and then I would tell him what is happening in Vrindavan at that time. So as time passed I started memorizing the verses and would recite them to him throughout the course of the day for him to meditate on as he engaged in his internal bhajan. Radhanath Swami would read with him from Srila Prabhupada's Chaitanya-charitamrita, especially the section on Madhavendra Puri's departure during the day, and I would read to him through the night.

I had gathered appropriate books, and organized the texts into various files. That way if I wasn't there, someone else could read them. One of the services we caretakers had was to create this Vrindavan atmosphere. Maharaja had an eclectic library suited to the type of outreach he did within the ISKCON community as well as within secular communities. One of them was full of secular books that continued to remind him of his own secular identity that he was trying to give up. We were thinking we should either remove the books or cover them to continue to help with the Vrindavan atmosphere. That's when he received a blanket with Radha and Krishna's feet and handprints on it. It was like a quilt. So his eyes saw Radha and Krishna, and his ears also bathed in the holy name; he was always chanting, and I would read these books to him.

Although Prabhupada's emphasis was clearly on the rules and regulations of Bhakti-yoga, he ultimately wanted devotees to enter into the Vrindavan mood, which necessitates reading about Krishna's pastimes as elucidated in his books. Encoded in the commentaries and sub-commentaries of the great Gaudiya Vaishnava theologians, advanced practitioners find inner wisdom and blueprints for esoteric procedures that remain hidden to the casual observer.

But this is not for everybody. Prabhupada argued that it was inappropriate to hear about the esoteric pastimes of Radha and Krishna if one was not first grounded in the fundamentals of spiritual life. Aware of these proscriptions, Maharaja would always gauge the esoteric literature against Prabhupada's books, asking Brahma-muhurta to find passages in his spiritual master's commentaries that confirm what the Vrindavan Goswamis say. Always the chaste disciple, Bhakti Tirtha Maharaja became absorbed in Krishna's pastimes, but only in the mood of Srila Prabhupada.

As his absorption in Krishna Consciousness became more intense, his time grew near.

June 13: After the New York Ratha-yatra, Lord Jagannath's devotees decided to bring Him to see Bhakti Tirtha Maharaja, driving several hundred miles out of their way to do so. Once they arrived, Maharaja, even though in a heightened state of physical pain, came outside to greet Jagannath, Baladeva and Subadhra, with whom he intimately interacted as a new Brahmin, so many years before in Philadelphia, and with whom he enjoyed special intimacy while in Puri as an aspiring renunciant. They would now give him audience one last time from a makeshift altar in a mini-van, parked outside the Institute house. There, from his wheelchair, he sang to the Lord, lovingly greeted all the devotees with his warm smile, personally distributed Jagannath *prasadam* to nearby disciples, and shared some final words of wisdom. This was the last time he would chant in public.

June 20: Something very special happened yesterday; another sweet manifestation of the Lord's great affection for his beloved devotee. Gurudeva has had a special connection with Tamal Krishna Goswami (TKG) since the days of Srila Prabhupada. TKG, as Srila Prabhupada's secretary, would read and reply to Gurudeva's famous preaching reports (the ones Srila Prabhupada would have read to him repeatedly). In fact, it was TKG who arranged for Gurudeva to meet with Srila Prabhupada in London, where Srila Prabhupada embraced Gurudeva and commended him for his important service of book distribution. Since the cancer set in, many times, especially recently, Gurudeva felt the presence of Tamal Krishna Goswami. He would often have dreams of him, as would some of the caregivers. In a recent dream, Gurudeva saw TKG coming to him with tears in his eyes, saying, "Srila Prabhupada is waiting for you."

Yesterday at noon, Ekavira Prabhu was told that devotees had arrived from Dallas, Texas, and wanted to show Gurudeva their Deities, Sri-Sri Radha-Damodara, Srila Tamal Krishna Maharaja's personal Radha-Krishna Deities. These particular forms of Krishna appeared mystically to TKG in 1980 or thereabouts. On a morning walk in

Juhu, Bombay, he saw a shiny object in the ocean. He sent his servant to investigate, and they came to see that it was a small Deity of Krishna. The experts he consulted said that it was at least 500 years old. Hearing the news, the Queen of Jaipur had a special Radharani Deity made out of pure gold, just to accompany this special Krishna Deity. TKG originally named them Radha-Gopinath, but later, out of great separation from his beloved Radha-Damodara, who now reside at Gita Nagari, he gave them that name instead.

The priest who is currently caring for them felt a tremendous compulsion to bring the Deities to Gurudeva. This feeling would come over her every time she dressed and worshiped them. Even though it was unlikely that it would ever happen, since she and her husband had absolutely no funds for travel, she arrived out of nowhere.

Shortly before noontime yesterday, Gurudeva woke up, after a fitful night's sleep. Seeing that he had awakened, Ekavira Prabhu told Gurudeva, "I have a surprise for you this morning, Gurudeva." No sooner could Gurudeva ask the obvious question, "What is it?" Ekavira responded: "Radha-Damodara are here to see you."

"Radha Damodara?" Gurudeva questioned. "Yes, but not the Gita Nagari Deities. These are Tamal Krishna Maharaja's Deities." At this point, Gurudeva motioned down from his seated position in bed to lie down. As he reclined back, he remarked, "This is amazing. This is so amazing. Krishna is so merciful. Krishna is so merciful." Immediately, Gurudeva arranged to go out to the living room to greet their Lordships, seeing them as the most honorable guests in his residence.

After coming out to view their Lordships, Gurudeva participated in the chanting that was led by the Dallas devotees. He was in tremendous bliss; smiling, chanting, crying and laughing simultaneously. He spoke for fifteen minutes, telling us that Krishna responds to our prayers, but that He responds based upon the mood in the heart. Gurudeva kept emphasizing this point—Krishna responds based upon what is in each individual's heart.

June 21: Today was a very special day. Yesterday evening, Gurudeva rested for about six hours. He awoke at 4:10 am and could not sleep anymore. He was in pain. He had perspired throughout the evening, and had symptoms of dehydration. The caregivers carefully sat him up and provided ice chips and water for his dry lips. His vitals had fluctuated, and later stabilized. He was enduring severe pain, and said that it increased to an extreme degree. The caregivers provided suitable medication, but the pain didn't subside.

At 8 AM, he expressed a desire to talk to the devotees. Despite his intense pain, he seemed determined to do this. And to ensure his clarity, he decided not to take his pain medication, even though it meant more pain than usual.

All the devotees assembled. Nanda Sunu Prabhu, Gurudeva's former secretary and one of his beloved Gurukuli disciples from England, was leading a very sweet Kirtan. As Gurudeva was getting ready to go out, Vraja-lila Prabhu said, "Go for it Gurudeva, go for it!" Gurudeva shook his head, like an innocent child.

Gurudeva entered the assembly of devotees carried on his chair—walking at this point was not possible. Since the prior week, when most devotees had last seen him, his physical appearance had markedly deteriorated. He is frail and weak, and it is difficult to see him like this. As he sat before the devotees, his face revealed great appreciation for all who were present. He spent some time catching his breath, and looked out at the devotees, with simple, sweet and charming glances. He took care to see that Radhanath Swami was situated comfortably, and then he spoke.

His voice was faint, and his cadence was in concert with his breath—slow and uneven. He said, "I do not have much breath left. That is a beautiful thing." Some moments went by. "Krishna is letting us know that our time is over. How wonderful this is; how glorious this is; how fortunate we are." He told us that his chariot was waiting for him.

He was sweating due to fever, and Ekavira and Dhruva Prabhu

were occasionally wiping his face. One devotee then fanned him with the peacock feathers, but it was a little too intense. Gurudeva then suggested, "Maybe use the *chamara* fan instead." After this, he made a joking comment that this was good, because the *chamara* is a little less prestigious than the peacock fan.

In his talk, he explained his situation to the devotees, expressing that, in his humble opinion, the pain was too much to bear, and from there he shared his concern for the pain of others. He remarked how he was aware of the pain and suffering of humanity and the devotees, and prayed to be used to help others deal with their pain. He said, "So many people are in pain, so many, and they don't have anyone to care for them; they don't have a support system." He was crying, going on for some time about the suffering and pain of others, and how his current affliction is something that has come forth to help others.

At this point, the devotees became emotional, so touched by his fathomless love and compassion. They of course knew of his deep feeling and empathy for living beings, but were amazed to see it expressed while he himself was in this condition, where he had every reason to be concerned with his own well-being.

Not wanting the devotees to be sad, he decided to return to his room. He ended by saying that he did not know when he would leave, but it would be some time soon—"today, tomorrow, a few days." By his request, Vakreshvara Pandit, the great Kirtan leader, led the devotees in chanting, much to their satisfaction.

June 22: This morning Gurudeva was stable. His resting patterns have changed. Even though he is taking pain medication (which causes drowsiness) and sleeping pills, he slept only lightly, maybe one hour at a time. He has not eaten in two days. He drank sixteen ounces of water on Monday and thirty-two on Tuesday. It is very difficult for Gurudeva to even drink water, as his esophagus is gradually collapsing. He told Radhanath Swami yesterday that tomorrow they will honor *prasadam* together.

364 / BLACK LOTUS

Gurudeva says that he doesn't know how much longer he can manage the pain, but at the same time he requests less pain medication each day. The caregivers see that Krishna is protecting him.

In the early afternoon, Radhanath Swami went in to meet with him. They were talking for some time. As Radhanath Swami mentioned Vasudeva Datta in the course of conversation, Gurudeva raised his hand to Radhanath Maharaja's head and pulled it to his heart. Keeping Maharaja's head pressed to his heart, Gurudeva started to weep. He trembled and repeated the name of Vasudeva Datta many times. After this, they continued to speak a little longer. Then Radhanath Swami left the room.

Kirtan then began. Initially, it was led by Bhava Bhakti Mataji from South Africa. She led by singing many of the tunes that Gurudeva likes. She was singing with great devotion and enthusiasm, and in response Gurudeva began to make soft gestures from his bed, as if he were dancing to her melodies. As far as possible he did his famous "jig"—circling his hand in time to the music, like a cowboy swinging a lasso, and moving his head to the beat. The devotees were deeply charmed.

June 24: Very faintly Gurudeva said: "So, just now Krishna has given me a house." Radhanath Swami replied softly, "Wow, did you hear that? Krishna just gave Maharaja a house. Yes, house also means home. Go back home Maharaja, back to Godhead. Krishna is there, and the cowherd boys and the forests, and Srila Prabhupada is holding the door for you!" Then Gurudeva's Godbrother Lokavarnotamma Prabhu came in and sat down close to him. Lokavarnotamma has been very supportive of Gurudeva's preaching in West Africa. Sitting there he began to cry.

"Lokavarnotamma says I must stay," smiled Gurudeva. But Radhanath Swami countered, "Go through the door, Maharaja," to which Gurudeva replied, "That's true, I must go through that door." It was very difficult for the devotees to understand what Gurudeva was saying as he could hardy move his mouth. He was straining to vocalize. Radhanath Maharaja was holding Gurudeva's hand.

Spontaneously, Radhanath Swami began to chant Hare Krishna in a soft voice. Soon all the devotees joined him. The collective consciousness was so focused. Already Gurudeva's compelling presence had captured the minds of everyone in the room, and now that focus was placed on the holy name of Krishna. After ten minutes the unison chanting stopped and Gurudeva commented, "Nice chanting." Then Radhanath Swami asked, "Would you like us to chant Kirtan for you?" Gurudeva replied with childlike eagerness, "Please!" And so Radhanath Maharaja began singing "Yashomati Nandana," a beautiful Vrindavan-based song, all the while holding Gurudeva's hand. Later, Gurudeva remarked that, "All that needs to be said has been said."

He has not taken food or water since yesterday morning. He just receives a soaked sponge to moisturize his mouth throughout the day (naturally he drinks some of that water). He was in a lot of pain this morning, so the caregivers repositioned him frequently. His vitals are stable, though they have fluctuated here and there.

Although he was experiencing intense pain, he wanted to walk. But with only one leg and weakness permeating his entire body, it was not entirely plausible. At that time, Radhanath Swami happened to be reciting the Mount Govardhan pastime, talking about how Lord Krishna had lifted the famous hill in Vrindavan on the pinky of His left hand. In the course of telling that story, he mentioned that when Srila Prabhupada was leaving his body, one of his last requests was to be taken to Govardhan Hill for a special pilgrimage—on a cart pulled by oxen. Just then, Radhanath Swami noted that there is a Govardhan Hill in Gita Nagari, too, since it is named after the original hill in Vrindavan. Thinking like this, he invited Gurudeva to go on pilgrimage, just as Prabhupada had wanted to go, so many years before.

"Would you like to go on a pilgrimage, Maharaja? The wheelchair can act as your cart and Ekavira can be your ox." Of course, weak though he was, Gurudeva enthusiastically responded in the affirmative. "Yes! Let's go!" Ekavira Prabhu immediately went to get the "cart" that he and Dhruva used for wheeling Maharaja here and there, and they started on their journey. Seeing Maharaja's pain, however, Vraja-lila suggested that they merely take him outside into the large living room, where he would be able to see Gita Nagari's Govardhan Hill through the window. She ran outside and immediately set up a small altar in the middle of the room with a small stone from Govardhan. Then Radhanath Swami, Ekavira, and Dhruva wheeled Maharaja outside, and they circumambulated Sri Giri Govardhan while chanting devotional songs. When Maharaja returned to his room, he was smiling and seemed happy.

June 26: This morning Gurudeva was resting. He had taken rest around 6 AM. He was up for most of the night, his pain persisting. He had been sustaining a fever for some time; this morning it was high. As the pain persisted yesterday, he had to be transported back and forth from his bed to his chair. The hospice nurse came to administer a subcutaneous (under his tissue) tube for his pain medication to be fed through. This tube is located on Gurudeva's chest. This simplifies the process of giving the pain medication, allowing him to continue to rest and avoid using his throat.

Yesterday he did have a significant change in his vital signs. His temperature and rate of breathing rose. When his vitals changed, there were some adjustments made in his room. Now the picture of Srila Prabhupada that Gurudeva cherishes so much is right in front of him.

The Kirtan continues, mostly in Gurudeva's room. The ambiance there contains such a vast array of moods: Gurudeva's physical pain with his profound devotion, the concern of the devotees with the sweetness of their love and care. All the while Krishna's holy names pervade everything, bringing forth the enchanting atmosphere of Vrindavan—with the presence of Krishna, what might appear to be a hospice becomes a place of pilgrimage.

Gurudeva's pain and rapid deterioration is intensifying the atmosphere. He hardly talks or responds to his external surroundings. The devotees are more reflective, and come together more and more in service and Kirtan. It is the best of times and the worst of times.

We have been informed by the doctor and the hospice nurse that Gurudeva has entered the active dying process. They said that his departure will occur between twenty-four and seventy-two hours. The nurse and doctor will inform us when it becomes clear that he has ten hours remaining. He could leave later than estimated, or sooner. It is in Krishna's hands.

The prior night (Saturday) was rough, with high fever and pain. Early this afternoon Mother Sangita arrived. By her care, his fever went down and his pain subsided to some extent. He has been resting the whole day. This is partly due to his lessened pain, but also due to the dying process.

As reported, Gurudeva is exhibiting one of the six symptoms of dying, namely, his eyes do not shut. The chanting in his room has become more intimate. There is very minimal instrumentation. It is a kind of choral *bhajan*. The devotees harmonize and unite in their offering of Kirtan. The mood is very serene and peaceful. Very reflective, and very sweet, bitter sweet.

Monday, June 27: Gurudeva lies on his bed surrounded by his caregivers. Radhanath Swami holds Gurudeva's hand, as his hand holds a Govardhan Shila, a sacred stone, nondifferent from Krishna Himself. Ekavira is on his left massaging his left hand; Dhruva is massaging his feet. Other caregivers take turns holding another Govardhan Shila on his head. Agni Prabhu fans him with a peacock fan at his right. A molding of Srila Prabhupada rests by his left arm. And he is adorned with *chandan*, a large *tulasi* garland from the Panca Tattva Deities and a beautiful flower garland from Radha-Damodara. The day is clear, and the room serene. The time is soon.

The sweet chanting of "Hare Krishna," in the classic tune, pervades the house. It is serene and stately. Srila Prabhupada looks upon Gurudeva from the altar that faces him above his feet. Beautiful images of Krishna with the cowherd boys and *gopis*, the transcendental maidens of Vrindavan, surround Gurudeva. He is peaceful and transfixed.

There is a slow queue of devotees coming in and offering respects. Many bring their Deities to show Gurudeva. They offer their prayers, their tears, and after a brief audience return to the living room where the majority of devotees are seated together in unison Kirtan. Everything is organized and harmonious. Fresh air circulates throughout Gurudeva's room.

Near to 1:00 PM the room filled with devotees again. Also outside of Gurudeva's room a sizable assembly of devotees are snuggled together in front of the door, getting a slight view of Gurudeva as he lies in his bed. Both groups of devotees are chanting the Mahamantra together, indicating the harmony that Krishna Consciousness has brought to their lives. There is a small path alongside to allow for devotees just arriving to come in and see him for one last time.

The caregivers continue to tend to his needs; keeping his mouth moist, his face clean and dry, lightly massaging his legs and foot, ensuring that proper circulation continues throughout.

Radhanath Swami stays fixed in front of Gurudeva, sometimes whispering into his ear, sometimes offering encouraging prayers. Often, he will tap Gurudeva lightly in time with the chanting, tapping his shoulder and arms. His affection radiates throughout the room.

Looking through the windows of Gurudeva's room, one can see the heads of various devotees popping in and out to get a different view of Gurudeva and to imbibe the holy atmosphere. Devotees from throughout the world continue to stream in: Dhanurdhar Swami, Rukmini and Anuttama, Brajabihari—so many are coming! They take their turn in fanning Gurudeva, glorifying him, and knowing he is always with Krishna.

On this day, June 27th, at 3:35 PM, His Holiness Bhakti Tirtha Swami passed away from the material world, and into the loving embrace of Srila Prabhupada and Sri-Sri Radha-Krishna. Just before his final breath, Sangita alerted Brahma-muhurta Prabhu, who immediately came and sprayed Radha-kunda water around his body and applied *tulasi* leaves on his tongue. Sangita and Madhvacharya, both professionally trained, checked his vital signs and confirmed that he had indeed left, that the life force was no longer in the body.

The Song Goes Ever On

After the proper mantras were chanted (led by Radhanath Swami) along with Vedic rituals for departed Vaishnava souls, a procession took place from the Institute house to the temple of Sri Sri Radha-Damodara, just down the road. By then, night had fallen, as devotees waited outside to accompany Bhakti Tirtha Swami to the temple. They held torches to light up the night sky, as Sri Chaitanya Mahaprabhu and His immediate followers had done in Bengal, some 500 years earlier. After several hours, close disciples, Godbrothers, and caregivers emerged from the house, along with Bhakti Tirtha Swami's body. He was on a palanquin, raised up by Madhvacharya, Garuda, Agni, and Pariksit, disciples who could scarcely believe they were carrying the remains of their Gurudeva's body. They battled to hold back tears, mostly unsuccessfully, as they performed their duty of carrying Bhakti Tirtha Swami to the temple amidst the chanting of loving devotees, initially led by Gaura-vani.

Once at the temple, a magnificent marble and wood bed, carved by Kalpa-vriksha, complete with ornamental Vedic embellishments, awaited Bhakti Tirtha Swami's body, which was gently placed in the bed and then brought before the deity of his spiritual master, Srila Prabhupada. After this, he was brought before Sri Sri Radha-Damodara, so they might witness the body of their dedicated devotee, soon after his departure from the material world. His body was inundated with flowers and garlands, befitting the great soul that he is.

All around him devotees sang in ecstatic Kirtan, with mixed happiness and sadness—they were gratified to know that a perfected life had reached its end on earth, to be rejoined with their Lordships in the spiritual world, or to go wherever he was needed most. They were sad that they would no longer have his association or see his smile. Still, they knew he would still be in their lives, one way or another, and that they would feel his love.

An elaborate Vedic ceremony then took place, with authentic rituals that his disciples had studied in anticipation of this inevitable moment. While his body lay on Kalpa-vriksha's ornate table-like bed, as the program ensued, devotees paid their final respects, offering prayers and thanks. They touched his foot and expressed appreciation for his life and work, which made theirs that much richer. Vakreshvara Pandit, Bhakti Tirtha Swami's Godbrother, famous throughout ISKCON for his pounding, resonant Kirtan, soon took over the lead singing, and devotees went wild.

And so, in accord with tradition, opulent festivities took place, with body washing, the chanting of mantras, carrying of the body to the local holy places, ecstatic Kirtan. Radhanath Swami then gave a lecture in remembrance of his dear friend and Godbrother and soulfully sang the traditional prayers for departed Vaishnavas. In this way, the event went on for almost four hours, until the director of the crematorium arrived. At that point, Bhakti Tirtha Swami's body was placed in a hearse, assisted by several devotees, as he was driven away. Throngs of well-wishers watched him go, their emotions palpable. Dry eyes were a thing of the past.

Still, the temple ceremony and his departure to the crematorium provided closure for many of his friends and disciples. They had time to process his departure, understanding that his life was well lived, and that his death was exemplary—for both were permeated with service to Krishna.

One of the few fortunate souls who accompanied his body to the crematorium, Jagannath Pandit remembers details of the cremation:

The cremation facility was in Lewistown, Pennsylvania, about one half-hour away from Gita Nagari. It's called Hoenstine Funeral Home, Inc. Ekavira, Dhruva, Brahma-muhurta, Vrindavan and I went to the funeral home in the morning. I drove the five of us in one car. The staff was very friendly and accommodating to our requests. The cremation room was in the back of the facility and we had to walk by empty coffins to get to it. When they opened the door to the room, which was the size of a large living room, Gurudeva's body was in the far corner. I don't recall my initial reaction, but he looked just the same as when he initially left the body. He had on new saffron and was still decorated with a Hari-nama chadar *and bright multi-colored flower petals and garlands around his face, chest and arms. His mouth was closed with a contented, slight smile. His forehead was still decorated with* candan *and beautiful Vaishnava* tilak. *Gurudeva always had the most perfectly applied* tilak. *He was always polished and meticulous about every aspect of his life.*

Brahma-muhurta brought bags of paraphernalia, mridanga, kartals, *and a* chamara. *I brought a video camera. Brahma immediately began chanting mantras and using ceremonial paraphernalia from his bag. For the first ten minutes, the staff watched in the back of the room. When there was a break in the chanting, they asked us to let them know when we were ready for them to do their part and they left the room. Brahma continued chanting and directed Dhruva to place fresh* candan *on his forehead. Brahma then led us in singing "Gurudeva," a traditional Vaishnava song.*

Then we each individually placed our head on the sole of Gurudeva's right foot and offered dandavats. *Everyone was very grave as we each placed* tulasi *leaves and* tulasi *branches from Krishna-Balaram Deities on his chest. Brahma also sprayed sacred Ganges water and sprinkled dust from the twelve forests of Vrindavan.*

Then we sang the prayers for a departed Vaishnava. This was very intense as we were getting closer to the end. I sensed a feeling of support and camaraderie amongst my Godbrothers as we moved through this difficult service.

Someone went and got the man in charge. He opened the doors to the chamber and instructed us how to place him inside. We each gripped a corner of the saffron sheet that he was lying on; as the fifth person, I held the area of the sheet supporting his head. He was placed in the chamber foot first. Once he was completely inside, we each placed tulasi *branches on his chest. The man asked if we were going to stay the entire time and of course we said yes. Later he told us that no one had ever stayed for the entire process before, and asked a number of questions about Krishna Consciousness.*

I had been in touch with my wife Chintamani, who was bringing the urn for the ashes. It was a beautiful golden color with "Sripad Bhakti Tirtha Swami" inscribed on the side. On the top was the inscription "sri-gaura-karuna-shaktaye namah"—he was the compassionate energy of Lord Chaitanya.

When we returned to the Institute, Bhakti-charu Swami, Chandramauli Swami and other sannyasis *were taking* prasadam. *They immediately rose from the table and offered obeisances to the urn. The urn was placed on Gurudeva's blue chair, which is in the right corner of his room and visible when you enter. A beautiful multicolored rose garland adorned the urn as Bhakti-charu Swami sat before the urn in meditation for some time. Across the room were Gurudeva's beloved Deities, Radha-Shymasundar, while Srila Prabhupada chanted* bhajans *on a tape in the background.*

Conservatives may question the cremation. Vedic texts say that children and ascetics, or *sannyasis*, should be buried in a tomb (*samadhi*). However, this is a general rule and not considered mandatory, as Brahma-muhurta Dasa, Maharaja's disciple in charge of funeral rites, makes abundantly clear:

I was asked by Srila Bhakti Tirtha Maharaja to do preliminary research on cremation in Mayapur and to oversee his final rites. Most of my research was conducted under the guidance of Bhakti-vidya-purna Swami in India, who is one of ISKCON's foremost authorities on rituals and Vedic culture.

While conducting this research, both Maharaja and I realized that because spiritual masters and/or sannyasis *did not traditionally depart in the West, there was not much precedence or clear way of performing these rites. One main dilemma was the burial itself. When a* sannyasi *passes, he is generally placed in a deep pit and covered with salt; afterwards, a monument (known as the* samadhi*) is built above the pit. In India, this is usually done with little or no threat in terms of legality or the future security of the site. However, in America, this is not so simple. Burial laws vary from state to state and there are many such laws. One must follow different local rules and detailed procedures. Gita Nagari still has an outstanding mortgage, and the land is technically owned by the bank. Our research indicated that it would not be advisable, nor permissible (Gita Nagari does not have local authorization for a cemetery site) to have a burial on land that is not privately owned.*

After careful research, contemplation, and lengthy discussions with Bhakti-vidya-purna Maharaja and full agreement by Srila Bhakti Tirtha Swami, it was concluded that we would cremate our guru's body and bring his ashes to Mayapur to be put into samadhi.

Now the question comes up of whether or not cremating a sannyasi *or spiritual master is a bona fide practice. Srila Gopal Bhatta Goswami (citing ancient texts in his* Hari-bhakti-vilasa, *a Vaishnava guidebook for procedure) specifically mentions that* sannyasis *and spiritual masters are eligible for "full body"* samadhi *and so many assume that such personalities cannot or should not be cremated. One point that should be emphasized: "full body"* samadhi *is an option for these personalities, but it is not abso-*

lute and mandatory. In his handbook for those in the renounced order, Samskara-dipika, which was translated and printed by Srila Bhaktivinoda Thakur, republished by Srila Bhaktisiddhanta Sarasvati Thakur, and is used by all Gaudiya Vaishnavas, Srila Gopal Bhatta Goswami gives instruction on the burial:

"The body may be placed in holy water or in a hole in the earth, which should be one step larger than the height of the deceased person. [Alternatively] If the body has been burnt, the ashes or bones should be taken to a holy place and there placed in earth."

Gopal Bhatta Goswami gives this instruction and adds that at the time of Samskara-dipika's compilation, cremation was common—and that this is why he included instructions regarding cremation of sannyasis and spiritual masters in his authoritative text.

To support his suggestion of cremation due to time, place, and circumstance, Srila Bhakti-vidya-purna Swami related that Srila Jiva Goswami cremated Srila Krishnadasa Kaviraja, Srila Raghunath Dasa Goswami and Raghunath Bhatta Goswami to avoid desecration by the Muslim invaders. In our more recent Vaishnava history, Srila Bhaktivinoda Thakur was also cremated and his ashes were sent from Jagannatha Puri (were he departed) to Mayapur to be put into samadhi some months after his death. Thus, it is clear that the bodies of the greatest spiritual masters in our own line were indeed cremated in the past.

Another common question that may need to be addressed is this: Why should his ashes go to Mayapur and not remain in Gita Nagari? The first and foremost answer to this, and to any other procedural question is, this is the desire of Srila Bhakti Tirtha Maharaja himself. Although he was quite weak toward the end of his stay on the planet, he has been personally involved with all of these arrangements—from picking out and approving his own urn to the spot of his flower samadhi, and so on. (So his ashes will be in Mayapur and an additional flower samadhi will be in Gita Nagari.) Secondly, as

with the "full body" samadhi, we are concerned with the permanence
of Srila Bhakti-tirtha Swami's samadhi; under some unfortunate po-
tential circumstance, we would not want to move his remains (body
or ashes) around unnecessarily. Instead, Maharaja chose to have the
flower samadhi in Gita Nagari. The samadhi will be constructed so
that the container with the flowers could be accessed and removed in
cases of emergency. Also, in Vaishnava tradition, there is no differ-
ence between the flower samadhi and the samadhi containing his
remains. His essence remains in both places.

Spiritual Warrior

What is death? Despite the numerous theories of deep thinkers, or even the bold proclamations of the world's religious traditions, it remains one of life's greatest mysteries. Still, there are certain things we can know for sure: Death is the cessation of life as we know it—a fate awaiting each of us, sooner or later. And yet, despite the fact that it is common to all, we react differently when confronted with it. For those with a spiritual dimension, imminent death is less bewildering. Because such people do not view daily life as the totality of existence, they can more easily adjust when faced with their inevitable mortality. Conversely, when death approaches materialistic persons, they tend to react with confusion, frustration, fright; often they are in painful denial. Both responses are perfectly natural.

If we don't ponder the questions of life and death while living, how much more confusing will these questions be when death makes its sudden appearance? Those who are wise, therefore, "die before they die," as Bhakti Tirtha Swami used to say. They explore inescapable questions before it is too late.

Some may feel that contemplating death is pointless, a morbid fascination with little or no purpose. After all, once death stands before us, there is nothing we can do about it. But the world's major religions, Vaishnavism included, argue that there is benefit in thinking deeply about our nature, our life, our unavoidable demise. One who learns certain "spiritual technologies," as Bhakti Tirtha Swami called them, can therewith make a smoother transition, and the painful process known as death can become manageable, even blissful.

Most people are products of their karma—they come into this world to enjoy or suffer the fruits of their past activities, to reap what they have sown. And they leave because of karma as well, when it is time for them to fulfill their destiny elsewhere, based on their desire and their just desserts.

For someone like Bhakti Tirtha Swami, karma has very little to do with his sojourn in the material world. A person who works on behalf of God functions according to different laws altogether. Depending on just how devoted to God they are, such persons are not forced to take birth, nor do they die because of a predetermined action/reaction schema. Rather, they come into this world to help others, to share love of God and to encourage people to raise their consciousness. They are emissaries of the Divine, and their business in the material world, though externally appearing much like anyone else's, is of an entirely different nature. So, too, is their death of a different nature. They leave when they hear the call of the Lord, when His divine flute signals them that there is work to do somewhere else.

Bhakti Tirtha Maharaja left the world like the great God conscious kings from days of old. One might think of the pious King Edward of Westminster, whose famous death story, replete with symbolism and holy imagery, may be summarized as follows:

He addressed his last words to Edith, his Queen, who was sitting at his feet, in this way: "May God be gracious to this my wife for the zealous watchfulness of her service. For she has served me devotedly, and has always stood close by my side like a beloved daughter." And stretching forth his hand to his governor, her brother, Harold, he said: "I commend this woman and all the kingdom to your protection. Let the grave for my burial be prepared in the Minster in the place which shall be assigned. I ask that you do not conceal my death, but an-

*nounce it promptly in all parts, so that all the faithful can beseech the
mercy of Almighty God on me, a sinner." He also occasionally com-
forted the queen, who ceased not from lamenting, to ease her natural
grief. "Fear not," he said, "I shall not die now, but by God's mercy
regain my strength." By saying this, he did not mislead the attentive,
least of all himself. For in reality, he has not died, but has passed from
death to life, to live with Christ.*

The Queen is comparable to Maharaja's many disciples, and Harold,
her brother, is like his many Godbrothers, who will now care for these
disciples as their own.

More to the point, perhaps, would be Grandfather Bhishma, the
Pandava elder in the *Mahabharata*. As he lay dying on a bed of arrows,
great souls came from around the world just to seek his blessings and
to ask questions on spiritual matters. This was the case, too, when
Bhakti Tirtha Maharaja met his end. Godbrothers and Godsisters,
Gurukulis, leaders from various religious traditions, and even successful secularists, whom he had touched along the way, came to hear
his words of wisdom. As he lay dying, he appeared to have access to
Krishna's world, and yet he was among us as well. Visitors were thus
hoping to get a glimpse of the eternal realm through his association,
and they were not disappointed. Friends and well-wishers poured in,
showing support, offering prayers, seeking blessings. Devotees from
around the world resolved long-standing differences in his name.

Like Grandfather Bhishma, he always lived and acted according
to religious principles. As a result, he and the Pandava grandsire were
able to recognize the actual identity of Krishna, who was God Himself.
Indeed, they perpetually offered the Lord unmitigated respect and worship, while many others—both on Bhishma's battlefield and on Bhakti
Tirtha's, including a plethora of pious souls—did not.

Following Bhishma's defeat in the Battle of Kurukshetra, when he
should have easily been dead, he was allowed to wait for an appropriate time to pass into the next world—a mystical blessing he had re-

ceived from his father. It was here, from his deathbed, that Bhishma demonstrated his knowledge and position as an exceptional teacher of religious principles, as he lectured on truth and virtue. A fitting end to the life of a great soul. Indeed, many would argue that Bhakti Tirtha Maharaja's concluding weeks reflected similar greatness.

Like the spiritual monarchs of Vedic times, Maharaja showed a step-by-step progression in his final days, resulting in the unfolding of his high spiritual position. Just as an onion's many layers are shed gradually, Maharaja's various identities—Johnny Boy, Ghanashyam, Bhakti Tirtha Swami, Krishnapada, even Gurudeva—fell away, revealing a soul totally dedicated to God. Dhanurdhar Swami, his close friend, noticed this gradual awakening at the end:

> If you look at the Srimad-Bhagavatam, you'll see that, in the end, Maharaja Yudhishthira traveled north. And these great kings, when they walked to the north, the first thing they would do—their liberation—would be to peel off their uniform, their medals of honor, and so on. The external identity, the false designations, are peeled away. In this way, they would gradually give up the bodily concept. The last part of liberation, says the Bhagavatam, is to amalgamate the false ego into the Maha-tattva, the aggregate of material elements, which reveals who we really are.
>
> In other words, you have to give up everything external to the self. That's liberation. So I saw that by his service to Prabhupada at the very, very end, he was taking part in an accelerated yogic process, and that he was actually at the last stage of the false ego. To be situated in the knowledge, not the knowledge—the realization—that I am an eternal servant of Krishna in Vrindavan is no ordinary thing. He seems to have achieved that goal.

His disciple Chintamani Dasi sums up:

> One of the things that was most striking to me during Gurudeva's

illness was how, from the very beginning, he had us all in the con-sciousness (1) to begin accepting his potential death and (2) that we should not pray for him to get better, but to surrender our will to Krishna's. I remember a phone conversation I had with Gurudeva on August 12, 2004, soon after he received the cancer diagnosis. He said, "I've been preparing everyone for a while. I'm ready to make changes in my own service. We know the philosophy. Different things happen in that process. Whether Srila Prabhupada will take me to another place or have me serve him more in this arena: we have to watch the process and see what goes on." Later in the conversation, he said, "Srila Prabhupada is deciding whether to keep me here or to take me away. The question is where I can have the most effect. Pray for whatever will bring about the best spiritual effect."

This mood was challenging us to a very high level of spiritual consciousness. Because he was open to Srila Prabhupada's plan either way, he did make efforts towards a possible cure or improvement. However, his classes and personal conversations focused on the fact that he was leaving—and that we should prepare our consciousness for that. It was quite difficult because of course I didn't want him to leave and a large part of me did hope that he'd get better. Yet his urging for us to not be attached to that result and to pray for Krishna's will to be done is what actually gave me strength—spiri-tual, mental and emotional strength.

In his 2004 Vyasa-puja offering to Srila Prabhupada, he offered this prayer: "Dear Lord, whatever we need to be better servants for Srila Prabhupada's mission, let it happen or come to us. Whatever we need to have taken away to become pure in Srila Prabhupa-da's service, let it be taken away." And that was his mood—"I am yours, Krishna. I am your puppet. Do with me what you will." Saying this prayer was my refuge and inspiration during those long months of his illness, and it remains so, even now. It connects me with Gurudeva and reminds me that Krishna is already control-

ling everything. By consciously turning my will over by saying this prayer, I just have less resistance when things happen that I don't expect or don't like. I tell myself: "Remember, you asked for this; you're saying that prayer . . ." Then I become more peaceful, because I know Krishna is arranging everything for my highest good. It is easy to forget that we asked for everything that is happening to us. Gurudeva is just reminding us of that reality and urging us to ask for the process to move faster, to get us Home faster! His whole life exemplified full surrender and dependence on the will of the Lord.

It was also quite challenging to constantly hear Gurudeva speak about his pending physical transition. Towards the last months of his life, I remember thinking: "This is so hard, thinking about death all the time." And then it hit me: That was intentional—Gurudeva was forcing us to think about death every day of our lives. Srila Prabhupada taught us that our lives should be lived in preparation for the time of death. By Gurudeva emphasizing death constantly, it forced me to face the reality of death in a way I hadn't before. One may think, "Of course, when you're around anyone who is dying it forces you to think about death every day." But, no. Often, even people who are very ill are thinking about trying to live and are avoiding thinking about—let alone, embracing—their death. They don't want to talk about their death and don't want others to talk about it. Often the caretakers are in a level of avoidance/denial as well. Gurudeva made me face the reality of my own mortality and to think very seriously and deeply about living a life in preparation for death. What a gift that he gave the world! It was a gift that he had inherited from his spiritual master. My small attempt is to live a life that he would be proud of—a life that would make his sacrifice worthwhile. This is my commitment and prayer.

As the author of this book, I too am committed to spreading his message in this world, and I pray that in doing so I can one day be the servant of the servant of his disciples.

AFTERWORD

"The legacy of heroes is the memory of a great name
and the inheritance of a great example."

—BENJAMIN DISRAELI

RELIGIONS DO NOT EXIST apart from the people who practice them. Historically, if not theologically, religions are what they are because human beings have made them that way. Even so, the most sincere of human beings will try to practice religion as it was originally intended, according to its own standards. And they will practice it as if their life depended on it. Bhakti Tirtha Swami, according to those who knew him well, was just such a person—he embraced Gaudiya Vaishnavism with heart and soul, if also in his own unique way.

381

There are many different types of practitioners who stand out in religious traditions. Founders and systematizers are important, certainly. But so are philosophers, visionaries, mystics, missionaries, ascetics, authors, miracle workers, and sincere exemplars. Bhakti Tirtha Swami was all of these and so much more.

The proof lay in the people he touched. Throughout his life, as we have shown, he provided a shining light for those fortunate souls who knew proximity to him—his siblings, friends, schoolmates, even his mentors. Martin Luther King noted his exceptional character, as did his teachers and colleagues at Princeton. Devotees in ISKCON found him to be of superior quality, and so did kings and queens in Africa.

But most important, it might be argued, are the disciples, or the people who will carry on his legacy. Unlike most of ISKCON's earlier converts, Bhakti Tirtha Swami seemed to attract a more seasoned clientele, well-established professionals, such as lawyers and doctors, accomplished people who already had direction in life. They will carry on his mission, his distinct mood of conveying Krishna Consciousness, and will bring great pleasure to their spiritual grandfather, Srila Prabhupada.

In conclusion, it should be noted that ISKCON's Governing Body Commission recently issued a decree acknowledging complete acceptance of Bhakti Tirtha Swami and his often revolutionary methods of spreading Krishna Consciousness. As one of their leading members, this should not come as a surprise. Still, the gesture of an official statement would have meant a great deal to him. Here, then, are their exact words, reproduced for posterity:

The departure of His Holiness Bhakti Tirtha Swami to join Srila Prabhupada's eternal pastimes has left ISKCON devotees worldwide with deep feelings of separation.

Today we reflect on his many extraordinary accomplishments in Srila Prabhupada's service and recall with deep gratitude the immeasurable ways, both great and small, that he inspired our Krishna

Consciousness, strengthened our communities, and, accordingly, touched our hearts.

During his thirty-three years of service to the International Society for Krishna Consciousness, His Holiness Bhakti Tirtha Swami:

• Was the founder of the Institute for Applied Spiritual Technology, which, molded by his hands, became a powerful instrument in spreading Krishna Consciousness

• Systematically developed bold and unconventional methods to spread Krishna Consciousness throughout the world and thus reach those unapproachable by traditional means

• As a dynamic member of the original BBT Library Party, introduced Srila Prabhupada's books to universities and libraries in the United States, Europe, and behind the "iron curtain" with deep conviction and enthusiasm, and often at great personal risk

• Wrote two dozen books that explore the techniques and substance of Krishna Consciousness, winning the acclaim of international experts for bringing his profound spiritual perspective into the fields of leadership and personal growth

• Was a spiritual counselor to heads of state, and developed the art of winning their support to facilitate the spread of Krishna Consciousness

• Was honored with the position of High Chief of an African tribe, and thus demonstrated his expertise in connecting foreign cultures to Vaishnavism and making them fertile grounds for offering Krishna Consciousness

• Set a profound example of being strict with himself while lenient with others, through his unparalleled habits of personal austerity and service and compassion for others

• Was chaste yet broadminded; chaste to Srila Prabhupada's ISKCON, while touching the hearts of those outside of ISKCON and spiritualists throughout the world

• Had compassion for suffering souls, and tried to help them by *offering seminars to honestly confront issues that plague us in the modern world, such as domestic abuse, depression, and suicide*

• *Provided regular guidance to hundreds of disciples in their spiritual life, and was a voice of insight, consultation and inspiration for many Godbrothers and Godsisters*

• *Was a voice for those who had no voice, and was a powerful example to all he met that no obstacle in this world is insurmountable if met with determination, enthusiasm, and full faith in the mercy of the Supreme Lord and His pure devotees*

• *Had a powerful and positive influence on ISKCON's Governing Body Commission, because he knew the art of dealing with understanding and affection, thus proving that loving dealings are the basis of our society*

• *Showed by his example how to develop intimate and caring relationships among devotees, and the importance of providing first and foremost for their necessities in devotional life*

• *In the last stage of his life he was absorbed in hearing Krishna-katha, and he left this world surrounded by loving devotees and the transcendental sound vibration of the Holy Name.*

We, the Governing Body Commissioners of ISKCON, express our profound bereavement at his passing. We miss him deeply as we remember and glorify his exemplary life of service to Srila Prabhupada. May his presence, wisdom and love be felt by all of us for many years to come.

TIMELINE

February 25, 1950
John Edward Favors is born at City Hospital, which has since been renamed MetroHealth Medical Center, located on the Westside of Cleveland,

1960
Met his first mentor and Bible teacher, Vivian DuBose Jordan.

1963
Met Martin Luther King Jr., for the first time, while in junior high school.

1966-67
Met King again, this time more intimately through his work with E. Randel Osburn and the Southern Christian Leadership Conference.

1967
Entered Hawken Preparatory School.

1968
Arrived at Princeton University.

1970
Became president of the Association of Black Collegians (ABC) and founded the Third World Center.

Summer, 1971
Took detailed instruction from Norman Anderson (Uncle Nanda) on nonsectarian spiritual sciences.

1972
Graduated from Princeton University and joined ISKCON.

February 16, 1973
Became an initiated disciple of His Divine Grace A. C. Bhaktivedanta Swami Prabhupada, receiving the name "Ghanashyam Dasa."

December 2, 1973
Received Brahminical initiation from Srila Prabhupada.

March 1974
The Library Party started in Boston.

1976
Made extreme sacrifices in Eastern Europe, distributing his spiritual master's books behind the Iron Curtain, and began chanting forty-two rounds on Japa beads every day.

November 12, 1977
Received the Bhakti-shastri Award, which was co-signed by Prabhupada himself.

November 14, 1977
Prabhupada left his mortal frame and Ghanashyam resolved to be more strict with himself.

March 1978
Became one of the few Westerners to have ever entered the Jagannath Puri temple in Orissa.

March 13, 1979
Accepted the *sannyasa* order of life from Kirtanananda Swami in New Vrindavan, receiving the name "Bhakti Tirtha Swami."

1979
Visited Africa for the first time and preached vigorously in Washington D.C., establishing a popular restaurant and founding The Committee for Urban Spiritual Development.

1980
Made his mission to Africa a priority.

1981
Met the honorable Pierre Adossama at the United Nations.

1982
Was appointed assistant Governing Body Commissioner for Africa.

1984
Was approved as GBC.

March 1985
Was approved for position of spiritual master in ISKCON and adopted the title "Krishnapada."

1985

Met and developed an ongoing relationship with Kenneth Kaunda, president of Zambia, and Muhammad Ali, world famous boxer. He also met His Honor Aiyadurai Sivanandan, Zambian High Court judge, who wore Vaishnava *tilak* marking while on the bench.

1986

Initiated his first disciples.

Fall, 1990

Was coronated as High Chief of Warri, Nigeria, affecting the lives of millions.

1990

Founded the Institute for Applied Spiritual Technology (IFAST).

1994

Met President Nelson Mandela of South Africa on several occasions and shared visions and strategies for world peace with him.

1994-1995

Was made Chairman of the GBC.

1995

Expanded IFAST to Gita Nagari and resolved to build community and work for self-sufficiency.

2000–2004

Emphasized global traveling, including twenty- to thirty-country world tours in three to four months' time, maintaining this pace repeatedly for five years.

August 2004
Began to feel pronounced pain in his left foot, which had plagued him for years. He went for a CAT scan in Detroit, which led to an "excision of mass" performed in Washington, D.C. by Dr. Stephen Kominsky. The mass was found to be cancerous.

Winter, 2004
Returned from treatments in Hawaii and resigned himself to amputation. Foot had swollen to three times its size, and he experienced fevers with violent tremors. His amputation was performed on December 23, 2004 by Dr. Robert Henshaw.

March 2005
Clear indicators that the cancer had spread.

April 2005
Relocated to Gita Nagari for the remainder of his life.

May 2005
Decided to enter *nirjana-bhajan*—solitary meditation—but also to let ISKCON view his death, hoping it will help her members in various ways.

June 27, 2005
Left his body in the holy realm of Gita Nagari.

INDEX

ALSO AVAILABLE

Four series of books by Bhakti Tirtha Swami

The Leadership for an Age of Higher Consciousness Series

Leadership in any capacity has taken on such awesome proportions that even the best leaders must find creative ways to deal with today's complex situations. This series includes groundbreaking self-help manuals written for those who seek to develop greater effectiveness in the leadership process. These books are relevant for heads of government, organizations, families, and for anyone seeking greater insight into self-leadership.

The Spiritual Warrior Series

The *Spiritual Warrior* series arms those who answer the call with the spiritual weapons and armor they need to battle debilitating plagues such as depression, anxiety, and hopelessness. These books include real world examples showing how attitude changes the way our challenges affect us. B.T. Swami provides us with a series of simple techniques to carry with us in our daily battles that help us maintain proper perspective, make better decisions, and achieve uplifting results.

The Beggar Series

Deeply penetrating reflections remind the reader of the necessity of dedicating time to spiritual growth along with secular pursuits. Written in an easily readable, non-sectarian style, the books in this series explore such topics as patience, humility, love, and compassion. The author presents these subjects not as quaint musings from another age but as necessary tools for maintaining sanity in a world of conflict and stress.

The Reflections On Sacred Teachings Series

Through the books in this series, B.T. Swami helps us delve deeper into many of the scriptural teachings of the Vaishnava tradition. In plain, easy to understand language, he allows the reader to apply texts such as *Sri Siksastaka*, *Madhurya-Kadambini*, and *Harinama Cintamani* to daily life. In other words, he provides us with ancient wisdom for modern times.

Please contact the publisher or check the website for other language editions.

Order on the web at www.ifast.net

Notes

Notes

Notes